Flowers, Dragons, & Pine Trees

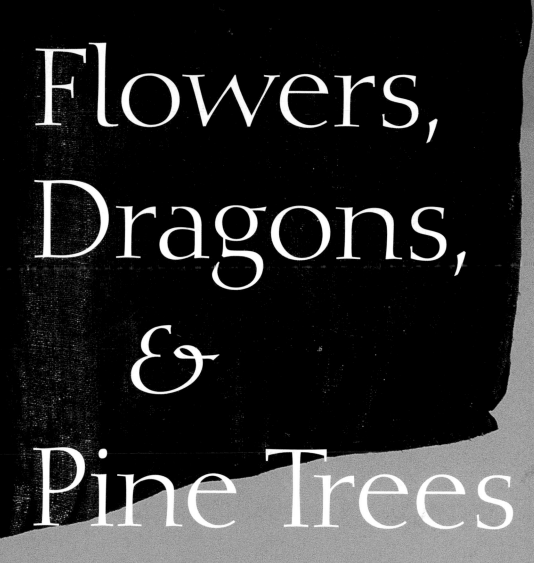

Flowers, Dragons, & Pine Trees

ASIAN TEXTILES IN THE SPENCER MUSEUM OF ART

MARY M. DUSENBURY

WITH AN ESSAY BY CAROL BIER

HUDSON HILLS PRESS, NEW YORK AND MANCHESTER

Published with the assistance of the Getty Grant Program, E. Rhodes and Leona B. Carpenter Foundation, and the Blakemore Foundation. Initial support for the project was provided by the Institute of Museum and Library Services, the Andrew W. Mellon Foundation, and The Japan Foundation.

First Edition

Published in the United States by Hudson Hills Press LLC, 74-2 Union Street, Manchester, Vermont 05254.

Distributed in the United States, its territories and possessions, and Canada by National Book Network, Inc. Distributed in the United Kingdom, Eire, and Europe by Windsor Books International.

Co-Directors: Randall Perkins and Leslie van Breen
Founding Publisher: Paul Anbinder

Editor: Melanie Drogin
Designer: Katy Homans
Photographer: Robert Hickerson
Map illustrator: Adrian Kitzinger
Proofreader: Laura Addison
Indexer: Karla Knight
Printed and bound by Toppan Printing Co.

frontispiece:
Kogin Overgarment
Japan (Tsugaru peninsula, Aomori Prefecture)
Late 19th century
Cotton and bast fiber (*asa*)
Kogin on plain weave cloth
37 x 21 in.; 94 x 53.3 cm
Museum Purchase: The Barbara Benton Wescoe Fund, 1993.9
see pages 243–247

Library of Congress Cataloguing-in-Publication Data
Dusenbury, Mary M.
  Flowers, dragons and pine trees : Asian textiles in the Spencer
Museum of Art / by Mary M. Dusenbury.—1st ed.
    p. cm.
  Includes bibliographical references and index.
  ISBN 1-55595-238-0 (alk. paper)
  1. Textile fabrics—Asia—Catalogs. 2. Textile
fabrics—Kansas—Lawrence—Catalogs. 3. Helen Foresman Spencer Museum
of Art—Catalogs. I. Helen Foresman Spencer Museum of Art. II. Title.
  NK8872.D87 2004
  746'.095'07478165--dc22
                    2004009225

Contents

Director's Foreword

The Spencer Museum of Art textile collection has long been a hidden treasure at the University of Kansas. The core of the textile collection, some 250 objects, came to the university with the museum's founding gift. In 1917 Sallie Casey Thayer, an advocate of the arts in Kansas City, Missouri, donated her collection of seventy-five hundred works of art from Europe, East Asia, and the United States to the University of Kansas in Lawrence.[1] Mrs. Thayer, the widow of Kansas City department store magnate William Bridges Thayer, believed that fine design from all over the world would inspire Kansas City's industrial designers in their efforts to produce functional and beautiful products. When she could not cajole Kansas Citians to build an art museum, William A. Griffith, founding chair of the art department at the University of Kansas, convinced Mrs. Thayer that the works in her collection would be an important inspiration and educational tool for students at the University.

It appears that Mrs. Thayer began collecting Asian art seriously in the years between 1908 and 1911, when she went to Chicago to study art history and art management. She began with Japanese prints, including a group of sixty-two *surimono* she purchased from architect Frank Lloyd Wright. A Japanese sword guard was followed by others, and by porcelain, jade, lacquer, snuff bottles, netsuke, inro, ivory carvings, Korean pottery, paintings, books on Asian art, Japanese stencils, and a diverse group of textiles. Mrs. Thayer continued to travel to New England, Europe, California, and Chicago in the years after she moved back to Kansas City, and Asian art often formed part of her acquisitions.

The textile collection was augmented in subsequent years primarily through donations from individuals in the region. When Mary M. Dusenbury became the honorary curator of textiles, she began to recommend objects that would be important to the Chinese and Japanese collection, and the Spencer Museum duly added some carefully chosen pieces during the 1990s. Dr. Dusenbury continued to recommend purchases through her tenure as acting curator of Asian art at the Spencer from 1999 through 2002.

We are very grateful to the Andrew W. Mellon Foundation for a 1996–1998 grant to encourage use of the Spencer Museum's collections in university teaching, part of which funded the research and writing of this catalogue. Without Mellon Foundation support it would have been impossible for the Spencer to engage Mary M. Dusenbury to produce the publication. Before her research began, the Institute of Museum and Library Services (IMLS) awarded the Spencer a grant (1994–1996) for survey of the collection and conservation of key objects. The Japan Foundation supported photography of the Spencer's Japanese textiles. Publication of this catalogue has been made possible through generous grants from the E. Rhodes and Leona B. Carpenter Foundation, the Getty Grant Program, and the Blakemore Foundation.

ANDREA S. NORRIS

1. Information on Sallie Casey Thayer and the Thayer collection is derived from Carol Shankel, *Sallie Casey Thayer and Her Collection* (Lawrence, Kansas: The University of Kansas Museum of Art, 1976). [The University's museum of art was renamed the Spencer Museum of Art in 1978.]

Author's Preface

This book documents a collection at the Spencer Museum of Art at the University of Kansas, a small group of Asian textiles that represent great geographical breadth as well as diversity of function, technique, and patronage. The original collection was part of Sallie Casey Thayer's gift to the University of Kansas in 1917 of seventy-five hundred objects of Western and Asian art, a gift that founded the museum. Since then, the Asian textile collection has grown through the generous gifts of museum patrons, with the addition of focused acquisitions in the 1990s.

The approximately three hundred objects that comprise this collection include court, merchant, military, theatrical, and folk costume, temple and household furnishings, and numerous discrete pieces of complex weaving, embroidery, and dyeing. The textiles range in date from the fifteenth to the late twentieth century. The largest number come from China, followed by Japan, the Indian subcontinent, Iran, Indonesia, Central and West Asia, and Korea. The collection has several focuses, each with considerable depth. These include late Persian textiles, Kashmir shawls, embroideries of northwest India and Pakistan, Chinese court costume, Buddhist and Daoist costume and temple furnishings, and Japanese cotton and bast fiber costume, furnishings, and festival textiles.

The collection raises a number of interesting issues that are addressed in the catalogue. These include interconnections between local tradition and regional and international trade; the role of the court or government in textile production; the use of textiles to designate rank, status, and power; the ritual use of textiles to legitimate, to protect, and to "bless"; interconnections between fashion, technology, and production; and the diverse functions of Asian textiles in nineteenth- and twentieth-century Asian and Western collections.

Research and writing were funded by the Andrew W. Mellon Foundation with a mandate that the book be written both for the specialist and for an interested general public. I have tried to do that.

MARY M. DUSENBURY

Acknowledgments

This book is the result of a request by Director Andrea S. Norris that I "do something" about the Asian textile collection in the Spencer Museum. That request quickly grew into a project to catalogue, conserve, photograph, research, and exhibit the collection, and finally to produce this publication. From the beginning, the project has involved many people, from undergraduate assistants to the museum director. Janet Dreiling, the museum registrar, played a key role throughout. I deeply appreciate her knowledge of the collection, sound advice, support of the project, and the excellent physical care that she gave the collection in the years before it received much notice. I learned a great deal from her. Cynthia Schira and Mary Ann Jordan, professors in the Department of Art and Design, participated in various ways and encouraged their students to apply for student assistantships in the museum. Three textile majors from the Department of Art and Design each spent many hours examining textiles and rehousing them. I am very grateful to Julie Custer, Jaminda Bass, and D'Arcy Jensen, who brought to their task skillful hands and a deep love of the objects.

Photographer Robert Hickerson's high standards occasionally drove those helping him to distraction, but his photographs silence protest. I am thankful to him for his discerning eye, uncompromising focus on excellence, and the many hours he spent working with each textile to show it to its best advantage. The Spencer Museum does not have a conservation/preparation department, so many people with other responsibilities took time to help prepare textiles for photography. Janet Dreiling supervised this process and often helped herself. In addition to the students mentioned above, graduate student interns in the registrar's office and in the Department of Asian Art spent many hours working with Robert Hickerson. My sincere thanks to Midori Oka, Laura Pasch, Cori Sherman, Sofia Galarza Liu, and Eric McNeal.

Sharon Shore, owner of the conservation laboratory Caring for Textiles, made two extended visits to the Spencer Museum to help survey the collection, to train staff in basic handling, cleaning, and housing practices, and to make suggestions about rehousing part of the collection. Sharon also conserved several objects in the collection and has remained an important consultant.

It was a pleasure to work with exhibition designers Mark Roeyer and Richard Klocke to design ways to show a wide variety of textiles and costumes to best advantage in the galleries and for photography. Dan Coester from the museum shop used his fine woodworking skills to build supports as well as new textile storage cabinets and furniture.

Asian Curators Patricia Fister and John Teramoto offered encouragement and provided office space. Carolyn Chinn Lewis, from her office next to the director, supported the project in numerous ways and always had words of encouragement. Museum Editor Sally Hayden gave valuable suggestions during the writing process and the search for an outside publisher. Museum Designer Valerie Spicher advised about ways to illustrate iconography. Asian intern Youmi Efurd read several sections of Chinese archaeological journals. Mary Ann Jordan; Doug Tilghman, assistant director; and Joe Lampo, assistant to the director, helped with grant applications. Joe also coordinated contact with the publisher and handled several aspects of the paperwork associated with reproductions borrowed from other institutions. In the final stages of production, Bill Woodard, director of communications, coordinated comments from several departments and Carolyn Chinn Lewis, now assistant director, oversaw the project for the museum.

The book is greatly enhanced by illustrations of objects in other collections. I thank the British Museum; the Metropolitan Museum of Art; the Philadelphia Museum of Art; the Peabody-Essex Museum; the Royal Ontario Museum; the temple Tōfukuji in Kyoto; and the Shōsōin Treasure House, Imperial Household Agency in Nara, Japan, for making these images available.

The project was supported throughout by Andrea S. Norris, who also raised the primary funds to make it possible. It has been supported at each stage by generous grants from a variety of agencies and foundations. I thank the Andrew W. Mellon Foundation for research and writing support, the Institute of Museum and Library Services (IMLS) for a key conservation grant,

The Japan Foundation for funds to photograph the Japanese textiles, and the E. Rhodes and Leona B. Carpenter Foundation, the Getty Grant Program, and the Blakemore Foundation for publication grants.

The publication team was a pleasure to work with. I am particularly grateful to the editor, Melanie Drogin, whose ability to clarify complex material, knowledge of Asian art history, and sensitivity to the material significantly improved the text. Designer Katy Homans's keen eye and superb skills further clarified the organization of the book, integrated text and image, and presented the objects to their best advantage. Mapmaker Adrian Kitzinger was faced with the task of making visual sense of a formidable array of place names and overlapping political entities from many different periods of history. His orderly and beautiful maps attest to his skill. Randall Perkins of Hudson Hills Press kept us all on task with grace, humor, and helpful suggestions throughout the process. My sincere thanks to all.

It was a real pleasure to work with my colleague Carol Bier, who analyzed the Iranian textiles and wrote the section on Iran. She also read the glossary and made valuable suggestions. Nora Fisher generously shared her intimate knowledge of Northwest Indian and Pakistani textiles. I am very grateful for her help with the initial identification of textiles from this area in the Spencer collection. Freelance editor Marian Weekly brought a fresh perspective to material that was quite unfamiliar to her. Marian's comments helped me clarify the text and open it to the non-specialist. Finally, I would like to express my deep appreciation to Verity Wilson and Monica Bethe, who read the sections on China and Japan, respectively, and to Dale Carolyn Gluckman, who read the entire text. Their careful reading and astute comments improved the manuscript considerably. Any errors, of course, remain my own.

MARY M. DUSENBURY

Notes to the Reader

This book follows accepted contemporary standards for romanizing Chinese and Japanese words—*pinyin* for Chinese and Hepburn for Japanese—with the exception of a few words that entered the English language in an earlier form (Noh drama rather than Nō drama). The romanization of Indian languages is less standard and is the subject of considerable debate in India today. The *pinyin* system for Chinese transcription is comparatively recent and includes pronunciations assigned to several letters and combinations of letters that are unfamiliar in English: "j" (soft "g" as in gin), "q" (ch as in cheap), "zh" (j as in jolt), "x" (s, between seat and sheet), and "z" (ds as in pads)[1]. In Japanese, consonants are generally pronounced as in English (with a hard "g"); vowels are: "a" (father); "e" (red); "i" (chief); "o" (tow); "u" (coo); and syllables receive equal stress. There are no silent letters in Japanese. Abe is a two-syllable name that is pronounced Ah/beh.

Words from Chinese, Japanese, and various Indian languages that appear in quotations are spelled as they were originally published. Diacritical marks are omitted for words that are well known in the English-speaking world—such as daimyo and sutra—and familiar place names (Tokyo, not Tōkyō).

Chinese and Japanese names are rendered in traditional style, with surname preceding given name(s). Dates in parentheses following personal names are birth and death dates. An "r" before a set of dates indicates that they are reign dates.

The names of many locations referred to in the text have changed over time. In the text, the name generally appears as it was in the time period discussed, sometimes with the modern name in parenthesis [Edo (Tokyo)]. On the maps, the modern name appears first with the name as it appears in the text in parentheses [Mumbai (Bombay)].

1. For a more complete guide to *pinyin* pronunciation see Sherman E. Lee. *A History of Far Eastern Art*, Fifth edition. New York: Prentice Hall and Harry N. Abrams, 1994, p. 16.

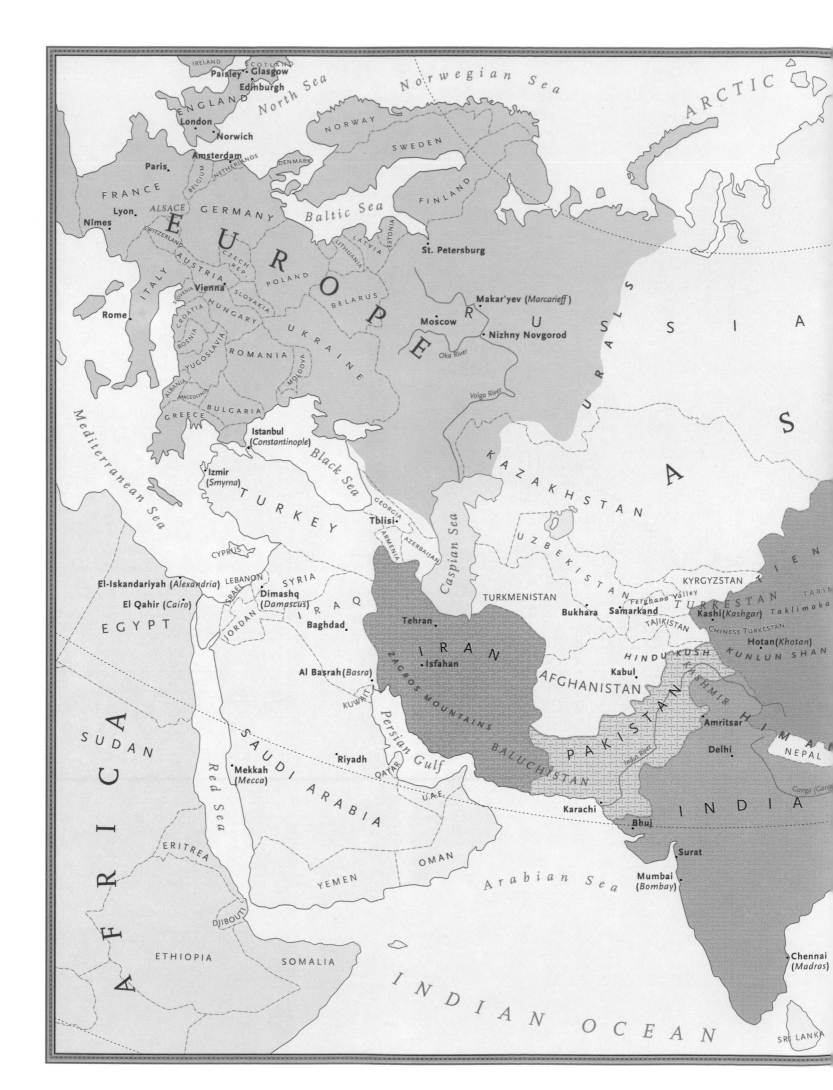

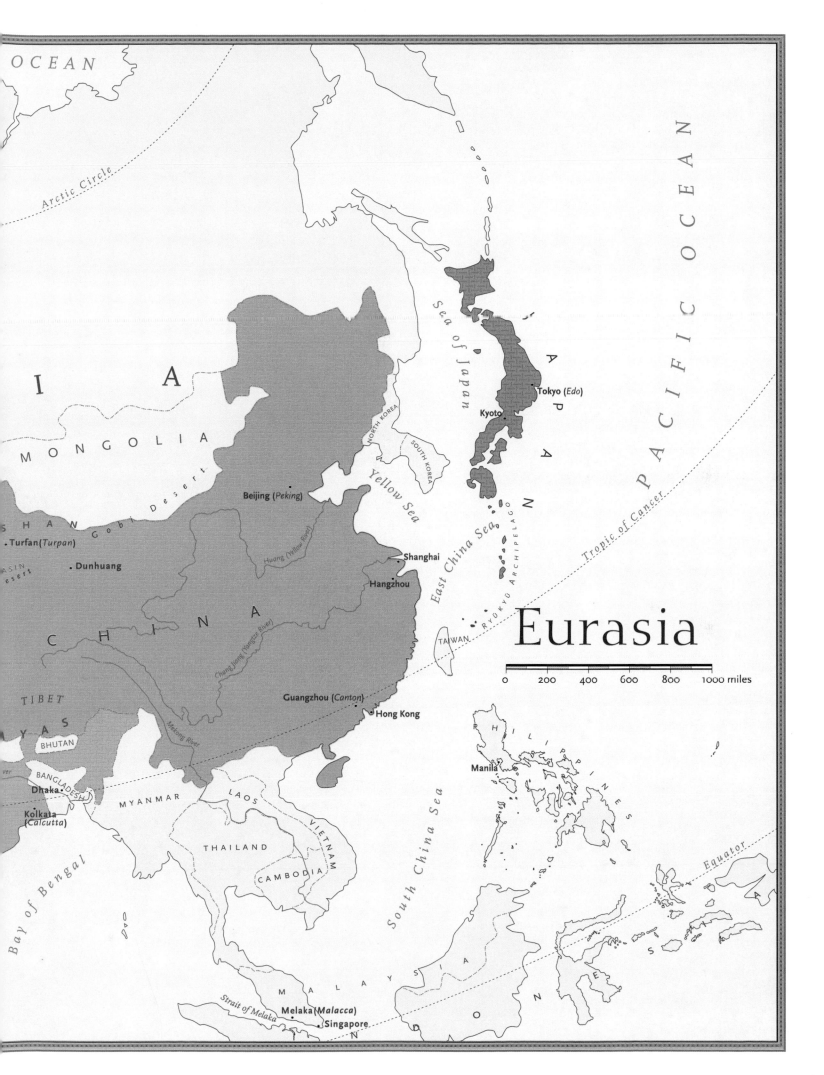

OCEAN

Arctic Circle

I A

MONGOLIA

SHAN

.Turfan(*Turpan*)

ASIN
esert

.Dunhuang

Gobi Desert

Beijing (*Peking*)

Huang (Yellow River)

C H I N A

TIBET

Chang Jiang (Yangtze River)

Y A S

BHUTAN

BANGLADESH

Dhaka

Kolkata
(*Calcutta*)

Mekong River

MYANMAR

LAOS

THAILAND

CAMBODIA

VIETNAM

Guangzhou (*Canton*)

Hong Kong

NORTH KOREA

SOUTH KOREA

Yellow Sea

Sea of Japan

J A P A N

Tokyo (*Edo*)

Kyoto

East China Sea

RYUKYU ARCHIPELAGO

TAIWAN

Shanghai

Hangzhou

PACIFIC OCEAN

Tropic of Cancer

Eurasia

0   200   400   600   800   1000 miles

P H I L I P P I N E S

Manila

South China Sea

Bay of Bengal

M A L A Y S I A

Strait of Melaka

Melaka (*Malacca*)

Singapore

N

I N D O N E S

A

Equator

11

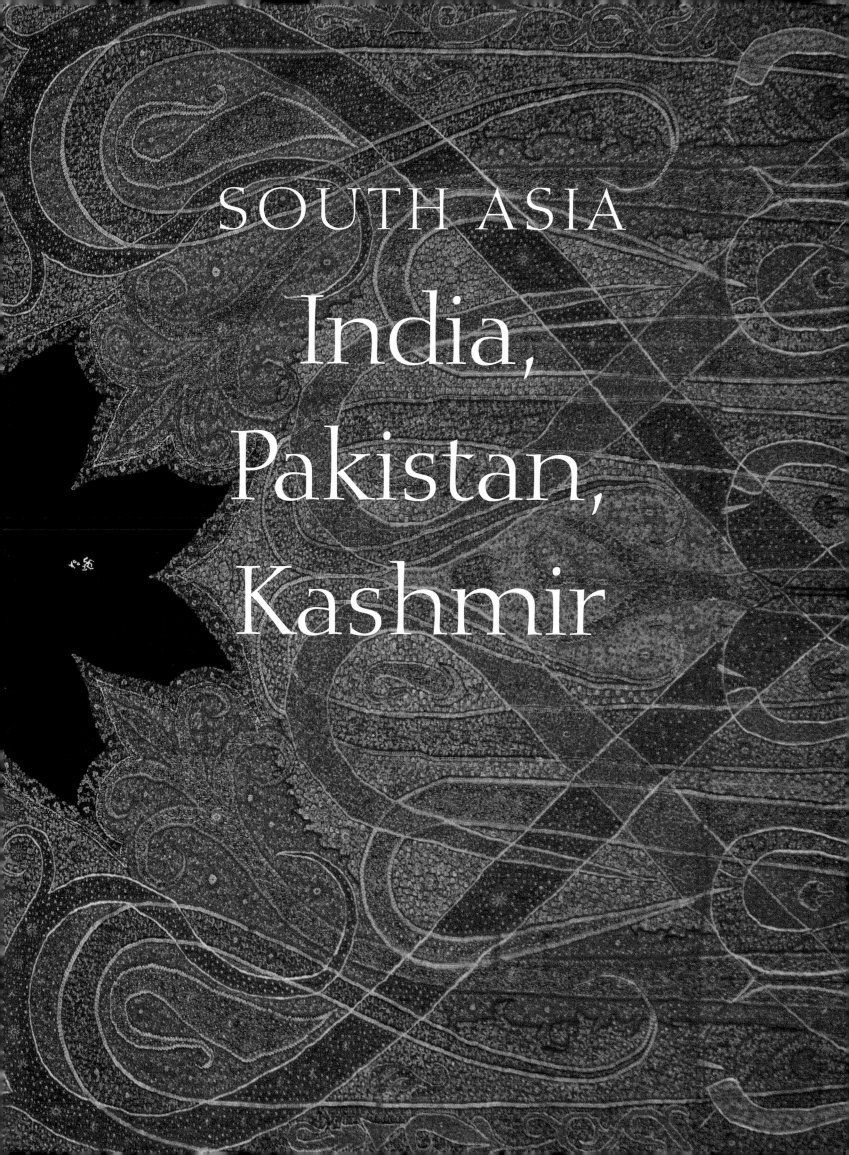

SOUTH ASIA

India, Pakistan, Kashmir

Contents

Chronology

Major Dynasties and Periods

Indus Valley civilization	ca. 2500–ca. 1500 BCE
Aryan invasions	ca. 2000–ca. 1500 BCE
Vedic age	1500–1000 BCE
Mauryan dynasty	332–185 BCE
Gupta era	320–520 CE
Northern kingdoms	648–1000
Chola empire (south)	ca. 800–ca. 1300
Turkish invasion	1000–1206
Mughal dynasty	1526–1857
Babur	r. 1526–1530
Humayun	r. 1530–1540, 1555–1556
Akbar	r. 1556–1605
Jahangir	r. 1605–1627
Shah Jahan	r. 1627–1658
Aurangzeb	r. 1658–1707
British India	1600–1947
Gandhian era	1917–1948
Modern India	1947–
Pakistan established as separate nation	1947
Bangladesh (formerly East Pakistan) established as separate nation	1971

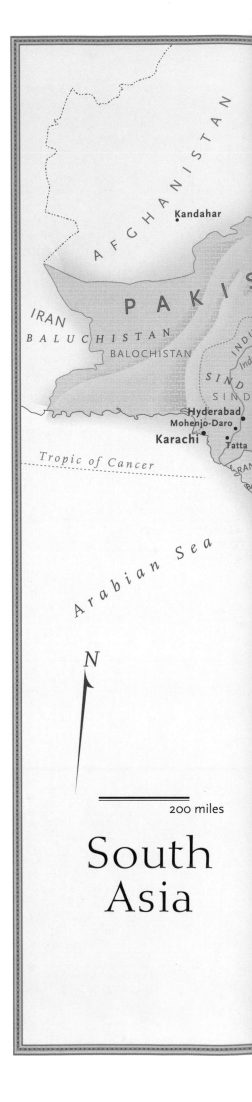

South Asia

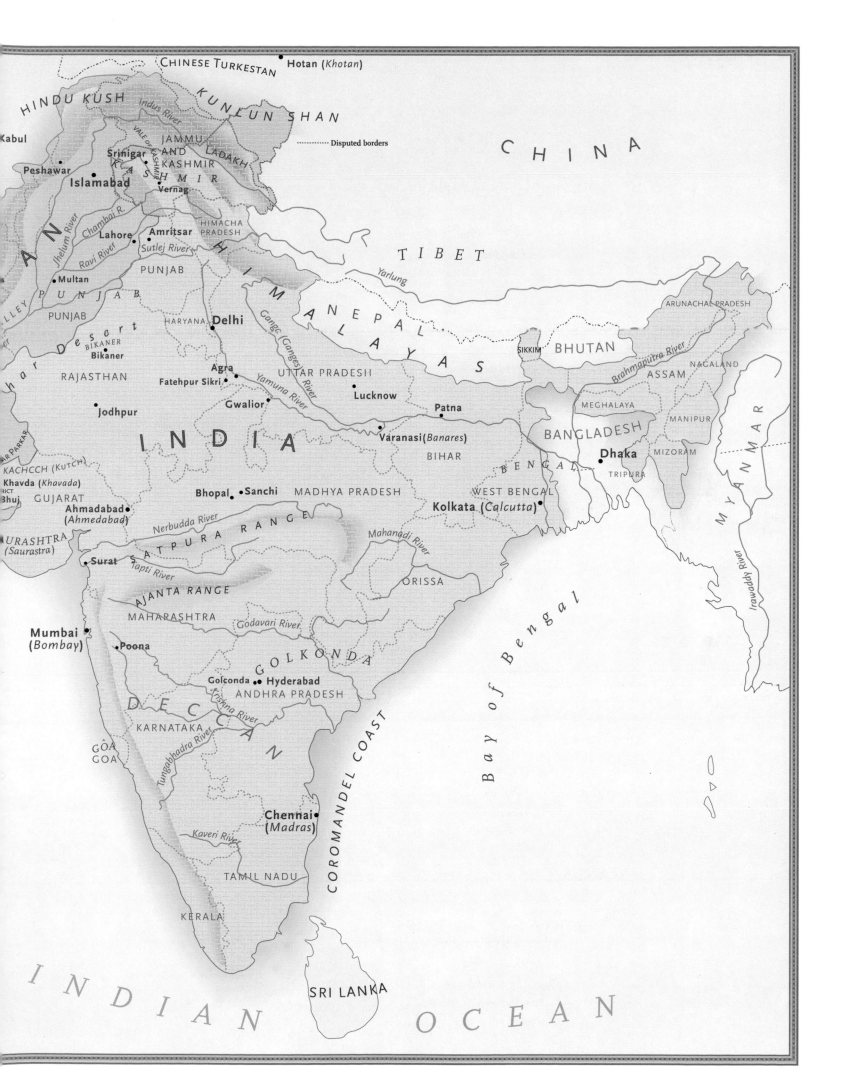

CHINESE TURKESTAN   Hotan *(Khotan)*

CHINA

HINDU KUSH   KUNLUN SHAN

Kabul

Indus River

Peshawar   JAMMU
Srinigar   AND   LADAKH
Islamabad   KASHMIR   KASHMIR
Vernag

- - - - - - Disputed borders

TIBET

Yarlung

Chambai R.

Jhelum River   Lahore   HIMACHA
Amritsar   PRADESH

Ravi River   Sutlej River

PUNJAB

Multan   PUNJAB

HARYANA   Delhi   H   I   M   A   NEPAL   A   Y   A   S   ARUNACHAL PRADESH

PUNJAB   Ganges   SIKKIM   BHUTAN
BIKANER   (Gangess)   River   NAGALAND
Bikaner   Agra   UTTAR PRADESH   Brahmaputra River   ASSAM
RAJASTHAN   Fatehpur Sikri   Yamuna River   Lucknow   MEGHALAYA   MANIPUR
Jodhpur   Gwalior   Patna   BANGLADESH   MYANMAR
INDIA   Varanasi *(Banares)*   Dhaka   MIZORAM
BIHAR   BENGAL   TRIPURA
Bhopal   Sanchi   MADHYA PRADESH   WEST BENGAL
Ahmadabad   Nerbudda River   Kolkata *(Calcutta)*
(Ahmedabad)
URASHTRA   SATPURA RANGE   Mahanadi River
(Saurastra)   Surat   Tapti River
AJANTA RANGE   ORISSA
MAHARASHTRA   Godavari River
Mumbai   GOLKONDA
(Bombay)   Poona
Golconda   Hyderabad
DECCAN   ANDHRA PRADESH
Krisna River
KARNATAKA
GÔA   Tungabhadra River
GOA

Irawaddy River

Bay of Bengal

KACHCH (KUTCH)
Khavda *(Khavada)*
Bhuj   DISTRICT
GUJARAT
THAR PARKAR

Thar Desert

Chennai
(Madras)

COROMANDEL COAST

Kaveri River

TAMIL NADU

KERALA

INDIAN   OCEAN

SRI LANKA

Introduction and Historical Overview

In 1928 Sallie Casey Thayer donated forty-three Indian textiles to the Spencer Museum of Art. Subsequent gifts augmented the museum's holdings, so that today the collection is comprised of approximately seventy textiles, including Kashmir shawls, brocades, block-printed fabrics, and a wide variety of embroideries. The textiles represent both the superb skill of professional craftsmen and the lively exuberance of folk designs. Some of the textiles were intended for local or regional use within India; others were produced for export to Europe or the United States. Most date from the nineteenth or very early years of the twentieth century.

Indian weavers and dyers were pioneers in many aspects of textile production, and Indian textiles were highly valued trade items in both the East and the West for more than two thousand years. They had a significant effect on diverse textile traditions, including those of Japan, southeast Asia, and Europe. With a few notable exceptions, very few early textiles have survived within India; therefore, any history of this rich tradition must be pieced together from extant paintings and written sources in India, trade documents, the observations of foreign travelers, mention in foreign literature and letters, and textiles that have been preserved in other countries.

For almost four millennia, the subcontinent that we now know as India has produced some of the world's finest textiles. At the site of the ancient city of Mohenjo-Daro in the Indus Valley, circa 1750 BCE, archaeologists found evidence of a well-established textile industry. A fragment of madder-dyed cotton cloth wrapped around a silver pot is the ancestor of a long tradition of beautifully colored fine cotton textiles. The site also yielded spindles, bronze needles, and dye vats as well as relief-carved stone sculptures clearly depicting figures wearing patterned cloth. The language of weaving was used as metaphor in India's earliest documents. In a hymn to Agni recorded in the *Rg Veda*, worshippers proclaim the mystery of the fire god:

I know not either warp or woof, I know not the web they weave.[1]

Inscriptions on Assyrian and Babylonian tablets suggest that by the seventh century BCE Indian cotton cloth had become a sought-after commodity in Middle Eastern trade. In the first century CE, Indian carpets, silks, and embroidered goods were important articles of trade at the Roman port of Alexandria, and Roman matrons clad themselves in fine Indian cottons, described as "venti" (fine as the wind) and "nebula" (misty). In Egypt, mummies were wrapped in Indian muslin and palaces were caparisoned with Indian silks, brocades, and embroideries.

The log book of an anonymous Greek trader, the *Periplus Maris Erythreae*, records the flourishing regional trade from Egypt along the Red Sea to the west coast of India circa 60 CE. The author describes a network of specialized textile centers throughout the Indian subcontinent.[2] Roman traders were stationed in India and, in at least one community, Indian weavers produced goods specifically designed for the Roman market three thousand miles to the west. Craft workers were organized in guilds and were well able to respond to the demands of a flourishing—and fluctuating—international trade.

Indian textiles were famous for their clear, brilliant, and fast colors, and as early as the fourth century, the skills of their dyers had become legendary. In an interpretive rendition of the Hebrew text for his fourth-century Latin translation of the Bible, St. Jerome has Job say that wisdom is even more enduring than "the dyed colours of India."[3] European dyers were not able to match the quality of these colors until well into the eighteenth century.

Although sheer muslin and beautifully dyed cottons appear to have dominated foreign trade (at least with the West), within India the vocabulary of weavers and dyers was much broader. Wall paintings in the Buddhist cave-temple complex at Ajanta in India, constructed between the fifth and eighth centuries, provide a detailed and lively chronicle of contemporary Indian court textiles. The murals depict aristocrats, dancers, musicians, and servants dressed in a rich array of resist-dyed and printed, ikat, tie-dyed, and brocade-woven textiles.

Indian rulers established royal workshops throughout the country to improve and promote textile production. A twelfth-century silk workshop (*karkhanah*) associated with the Delhi sultanate is reported to have employed more than four thousand workers. A fourteenth-century traveler from Damascus described the output of weavers associated with the court of Muhammed Tughlak (1325–1350), a sultan in the region of Banares, which had benefitted from the immigration of Iranian pattern weavers: "The Sultan keeps in his service 500 manufacturers of golden tissues, who weave the gold brocades worn by the wives of the Sultan, and given away as presents to the Amirs and their wives."[4] Abdul Fazil, a writer at the court of the third Mughal ruler Jalal-ud-din Muhammad Akbar (1542–1605), described Akbar's keen interest in textiles and the Kashmir shawls, silks, velvets, brocades, and fine muslins that graced his court:

> His Majesty pays much attention to various stuffs; hence Irana [Iranian] and European and Mongolian articles of wear are in abundance. Skillful masters and workmen have settled in this country to teach the people an improved system of manufacture. The imperial work-shops, the towns of Lahor, Agra, Fathpur, Ahmadabad, Gujarat, turn out many masterpieces of workmanship; and the figures and patterns, knots, and variety of fashions which now pre-vail, astonish experienced travellers. His Majesty himself acquired in a short time a theoreti-cal and practical knowledge of the whole trade; and on account of the care bestowed upon them the intelligent workmen of this country soon improved. . . . A taste for fine material has since become general, and the drapery used at feasts surpasses every description.[5]

In 1498 Vasco da Gama rounded the Cape of Good Hope and ushered in a new age of European exploration and trade. Portuguese (and later Dutch and English) merchant fleets joined those of well-established Arab and Indian merchants plying their wares in the Indian Ocean and southeast Asia. The Portuguese traveler Tomé Pires described the beauty, diversity, and high monetary value of the Indian textiles that acted as currency in the complex network of trade that, among other things, procured spices for Europe from the islands of southeast Asia. Writing in 1515, Pires noted the high value of the textile cargo of ships arriving in Malacca from Gujarat on the northwest coast of India. He remarked that they carried thirty different kinds of cloth (many of which were specifically made for particular markets), and described "very rich bed canopies, with cut-cloth work in all colours and very beautiful" and "wall hangings like tapestry" from Bengal; he also noted "rich cloths of great value" from the Coromandel coast.[6] Indian textiles became a mark of royal prestige and power; they often acquired ritual signifi-cance; and they profoundly affected the development of local textile traditions in mainland southeast Asia and the island archipelagos.[7]

Dyers along the Coromandel coast of southeast India, and elsewhere, not only catered to a variety of specific markets in southeast Asia, but by the late seventeenth century were respond-ing to an ever-increasing demand from Europe as well, first for household furnishings and soon for cloth to be fashioned into garments. Correspondence between the English East India Company and its representatives in India suggests the great popularity of the beautifully dyed Indian cottons. A memo from London to India in 1686 states, "You may exceed our former orders in Chintz broad of all sorts, whereof some be of grave and cloth colours, with the great-est variety you can invent, they being become the weare of ladyes of the greatest quality, which they wear on the outside of Gowns Mantuoes which they line with velvet and cloth of gold."[8]

In the eighteenth and nineteenth centuries, Indian textiles became more widely available in Europe and in the American colonies. Painted chintz or embroidered bed hangings graced the stately mansions of Europe and the colonies, and women from many walks of life dressed in sprigged muslins and printed calicos. In 1809 Empress Josephine had her portrait painted wearing a Kashmir shawl. Within fifty years, Kashmir shawls and their European jacquard-woven imitations had become an indispensable article of female attire in salon and marketplace alike. From the 1720s until 1833, when it stopped dealing in textiles, the English East India Company annually imported thousands of silk tie-dyed *bandhani* from Bengal, which were sold as neck-cloths to sailors, traders, and agricultural laborers. The printed cotton bandana later became so closely associated with the American West that its Indian origins were forgotten. Calico, chintz, sash, shawl, pajama, gingham, dimity, dungaree, bandana, and khaki . . . a cursory look at a few terms that originally designated Indian fabrics suggests the indebtedness of European and American fashion and household furnishings to the rich heritage of Indian textiles.[9]

Flowers and Flowering Plants as Design Motifs

Images of flowers and flowering plants form a leitmotif that runs through the textiles of northwest India, Pakistan, and the Kashmir Valley, whether made by a village woman for her family, by a court artisan, or by a professional weaver for the export trade. Although some of the most common flower motifs, such as the *buta* on Kashmir shawls, are so stylized that they may appear to be simply abstract forms, their roots are firmly embedded in a love of gardens and flowering plants that dates back at least to the court cultures of the early years of the Safavid dynasty in Iran (1501–1732) and the Mughal dynasty in India (1526–1857).

Flowers filled the gardens of the Mughal court and spilled over into paintings and textiles. The first Mughal emperor, Babur (r. 1526–1530), established gardens in his new land. He wrote precise descriptions of unusual plants, which he commissioned court artists to paint. His personal writings include poetic descriptions of an apple tree in autumn and spring flowers in the foothills of the Hindu Kush. His grandson Akbar (r. 1556–1605) chose a painting of Babur supervising the construction of an Iranian-style garden to illustrate his grandfather's diary, the *Baburnama*. This might seem an unusual choice to depict the life of a conqueror who, from the time he left Ferghana at age fourteen, spent most of his life fighting. It certainly underscores the pleasure Babur took in his gardens.[10]

Babur, his son and heir Humayun (r. 1530–1540, 1555–1556), and Akbar were patrons of the arts and keenly interested in intellectual matters, and all three maintained contact with the Iranian court; Humayun was once granted asylum there after a series of military defeats in India. All three invited Iranian artists and craftsmen to India. Gradually a distinctive Mughal style developed that combined the naturalism of pre-Islamic India with the formalism, grace, and delicacy of the Islamic Iranian style. Depictions of flowers blended the elegance of fifteenth-century Iranian models with the Indian interest in the natural world. At its best, the style balances delicacy, exuberance, and restraint.

Beginning in Akbar's reign, the influence of European artistic styles was added to the already eclectic style of the court. Akbar actively sought out European art and provided opportunities for his craftsmen to study European artistic ideas and skills. In 1575, for example, he sent a group of craftsmen to the Portuguese settlement in Goa to learn foreign craft skills. Akbar welcomed European travelers to the court, listened to their ideas, and along with his artists, studied the paintings, textiles, and other artifacts that the travelers brought with them. Indian artists began to experiment with certain European concepts like perspective in their paintings, but it was sixteenth- and seventeenth-century Dutch botanical drawings—rather than portrayals of plants in a natural setting—that would have the greatest influence on the depiction of flowers in Mughal painting, textiles, and other media.[11]

Akbar's son Jahangir (r. 1605–1627), like his great grandfather Babur, was a keen observer of the natural world. Like his forebear he traveled with court artists who documented the flora and fauna that he described in careful detail. One of the best known of the artists working under Jahangir was Mansur, who was known for paintings that combined the elegance of Iranian style with an acute observation of nature.[12] R. Skelton believes that it was probably this artist who developed the Mughal-style flowering plant motif that became so closely associated with Mughal court arts during and following the last years of Jahangir's reign.

In a study of the evolution of this flowering plant motif, naturalistically depicted yet formally disposed, R. Skelton suggests two specific factors that led to the emergence of the motif during Jahangir's reign. The first was the influence of a French herbal by Pierre Vallet that

FIG. 1

Chitarman

Shah Jahan on a Terrace Holding a Pendant Set with His Portrait, 1627–1628

India
Mughal period, reign of Shah Jahan (r. 1627–1658)
Leaf from an album made for the Emperor Shah Jahan
Ink, opaque watercolor, and gold on paper
15.4 x 10.1 in.; 39.9 x 25.6 cm
The Metropolitan Museum of Art, Purchase, Rogers Fund and the Kevorkian Foundation Gift, 1955 (55.121.10.24)
[Photograph © 1980 The Metropolitan Museum of Art]

Jahangir probably received circa 1618. The second was Jahangir's trip to Kashmir two years later, during which he commissioned Mansur to paint one hundred of the spring flowers that graced the foothills of the Himalayas, the same flowers that had moved Babur to poetry several decades earlier. Skelton suggests that Jahangir not only commissioned Mansur to paint these flowers, but ordered his court artist to follow the style and format of the Vallet herbal—i.e., to paint naturalistically depicted plants formally posed against a plain background. Although Mansur's paintings have been lost, other flower studies that appeared after the 1620 Kashmir trip depict flowering plants described in this manner, arranged singly or in regularly ordered groups.[13]

This formalized flowering plant motif was quickly adopted throughout Mughal art. The change was seen first in the border decoration of Jahangir's picture albums, which changed from arabesques and landscapes to rows of discrete flowering plants. By Shah Jahan's reign (r. 1627–1658) it had become a major theme in architecture and had permeated the decorative arts.[14] Although the plants continued to look naturalistic, they were altered freely and combined with one another. Skelton states that even by the second quarter of the seventeenth century some flowering plant motifs displayed "[t]he most astonishing juxtapositions of flowers and leaves," and asserts that "[m]any of the resulting creations would lead to the despair of any botanist foolhardy enough to attempt their identification."[15]

During the reign of Shah Jahan, perhaps best known for building the Taj Mahal, flowers surrounded and inundated the Mughal court. From the gardens surrounding his new palace in Delhi to the carved marble of the audience hall, to wall hangings, floor coverings, jewelry, manuscript illumination, and even weapons, the flowering plant and other floral motifs defined exalted spaces and intimate objects alike.

Shah Jahan, like his predecessors, traveled several months of the year to hunt, campaign, and observe his vast empire. During his travels, he and his extensive retinue were housed in one set of elaborate tents while a second set was erected at the next site. The tents were constructed in a specialized imperial workshop that employed architects, textile specialists, and artists, all under the interested eye of the Shah. One imperial tent from Shah Jahan's reign has been preserved in the fort at Jodhpur. Serving at once as palace and audience hall, the tent has a large, domed interior space made of red silk velvet and partitioned with arches and columns of the same material. Domed ceiling, walls, columns, floor coverings, cushions, and table cover are all made of the same thick red velvet and adorned with scrolling flowers embroidered with metallic threads in gold and silver, creating a dazzling interior.[16]

Mughal court style set the tone for styles at regional courts, including the court at Bhuj in Gujarat. Paintings of flowers made by Mughal court artists for copying in other media were distributed to regional courts throughout the country, where they were used as models by artists and craftsmen. The regional courts, in turn, influenced tribal and village design. Nora Fisher notes that in Gujarat, village women as well as the Mochi professional embroiderers referred to drawings in creating their designs in the late nineteenth and early twentieth centuries.[17]

The floral motifs (*buta*) on the end borders of a shawl such as Plate 3 thus situate it within a long and complex interchange of ideas about the depiction of flowers. Variants of this formalized flowering plant could be seen throughout the Mughal world in palaces and villages. Like the closely related *buta* motifs on early Kashmir shawls, the description of flowers on this embroidered shawl is the product of influences as diverse as a pre-Islamic Indian interest in depictions of nature, flower imagery in fifteenth-century Iran, and sixteenth- and seventeenth-century Dutch and French botanical drawings. These influences were all filtered through an Islamic Mughal court whose rulers were interested in understanding diverse foreign philosophical and artistic ideas and incorporating them into the life of the court and state. They appear, in varied and vibrant forms, on textiles as diverse as this embroidered shawl probably made by a village woman for her own use, and the highly elaborated *buta* executed in twill tapestry by Kashmiri craftsmen for sale to fashionable customers in Europe.

Embroideries of Northwest India and Pakistan

OVERVIEW

In the semi-arid desert regions of northwest India and eastern Pakistan, clusters of thatched mud houses are separated by miles of roadless desert and blowing yellow sand. Villages seem to rise unbidden from the surrounding desert, their forms and dull ochre color reflecting the earth from which they are molded. Like the landscape, the basic forms of the village reflect the forms and colors of the earth; but both landscape and village are embellished with pattern and brilliant color—the landscape through the changing play of light, and habitat and costume through human skill and ingenuity.

As one enters the village, one is struck by the color and pattern with which women embellish themselves, their loved ones, and their habitat. Some observers see the patterns and colors of textiles and wall ornamentation as standing in contrast to the desert, providing relief from a monotonous landscape. Others argue that these forms and colors are derived from the desert. The patterns are there for the eye to see, and the colors reflect the swift, dramatic changes that light brings to the desert landscape—from the crimsons and deep reds of sunrise and sunset to the shimmering white of high noon and the silvery blue-grey of evening.[18] In some places, outside walls and the surrounds of doors and windows are painted, often in large geometric patterns depicting ritual motifs, rendered in white on red or the reverse. Both outside and inside walls may be decorated with relief patterns, molded from the same plaster of mud and cow dung that prepares the mud surfaces for painting. The relief patterns are sometimes further embellished with color and/or embedded mirrors and other objects.[19]

Highly ornamented embroidered textiles are used throughout the house; hanging in doorways, they define and protect the threshold between the public and private domains. Women and young girls dress in layers of colorful, patterned clothing. If the textiles are locally embroidered, as per traditional practice, their colors and patterns are closely related to those of the wall decoration, and the vocabulary used to describe them is often the same. Many textiles as well as some wall decorations are embellished with tiny bits of mirror glass intended to ward off evil spirits by confronting them with their own images.[20]

Even today, styles, color schemes, motifs, and even certain embroidery techniques identify specific groups of people and have complex social meanings. Judy Frater has pointed out that, although both migration and the movement of a bride from one community to that of her new husband have served to disseminate styles and practices to a certain extent, embroidery styles still generally serve to identify a person with a particular group, and with all the connotations of relative status that this identification implies. Frater has observed a group of high-status Sodha Rajputs from Thar Parkar, who migrated to border areas of Gujarat and Rajasthan in the 1970s, begin to abandon their distinctive embroidery because, in their new land, some of its techniques and styles were associated with low-status Marwada Meghwas and Muslim communities that had also migrated from Thar Parkar to the region much earlier. Other groups have adopted embroidery styles and techniques emblematic of higher-status groups within their communities in a deliberate attempt to elevate their own status.[21]

Throughout the region, a woman is understood to contribute significantly to the health and welfare of her household and its guests through her adornment of clothing and household furnishings, and her daily and seasonal re-adornment of the mud walls and threshold of her house. She works creatively within an established tradition, re-interpreting time-honored patterns in her own vocabulary. Motifs, techniques, and overall style are handed down from mother to daughter throughout the generations. Many patterns are ancient, their specific meanings long forgotten. Some have a protective function, often invoking a deity such as Lakshmi, guardian of the home and family.[22] Some are created in conjunction with a specific request of a deity; others in thanks for a request granted. Some follow a prescribed formula. Others, such as threshold diagrams, exhibit a great range of expression that pushes the boundaries of the established vocabulary. Some diagrams are designed as an integral part of a cycle of ornamentation and recitation, each requiring the other for completion.

Adornment and ornamentation in Northwest India do not simply add pattern and color to what might otherwise seem a dull and monotonous landscape. They do not merely serve a decorative function. They are seen, rather, as playing an essential role in establishing and maintaining the basic humanity of the community—of locating and grounding a person and family within a very specific social, historical, and cultural matrix. They offer protection from the forces of evil within and without the individual or household; provide a threshold, or entryway, for the deities; and form a means of communication with the deities.

Nora Fisher has summarized the functions of adornment in rural India as follows:

> In India, adornment serves mankind in innumerable ways: attracting gods, protecting people and communities, identifying ethnic groups, or revealing the history and daily life of those groups. Adornment gives men and women a creative outlet that supports society; it grants those of even the lowest classes a meaningful place in the social structure. Adornment and ornamentation are intricately intertwined with the whole fabric of Indian life, particularly in rural India.[23]

Because the adornment of cloth and habitat had ritual importance, women traditionally prepared themselves before starting the work. In the parts of India where these traditions are still followed, women habitually rise early, wash, and recite the morning prayers before beginning the day's work. In the Punjab, a grandmother traditionally started work on a wedding shawl for her granddaughter when the child was born. The act of embroidery itself had religious significance and the woman began work on the shawl only after a ceremony of prayers and ritual gifts.

In his writings, the Indian art historian Ananda Coomaraswamy emphasized the transformative power of ornamentation, stating that its primary function was not simply to decorate an object for the viewer's pleasure, but to give that object the ability to function spiritually as well as physically.

> We must not think of ornament as something added to an object which might have been ugly without it. The beauty of anything unadorned is not increased by ornament, but made more effective by it. It is generally by means of what we now call its decoration that a thing is ritually transformed and made to function spiritually as well as physically.[24]

HEADCLOTHS

1. Woman's Headcloth (*Odhani*)

◆

India (Banni district, Kutch, Gujarat)
Late 19th or early 20th century
Silk and mica
Embroidery (chain stitch and mirrorwork) on satin ground
67 x 75 in.; 170 x 190.5 cm
The William Bridges Thayer Memorial, 1928.854

In the vast, dry landscape of contiguous regions of Kutch in Gujarat and western Rajasthan in India, the Sind in Pakistan, and the Punjab in India and Pakistan, village and tribal women cover their heads—and sometimes envelop their bodies—with beautifully decorated body-length shawls, variously known as *odhani* in Hindi, *abocchnai* in Tharri, and *bochini* in parts of Pakistan. The headcloth is worn over blouse, bodice, or tunic (with skirt or pants). The color, design, materials, technique, and manner of wearing the headcloth, as well as the construction and other aspects of costume and jewelry, define a woman's identity, suggesting her religious and village or tribal affiliation as well as her age, family occupation, marital and social status.

Headcloths vary from simple, monochromatic, and undecorated lengths of fabric to intricately block-printed, tie-dyed, or embroidered cloths in a rich array of colors. All eleven of the headcloths in the Spencer collection are embroidered. They represent a wide range of styles, materials, and skill, from a rough cotton shawl with an exuberant mass of casually executed flowers strewn profusely, but randomly, over the surface (Fig. 2) to the geometric precision and meticulous workmanship of a professional Mochi craftsman working in fine silk (Plate 1).

The dark blue satin central field of this *odhani* is dominated by an elaborated medallion set into a field of abstracted *buta*, or flowers, in rows that are precisely aligned to alternate red flowers with flowers outlined in white in the horizontal, vertical, and diagonal directions. The central field is bordered by red satin with a row of inset mirrorwork in the top and bottom

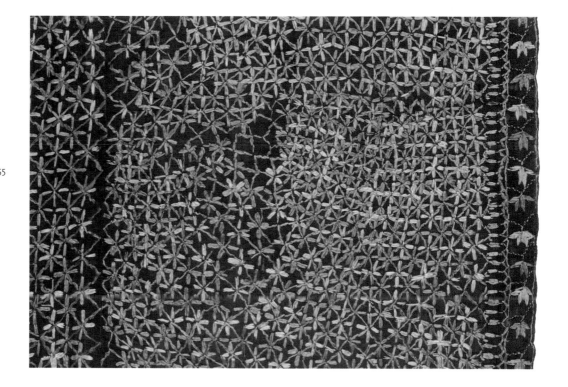

borders. The central medallion, composed of an intricate arrangement of floral *buta*, is the predominant motif in the work of the Lohana craftsmen of Khavada in the Banni district of northern Kutch.[25] The medallion represents a stylized eight-petalled lotus flower, an ancient and pervasive symbol for Lakshmi, consort of the Hindu creator god Vishnu and a beloved household goddess worshipped throughout the desert regions of northwest India and Pakistan.[26]

The meticulous craftsmanship of this headcloth, the high quality of the materials, and the strong association of the central motif with Lakshmi, beloved goddess of fertility, prosperity, and good fortune, suggest that this *odhani* may have been a wedding veil. As such, it would have been worn with the medallion centered on the bride's head, enveloping her and hiding her from view until after the ceremonies were completed.

Two edges of the headcloth have been trimmed. Only portions of the outermost row of *buta* are visible within each of the mirrored borders. It is unclear whether the *odhani* was only slightly trimmed and was originally made in its present, unusual square shape; or whether it was significantly reduced from the more common long rectangle. The latter is suggested by the fact that it has been carefully repaired in places by inserting identical passages of embroidered motifs to replace damaged or missing sections of cloth. Although these could have come from another textile, it is more likely that they are from one of the missing ends of this *odhani*.

2. Woman's Headcloth (*Orhni*)
◆

Jat women of Bikaner in the Thar desert of northern Rajasthan were known for the quality of their wool fiber and for the products they made from it. In the nineteenth century they exported wool to Europe and woolen products to other parts of India.[27] They typically embroidered their own headcloths and ceremonial cloths in white, or white and polychrome, cotton on a reddish brown handspun cotton or wool ground. Motifs are highly abstracted, and the overall composition shows the complex geometry that suggests the influence of Islamic design.

The ground fabric of this *orhni* is woven of tightly spun "z" twist warp and weft, providing a firm foundation for the embroidered ornamentation. The embroidery is executed primarily with flat stitches based on the running stitch, making full use of the negative spaces of deep red that show through the white, light yellow, and light blue embroidered motifs at the intervals where the cloth is left unworked. The headcloth is composed of two primary panels, each a

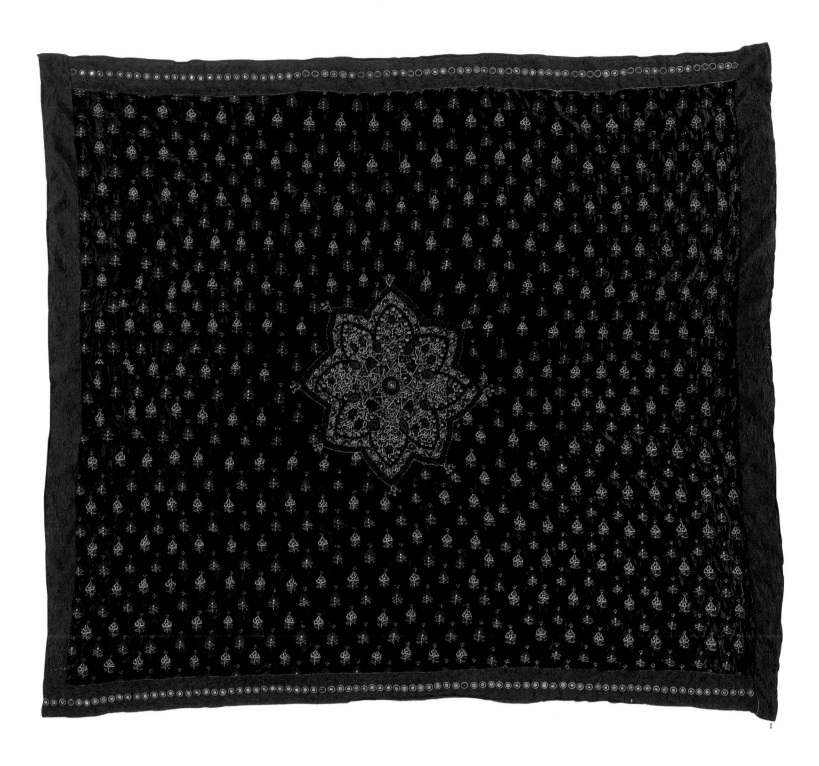

2

width that could be woven comfortably on a handloom. The panels are stitched down the center and each appears to have been embroidered before they were stitched together. It would have been easier to make the patterns match across the seam if they were embroidered after the panels had been stitched together, but the whole piece would have been heavy and cumbersome to work on. Most extant *orhni* exhibit some discrepancies on the two sides of the center seam, suggesting that the panels were customarily worked separately and then stitched together. Here the discrepancies are very slight despite the unusual complexity of the design, and the woven border stripes match almost exactly.[28]

Nora Fisher has suggested that a Jat ceremonial cloth in the Museum of International Folk Art in Santa Fe may represent a ritual diagram of walled village compounds.[29] The motifs on the Spencer *orhni* more closely resemble the common abstracted stars, flowers, and crosses—and the motifs built of these elements—that are also found, for example, on a Jat headcloth in the Museum of Ethnography in Basel.[30] The complex interrelationship of the various design motifs and groupings of motifs on the Spencer *orhni*, however, suggest the possibility that this design also represented a ritual diagram.

3. Woman's Shawl (*Abocchnai*)

◆

Pakistan (Sind)
Late 19th or early 20th century
Silk embroidery thread on cotton ground
Embroidery (stem, chain stitch) on plain weave ground
75.5 x 51.5 in.; 191 x 131 cm
The William Bridges Thayer Memorial, 1928.848

The vibrant red flowers, executed with silk embroidery floss on a plain woven cotton ground, exemplify the widespread dissemination and adaptation of courtly motifs. The flowering plants at the borders are related in form to early prototypes of the motifs that developed into the familiar *boteh*, or "paisley cone," found on nineteenth-century Kashmir shawls.[31] Both the Kashmir *boteh* and these brilliant flowers are derived from flowers and flowering plant motifs popular at the Safavid court in Iran and at the Mughal court in India. The embroiderer of this shawl has taken this conventional imagery, crowded the central motifs into slightly irregular rows, and executed the whole in brilliant red with touches of green. The luster of the silk floss, vibrant color, sheer plentitude of motifs, and their slightly irregular placement in otherwise orderly rows, convey an impression of joyful exuberance.

3

TUNICS

4. Woman's Tunic (*Aba*)

✦

India (Banni district, Kutch, Gujarat)
Late 19th or early 20th century
Silk and mirror glass
Embroidery (variety of looped and flat stitches,
mirrorwork [*shisha*], and detached interlacing)
on red satin ground
43.5 x 41.3 in.; 110.5 x 105 cm
The William Bridges Thayer Memorial,
1928.873

The deep red of this tunic, as well as its exquisite workmanship, suggest that it may have been a wedding garment. In many communities in northwest India, the wedding tunic was an important part of a woman's dowry, often given to her by the groom's family. This *aba* would have been worn with an *odhani* headcloth and the wide, embroidered pants with narrow cuffs (*ezar*) typical of women from Hindu families that had converted to Islam.[32]

Sallie Casey Thayer purchased the tunic from Marshall Field's department store in Chicago sometime before 1928, when it was included among the objects she donated to the University of Kansas. Small signs of wear and repair on the tunic suggest that it was not new when it was purchased.

The design on this tunic is closely related to that on a tunic that won first prize for embroidery in a nationwide competition of Indian handicrafts in Bombay in the winter of 1885–1886. The Mayo Prizes for Art-Workmanship were designed to encourage traditional Indian arts during a time when the influx of cheap European industrial products, particularly textiles, threatened the economics of native industries. At the same time, Western demand for Europeanized styles and Indian interest in things European were displacing traditional aesthetic sensibilities. Many nineteenth-century travelers and British public servants described with pleasure and respect the various crafts they observed, and lamented the factors that undermined their economic viability and, in the eyes of some European observers, the aesthetic value of the work. The annual Mayo Prizes were designed to reward "those specimens which are truly Oriental in character, and which exemplify in the highest degree elegance in design with excellence in workmanship." The notice was signed by the British public servant J. B. Richey, acting chief secretary to government.[33]

The *aba*—or *kudti*, as it was called in the citation—that won first prize for embroidery in 1885–1886 was submitted by a woman named Hurbai from Bhuj, the capital of Kutch in Gujarat. Hurbai is identified only as "the mother of Nur Mahammad Khamesa of Bhuj." The citation briefly describes the red silk *kudti*, "embroidered with native dyed silk thread" and with "[s]mall pieces of looking-glass (*Shishadar*) . . . very effectively introduced in the design." Hurbai's work is praised as being "excellent in design, colour and workmanship." The citation concludes with surprise and satisfaction that the prize was won by a woman:

> As the subject of the education and employment of native women forms one of the
> public questions of the day, it is interesting to note that this prize should be carried off
> by a woman.[34]

The Spencer tunic is almost identical to Hurbai's 1885 tunic in the shape and ornamentation of the rectangular neck panel and the mirrored interlacing of the breast panel, even down to such details as the composition and arrangement of each narrow band in the rectangular neck piece. Both, for example, include two bands of detached interlacing that border two rows of mirrorwork. Their prominent position in the neck panel appears to be distinctive to a particular group of closely related *aba* from Bhuj.

The Spencer tunic is not only closely related to the Hurbai tunic, but also to several other tunics that are generally considered to be of more recent date. Among the *abas* in museum collections are one on green satin ground in the Calico Museum in Ahmedabad; an *aba* on blue satin ground in the Hiroshima Prefectural Museum; and four on red satin ground: one in the Museum of International Folk Art in Santa Fe, another in the Museum of Ethnography in Basel, a third in the Indianapolis Museum of Art, and a fourth in the Victoria and Albert Museum in London. All eight have rectangular neck panels with similarly placed pattern bands, including two bands of detached interlacing. All eight also employ a similar interlacing pattern interspersed with tiny mirrors for the large breast panel, and a form emanating from the pointed end of the breast panel. In all but the Hurbai tunic this is a scalloped medallion. The Spencer and the Victoria and Albert *abas* have an elaborate embroidered border at the hem;

the others have undecorated hems. The Spencer, Santa Fe, Basel, Indianapolis, Victoria and Albert, Ahmedabad, and Hiroshima tunics are all executed on a finer scale than the Hurbai tunic, with more meticulous workmanship and greater geometric precision.

From the treatment of the neck closure, Nora Fisher has identified the Santa Fe tunic as probably belonging to a Memon merchant-class Muslim woman. Marie-Louise Nabholz-Kartaschoff, keeper of Asian textiles and East Asia at the Museum of Ethnography in Basel, and the late Peggy Stoltz Gilfoy, past curator of textiles and ethnographic arts at the Indianapolis Museum of Art, associate the Basel and Indianapolis tunics, respectively, with Jat embroiderers. The Jats were a group of Islamic people who immigrated from Baluchistan and Sind several centuries ago. The Muslim Jats were known for the high quality of their embroidery and for a long tradition of creating intricate geometric patterns. Jat women traditionally embroidered not only for their own households, but for the marketplace as well.

On the basis of these comparisons, it is likely that the Spencer tunic was commissioned by a family of the Memon merchant class, and that the work was done by Jat embroiderers.

The Hurbai tunic can be dated prior to 1885. As it was submitted to a competition for current work, it was probably made not much before that date. The seven tunics in museum collections have ascribed dates ranging from the nineteenth to the early twentieth century, clustering around 1900: the Ahmedabad tunic, nineteenth or early twentieth century; the Victoria and Albert tunic, early twentieth century; the Basel tunic, late nineteenth century; the Indianapolis tunic, circa 1900; and the Santa Fe tunic, nineteenth century. The Hiroshima tunic has no ascribed date. The Hurbai tunic appears to be the oldest of the group. If this dating is correct, and if we can take the first-prize Hurbai tunic as typical of the best work of its kind, it would appear that *aba* tunics in Bhuj and the surrounding area of northern Kutch became more complex—and the workmanship finer and more meticulous—toward the end of the century. Such a finding is in direct contradiction to the lamentations of many contemporary observers that skills were being lost and workmanship deteriorating during this period. Perhaps the contests were a factor in the increasingly fine and more complex workmanship.

5. Woman's Tunic (*Aba*)

◆

India (Gujarat)
19th or early 20th century
Silk and mirror glass
Embroidery (variety of looped and flat stitches and mirrorwork) on deep blue satin ground
49.5 x 41.5 in.; 126 x 105.5 cm
The William Bridges Thayer Memorial, 1928.874

This tunic is the most intricately worked of the three Spencer *aba*. Although red was the most common color for wedding apparel, this *aba* probably was part of a wedding ensemble in Kutch, Gujarat. The minute detail of the design and exquisite craftsmanship suggest the work of a professional embroiderer. The wide variety of looped and flat stitches used here to create subtle differences in texture include chain stitch, open chain, couching, cretan, dot, fly, long armed cross, stem, Roumanian, and *shisha* mirrorwork.

The tiny "mirrors" traditionally were made by blowing glass into spheres, silvering the spheres on the inside, and then splintering them.[35] Sometimes bits of mica were substituted for glass. Glass-making was a specialized occupation, and mirror glass was often sold in open-air markets.

In the Banni district of Kutch, the small, white three-petalled flower motifs used to border certain areas such as the sleeve bands are associated with the Islamic holiday Mohuram. They are referred to as "the hand," and appear also on the Spencer red *aba*.[36]

An *aba* in the Hiroshima Prefectural Museum resembles the Spencer red *aba* in design, but like this one, has a deep blue satin ground. The Hiroshima *aba* is identified as an Islamic woman's wedding dress from Kutch in Gujarat.[37]

4

5

6. Woman's Tunic (Aba) (detail)

✦

India (Banni district, Kutch, Gujarat)
19th or early 20th century
Silk and mirror glass
Embroidery (chain stitch and mirrorwork) on mustard yellow satin ground
40.5 x 40.5 in.; 103 x 103 cm
The William Bridges Thayer Memorial, 1928.872
Note: This *aba* has a small Marshall Field and Co. tag attached to it with a handwritten inscription: "antique embroidered silk dress" and "over 100 years."[38]

The mustard yellow ground of this tunic, the comparative simplicity and coarseness of the embroidery, and the imprecise rendition of its geometric patterns are unusual among extant examples of nineteenth- and early-twentieth-century *abas*. Perhaps such *abas* were simply considered less collectible (or publishable) than the exquisite deep blue and red wedding *abas* scattered in museum collections around the world. Within the community of its origin, however, this *aba* appears to have been highly valued, and the evidence suggests that the color was probably not an anomaly. The embroidered panels on their mustard yellow ground have been reappliqued to a ground satin of similar color. The ground satin itself has been pieced and repaired with other fragments of a similar satin, suggesting that mustard yellow satin was available in the community. The border of the main breast panel has been unevenly trimmed, causing the pattern to appear and disappear at the edge of the medallion. This suggests that the panel may have been reused more than once, an idea reinforced, although not proven, by several carefully darned repairs to the ground fabric of the panels.

The lack of geometric precision in the patterning of this *aba,* as well as the comparatively large scale of the motifs and simplified design, suggests that it was embroidered by members of a household, rather than by professional embroiderers.

6

34

7. Child's Hooded Cap

✦

India (Kutch or Saurastra, Gujarat)
19th or early 20th century
Silk
Embroidery (chain and other looped stitches)
on red satin ground
17.3 x 9.3 in.; 44 x 24 cm
The William Bridges Thayer Memorial,
1928.875

This little hood, adorned with imagery from the Mughal court and creatures from Hindu mythology, is called a *nati* in Kutch and a *kathi* in Saurastra.[39]

Flowering plants in full bloom dwarf the figures of peacocks, parrots, elephants, and courtly women in a parody of scale that nevertheless evokes images of gardens associated with the Mughal and Rajput courts. Peacocks, a flamboyant presence in those gardens, symbolize the beauty of the court. By dancing, they brought rain and thus prosperity.[40] Parrots perch on the flowering plants as if they were trees, on the ground beneath them, and on the flowers the women hold in their veiled left hands. Both parrots and women are portrayed with dark, projecting profile eyes made more pronounced by a white surround. The projecting profile eye was a distinctive feature of a medieval Jain and Hindu manuscript tradition in Gujarat, a tradition that influenced later Rajput painting.[41] Here we see a later manifestation of this enduring stylistic feature in a small folk embroidery from the region.

Elephants, majestic and powerful, were fitting mounts for Indian rulers both in war and in peace. Originally descended from heaven, elephants were considered to be cousins of the clouds and to have the power to bring rain.[42] The caparisoned elephant in this lush garden setting evokes the ruler of the garden in his role as preserver of peace and harmony.

The woman who embroidered this little hood created a world of harmony, beauty, and abundance to envelop a small child.

7

HOUSEHOLD FURNISHINGS

8. Household Furnishing

◆

India
19th century
Silk
Embroidery (chain stitch) on satin ground
78.5 x 57 in.; 199 x 145 cm
The William Bridges Thayer Memorial, 1928.853

9. Household Furnishing

◆

India
19th century
Silk
Embroidery (chain stitch) on satin ground
40.5 x 76.5 in.; 103 x 194 cm
The William Bridges Thayer Memorial,
1928.856

Flat textiles were used for many purposes around the house. They were hung in doorways and on walls, and used as covers for other objects. These might have been used to cover piles of quilts.

These two textiles have been recycled from articles of women's costume. The first (Plate 8) probably started life as an *odhani*; the second (Plate 9), as a skirt. Both have been strengthened and made into household furnishings by the addition of linings and one or several plain satin borders.

The first textile retains the long, rectangular shape and almost full size of most *odhani*. In style it closely resembles Plate 1, with red and multicolored *buta* and central medallion. The ground, however, is yellow satin rather than blue, and the flowers are more widely spaced and somewhat less abstracted and compact than in the preceding example. The central medallion has eight lobed petals that narrow to long points, giving it a sharper, more star-like, appearance. It is surrounded by three wide satin borders, pieced from recycled satin fabric—the innermost yellow, the second red, the third pale blue. The borders are separated by fine edging with a final narrow red border on the outer edge.

The second textile (Plate 9), probably constructed from a skirt, is the most worn and has been cut down and carefully repaired. The central panel is composed of alternating rows of women with nose rings, flowers, and peacocks in full display. The upper two rows are inserted, pieced from a similar textile or from a cut-off section of this one. Depictions of women with nose rings, flowers, and peacocks, motifs derived ultimately from imagery associated with the Mughal court, were popular throughout northwest India and Pakistan. Even within the strict constraints of highly conventionalized imagery, however, artisans were able to interpret these motifs in their own way. Here, the women's headcloths envelop their bodies, half hiding the clothing beneath. The women turn slightly to the left and appear to be moving in horizontal rows, walking or even dancing. Their skirts flare slightly and they stand on the balls of their feet. Every other woman wears a red *odhani*, which unifies a complex interplay of blue, purple, green, and gold, colors that variously define headcloths, bodices, and skirts against the golden yellow satin ground. The woman who embroidered these figures emphasized movement and color within the strictures of conventional format.

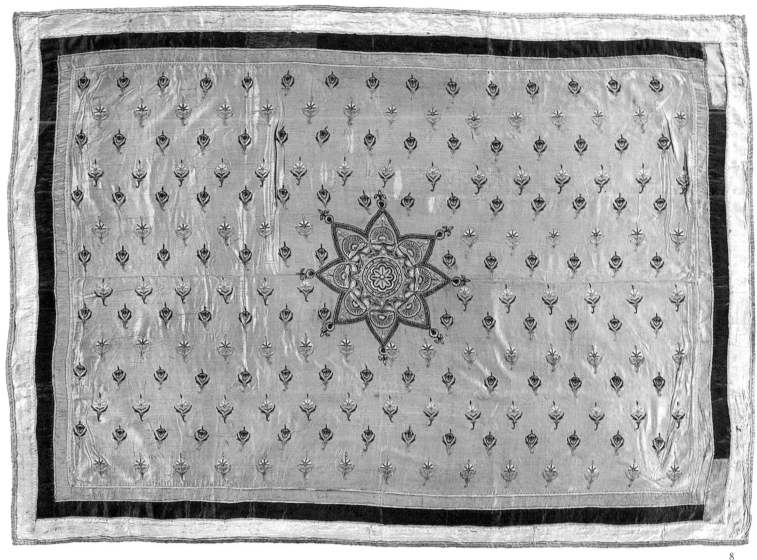

8

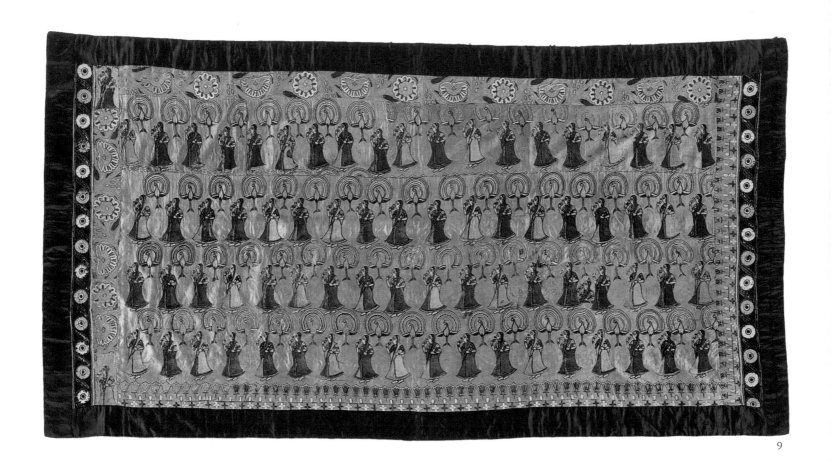

9

10. Embroidered Panel

✦

India (Kutch) or Pakistan (Sind)
19th or early 20th century
Cotton
Embroidery (detached interlacing) on plain
weave ground
41 x 21.5 in.; 104 x 54.5 cm
The William Bridges Thayer Memorial,
1928.881

The motifs on this small household textile were made with the needle technique known as detached interlacing. Using a needle, the stitcher first sets up scaffolding warps on the surface of the ground fabric, and then darns wefts into the warps, creating separate layers of plain weave fabric that float over the surface of the ground fabric. A distinguishing characteristic of detached interlacing is that the embroidery thread shows on the reverse only as a series of tiny stitches marking the points where the scaffolding threads are anchored to the ground fabric at the edges of the motifs.

This distinctive technique, called *hurmitch* in the Sind and *bavaliya* in Kutch, was practiced in Dhat and the area surrounding Hyderabad at the center of the province of Sind and in parts of Kutch, particularly in Vaghad in eastern Kutch. Detached interlacing was also used in conjunction with other embroidery stitches in the Thar Parkar regions of Pakistan and Rajasthan, India, as well as in Kutch.[43] For border motifs and space fillers, detached interlacing added yet another element of variety to the already large vocabulary of stitches used throughout the desert regions of northwest India and eastern Pakistan.

On this small textile, created almost entirely of detached interlacing, a web of motifs based on circles and ellipses is set within a doubled rectangular border. Cross and abstracted flower motifs alternate in a scrolling vine-like manner within the double border. The border is flanked on the vertical ends with alternating interrupted circles and three pairs of half ellipses. The web is predominantly red with light blue and white accents, skillfully used to reinforce the geometric scheme. The deep blue indigo ground is incorporated visually into many of the motifs so that it is read sometimes as part of the design, sometimes as the ground.

In this design scheme, the large central medallion, six surrounding medallions, and quarter circles in the four corners completely fill the central panel. The theme of central medallion with six orbiting medallions is reinforced by a double circle, in natural white, enclosing the central portions of the medallions, and by white ellipses with attached crosses pointing diagonally toward the central medallion from within each of the four quarter circles in the corners. The central medallion is enlarged—and made dominant—by a wide circle of light blue outlined in white just inside its outer red border. Pairs of light blue half ellipses surround the central motif in the intervals between the surrounding medallions, and the three pairs of half ellipses at the vertical borders draw further attention to the central medallion. The interstices between major motifs are completely filled, mostly with small motifs that are primarily varieties of crosses and their multiples. Although there are a few places where the motifs do not meet as apparently planned, the overall design—created through the layout of motifs and the skillful use of color—is so strong, and the use of sub-motifs in the interstices so skillful, that these discrepancies are almost unnoticeable.

There is one striking anomaly. One of the surrounding medallions lacks the double white circle of connected crosses that characterizes the central and other five subsidiary medallions. Although in other respects this medallion is similar to the others, the lack of the prominent white band defining the center causes the whole medallion to blend into the red web of the ground, which creates a strange disquiet in the viewer at the ambiguity posed by the almost missing medallion, a crucial element within the dominant geometric scheme set up by the artist.

10

Embroidery for Export

11. White-on-White Embroidered Fabric (detail)

◆

India
19th or early 20th century
Cotton on raw silk
Embroidery (double-face satin stitch) on plain
weave ground
324 x 33.5 in.; 823 x 85 cm
Source Unknown, 0000.2433

This long piece of fabric is embroidered with several sets of floral designs. Each forty-inch pattern unit is set off from the others by a border of five naturalistically portrayed flowers set within a double border of tightly scrolling vines. Most of the pattern units are made up of a pyramid of isolated floral motifs. A few display a pyramidal flowering plant, fully depicted with leaves and stems. The embroidery is executed with loosely plied cotton embroidery thread with a long, smooth, and lustrous surface. The predominant embroidery stitch is satin, worked to create a double-face fabric; in other words, the pattern shows equally well on front and back. The embroiderer has created a three-dimensional, embossed effect by the sheer density of the stitches and by partially stitching over areas already stitched (i.e., encroaching satin stitch). The direction of twist and ply affects the way light bounces off the pattern threads. Stitches lying in different orientations reflect light differently, creating the effect of shading as light glances across the surface of the fabric.

A distinctive type of white-on-white embroidery, intended primarily for export, was developed in urban workshops in Calcutta and Dhaka (now in Bangladesh) and seems to have spread from there to Lucknow near Varanasi (Banares) in the mid-nineteenth century.[44] The white-work embroidery in these regions was probably influenced both by the tradition of white-on-white cotton brocade weaving of Dhaka and by European whitework, particularly embroidery of the "Dresden" and Ayrshire styles, brought to India by European women in the early nineteenth century.[45] The most well known whitework embroidery from the region, known as chikan work, was executed with cotton or silk thread on fine Indian muslin. Before stitching began, the pattern was usually block printed on the ground fabric. A trader or middleman typically chose or created the design by selecting one or a combination of several pattern blocks from an established repertoire. The piece would then be block printed, given to the embroiderer, and washed afterwards by another specialist to remove all traces of the printed pattern. Although the stitching could be done from the front or from the reverse, chikan work embroideries were characteristically one sided.

Chikan work embroiderers used a wide variety of stitches in prescribed ways to create complex, generally floral, designs. Chikan work textiles often have mesh-like sections in the design created by gently pulling threads in the ground fabric apart with a needle and working around the spaces. Patterns appear dense against the translucency of the delicate muslin ground.

Although this textile exhibits the high skill of the best of the chikan work embroiderers, it is quite different from typical chikan work in several respects. The pattern is executed on a translucent raw silk instead of cotton. The embroiderer relied primarily on a single stitch, the satin stitch, to achieve all of the various texture and shading effects of the pattern. There is no evidence of a block-printed pattern underneath the embroidered pattern, although there are traces of pencil markings. It is a double-sided piece.

The unusual combination of cotton embroidery on a silk ground, coupled with other discrepancies from typical Indian white-on-white embroidery, suggests that this length of fabric was specially commissioned; the merchant (or private person) placing the order made use of the skills of embroiderers accustomed to working with cotton, but requested (or supplied them with) a different ground fabric. The careful layout of discrete but related pattern units suggests that the fabric was designed for a specific purpose. The use of free-hand pencil markings instead of block-printed patterns suggests that this pattern was not part of an established repertoire, and supports the idea that the piece was commissioned to fit a specific purpose and space. The fabric would have been appropriate for a European woman's summer dress, or for bed or bedroom furnishings in a European house. Perhaps it was designed for bed furnishings, as it was so carefully worked to be seen from both sides.

Kashmir Shawls

INTRODUCTION

Shawls from Kashmir made of fine lustrous wool and decorated with cone-shaped motifs dominated the European fashion world from the late eighteenth century through the third quarter of the nineteenth. Dress fashions changed radically during this period of empire building and industrial revolution, but a close collaboration between Kashmiri and French designers, the adaptability and ingenuity of Kashmiri craftsmen, and a continuing European fascination with the exotic ensured a remarkable longevity for the Kashmir shawl among fashion-conscious European women.

The Vale of Kashmir is nestled high in the Himalayas, a lush, fertile valley situated at the crossroads of several ancient trade routes. Its most famous product was a cloth of exceptionally high quality that was made from the wool of several species of mountain sheep and goats found at high altitudes in Ladakh, Tibet, and Xinjiang. Although the fleece had to be imported, and although other countries—such as Iran—also wove fine articles of clothing from similar fleece, Kashmir gained the greatest fame for the skilled spinning and weaving of this precious fiber.[46] Rulers from India to Iran and Russia, and from the Near East to Europe, admired the lustrous sashes, shawls, and turbans woven on Kashmiri looms.

The highest-quality wool was light, warm, and glossy. It was so fine that merchants in Kashmir, even today, customarily pull a large shawl through a finger ring to prove that a particular piece is of premier quality.[47] The highest-quality fleece, known as *asli tus*, was from the Himalayan ibex (*Capra ibex*), which lived in the wild above fourteen thousand feet in Ladakh and western Tibet. The fleece was collected from rocks and shrubs where the ibex rubbed off its precious winter undercoat at the beginning of spring. The fleece of wild mountain sheep—the Shapo (*Ovis orientalis vignei*), the Argali (*Ovis ammon*), and the Bharal (*Pseudois nayaur*)—was collected in the same manner, and also was considered of premium quality.[48]

Wild animals yield very little fleece, and despite its high value, an English observer noted in 1821 that only two looms in all of Kashmir specialized in weaving *asli tus*.[49] Most high-quality shawls were woven from the fleece of a Central Asian species of mountain goat, the *Capra hircus*, that lived in the mountains of Ladakh, Tibet, and Chinese Turkestan. Like their wild counterparts, these domesticated goats produced a soft undercoat beneath a coarse layer of outer hair. Shepherds combed the goats in the spring to harvest the soft lustrous underfleece. The preferred habitat of the goats was lower than that of their wild counterparts, but they still had to live above ten thousand feet to thrive, five thousand feet higher than the Kashmir Valley. The *Capra hircus* is the goat known to the West as the cashmere goat, a name derived from old European spellings of Kashmir. Cashmere is, and was, also known as *pashmina*.

Until the early nineteenth century, when a severe epidemic decimated the herds, most cashmere fleece was imported to Kashmir from Ladakh and Tibet. After the epidemic, fleece from the flocks of nomadic Kirghiz herders was imported through Yarkand and Khotan, cities on the southern branch of the Silk Road at the base of the Kunlun mountains in Central Asia (present-day Xinjiang). After mid-century, most cashmere fleece came from Turfan on the branch of the Silk Road that skirted the Taklamakan Desert to the north, at the base of the Tien Shan mountain range in Xinjiang.[50] Fleece from the *Capra hircus* was sometimes mixed with fleece from sheep flocks in Kashmir, Iran, the Punjab, and other shawl-producing areas in order to meet high export demands and control prices. Kirmani sheep from Iran produced a wool so fine that some nineteenth-century European travelers mistook these sheep for cashmere goats.[51] Although neither the wild nor the domesticated goats were native to Kashmir, Kashmir controlled the mountain passes and monopolized the supply of cashmere throughout much of the nineteenth century.

FIG. 3

Abdullah Qutb-Shah of Golconda
Wearing a Kashmir Shawl

India
ca. 1670
Leaf from an album
Ink and pigment on paper
20 x 37 cm
The British Museum, 1974.6-17.02 (7)
[© The British Museum]

سلطان عبدالله

HISTORY

One of the earliest documented products of the Kashmiri looms was a long, narrow sash, decorated at both ends, that was worn by men as a turban, wrapped several times around the waist, or folded and worn over the shoulder. Paintings and written records show that it was incorporated into both Mughal and Iranian male royal attire in the seventeenth century. References in paintings and documents, as well as the comments of most European observers, suggest that Kashmir shawls, in India, were worn exclusively by men. François Bernier (1620–1688), a French doctor who served as personal physician to the Mughal ruler Aurangzeb (r. 1658–1707), however, also saw them used by women and children: "The Mughals and Indian men and women wore [Kashmir shawls] in winter around their heads, passing them over the shoulders as a mantle."[52]

EARLIEST DEPICTIONS AND DOCUMENTARY EVIDENCE

Kashmir shawls are depicted in seventeenth-century Indian miniatures, where they appear as part of Mughal court dress. Several rulers of Golconda in the Deccan, for example, dressed for their official portraits with meticulously rendered Kashmir shawls prominently draped over their shoulders. In these portraits, the shawls are long and comparatively narrow with a shallow band of decoration at each end. The decorated panel consists of a row of slender, naturalistically depicted flowering plants presented as discrete entities against a plain ground (see Fig. 3).[53] The paintings match a written description by François Bernier, who stated that the shawls measured about five feet by two and a half feet. They had plain fields with decorated borders at the ends, measuring less than a foot in height.[54] These shawls were also worn with Iranian royal attire, according to another seventeenth-century French traveler, Jean Baptiste Tavernier (1605–1689).[55]

The earliest written reference to the Kashmir shawl is in the records of the Mughal ruler Akbar, compiled by the court chronicler Abul Fazl 'Allami. From the *Ain-i Akbari* we learn that Akbar sent Kashmir shawls as gifts to the rulers of other countries, and that he introduced new styles of wearing the shawls at court. Fazl reported that shawls formerly were worn folded in four, but now were worn simply draped around the shoulders. He wrote that Akbar also instituted the practice of wearing a pair of shawls stitched back to back in order to hide the underside of the shawl, a practice that his son, Jahangir, noted was still popular in his day.[56] Until the division of a single shawl between several different looms in the mid-nineteenth century, most Kashmiri looms were set up to weave not one, but an identical pair of Kashmir shawls on each warp.

EARLIEST EXTANT KASHMIR SHAWLS

The earliest extant Kashmir shawls also date from the seventeenth century. Like the Mughal painted depictions and Bernier's written description, they are long shawls with shallow borders of discrete flowering plants at each end. Perhaps the earliest is a fragment of a border, or *pallov*, in the Jagdish and Kamla Mittal Museum of Indian Art in Hyderabad. Jagdish Mittal states that it is woven of *shah tus*, the highest quality of wild fleece—fleece "fit for a shah." On the narrow seven-inch border, seven slender flowering plants, perhaps wild roses, rise gracefully from their roots, swaying slightly under the weight of the blossoms. The depiction appears to be carefully, and brilliantly, copied from a Mughal painting, one perhaps executed for the purpose. Stylistically, the depiction of the flowers resembles that on carpets and velvets from the reign of Shah Jahan. For this reason, Mittal dates this fragment to 1640–1650, and suggests that the shawl's high aesthetic qualities, the exceptional quality of the fiber, and technical virtuosity might point to a royal patron, perhaps Shah Jahan himself.[57]

Another seventeenth-century fragment, divided between the Calico Museum in Ahmedabad and the Victoria and Albert Museum, displays a shorter, fuller rendering of the same flower with more bend in the stalk. It is generally dated to the late seventeenth century. A complete shawl in the Museum of Fine Arts, Boston, dating from the late seventeenth or early eighteenth century, has a double border of flowering plants at each end. While still naturalistic, the plants are beginning to bend in a more abstract manner and to point toward the "cone" shape that became characteristic during the eighteenth century.[58]

Akbar actively stimulated the Kashmir weaving industry.[59] From the *Ain-i Akbari* we learn that he imported skilled weavers from Andizhan in Eastern Turkestan, sponsored experiments to improve the quality of dyes, and encouraged shawl weaving in Lahore, probably by immigrant communities of Kashmiri weavers.[60] We know from other sources that Akbar treasured his collection of Kashmir shawls, and kept them with other royal textiles in the *toshkana* (imperial wardrobe) in a manner that anticipated the concerns of modern museums.[61]

Many Mughal rulers maintained residences in Vernag in the Kashmir Valley and continued Akbar's active support of Kashmiri weaving. Akbar's son Jahangir stated that his Kashmir residence was his favorite, and that he would rather lose his empire than the province of Kashmir. Sick with palsy, he asked to be carried to Kashmir so that he could die in Vernag.[62] Jahangir first visited the province of Kashmir in 1589 when, as a young man of twenty, he accompanied Akbar on a tour of the province. The prince admired the beauty of the Kashmir Valley and described the charm of its flowers in his memoirs, the *Tuzk-i-Jahangir*:

> The red rose, the violet, and the narcissus grow of themselves; in the fields there are all kinds of flowers and all sorts of sweet, scented herbs, more than can be calculated. In the soul-enchanting spring the hills and plains are filled with blossoms, the gates, the walls, the courts, the roofs are lighted up by the torches of banquet-adorning tulips.[63]

Jahangir also described the shawl industry, noting the well-deserved fame of the Kashmir shawls that his father used so extensively at court, and exhibiting his knowledge of the industry by stating that the best fleece was imported from Tibet and made from the wool of a Tibetan goat.[64]

Kashmir prospered under Jahangir's rule. He followed Akbar's precedent in favoring the province, and used the products of its looms for royal gifts. Jahangir once gave a shawl from Kashmir to a man named Mirza Raja Bhao Singh. He recorded the gift in the *Tuzk-i-Jahangir*, noting that the shawl was a particular type called a *phup*, a word derived from the Sanskrit *pushpa*, meaning "flower."[65] The fact that Jahangir made a point of identifying the shawl as a "flower" shawl suggests that not all shawls exhibited floral patterns at the time. It is also possible that the word *phup* referred not just literally to flowers, but to patterning in general; hence a *phup* might simply refer to a patterned, as opposed to an unpatterned, shawl. In any case, we know from visual and written records that most of the patterning was floral.

As long as they maintained power, Mughal rulers continued their protection of Kashmir and patronage of its weavers. George Forster (d. 1792), an Englishman traveling in the late eighteenth century, was impressed by the attention paid by the rulers to this province on the outskirts of the empire. He observed that

> the interests of this province were so strongly favoured at the Mughal court that every complaint against its governors was attentively listened to, and any attempt to molest the people was restrained or punished.[66]

Famine and factional warfare ravaged the Mughal empire in the early eighteenth century. In 1739 the Iranian ruler Nadir Shah invaded Delhi, pillaging the great capital and slaughtering its inhabitants. He returned to Iran, leaving the current Mughal ruler on the throne, but with reduced territories, an empty treasury, many of the dynasty's treasures—including the famous Koh-i-Noor diamond—confiscated, and some of India's best craftsmen commandeered to work in Iran. Although the Mughal dynasty survived in name until 1857, real power passed to the hands of regional courts and to the British. Kashmir could no longer rely on the old combination of court patronage and protection that had supported the development of its shawl industry.

Fourteen years after Nadir Shah devastated the Mughal capital, a warlord named Ahmad Shah Abdali invaded Kashmir from his base in Afghanistan and added the province to his expanding empire. Afghani rulers controlled Kashmir from 1753 until 1819, and Afghan rule was harsh. The Afghan overlords taxed Kashmir shawls heavily but provided little support for the industry. During this period Kashmiri weavers and merchants turned increasingly to foreign markets to sell their shawls and to meet their heavy financial obligations to their Afghan overlords. Late-eighteenth-century paintings depict male rulers of the Qajar dynasty in Iran and French noblewomen alike draped in Kashmir shawls. The European fashion industry, in particular, would have a profound influence on the subsequent development of Kashmir shawls.

Kashmir shawls had first come to the attention of Western travelers, such as the Frenchmen Jean Baptiste Tavernier and François Bernier, in the seventeenth century. By the end of the eighteenth century they had attracted the attention of the fashion-conscious in Europe. The youthful Marquise de Sorcy de Thélusson, however, was ahead of French fashion when she sat for her portrait in a Kashmir shawl in 1790. Jacques-Louis David depicted her dressed in white and draped in a long, narrow shawl of natural white cashmere, with end borders of discrete cone-shaped motifs with bent tips and floral interiors.[67] The bent-tip cone motif became known in Europe by the Persian word *boteh*. In India and Kashmir it was referred to by the related term *buta* or "flower pattern." (See Plate 3 for a discussion of the *boteh* motif.) In Europe the pattern was also referred to as the "pine cone," "pine," "cone," "mango," and "Paisley" pattern, the latter after Paisley, Scotland, one of the many places in Europe and Britain where pattern looms (first draw looms and then jacquard looms) were used to weave less costly imitations of the prized tapestry-woven shawls from Kashmir.

The Marquise's shawl is very similar to shawls depicted in Indian miniatures from the sixteenth to the eighteenth century, but after the beginning of the nineteenth century, the shawl—in size as well as in ornamentation—changed quickly and radically in response to the constantly shifting vagaries of European high fashion.[68]

From the mid-seventeenth until the beginning of the nineteenth century, borders became slowly but progressively larger. At the same time, the naturalistic flowers with roots that bordered seventeenth-century shawls became fuller and evolved into a vase filled with a tightly packed, stylized display of assorted flowers. The vase of flowers motif, in turn, merged with an Iranian abstracted leaf pattern expressed as a "cone" with a bent tip. By the late eighteenth century, a discrete row of abstracted flower-filled cones with bent tips had taken the place of the naturalistic flowering plants of the seventeenth century, but the general composition remained the same.[69] The shawls were long and comparatively narrow, with a plain field and borders at each end filled with a row of discrete pattern units. The patterned borders are wider than in earlier prototypes.

During the course of the nineteenth century, shawls became larger and more colorful, and the end borders expanded until, by mid-century, richly colored swirling motifs encroached on a central medallion. At the same time, the *boteh* motif became increasingly abstracted, elongated and interconnected with other *boteh* and background motifs.

In the early nineteenth century, Empress Josephine set the tone for fashion of the day. She owned more than sixty Kashmir shawls, and in 1809 had her portrait painted wearing one as a dress and another over her shoulders.[70] A meticulous description of an early-nineteenth-century Kashmir shawl may be seen in the portrait of Madame Philibert Rivière by the painter Ingres. The shawl is long and narrow with a plain central field, but the borders have widened to accommodate a single row of enlarged, flower-filled *boteh*. Although the background is undecorated, the cones nearly fill the space, pushing against each other and the edges of the borders.[71] A similar shawl is draped over the seated wife and mother in Ingres's 1818 drawing of the Stamaty Family.[72]

In 1810 Napoleon gave seventeen Kashmir shawls to his new bride, Marie-Louise of Austria. A watercolor by Benjamin Dix depicts a crowd of noblewomen attending the wedding, most with a Kashmir shawl folded over one arm. Kashmir shawls were also collected by wealthy

women in England and Russia. They not only were worn as part of a stylish costume, but also were used in multiples as props for parlor dramas.[73]

William Moorcroft (1767–1825), an Englishman who worked for the East India Company, carried out a detailed survey of the Kashmir shawl industry between 1820 and 1823. In 1823 he returned to England with a manuscript and a set of drawings that have proved invaluable to scholars.[74] The eight drawings that survive represent particular designs commissioned by various patrons. All are variants of the bent-tip cone. The name of the design as well as the patron's name and country are inscribed on the back. Three of the extant drawings were commissioned by Mahummud Azeen Khan of Russia. Three others were for the Iranian market, one commissioned by Shooguoob Moolkh, and two others by Shah Zuman. The final two, intended for the Indian market, were simply labelled "Hindoostan."[75] The design motifs differ in shape and style, but all represent variants of the bent-tip cone, and all are not only filled with flowers, but imbedded in a floral ground. Already by 1823, the discrete motifs and large empty central field of the late eighteenth century had given way to a *horror vacui* exuberance of embellishment.

European enthusiasm for Kashmir shawls in the early decades of the nineteenth century increased demand for the shawls beyond the traditional capacity of Kashmiri weavers.

European patronage stimulated the industry and spurred the development of new formats and designs. While the complexity of the designs increased, Kashmiri weavers, workshop owners, and shawl brokers invented new manufacturing techniques to speed production.

The popularity of Kashmir shawls in the early nineteenth century prompted weavers in France (Nîmes, Lyon, Alsace) and Great Britain (Norwich, Edinburgh, Paisley) to enter the market with shawls of their own. These European shawls were often closely related to their Kashmiri prototypes in design, but were woven on pattern looms with the design preset into a complex threading arrangement. Once the pattern was set up on the draw loom, these shawls were much quicker to weave than the interlocking twill tapestry of true Kashmir shawls in which each tiny color area was handpicked with an eyeless wooden needle wrapped in thread. The widespread adoption of the semi-mechanized jacquard loom in the second half of the nineteenth century speeded production in Europe even further. In France, designers such as Amédée Couder (1797–1864) and Antony Berrus (1815–1883) reinterpreted traditional Kashmiri designs to meet the demands of French (and English) fashion. The French agents stationed in Kashmir from the 1840s facilitated a flow of goods and information between the two countries. A lively interplay developed in which Kashmiri weavers, workshop owners, and shawl dealers responded to the latest Parisian fashions at the same time that European designers emulated Kashmiri patterns.

FIG. 5
Border Detail of a "Cachemire" Shawl, 1861
Antony Berrus (1815–1883) or workshop

France
Graphite and chalk on paper
26.1 x 13.2 in.; 66.5 x 33.5 cm
Museum Purchase: The Barbara Benton Wescoe Fund, 1994.16

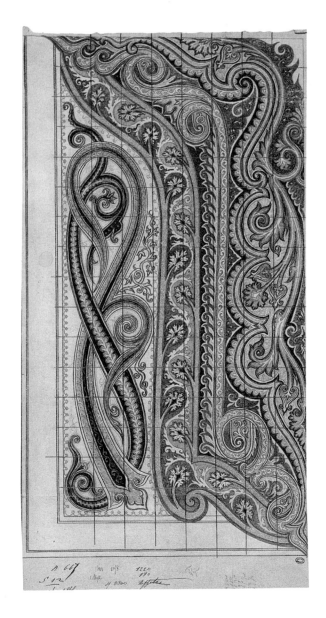

MANUFACTURE

The format (long and narrow), technique (tapestry), and patterning (floral borders) of so-called Kashmir shawls appear to have changed only slowly and in comparatively minor ways from the first solid documentation of the shawls in the seventeenth century to the late eighteenth century, when they were introduced to Europe. During their long popularity in Europe, however, which extended from the late eighteenth through the third quarter of the nineteenth century, format, fiber, patterning, technique, and the organization of a shawl's manufacture changed radically to meet the rapidly changing demands of a fashion-conscious European clientele.

Kashmir shawls were patterned in the intricate technique of interlocking twill tapestry, or *kani* as it was known locally. Twill weaves, with a structure based on warp and weft floats set on a diagonal, create a cloth that drapes well and shows to advantage the lustrous quality of the fiber. Tapestry is a technique in which each color area is woven separately using a small bobbin. The tapestry wefts of adjacent sections may or may not loop around each other or a common warp. Despite the difficulty of working on a diagonal twill structure, Kashmiri weavers interlocked adjacent wefts. A complex Kashmir pattern required hundreds of *tojis*, tiny bobbins resembling eyeless needles that carried the colored weft threads. A French botanist traveling in Kashmir in the 1820s observed as many as three thousand *tojis* in use on a single shawl.[76] Weaving progressed very slowly; even with two men working long hours each day at the loom, a Kashmir shawl typically took eighteen months to complete, while a particularly complex shawl required up to three years.[77]

The earliest substantive evidence for the use of the *kani* technique in Kashmir is that provided by extant seventeenth-century shawls. The fact that the earliest of these is woven with consummate skill, however, suggests that the technique is older. The art historian Moti Chandra cites documentary evidence to suggest that the *kani* weave was practiced as early as the eleventh century, but other scholars question his interpretation of the relevant texts.[78] According to Baron Karl Von Hügel (ca. 1795–1870), who visited Kashmir in 1836, Kashimiri weavers credited the fifteenth-century ruler Zain-ul-'Abidin (1420–1470) with importing skilled weavers from Turkestan, particularly a man named Naghz Beg, to introduce the *kani* weave. Von Hügel noted that Kashmiri weavers still laid flowers on Zain-ul-'Abidin's grave, honoring him as the founder of *kani* weaving in Kashmir.[79] A seventeenth-century history of Kashmir, the *Rajatarangini* by Srivara Pandita, notes that Zain-ul-'Abidin introduced new weaving techniques, but doesn't specify the techniques or their provenance except to say that they came from distant countries.[80]

Hajji Mukhtar Shah, whose family had been shawl dealers since the seventeenth century, wrote a history of the industry after its collapse in the 1870s. He credited Mirza Haider Dughlat, the de facto ruler of Kashmir in the mid-sixteenth century, with making *asli tus* and *pashm* available to the already skilled Kashmiri weavers. Mukhtar Shah attributed the beginnings of *kani* pattern weaving to the ingenuity of Haider's attendant and cook, Naghz Beg. According to Mukhtar Shah, it was Beg who introduced the idea of small bobbins to carry colored threads for use in discrete areas of the weaving. The early patterns were very simple, such as regular rows of red and green dots.[81]

In his history of the Kashmir shawl, Mukhtar Shah states that although the beginnings of the *kani* weaving of *asli tus* and cashmere wool can be traced to the mid-sixteenth century, it wasn't until after the Mughal conquest of Kashmir in 1586 that Kashmiri weavers began to develop the full potential of the technique.[82] François Bernier visited Kashmir with the Mughal ruler Aurangzeb in the mid-seventeenth century. Bernier described an active shawl industry that even employed children. He states that the shawls were patterned "with a sort of embroidery made in the loom," a pithy description of *kani* weaving.[83]

Observers in the early nineteenth century noted that the Kashmir shawl industry was organized into a number of discrete occupations. In the account he wrote in 1823 after a three-year study of the industry, William Moorcroft reported that twelve or more specialists were involved in the production of a single shawl. First the fleece was given to spinners, women working at home. They sorted the raw material into fine fleece, inferior fleece, and hair, and then further subdivided the fine fleece into two grades. Every category was used, but generally only the top two categories were woven into shawls. After the fleece was sorted, the women spun and then plied it. The thread was then dyed by a separate group of specialists who often also operated as brokers. One shawl required between two and three thousand warp threads.[84]

Dyers told Moorcroft that in Mughal times their forebears had used more than three hundred colors, but that now they only used sixty-four.[85] Although the number may be an exaggeration, Mughal textiles do display a wide chromatic range of beautifully rendered, fast colors. In the early nineteenth century major dye stuffs included indigo for blue; cochineal, kermes, and logwood for a range of colors from crimson to violet; safflower and saffron for oranges and yellow; and iron filings, iron sulphate, and wild pomegranate skins for black. Some of these dyestuffs were mixed to yield additional colors. Alum was the primary mordant. Green was extracted from English broadcloth and reused to dye shawl yarns. At some point, according to Hajji Mukhtar Shah, a merchant from Kabul named Yusuf Armani introduced new techniques to the Kashmiri dye industry, including the use of purified sulphuric acid with indigo and nitric acid with red.[86]

According to Moorcroft's 1823 account, three different specialists wound the warp, starched it for added strength, and dressed the loom. The pattern drawer, or *naqqash*, drew the patterns in black and white. His role was considered crucial, and he was highly paid and respected. Even at the height of the industry there were only five or six families of *naqqash* in all Kashmir.[87] It was probably *naqqash* drawings that Moorcroft brought back to England in 1823. Some pattern drawers colored their own designs, but that task was generally left to the color caller (*tarah-guru*) who worked in tandem with a pattern master. Looking at the black-and-white drawing prepared by the *naqqash*, the color caller called out the colors. He started at the bottom, calling out each color and the number of warps it extended across, and worked across each row from the bottom of the design to the top. The pattern master (*talim-guru*) transcribed his rapid chant into a shorthand notation (*talim*) that the weavers read somewhat like a musical score.[88]

Most weavers did not own their own looms. Some worked on a piece-work basis for a loom owner; others paid the owner a percentage of the price of the shawl in return for the use of the loom and a supply of wool. Moorcroft reported that most loom owners in the early 1820s had about twenty or twenty-five looms, although he had seen some establishments with fifty. By the second half of the century, some loom owners had huge manufactures with one hundred or more looms. A Colonel Grant inspected one of them in the 1860s and reported,

> The proprietor, a Mohammedan, employs 300 hands. His house is a handsome, three-storied building, well aired and lighted, and the workers are seated at their looms like clerks at their desks. . . .[89]

In the 1830s, the shawl industry suffered a significant set-back when a severe famine devastated the region and many skilled weavers and dyers perished or emigrated. By mid-century, under the stimulus of continued European demand, the industry recovered and appeared to be thriving. In 1859, Sir Richard Temple (1826–1902), a resident officer of the British government, wrote in his journal entry for Friday, July 8:

> Early in the morning I went out on an elephant with Diwan Kirpa Ram [son of the Prime Minister of Kashmir], who talked a good deal about the former Governors of Kashmir. . . . He said there was a great famine in the Sikh times [1819–1846], in which thousands of Kashmiris emigrated and the shawl manufacture suffered greatly, and that the valley had by no means recovered from the shock, when the country was made over to Gulab Singh. He also said that the records of his office would show a great revival of the shawl trade since then, and that there were now [in 1859] 6,000 families engaged in it.[90]

French agents had begun arriving in Kashmir in large numbers in the 1840s, bringing with them the latest Parisian shawl patterns for Kashmiri weavers to copy or adapt. Meanwhile, European weavers, using the new jacquard looms, were able to imitate complex Kashmiri tapestry woven designs quickly and for a comparatively modest price. Kashmiri and European designers borrowed freely from one another's repertoire, and competition was fierce.

The European market demanded a quick response to fashion trends. The eighteen-month period required to produce a typical shawl was too long. To meet the challenges of an appreciative but demanding European clientele, the shawl industry broke production into ever smaller units. A single shawl, or pair of shawls (for shawls were usually woven in pairs), instead of being woven in one piece on one loom by two weavers working together, was divided between several looms, each of which produced a segment of the shawl. This system had been used in the eighteenth century after the Afghan invasion of 1753 in order to evade the heavy shawl tax imposed by the Afghan rulers.[91] At that time, the system was not very successful; the segments were often not the same size and didn't fit together well. The finest shawls were still woven in one piece, probably in a royal workshop. In the nineteenth century, the purpose for the division of production was different, and with the stimulus of lively market demand for high-quality shawls, designers, weavers, and needleworkers conspired to produce shawls in segments that could be made into a visually unified whole. In the 1820s, Moorcroft reported seeing a shawl that had been woven on eight looms.[92] In 1836 a visitor to Kashmir described a workshop in which twenty-four weavers worked simultaneously at eleven looms to produce a single pair of shawls. He recorded the division of labor as follows:

2 looms with 3 weavers each for the large pines
4 looms with 2 weavers each for the small pines
1 loom with 2 weavers for the field
4 looms with 2 adolescent weavers each for the borders.[93]

An 1875 description of a Kashmir shawl notes that it was assembled from fifteen hundred separate pieces.[94]

Assembling a shawl from even eight segments required considerable skill on the part of designers and weavers to assure that the patterns and sizes fit together. Shawls composed of hundreds of small pieces, dating mostly to the third quarter of the nineteenth century, required astonishing skill to assemble into a coherent unit. The craftsmen responsible for this task were the *rafugar*, needleworkers who received the individually woven segments of a shawl and joined them together like a jigsaw puzzle with such skill that the seams are very difficult to detect. The *rafugar* also embellished the design as necessary to make the parts work together as a whole. They worked in a technique closely allied to *kani* weaving so that their work was well integrated with that of the weavers.

After work was finished on the shawl, it was washed by yet another group of specialists, and then sent to a final group of craftsmen who added embellished borders and fringes before the shawl was bundled with others and packed for shipping. In the nineteenth century, a number of groups of *rafugar* and finishing specialists worked in the Punjab, including many Kashmiri emigrants who had fled the valley in hard times. Craftsmen in Amritsar were particularly well known for the high quality of their embroidered borders and fringes.[95]

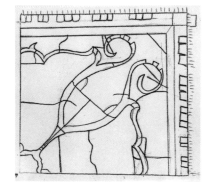

FIG. 6
D'Arcy Jensen (b. 1970)
Sketch of construction detail of
Plate 18

ca. 1994
U.S.A.
Pencil on paper
11 x 8.5 in.; 27.9 x 21.6 cm
Spencer Museum of Art, filed under 1928.971

Despite Colonel Grant's pleasant description of weavers working in a well-aired, well-lit building "like clerks at their desks," most nineteenth-century Kashmiri weavers were exploited by the government of the moment, as well as by upper levels of their own shawl industry. Weavers were taxed heavily, often with additional money extorted from them by unethical officials. They were forced to buy overpriced grain from their employers. They were unprotected from the bouts of famine and cholera that scourged the country several times in the nineteenth century. Born into their occupation, they were forbidden from leaving it; in any case, years of long hours at the loom delicately manipulating tiny bobbins of gossamer-fine threads left Kashmiri weavers completely unsuited for other occupations and, indeed, unable to perform any but their own. Although they also were often forbidden from emigrating, the large number of Kashmiri craftsmen associated with the shawl industry in the Punjab attests to the numbers of those who risked their lives to slip through the mountain passes, and underscores the severity of their situation in Kashmir.

Writing in 1887, in an introduction to the journals his father, Sir Richard Temple, had kept in the 1860s and 1870s, Richard Carnac Temple (1850–1931) noted the effects of deprivation and hard, delicate work on the health and physique of generations of Kashmiri weavers. Their condition in itself might not be so striking if it were not so different from that of their other countrymen:

> The Kashmiris, if we except the weakly shawl-makers, are one of the finest races physically in all India; robust, broad-shouldered, muscular, and well-featured, but of not more than middle height as a rule.[96]

Throughout the nineteenth century, the manufacture and export of shawls was one of the primary sources of income for Kashmir and its rulers, and this was the reason behind the strict government control of the weavers. The shawl industry as a whole was divided into many levels that included producers, owners, middlemen, merchants, and official supervisors. Each stage of production was watched with eagle eyes by tax collectors who, along with supervising officials, often exacted payments beyond that required by law. Temple described this system as he observed it in the final years of the industry:

> When the shawl is so far completed that its value can be estimated, it gets thoroughly into the grip of the tax-gatherer; indeed, throughout every process, from the growing of the wool to the final sale, this official never lets go his hold of it. It is this fact that has rendered the workmen connected with this manufacture so wretched, though their work is of surpassing excellence and their skill unrivalled. The shawl being the sport—legitimate and illegitimate—of a host of officials. . . .[97]

As early as 1823, Moorcroft noted that without the wages of his wife and children, the Kashmir shawl weaver could not provide the bare necessities for his family.[98] The situation was worse in the final years of the shawl industry when the defeat of the French in the 1870–1871 Franco-Prussian war, coupled with a change in European fashion, brought an end to the long popularity of the Kashmir shawl. Physically weak, masters of a craft for which there was no demand, and unfit for other occupations, many of the superbly skilled weavers of Kashmir did not survive the devastating famine of 1877.

TRADE AND TRADE ROUTES

Finished shawls were packed in tight bundles for transport. They were sent out from Kashmir in several directions and were customarily traded, and taxed, several times before they reached their final destinations.[99] One route went from Kashmir through Lahore to Multan in Pakistan, an important trading center in the eighteenth and nineteenth centuries and the meeting point for caravans from India and Iran. From Multan some shawls went on to Baghdad in Iraq, and from there to Constantinople (Istanbul). Others went south to the port cities of Surat in Gujarat, India, or Tatta near Karachi in present-day Pakistan. From there they traveled by ship via a network of Indian colonies to Basra (Al Basrah, Iraq) at the western end of the Persian Gulf, and to other trading cities in Iran and Turkey. Other routes went north from Kashmir to Tibet and Russia. A northwestern route went to Kabul and on to Bukhara, an important oasis and trading city on the main east-west caravan route. James Baillie Fraser (1783–1856), an English traveler in the early 1820s, stated that caravans of four to five thousand camels each left Bukhara for the three-month journey to Russia twice each year.[100] Many of these shawls passed through Tiflis (Tblisi) in Georgia, midway between the Black and Caspian Seas, and from there to Amsterdam, London, Saint Petersburg, and Moscow. In Russia, the Nizhny Novgorod fair, strategically located at the confluence of the Oka and Volga rivers, attracted merchants from far afield, including French shawl merchants from Paris.[101]

Even a cursory look at the vast network of trade routes by which Kashmir shawls were transported from Kashmir and the Punjab to Iran, Russia, the Near East and Constantinople, Germany, and Austria, as well as England and France, reveals the extent of the trade and the popularity of the shawls from the western edges of Xinjiang in Chinese Turkestan to the Atlantic Ocean.

In fashion-conscious France, Kashmir shawl dealers faced keen competition not only from each other, but also from locally produced draw loom and later jacquard-woven imitations of Kashmir shawls. French dealers scoured the world markets for fashionable shawls, importing from Constantinople, Alexandria, Smyrna, Marcarieff, Moscow, and Vienna. There were French shawl merchants based in Constantinople and Moscow, and French merchants were a noticeable presence at the annual market in Tblisi. Major French companies kept their own agents in Kashmir who worked closely with producers and bought shawls directly from them.[102]

England, on the other hand, received most of its Kashmir shawls through the East India Trading Company, which controlled British trade with the Indian subcontinent. The company normally shipped the shawls by sea from Bombay around the Cape of Good Hope to London. In London, shawls were distributed through two three-day auctions held in December and June of each year, auctions that attracted dealers from many countries.

THE KASHMIR SHAWL AFTER 1870

Kashmir shawls survived many changes in women's dress to maintain their status as symbols of high fashion until the early 1870s. The development of the bustle in the late 1860s and the availability of inexpensive European copies of Kashmir shawls, hitherto the exclusive property of a fashion-conscious elite, led to a decline in sales. Claude Monet's 1868 portrait of Madame Gaudibert in a large and colorful Kashmir shawl is one of the last of a long series of paintings of fashionable women wearing the garments.[103] In *Art-Manufactures of India*, a study that he compiled for the Glasgow International Exhibition of 1888, T. N. Mukharji stated:

> The warehouses of London and Paris are full of shawls which find no purchasers, and their value in Kashmir has consequently fallen to a third of what it was ten years ago [1876].[104]

Through the mid-1870s magnificent shawls continued to be made and given as wedding gifts, but most of these were folded carefully away and never worn. A few decades later, during the Arts and Crafts Movement, Kashmir shawls and their European counterparts were brought out of trunks and closets, cut up, and remade into newly fashionable articles of clothing such as

waisted jackets; they were also used for household furnishings—as piano covers, throws, and wall hangings. Kashmir shawls seem to have been treasured even when they were not in style. If they were not kept as family heirlooms, they were often donated to museums, where they remain a legacy of the unrivalled skill and creative adaptability of the Kashmiri weaver.

Kashmir shawls had evolved to suit European tastes, and the industry never recovered from the loss of the European market in the early 1870s. Shortly afterwards, many of the most skilled weavers and other craftsmen associated with the production of Kashmir shawls died in the severe famine of 1877. The industry did not, however, die out overnight. In the Delhi exhibition of 1902–1903, Kashmir shawls won first prize in several categories. Old shawls were especially admired, and the exhibition included a number of fine collections loaned by the descendants of provincial rulers and by old trading houses. Sir George Watt, who compiled the catalogue, noted particularly the variety of the two hundred shawls sent by "His Highness the Maharaja of Kashmir," the "charming, fine old shawls" sent by "His Highness the Maharaja of Bikanir," and several "very excellent collections" from Amritsar, which included a group of shawls sent by a trading company there. Watt states that merchants of the firm of Khan Muhamed Shah and Saifuddin were "merchant princes" when the shawl trade was at its height, but that they had "for some years practically ceased to trade in shawls . . . ." The outstanding collection they sent was composed almost entirely of old shawls that had been kept in the company for several generations as models of excellence.[105]

12

THE WOVEN SHAWL

12. Kashmir Shawl

◆

Kashmir
1820s
Cashmere
Twill tapestry
125 x 49 in.; 317 x 124.5 cm
The William Bridges Thayer Memorial, 1928.751

13. Kashmir Shawl

◆

Kashmir
1815–1830; reconstructed late 19th or early
20th century
Cashmere
Twill tapestry and embroidery
117 x 25 in.; 297.3 x 63.6 cm
The William Bridges Thayer Memorial,
1928.756

Both of these shawls date from the first half of the nineteenth century, or in the case of Plate 13, are assembled primarily from pieces of at least two different shawls that date from this period. Both are woven from cashmere fleece in a format only slightly changed from eighteenth-century prototypes. Both are long rectangles with a large, plain central field bordered on the ends by a tidy row of discrete *buta* motifs. Both have comparatively narrow side borders. French paintings and fashion plates of the late eighteenth and first third of the nineteenth centuries show many examples of Kashmir shawls in this format.

Kashmir shawls originally were valued primarily for the properties of the cashmere fiber from which they were woven. Their format and twill weave structure showed the fiber to its best advantage. Kashmiri weavers generally chose the highest-quality cashmere for the center panel, and a slightly lower quality for patterned borders. The finest cashmere is fragile and would not have stood up well to the many manipulations necessary to produce twill tapestry patterning. Also, inferior fiber could be hidden within complex patterning, but a plain field showed the fiber for what it was. The central fields and plain outer borders of these two shawls have the lustrous sheen and fine hand typical of high-quality cashmere, while their comparatively narrow, unobtrusive borders serve to define and enhance the central field rather than to dominate it, as in later shawls.

Plate 12 is almost twice as wide and somewhat longer than Plate 13. It represents a response to European demand for a larger, wider shawl that could be used by fashionable

European women in place of a cloak. This wide rectangular shape remained popular in Europe until the shawl went out of fashion in the 1870s. There are practically no examples of narrow shawls in European collections that date after the 1840s.

The *buta*, or cone motifs, on both of these shawls are filled with floral patterns and imbedded in a floral ground. Only a narrow outline of unpatterned ground defines the primary *buta* shapes. This *horror vacui* treatment of the primary motif is a radical departure from earlier Indian styles in which the flowering plant (or, later, the cone motif depicted here) was invariably set against a plain ground.

The *buta* in Plate 13 are filled with colorful flowers of various types and a barely distinguishable second cone, defined only by its narrow red outline and the differing arrangement of the interior and exterior flowers. The ground exhibits an exuberant variety of densely packed, multicolored flowers.

By contrast, the *buta* motifs on Plate 12 are more clearly defined and simpler than those in Plate 13, and the palette is more restrained. Each cone is filled with orderly rows of tiny blue *buta*. A red flower at the base of the cone has abstracted leaves and roots reminiscent of early depictions of flowering plants. Here, however, the "roots" descend from the cone and form interlocking meanders that, with the addition of an abstracted leaf pattern, fill the background space with slender leafy branches.

In both of these shawls, the various borders and the central field were woven separately and then stitched together. Plate 12 is still in its original configuration except for the narrow outermost borders, which are a later addition or replacement. The frayed selvages of the main panel have been turned under, and narrow borders added, stitched together end to end to strengthen the fragile selvages. Some contain patterns dyed with aniline dyes, chemical dyes that were not available until decades after the shawl was woven. The tapestry-patterned end borders of this shawl share the same warp as the central field. In later shawls, this visually encroaching pattern is either a separately woven band, embroidered, or a combination of the two.

By contrast, Plate 13 is a reconstruction probably dating from the last third of the nineteenth or even the early years of the twentieth century. Some of the threads used for decorative top stitching on the narrow side borders are dyed with analine dyes, and the border is edged with commercial trim. The central panel and end borders, however, are woven of the fine

cashmere typical of early shawls, and may have been cut from a single old shawl. A small addition at one side of each of the plain cashmere borders was cut from a piece of cashmere with slightly thicker threads and coarser weave. The style of the cone borders is consistent with a date in the first third of the nineteenth century. The idea of a flower-filled cone outlined only by the ground color and imbedded in a densely packed floral field is seen in all of the designs Moorcroft sent to England from Kashmir in 1823.[106] The border of this shawl is slightly more complex than that of a shawl in the Musée National des Techniques in Paris that appears to have an inscribed date of 1815, but the two shawls share the idea of one cone imbedded in another.[107] The style is consistent with other shawls from the same period, and with shawls depicted in dated paintings. An unidentified number is stamped in the central field.

At the time Plate 13 was reconstructed, the fragile cashmere pattern panels were backed with black mesh, possibly made from silk. A single row of black whipstitching secures both the net and the white cashmere end borders. The reconstruction is consistent with shawl construction techniques in Kashmir and India, but the visually obtrusive mesh backing suggests that the reconstructed shawl was not meant to be worn. This shawl was probably constructed primarily from early-nineteenth-century pieces by a Kashmiri or Indian merchant, perhaps working in conjunction with a Western dealer, for sale to a Western collector looking for an "early" shawl.

By the time the border cones were as complex as those in Plate 13, shawls typically had elaborate cones in the four corners of the central field.[108] Not only would it have been difficult for a dealer to reconstruct stylistically consistent corner ornaments in a new field, but the plain central field suggests an earlier date for the shawl—and a buyer unaware of the discrepancy between the plain central field and the complexity of the border cone patterns.

In later shawls, embroidery was used with great skill to correct errors in weaving, to embellish patterning, and to join together patterns that were woven on separate looms. There is no embroidery on any of the main panels of either of these shawls, confirming a comparatively early date for both.

14. Kashmir Shawl

✦

Kashmir
Second quarter of 19th century
Cashmere/wool with some silk thread for
piecing
Twill tapestry and embroidery
131.5 x 55 in.; 333.5 x 140 cm
The William Bridges Thayer Memorial,
1928.965

15. Kashmir Shawl

✦

Kashmir
ca. 1840
Wool with cashmere end tabs
Twill tapestry and embroidery
56 x 119 in.; 142.5 x 302.5 cm
The William Bridges Thayer Memorial,
1928.748

16. Kashmir Shawl

✦

Kashmir
Third quarter of 19th century
Cashmere/wool
Twill tapestry and embroidery
125 x 54 in.; 320 x 137 cm
The William Bridges Thayer Memorial, 1928.752

17. Kashmir Shawl

✦

Kashmir
Third quarter of 19th century
Cashmere/wool
Twill tapestry and embroidery
125 x 56 in.; 316.8 x 142.3 cm
The William Bridges Thayer Memorial,
1928.754

In the second and third quarters of the nineteenth century, the patterned borders of Kashmir shawls expanded into the central field, finally reducing it to a small medallion in the 1860s. The *buta*, or cone motif, became increasingly elongated, enhancing the fashionable silhouettes of Parisian women. Used as an element of abstract design, the motif changed orientations and size within a single shawl, intertwined with adjoining cones, and visually moved in and out of an elaborate field. On later shawls there is less emphasis on the quality of the fiber itself, and more on the design. Like these, most Kashmir shawls in Western collections from this period were probably made from a combination of cashmere and sheep's wool.

Plate 14 has the same series of end borders as Plate 12, but each border is wider and the distinction between the succession of end borders is less clearly defined. An additional interior side border frames and further reduces the central panel. In Plate 12, a tiny *buta* motif graces the transition between border and central field. Here these grace notes have become a substantive additional border area of flowers, ellipses, and wave-like cone tips, and four large cones have been appliqued to each corner of the central field. The shawl was constructed from a series of separately woven borders around a plain central field. Even the pattern that appears to be encroaching on the central field was actually woven as a separate border with tapestry motifs. The ground fabric around the inner edge of the pattern was cut away; the decorative border was then stitched to the central panel about four and a half centimeters from the inner edge of the border, and the tips of the motif were almost invisibly appliqued to the central panel.

The outer side borders and the encroaching border on the central panel are stylistically distinct from each other and from the other border areas of the shawl. These four sets of units—outer side borders, main pattern borders, encroaching border, and central field—were probably woven in four different workshops, with the shawl eventually designed and constructed from previously finished units. This shawl relied on the skills of the *rafugar*, whose meticulous and barely discernable stitchery joined panels and smoothed transitions from one pattern area to another.

The central field in Plate 15 has become a flower-like medallion set in a square panel of abstracted trees, wave-like cone patterns, and meanders. The outer and inner side borders resemble those of Plate 14, but the cone motifs on the ends of the shawl have become greatly abstracted and elongated, breaking the boundaries of the separate borders. The resemblance of the side panels to those of Plate 14 and the stylistic dissimilarity of the central panel to any other area of the shawl suggest that this shawl also was constructed of elements woven in three or four different workshops, and that different workshops may have specialized in different parts of the shawl. The narrow outer side borders in all four of these shawls are quite distinct in color and style from other parts of their respective shawls. The greatest stylistic change appears in the several end borders which, by mid-century, came to dominate the field. It would appear that the most innovative designers and weavers, working in conjunction with European designers, were responsible for the main panels, while smaller, less innovative workshops continued to supply supporting elements.

Plate 15 has a series of discrete, colored cashmere tabs as a final border, or fringe gate, at each end. Monique Lévi-Strauss dates the appearance of these harlequin shawl ends on European shawls to the 1830s and 1840s, and of embellished tabs to the period after 1848.[109] Kashimiri styles probably follow a similar dating scheme.

The tabs on Plate 16 are embroidered with flowers set in *mihrab*-shaped arches. These embellished tabs became a standard feature of Kashmir shawls produced towards the end of the second quarter and in the third quarter of the nineteenth century. In format, this shawl closely resembles Plate 15. Both have a similar arrangement of pattern and border sections, and a plain central field defined by encroaching motifs and set into a square. The defining element of both shawls is the patterned areas of abstracted, elongated cones at the shawl ends. Outer and inner side borders appear to be standard stock-in-trade. Of secondary interest is the central medallion

14

15

16

17

set into a square. The whole central unit is unrelated in color and style to the main body of the shawl; these medallion squares could have been easily replaced if the buyer preferred a black medallion to a white circle, for example. Records indicate that buyers and middlemen sometimes requested such substitutions.[110]

In this shawl, the central panel seems older and more worn than the rest of the garment. Shawls were refashioned and even radically reconstructed, with usable parts saved and worn portions replaced. It is possible that this shawl is a reconstruction, setting an old medallion into a new field.

In contrast to the patchwork appearance of Plates 14 and 15, Plate 17 presents a unified composition and suggests direct cooperation among designers working in France (such as Antony Berrus and Amedée Couder), French agents stationed in Kashmir, and Kashmiri designers and weavers. Two slender cones rise from each end, cross, and sweep to the center of the shawl, breaking the barriers imposed by earlier borders. Throughout the field, mauve, green, and orange cones cross and recross each other in a transparent layering of forms. The outer side borders and narrow end borders relate to each other in style, color, and motif, and to the main field in color and style. The central black medallion is incorporated into the overall design rather than being isolated in a separate square inset.

Despite its visual unity, this shawl was constructed of a greater number of independently woven panels than any of the other three shawls. In Plates 14, 15, and 16, most of the discrete panels were also discrete pattern areas. Here that is not the case. The central field was constructed of fourteen separately woven rectangular panels to create a unified design scheme, a feat that required technical virtuosity and close cooperation among designer, weaver, and *rafugar*.

All four shawls have one or more inscriptions, or traces of old inscriptions, in the center medallion. Plates 14, 15, and 16 have one each. Plate 17 has three, a further indication that its production was carefully monitored at each stage of construction.

To date, no one has been able to read the inscriptions on Kashmir shawls or to identify the workshops or middlemen to whom they belonged. A compilation and careful study of shawl inscriptions, and comparison of shawls with similar inscriptions, might help identify particular workshops or an individual merchant house, such as that of Mukhtar Shah. This, in turn, might help us learn more about stylistic development in Kashmir, and perhaps aid in dating individual shawls with greater accuracy.

18. Kashmir Shawl

◆

India/Pakistan (Kashmir or the Punjab)
ca. 1870
Cashmere/wool
Twill tapestry, embroidery
83 x 81 in.; 210 x 205 cm
The William Bridges Thayer Memorial,
1928.971

This heavy square shawl was designed to be worn folded diagonally across the shoulders, with the point of the triangle at center back. Some square shawls were designed so that, when worn in this fashion, both the triangle on top and the layer beneath revealed the front, or "right" side, of the garment. To achieve this, one half of the shawl, measured on the diagonal, was woven front side up on the loom, and the other half was simultaneously woven with the front side down. In other shawls, the central inset square is divided diagonally into black and white grounds, giving a single shawl the versatility of two.[111]

Visually the central field of Plate 18 presents a unified composition. Four corner ornaments extend to and encircle the central medallion, incorporating it closely into the composition as well as emphasizing its position as geometric center of the shawl. Technically, however, the shawl is a veritable jigsaw of small, odd-shaped pieces. Weavers worked apparently miscellaneous motifs into narrow strips of background fabric that, when cut off the loom, looked somewhat like small pieces of clothing patterns arranged at odd angles to take advantage of every possible inch of cloth.[112] The finished strips were given to a *rafugar*, who cut the patterns out of the ground cloth and pieced them together, using his needle to correct the inevitable discrepancies and, in this shawl, blending more than two hundred pieces into a coherent whole. The completed shawl was necessarily bulkier and heavier than shawls put together from only a few large rectangles.

It was difficult and time consuming for the *rafugar* to construct a complex shawl from a series of small cut-outs. For the weaver, too, it was extremely inefficient to keep cutting the pattern off the loom and then having to retie and retension the warp threads before starting on the next small strip. This strange and inefficient construction method can be traced primarily to European demand for quick responses to continental fashion trends. The strip method allowed a large number of weavers to work simultaneously on one shawl, drastically reducing the eighteen or more months that two weavers working together typically required to complete one. The strip method also accommodated less skillful weavers. On early shawls, like Plates 13 and 12, constructed of very few pieces and with almost no embroidery, any mistake by the weaver stood out; furthermore, such mistakes could not be corrected except by unweaving and reweaving the section in question, which was impossible to do after a shawl left the loom. In the strip method, if a weaver made an error on a motif, the *rafugar* could simply reject that motif, or section of motifs, and substitute another. He also had the option of correcting the error by top stitching, a correction that would probably be unnoticeable in a dense ground composed of juxtapositions of woven patterns stitched together and already embellished with additional stitching.

Contemporary Europeans viewed this construction method with astonishment. The cover of the fifteenth journal (of a series of thirty) of the Paris Exposition of 1878 features a print of an Indian or Kashmiri weaver and *rafugar* constructing a shawl of this type. They are surrounded by an interested mob of people, including one small boy with eyes and mouth wide open in wonder. The loom depicted is small and narrow, something that could only be used for weaving narrow bands of discrete motifs. The shawl on which the *rafugar* is working appears as thick and textured as a bearskin, a completely different article of clothing than the simple, almost translucent shawls popularized by Empress Josephine sixty years earlier.[113]

18

The *amli*, or needleworked shawl, was a product of the nineteenth century, a cost-cutting innovation that has been attributed to Khwaja Yusuf, an Armenian shawl merchant who was sent to Kashmir in 1803 as an agent for a firm based in Constantinople. Yusuf has also been credited with playing an early and important role in adapting Kashmiri designs for a Western market.[114] Upon observing shawl production in Kashmir, Yusuf soon realized that it would be much quicker, and therefore less expensive, to imitate the laborious twill tapestry-woven patterns with embroidered ones. Moorcroft reports that Yusuf worked with a needleworker named 'Ali Baba to produce the first completely needleworked shawls, which he was able to sell for one third the cost of a woven shawl. In addition, the embroidered shawls initially escaped the government tax, more than a quarter of a shawl's value in 1826. Consequently, the production of needleworked shawls expanded rapidly. In 1803, Khwaja Yusuf found only a few needleworkers in Kashmir with the necessary skill to make an entirely needleworked shawl; but when Moorcroft reported on the industry in 1823, there were almost five thousand. Moorcroft also stated that many of these new needleworkers were drawn from the ranks of old landholding families, dispossessed by the Sikh ruler Ranjit Singh (1780–1839), who conquered Kashmir in 1819 from his base in the Punjab.[115]

Richard Carnac Temple suggests that the weavers who produced unpatterned cashmere (*pashmina*) ground cloth for embroidery worked more independently than those who wove patterns into the cloth:

> The shawls are of two descriptions, loom-made and hand-made [embroidered]. . . . In the hand-work system the ground cloth (*pashmina*) is made by workmen (*sadabafs* [weavers]), who procure their materials themselves, and then hand over the manufactured article to *rafugars*, or fine drawers, to work in the coloured threads.[116]

19. Embroidered Kashmir Shawl

◆

India/Pakistan (Punjab)
19th century
Cashmere/wool
Embroidery on twill ground
47 x 46 in.; 119.5 x 117 cm
The William Bridges Thayer Memorial, 1928.451

20. Embroidered Kashmir Shawl

◆

India/Pakistan (Punjab)
Sikh period (1819–1846)
Cashmere/wool
Embroidery on twill ground
71.5 x 69 in.; 179.5 x 175.5 cm
The William Bridges Thayer Memorial, 1928.460

21. Embroidered Kashmir Shawl

◆

India/Pakistan (Punjab)
19th century
Wool
Embroidery on twill ground
67 x 66 in.; 170.3 x 167.8 cm
The William Bridges Thayer Memorial, 1928.455

These three embroidered shawls relate both to contemporary woven shawls from Kashmir and to other embroidered textiles of northwest India and Pakistan. The cone motifs are similar to contemporary styles in Kashmir, and like their woven counterparts, these shawls are made of cashmere or a combination of cashmere and wool. The elaborated central medallions and naturalistic depiction of flowers, however, are quite different from contemporary Kashmiri work and relate, rather, to Indo-Islamic styles developed at the Mughal court and popularized through provincial courts in what is now northwest India and Pakistan.

All three of these embroidered shawls feature a cone motif organized around a highly elaborated central medallion that is visually as well as geometrically the central focus of interest. On woven Kashmir shawls the central medallion is left empty to feature the quality of the unadorned cloth, while the main focus of visual interest is the deep border panel. By the second quarter of the nineteenth century, when these three embroidered shawls were produced, designs on woven Kashmir shawls had become quite abstract. Although the cone motifs in the three shawls shown here are also somewhat abstracted, they refer additionally to earlier motifs—such as the "vase of flowers" motif and isolated, somewhat realistically depicted flowering plants—in which the flowers are more recognizable.

These features point to an origin in the Punjab, possibly during the quarter century (1819–1846) when Kashmir was ruled by a Sikh kingdom based there. During this period the two regions became quite closely interconnected, because of the interest of the Sikh rulers in the products of Kashmiri looms and because of a large emigration of Kashmiri people to the Punjab during the severe famine of 1834.

The city of Amritsar, for example, was one of several centers of fine embroidery in the Punjab that had close ties to Kashmir. It had a large emigré Kashmiri population that was deeply involved in various independent aspects of shawl production, particularly tasks related to finishing the shawls, such as washing, bleaching, and dyeing the finished product;

21

embellishing the woven patterns with needlework; and adding embroidered borders and fringes. Amritsar was also famous for the production of fine *amli* such as these.

Plate 19 is constructed of four panels stitched together, two of a deep red and two of pale indigo. The four panels were either joined before the shawl was embroidered or worked separately, joined, and then embellished with motifs that extend across the seams. The four corner motifs transform a graceful adaptation of the cone into a contemporary interpretation of the old vase of flowers motif. A stylized flower rises from the "vase" and is surrounded by two other flowering plants. The central medallion, possibly with a lotus flower at its core, is surrounded by cones and teardrops. On all three shawls, the central medallion has an importance that is lacking in shawls woven in Kashmir, where the primary function of the plain central field—whether a large rectangle or a small medallion—is to show off the quality of the fiber.

Plate 21 is also constructed of several pieces of ground cloth. The large central panel has a seam about one-third of the distance from one end, and is surrounded by three intact borders. The fourth border is made of two strips of fabric of unequal lengths. The irregular piecing of the ground cloth suggests that this shawl was made of viable pieces rescued from an older shawl that had become too worn for use. Visually the shawl is divided into four quadrants, each organized around a central medallion with a lotus flower center. Four cones point towards the central medallion from the four corners of each quadrant. Radiating from the lotus flowers at the cardinal points, four tear drops act as stems for an abstracted depiction of a flowering plant. More naturalistically rendered flowering plants encircle the medallion, their heads bent towards the stems in reverse imitation of the cones pointing towards the center.

The popular *buta*, or cone motif, dominates the large interior border of Plate 20, and the treatment of the motif here is closely related to that on contemporary woven Kashmir shawls. The highly elaborated central medallion, however, is related only in general format to the empty medallions on Kashmir shawls. This medallion relates rather to Indo-Islamic medallions from the Mughal period that found their way into the design vocabulary of northwest India through the arts of the provincial courts.

Although it would not have been difficult to work this shawl as a single piece, it was embroidered in several panels; the borders were each embroidered separately, and the central panel is composed of four pieces. The shawl is woven of high-quality cashmere with a slightly lower-quality cashmere or wool embroidery floss. It was typical of both woven and embroidered shawls to reserve the highest-quality fiber for the ground, employing a secondary quality for pattern areas. The shawl appears to be in very good condition, but the ground cloth is actually extremely fragile. It was probably constructed of old shawl fragments, dyed anew, and then embroidered to give new life to parts of one or several old shawls too worn for use.

ENDNOTES

1. Shanti Swarup, *The Arts and Crafts of India and Pakistan* (Bombay: Taraporevala's, 1957), 80.

2. Cited in M. H. Kahlenberg, "A Study of the Development and Use of the Mughal Patkā (sash) with Reference to the Los Angeles County Museum of Art Collection," in *Aspects of Indian Art: Papers Presented in a Symposium at the Los Angeles County Museum of Art*, ed. Pratapaditya Pal (Leiden: E. J. Brill, 1972), 158.

3. John Irwin, "Indian Textiles in Historical Perspective," in *Textiles and Ornaments of India*, ed. Monroe Wheeler (New York: Museum of Modern Art, 1956), 26.

4. Pupul Jaykar, "Naksha Bandhas of Banares," in *Handwoven Fabrics of India*, ed. Jasleen Dhamiya and Jyotindra Jain (Ahmedabad: Mapin Publishing, 1989), 48.

5. Quoted in John Irwin and Margaret Hall, *Indian Embroideries* (Ahmedabad: S. R. Bastikar on behalf of Calico Museum of Textiles, 1973), 5.

6. Cited in Mattiebelle Gittinger, *Master Dyers to the World* (Washington, DC: The Textile Museum, 1982), 13.

7. Robyn Maxwell, *Textiles of Southeast Asia: Tradition, Trade and Transformation* (Melbourne, Oxford, Auckland, New York: Australian National Gallery and Oxford University Press, 1990). See especially chapter 3, "Indian Transformations," 149–238.

8. Cited in Gittinger, *Master Dyers*, 180.

9. Irwin, "Indian Textiles in Historical Perspective," 26.

10. John Guy and Deborah Swallow, eds., *Arts of India: 1550–1900* (London: Victoria and Albert Museum, 1990), 59 and pl. 41.

11. Ibid., 79.

12. Stuart Cary Welch, *India: Art and Culture, 1300–1900* (New York: The Metropolitan Museum of Art and Holt, Rinehart and Winston, 1985), 169.

13. R. Skelton, "A Decorative Motif in Mughal Art," in *Aspects of Indian Art*, 145–152.

14. Victoria and Albert Museum, *The Indian Heritage: Court Life and Arts under Mughal Rule* (London: Victoria and Albert Museum, 1982), 25.

15. R. Skelton, "A Decorative Motif in Mughal Art," 152.

16. Welch, *India: Art and Culture, 1300–1900*, 252–256 and pl. 165.

17. Nora Fisher, ed., *Mud, Mirror and Thread: Folk Traditions of Rural India* (Ahmedabad: Mapin Publishing in association with Museum of New Mexico Press, 1993), 31.

18. Masatoshi A. Konishi, "Colour and Forms of the Semi-Arid India," in Hiroko Iwatate, *Desert Village, Life and Crafts: Gujarat, Rajasthan* (Tokyo: Yobisha, 1985), 182–185.

19. See Stephen P. Huyler, "Creating Sacred Spaces," in *Mud, Mirror and Thread*, 172–191.

20. Eleanor Olson, "The Textiles and Costumes of India: A Historical Review," *The Museum*, Summer/Fall 1965: 15.

21. Judy Frater, "Elements of Style: The Artisan Reflected in Embroideries of Western India," in *Mud, Mirror and Thread*, 106–107.

22. Fisher, ed., *Mud, Mirror and Thread*, 174.

23. Ibid., 27.

24. Ananda K. Coomaraswamy, *Christian and Oriental Philosophy of Art* (New York: Dover Publications, 1956), 18. First published in 1943 under the title *Why Exhibit Works of Art*.

25. Irwin and Hall, *Indian Embroideries*, 80. See plate 49 for a very similar *odhani* in the Calico Museum in Ahmedabad.

26. Lakshmi and the lotus are closely associated in the Vedic hymns of the *Rg Veda* (ca. 1500–800 BCE) and appear together in religious sculpture and painting throughout Indian history. In Hindu symbolism, the lotus flower is evidence of the life-supporting potency of the fecund mud from which it grows (the "cosmic ocean" of the creator god Vishnu) and of the power of the goddess Lakshmi, Vishnu's consort, to channel that undifferentiated energy into individual life forms on earth. Hence Lakshmi is worshipped as goddess of fertility and, by extension, of prosperity and good fortune. See, for example, Veronica Ions, *Indian Mythology* (London: Paul Hamlyn, 1975), 91; and Heinrich Zimmer, *The Art of Indian Asia: Its Mythology and Transformations*, completed and ed. Joseph Campbell, Bollingen Series, vol. 39 (New York: Published for Bollingen Foundation by Pantheon Books, 1955), 1:158 ff.

27. Marie-Louise Nabholz-Kartaschoff, *Golden Sprays and Scarlet Flowers: Traditional Indian Textiles from the Museum of Ethnography Basel, Switzerland* (Kyoto: Shikosha, 1986), 194.

28. See, for example, John Gillow and Nicholas Barnard, *Traditional Indian Textiles* (London: Thames and Hudson, 1991), 70; and Nabholz-Kartaschoff, *Golden Sprays*, 194 and pl. 38.

29. Fisher, ed., *Mud, Mirror and Thread*, 27 and plate following on 28–29. This intricately patterned head-cloth in the Museum of International Folk Art in Santa Fe is made of two pieces of ground cloth stitched approximately one-third of the distance from one selvage. The seam falls at the inner edge of a vertical pattern block and there are very few places where the pattern is misaligned.

30. Nabholz-Kartaschoff, *Golden Sprays*, pl. 38.

31. See John Irwin, *The Kashmir Shawl* (London: Her Majesty's Stationery Office, 1973), pl. 2–3.

32. Fisher, ed., *Mud, Mirror and Thread*, 34.

33. B. A. Gupte, "Description of the Illustrations," *Journal of Indian Art* 2, no. 18 (Oct. 1888): 16 and pl. 15.

34. Ibid., 16.

35. Olson, "The Textiles and Costumes of India," 15.

36. Fisher, ed., *Mud, Mirror and Thread*, 34.

37. Hiroshima Prefectural Art Museum, ed., *Textile Arts of Asia* (Hiroshima: Hiroshima Prefectural Art Museum, 1996), pl. 75, 31.

38. Marshall Field and Co. was a Chicago department store. In the early twentieth century, following the popular enthusiasm for Asian textiles and other arts generated by the world fairs (e.g., St. Louis, 1904), the store began selling antique (or simply old) textiles from Asia. Several other textiles from China and South Asia in the Spencer collection have Marshall Field tags. Although this is the only *aba* with a tag, the other two might also have come from the same store.

39. Nora Fisher, oral communication, April 8, 1994.

40. Chelna Desai, *Ikat Textiles of India* (Tokyo: Graphic-sha, 1988), 148.

41. Sherman A. Lee, *A History of Far Eastern Art* (Englewood Cliffs and New York: Prentice Hall and Abrams, 1994), 257.

42. Zimmer, *The Art of Indian Asia*, 160.

43. Fisher, ed., *Mud, Mirror and Thread*, 86.

44. Rosemary Crill, *Indian Embroidery* (London: Victoria and Albert Publications, 1999), 11.

45. Ibid.; and Gillow and Barnard, *Traditional Indian Textiles*, 119.

46. The seventeenth-century French traveler Jean Baptiste Tavernier, for example, noted the rare wool woven in Kerman, Yezd, and Alep in "Persia." Most of this was made into articles of clothing such as the sashes used at the Iranian court and the prayer veils used by high-ranking Islamic holymen. See Tavernier, *Les six voyages de Jean Baptiste Tavernier . . .* (Paris, 1676–1677), 1:172; cited in Frank Ames, *The Kashmir Shawl and Its Indo-French Influence* (Woodbridge, Suffolk (England): Antique Collectors' Club, 1988 [1986]), 102. Vigne, traveling in 1842, remarked that fine shawls were made in the Caucasus. See G. T. Vigne, *Travels in Kashmir* (London: H. Colburn, 1844). Ames reports that Bokhara, Meshed, Kabul, and Andijanin also produced shawls (*The Kashmir Shawl*, 105 and 111).

47. Ames, *The Kashmir Shawl*, 61–62.

48. Irwin, *The Kashmir Shawl*, 5.

49. William Moorcroft, MSS (Eur, D, 260), 1–2. Cited in Irwin, *The Kashmir Shawl*, 5. Moorcroft's manuscript is preserved in the India Office Library in London.

50. Irwin, *The Kashmir Shawl*, 5–6.

51. Ibid., 22.

52. François Bernier, *Travels in the Mogul Empire, 1656–1658* (London: Archibald Constable, 1891), 402–403; cited in Ames, *The Kashmir Shawl*, 22–23.

53. See also the portrait of Sayyid Raju Qattal, ca. 1680, at the Musée Guimet in Paris; illustrated in Monique Lévi-Strauss, *The Cashmere Shawl* (New York: Harry N. Abrams, 1986), 17.

54. Bernier, *Travels in the Mogul Empire*, 43; cited in Irwin, *The Kashmir Shawl*, 10.

55. Tavernier, *Les six voyages de Jean Baptiste Tavernier . . .*, 2:268; cited in Ames, *The Kashmir Shawl*, 102.

56. *Ain-i Akbari*, 1:32 and 2:15; in Irwin, *The Kashmir Shawl*, 10. *Tuzk-i-Jahangir*, 2:147–148; in Ames, *The Kashmir Shawl*, 20–21.

57. Welch, *India: Art and Culture, 1300–1900*, 264–265 and pl. 174. Dale Gluckman has pointed out that the fiber of this shawl has not been analyzed, and that, generally, *asli* is considered to be too fine to withstand the manipulation required to pattern a shawl. Most modern shawls made of *asli* are neither patterned nor dyed. Dale Gluckman, written communication, December 2001.

58. These shawl fragments are illustrated in Irwin, *The Kashmir Shawl*, pl. 5–6.

59. *Ain-i Akbari*, 1:120; cited in Susan Stronge, "The Age of the Mughals," in *Arts of India: 1550–1900*, ed. Guy and Swallow, 75.

60. *Ain-i Akbari*, 1:32; cited in Irwin, *The Kashmir Shawl*, 9. See also Ames, *The Kashmir Shawl*, 19–20.

61. Stronge, "The Age of the Mughals," 75. Ames, *The Kashmir Shawl*, 18–19.

62. In fact, Jahangir died en route to Kashmir. Sir Richard Temple, *Journals Kept in Hyderabad, Kashmir, Sikkim, and Nepal*, ed. Richard Carnac Temple (London: W. H. Allen, 1887), 2:79; Ames, *The Kashmir Shawl*, 20.

63. Quoted in Ames, *The Kashmir Shawl*, 20.

64. *Tuzk-i-Jahangir*; cited in ibid., 20–21.

65. Ames, *The Kashmir Shawl*, 21–22.

66. George Forster, *A Journey from Bengal to England . . .* (London, 1798); quoted in Ames, *The Kashmir Shawl*, 20–21.

67. Illustrated in Lévi-Strauss, *The Cashmere Shawl*, 18.

68. In India styles also changed in the early years of the nineteenth century. A watercolor of *Eight Horse Merchants* painted in Delhi, ca. 1816–1820, depicts six of the eight merchants wearing shawls of some kind; only the two servants do not wear shawls. Three of the eight wear what appear to be Kashmir shawls draped around their shoulders or bundled around their waists. The painting was commissioned by William Fraser, an employee of the British East India Company, who identified each man by name, tribal or group affiliation, place, and occupation. Of the three men wearing Kashmir shawls, two are identified as "a rich merchant" and "a very rich merchant," respectively; the third, as the nephew of the former. The three men are dressed quite differently in other respects, but all three shawls are red with a long central field. Two have borders completely filled with small flowers, one with a glimpse of a corner *buta* in the central field. Only on the nephew's shawl are the flowers organized into indistinct *buta* forms that blend to create a completely floral field where the shawl drapes.

A second painting dating to 1815 depicts the commander of a Ghoorka company who accompanied William Fraser on a trip to Kashmir in 1814–1815. He wears a red Kashmir shawl wound around his waist and hanging down in front, a striking contrast to his white costume. The shawl has a plain central field with a single row of clearly defined *buta*. The borders of these shawls are deeper and fuller than those of earlier shawls, and no longer feature a row of clearly depicted flowering plants isolated in a plain field. The fields are more crowded, but there is less emphasis here on the developing *buta* as cone motif than in the shawls woven for European customers, and more emphasis on the flowers themselves.

The paintings are reproduced in Mildred Archer and Toby Falk, *India Revealed: The Art and Adventures of James and William Fraser 1801–35* (London: Cassell, 1989), 111, pl. 99 and 129.

69. See figs. 1–8 in Irwin, *The Kashmir Shawl*, 11–14.

70. Antoine-Jean Gros (1771–1835), *L'Impératrice Joséphine*, 1809, is now in the collection of the Musée Massena in Nice, France. Reproduced in Lévi-Strauss, *The Cashmere Shawl*, 24.

71. The *Portrait of Madame Philibert Rivière*, by Jean-Auguste-Dominique Ingres (1805) is reproduced in *Jean-Auguste-Dominique Ingres* (New York: Skira/Rizzoli, 1980), 16.

72. This "Group Portrait of the Stamaty Family" is now in the Cabinet des Dessins, at the Louvre in Paris. Reproduced in *Jean-Auguste-Dominique Ingres*, 40.

73. Lévi-Strauss, *The Cashmere Shawl*, 16–19.

74. The eight extant drawings are at the Metropolitan Museum of Art in New York City.

75. Illustrated in Irwin, *The Kashmir Shawl*, pl. 6–13.

76. Victor Jacquemont, *Voyages dans l'Inde pendant les années 1828 a 1832*, 4 vols. (Paris, 1841); cited in Ames, *The Kashmir Shawl*, 66 n. 5.

77. Irwin, *The Kashmir Shawl*, 2; Lévi-Strauss, *The Cashmere Shawl*, 15.

78. Irwin, *The Kashmir Shawl*, 1–2.

79. See Baron Charles Hügel [Karl Von Hügel], *Travels in Kashmir and the Panjab* (London, 1845), 118; cited in Irwin, *The Kashmir Shawl*, 1 n. 3. Hügel's book, which was originally translated from the German and annotated by Major T. B. Jervis, was reprinted by Laurier Books Ltd/AES in 1995. See also Lévi-Strauss, *The Cashmere Shawl*, 14; and Ames, *The Kashmir Shawl*, 17.

80. Irwin, *The Kashmir Shawl*, 1 and n. 4. The original *Rajatarangini* (River of Kings) was an historical chronicle of early India written in 1148 by Kalhana, a Kashmir Brahman. The text known today as Srivara Pandita's *Rajatarangini* continued this history up to the reign of King Zain-ul-'Abidin; the authors were Jonaraja (d. 1659) and his pupil Srivara (dates unknown). The term *pandita* refers to a scholar (particularly one versed in Sanskrit), and in Kashmir, to an official.

81. Ames, *The Kashmir Shawl*, 17–18.

82. Ibid., 18.

83. Bernier, *Travels in the Mogul Empire*, 402–403; cited in Ames, *The Kashmir Shawl*, 22.

84. See Irwin, *The Kashmir Shawl*, 6.

85. Ibid.

86. Ames, *The Kashmir Shawl*, 68.

87. Charles Ellison Bates, *A Gazetteer of Kashmir and the Adjacent Districts* (Calcutta, 1873), 56; cited in Irwin, *The Kashmir Shawl*, 7.

88. See Irwin, *The Kashmir Shawl*, 6–8, for a synopsis of Moorcroft's description of the shawl industry.

89. Colonel J. A. Grant, quoted in *Kashmeer and Its Shawls* (London, 1875), 48; cited in Irwin, *The Kashmir Shawl*, 8.

90. Sir Richard Temple, *Journals Kept in Hyderabad, Kashmir, Sikkim, and Nepal*, 95–96.

91. Ames, *The Kashmir Shawl*, 51.

92. Irwin, *The Kashmir Shawl*, 2–3.

93. Karl Von Hügel, in an account of a visit to Kashmir in 1836, *Kaschmir und das Reich der Siek*, as quoted in Lévi-Strauss, *The Cashmere Shawl*, 43.

94. Colonel Grant, quoted in *Kashmeer and Its Shawls*, 48; cited in Irwin, *The Kashmir Shawl*, 2–3.

95. Ames, *The Kashmir Shawl*, 40.

96. Richard Carnac Temple, "Introduction: Diaries of Travel in Jammun and Kashmir," in Sir Richard Temple, *Journals Kept in Hyderabad, Kashmir, Sikkim, and Nepal*, 1:275.

97. Ibid., 1:299–301.

98. Cited in Irwin, *The Kashmir Shawl*, 8–9.

99. See George Forster's *A Journey from Bengal to England . . .*, published in London in 1798, for a detailed account of portions of the trading routes. Forster, disguised as a Turkish shawl merchant, traveled from Srinagar in Kashmir to Lucknow in Uttar Pradesh. In that comparatively short distance he passed thirty duty stations, each of which charged three or four percent of the value of the shawls. Cited in Ames, *The Kashmir Shawl*, 109.

100. Ames, *The Kashmir Shawl*, 111.

101. For a synopsis of information about these trade routes from the accounts of nineteenth-century travelers, see ibid., 108–111. Ames draws on the following nineteenth-century journals: Jean Deloch, ed., *Voyage en Inde du Comte de Modave 1773–1776* (Paris, 1971); Adrien Duprès, *Voyages en perse faits dans les années 1807, 1808, 1809*, 2 vols. (Paris, 1819); George Forster, *A Journey from Bengal to England . . .* (London, 1798 [1790]); Victor Jacquemont, *Voyages dans l'Inde pendant les années 1828 a 1832*, 4 vols. (Paris, 1841); Heinrich Julius von Klaproth, *Voyage dans les steppes d'Astrakhan et de Caucase par le Comte Jean Potocki*, 2 vols. (Paris, 1829); Jean Baptiste Tavernier, *Les six voyages de Jean Baptiste Tavernier . . .*, 2 vols. (Paris, 1981 [mid-seventeenth century]); H. H. Wilson, ed., *Travels in the Himalayan Provinces by Moorcroft and G. Trebeck, 1819 to 1825*, 2 vols. (London, 1841); and a history of Kashmir by Dr. G. M. (Al-Hajj) Sufi, *Kashmir*, 2 vols. (New Delhi, 1974).

102. Ames, *The Kashmir Shawl*, 110–111.

103. Claude Monet (1840–1926), *Madame Gaudibert, Wife of a Le Havre Shipowner*, 1868, is now in the Musée d'Orsay in Paris. Reproduced in Lévi-Strauss, *The Cashmere Shawl*, 49.

104. T. N. Mukharji, *Art-Manufactures of India* (New Delhi: Navrang, 1974), 374–375. This is an unreferenced quotation.

105. Sir George Watt, *Indian Art at Delhi, 1903* (Calcutta: The Superintendent of Government Printing, India, 1903), 351–355.

106. See especially Irwin, *The Kashmir Shawl*, pl. 6, 7, and 9.

107. Illustrated in Lévi-Strauss, *The Cashmere Shawl*, 58.

108. See, for example, the end border on the shawl in Joseph Tominz, *Portrait of Maria Louis, Ritter von Brucker, his Wife Amelia, née Holzknecht, and their Son Friedrich*, ca. 1830. Lévi-Strauss states that the shawl, possibly a wedding gift, was probably woven about ten years before the portrait was painted (*The Cashmere Shawl*, 35).

109. Lévi-Strauss, *The Cashmere Shawl*, 189.

110. Watt, *Indian Art at Delhi*, 349. Watt is quoting from Moorcroft's 1823 account. He states that, of the many technical works that exist on the manufacture of Kashmir shawls, Moorcroft's is among the most interesting.

111. Two shawls in the Spencer collection, 1928.790 and 1977.5, illustrate the first and second of these two distinctive constructions, respectively.

112. See illustration of a woven strip with miscellaneous twill tapestry motifs designed to be cut out in Lévi-Strauss, *The Cashmere Shawl*, 51.

113. Reproduced in ibid., 50.

114. Irwin, *The Kashmir Shawl*, 13–14. See also Crill, *Indian Embroidery*, 10.

115. Irwin, *The Kashmir Shawl*, 3.

116. Richard Carnac Temple, "Introduction," in Sir Richard Temple, *Journals Kept in Hyderabad, Kashmir, Sikkim, and Nepal*, 299.

IRAN

Contents

Chronology

Achaemenid empire	550–330 BCE
Seleucids and Parthians	330 BCE–224 CE
Sasanian empire	224–642
Islamic empire	642–750
Abbasids	750–1258
Buyids 932–1062	
Seljuqs 1038–1194	
Mongol conquest	1256
Ilkhanids	1256–1353
Timurids	1370–1506
Safavids	1501–1732
Shah 'Abbas I r. 1588–1629	
Afghan invasion	1722
Afsharids	1736–1795
Nadir Shah r. 1736–1747	
Zands	1750–1794
Karim Khan r. 1750–1779	
Qajars	1779–1924
Fath 'Ali Shah r. 1797–1834	
Pahlavi period	1924–1979
Islamic Republic of Iran	1979–

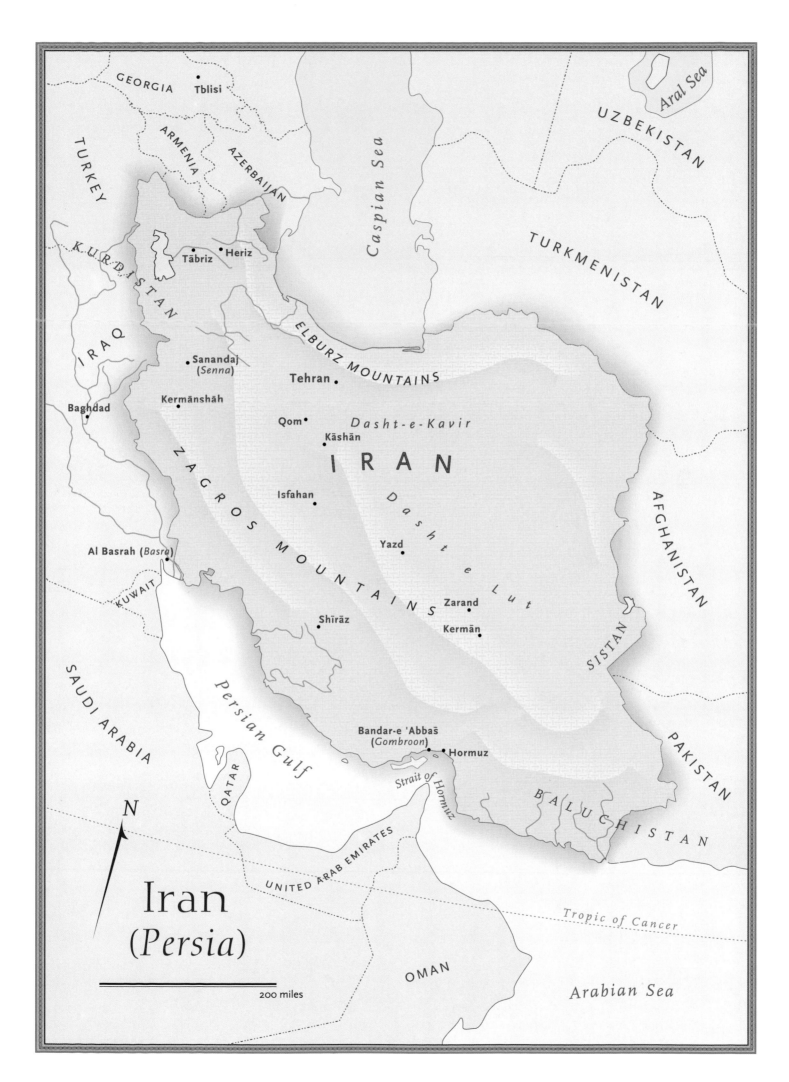

Textile Arts of Iran after the Sixteenth Century

The Persian carpet in the Western mind is associated with opulent interiors, luxurious textures, vibrant colors, and a riot of pattern. Received by royalty, Persian textiles, including carpets, arrived from Iran with the emergence of modern Europe, and contributed to an evolving appreciation of luxury goods—and to fantasy. In the sixteenth and seventeenth centuries, the exoticism of the Orient captured European fancy, which stimulated the expansion of horizons for trade and commerce. From the moment that the textile arts of Iran first began to dazzle and enthrall, these arts gained fame throughout the world, and they continue to be recognized and appreciated today for their amazing intricacy of design and high quality of craftsmanship.

Before the carpet achieved world-renowned status, Persian textiles were traded far and wide. Early commerce through overseas trade was promoted and protected by the advent of diplomatic exchanges. Subsequent industrialization in Europe helped to transform this trade, shifting the balance of power toward European enterprise and precipitating colonial domination, prefiguring the global economy of today.

Looking back, the Safavid period in Iran (1501–1722) was a golden age for textile arts. Iran was both a producer and exporter of fabulous textiles, drawing upon a rich artistic heritage that for centuries had included magnificent fabrics. In the sixteenth century the classical Persian carpet achieved its fully developed form under royal patronage; it was then that woven silks and velvets reached the pinnacle of their technical and aesthetic advancement. In subsequent periods, Persian textiles reflected the extraordinary achievements of the Safavid era, achievements that have never been exceeded.

Within Iran, textiles were expressive forms through which to reflect upon a glorious past, illustrating themes drawn from poetry, literary epics, and pictorial narrative. Weavings could depict metaphors of love, such as intertwined trees or birds and roses. Intricate designs of winding branches, sinuous stems, and abundant blossoms on carpets and fabrics spoke to the Persian appreciation of beauty and form. Other arts also flourished under court patronage, and together they composed an environment richly textured and patterned with ensembles of colorful tiles, painted stucco, polychrome panels, monumental carpets, and resplendent textiles for garments and furnishings. Public spaces saw the repeated volumetric shapes of arches, vaults, and domes, some clad in shiny glazed bricks and ornamental tiles. In the Shah's private quarters there were painted albums and illustrated books, elaborately inscribed and illuminated in ink, pigments, and gold.

Shah 'Abbas I (1588–1629) established his capital at Isfahan in 1598 and soon entertained ambassadors from all over the world. Isfahan was considered a beautiful city, filled with large buildings with tiled exteriors and set amidst sweet and verdant gardens. Fragrant blossoms and shade trees stood beside high walls with columns, reflected in large pools of still water in which the brilliant colors of mosques and palaces shimmered. European visitors to the Safavid court were impressed by the magnificence of the city of Isfahan and by the expanse of its gardens and planned open space. In the bazaar, carpet and cloth merchants offered a rich array of textile arts from the famous weaving centers of Tābriz, Kāshān, and Kermān, as well as from the looms of Isfahan and neighboring towns and villages. Silk weavers and other craftsmen practiced their crafts, and textile printers set up shop. One came to the bazaar not only to buy merchandise but also to seek adventure, knowledge, or fortune. Adam Olearius went to Persia in 1637 and was struck by the wealth and cosmopolitan nature of Isfahan: "There is not any nation in all Asia, nor indeed most of Europe, who sends not its merchants to Isfahan . . . besides . . . Indians, there . . . [are] Tartars . . . Turks, Jews, Armenians, Georgians, English, Dutch, French, Italians, and Spaniards."[1]

Shah 'Abbas was justly proud of his international capital. He encouraged artistic production on a monumental scale, and all of the arts flourished during his reign. Not only did he support architectural projects and the development of the urban environment, but he was also a strong instigator of commercial enterprise. He encouraged and established the commercial production of textiles and carpets in centers throughout the country, and sent embassies abroad from Iran to stimulate the demand for Iranian silk. Shah 'Abbas had his own interests in mind: from favored status in trade, he sought economic advantage and political alliance.

In 1600 the English East India Company was founded by royal charter, and thereafter ships set sail yearly for the East to bring back spices, silk, and exotic goods. By 1602 the Dutch East India Company had been established, and their ships, too, sought to control trade to and from the East. As English and Dutch maritime strength grew, so did the competition with the Portuguese, who held supremacy of the seas and controlled several ports along the Persian Gulf. Shah 'Abbas sought the assistance of the English in an effort to restore Safavid rule along the coast, and to build support against the Ottoman Turks, who controlled the overland trade routes. In 1621, with the aid of the English, he ousted the Portuguese from the port of Hormuz and founded the port of Bandar 'Abbas (Gombroon), thus establishing a Safavid presence in international trade along the Persian Gulf. There the English and the Dutch built trading stations. Textiles and goods associated with the production of textiles were sought and traded in every direction: furs; raw silk; calico, chintz, and other dyed cottons; carpets by commission; woolen broadcloth; gums for sizing; and dyestuffs such as indigo and lac. Iran had ports of call on the route to India, where the cities of Calcutta, Bombay, Surat, Goa, and Madras flourished during this intense period of commercial rivalry among the Portuguese, the Dutch, and the English.

In the next hundred years the explosion of global trade affected the regional economies of virtually all nations. To promote and mediate this mercantile activity, a new diplomacy evolved as political interests sought to balance and protect commercial stakes.

Throughout the seventeenth and early eighteenth centuries, and again in the nineteenth century, treaties, contracts, royal decrees, and merchants' reports focused upon the status of—and prognosis for—textiles: the circumstances of their production, the state of their markets, and the means of their distribution. The focus of so much commercial activity, both for import and for export, textiles emerged in the nineteenth century as key commodities in the international market, and provided a basis for commercial rivalry and competition that led to the mechanization of spinning and weaving, as well as to the development of steam-powered looms in the race for faster technologies and quicker profits.

As for textiles from Safavid and post-Safavid Iran, a wide variety of techniques were used to produce many distinct woven structures. The most complicated weaves, technically, are the velvets, which rely upon supplementary warps to form the pile by pulling loops into the fabric. The loops may be cut after weaving, or left uncut. Areas of the textile may be left plain (i.e., without loops), in which case the velvet is described as "voided." In the Safavid period, velvets were often very colorful because the weavers knew how to substitute different colors in the warps used to create the pile; but these exceptional velvets proved to be so labor intensive that they were not economically viable. Velvets (see Plates 22 and 23) from the Qajar period (1779–1924) show the use of one or two colors in the pile, combined with metal-wrapped threads in the voided areas. The patterns are reduced in scale and pleasing in appearance, but have none of the complexity of their Safavid forebears.

Many textiles from Iran were produced on a drawloom, in which the pattern harness is distinct from the foundation harness, lending complexity to the woven structure. Presumably, all of the figured silks with a metal ground, which were so favored at the Safavid and Qajar courts, were made on a drawloom. The term "metal ground" is a stylistic designation, for "metal-ground" textiles show a variety of compound weave structures (see Plates 24, 25, and 26). In the Safavid period, the elaborate designs are often large with fancy floral motifs and birds, richly colored in varied hues of pink, orange, green, and yellow. Repeated design elements may alternate with striped sections (see Plate 27), which are equally bold in their execution. In silks from the Qajar period, a darker palette and fewer colors are seen; patterns tend to be more rigid with smaller design elements scattered on a plain field (see Plate 28). Numerous printed cotton textiles from the nineteenth century are preserved, and these comprise a mixture of European imports and Iranian products. For garments, printed cotton textiles show patterns with small-scale motifs using few colors, predominantly red and blue, often with black outlines (see Plate 29).

Other silk textiles exhibit simpler weave structures. The primary textile structures, "plain weave," "twill," and "satin," represent basic binding systems (in regular ordered sequences of warp and weft: over one/under one, over two or three/under one, and over five/under one, respectively) that were used for the vast majority of utilitarian textiles. Such textiles could be ornamented after weaving by such techniques as painting and printing, embroidery, applique, quilting, and patchwork, all of which are well represented among textiles produced in the Safavid and post-Safavid periods. Different sequences of interlacing warp and weft, known as "float-patterning," were used to create figural, floral, and geometric patterns in Safavid and post-Safavid textiles.

Textile structures that are technically less complex include "brocaded satin," which utilizes discontinuous supplementary wefts to create the pattern by floating them over a satin foundation (see Plate 27); and "brocaded taffeta," which also utilizes discontinuous supplementary weft patterning, but on a plain weave foundation (see Plate 28). "Tapestry" is a plain weave structure with discontinuous wefts of different colors; each colored weft yarn is used both structurally and decoratively to create the pattern (see Plate 30). Carpets generally have a pile structure, in which discontinuous supplementary weft elements are wrapped around adjacent warps, or pairs of warps, and then cut to form tufts of color that carry the patterns (see Plates 31, 32, and 33). (The tufts are called "knots," although they comprise a wrapped structure, which is not actually knotted.)

In the mid-eighteenth century the Safavid empire fell, due to political turmoil and invasions from the East. In the aftermath of the fall of the Safavid dynasty in Iran, changes such as the decentralization of administration, the increase of regional powers, and the strengthening of tribal groups affected the availability of raw materials for textile production. In general, the economy suffered. Periods of internal stability and development occurred under the rule of Karim Khan Zand (1750–1779) and the subsequent Qajar dynasty, but overall, quality in the textile arts of the nineteenth century declined and cheap European imports became more and more plentiful. The textile industry in Iran, no longer masterfully innovative as it was under the imperial patronage of the Safavid rulers, was beset by competition from textiles manufactured abroad. As the economy declined, new products were sought to balance growing trade deficits. Resultant efforts saw the extraordinary development of the Persian carpet industry, which has remained a key component of Iran's economy. Under the Qajars, with European capitalization and management of production, the Persian carpet industry developed rapidly to meet the desires of the newly emerging middle classes in Europe and America.

From royal patronage of court and commercial products under the Safavids in the sixteenth and seventeenth centuries, to the proliferation of commercial production in the nineteenth century, carpets were produced in a wide range of contexts and circumstances, including city workshops, as a cottage industry for commercial distribution, and by village and nomadic women for use by their own families. In the cities and towns, the artistry of later Persian carpets drew upon the repertory of Safavid designs; stylized floral forms were particularly favored. Smaller units of design were repeated to form a variety of patterns (see Plate 31), or designs were simplified by enlarging the motifs (see Plate 32). In both cases, the apparent complexity of design and pattern was achieved by a simple technology, which used to great effect methods of counting and repeating sequences of knots.

Alongside political and social developments, which depended more or less upon a centralized administration and court-instigated enterprise, much of Iran's population adhered to a nomadic way of life, deriving its livelihood from herding and the breeding of livestock in areas marginal to the courts and cities, and their orchards and fields. In dry areas of the Iranian plateau and along the slopes of the surrounding mountain ranges, herders sought pasture for their flocks. The remarkable textiles and carpets they produced, some for their own use and some to sell at market, attest to many of the same historic changes occurring in the cities, and also reflect the development of an international exchange. In very general terms, the tribes grew stronger as the highly centralized Safavid state weakened during the eighteenth century. International trade declined, and it appears that the economy of Iran shifted more towards agricultural and pastoral pursuits closer to subsistence level by the end of the century. In the nineteenth century commercial ties were renewed with European markets, but urban artisans may have held less sway. The quantity and variety of tribal and ethnographic woven products surviving from the nineteenth (see Plate 30) and early twentieth centuries may represent a different path of development. They give evidence of the continuity of tradition in quality of materials and craftsmanship, but they nonetheless show the response in the production of textile arts to changing economic and social conditions in Iran and the world beyond.

ENDNOTE

1. Adam Olearius, *The Voyages and Travels of the Ambassadors Sent by Frederick, Duke of Holstein, to the Great Duke of Muscovy, and the King of Persia, Begun in 1633 and Finished in 1639* (London, 1669), 223.

22. Textile Fragment
✦

Iran
Qajar period, 19th century
Silk and metal strips
Cut and voided velvet (right selvage)
7 x 4.5 in.; 18 x 11.5 cm
Source Unknown, 0000.2089

22

23. Textile Fragment
✦

Iran
Qajar period, 19th century
Silk and metal strips
Cut and voided velvet (right selvage)
4.5 x 9 in.; 11.8 x 23 cm
Source Unknown, 0000.175

23

24. Textile Fragment

✦

Iran
Safavid period, 17th century
Silk and metal-wrapped silk thread
Compound weave with metal ground; discontinuous and continuous supplementary weft patterning (weft floats on back)
10.3 x 10 in.; 28 x 25.3 cm
Source Unknown, 0000.2084

24

25. Ceremonial Horse Cover

✦

Iran
Safavid period, 18th century
Silk and metal-wrapped silk thread
Compound weave with complementary weft
patterning and metal ground
54.5 x 34 in.; 138.5 x 86.5 cm
The William Bridges Thayer Memorial,
1928.877

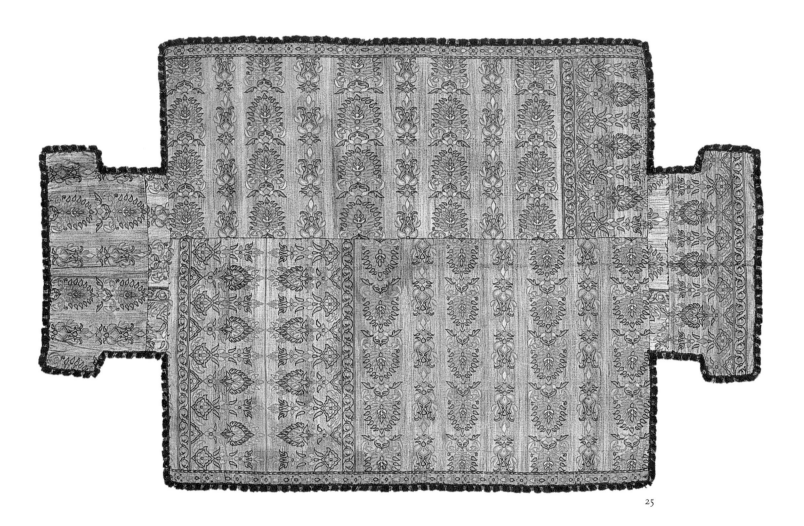

25

26. Textile Fragment

✦

Iran
Qajar period, 19th century
Silk and metal-wrapped silk thread
Compound weave with metal ground;
continuous complementary weft patterning
(left selvage)
10.3 x 7.3 in.; 26 x 19.5 cm
Source Unknown, 0000.2085

26

27. Textile Fragment

✦

Iran
Safavid period, first half of 18th century
Silk and metal-wrapped silk thread
Brocaded satin with warp-resist stripes;
discontinuous supplementary weft patterning
23 x 15.3 in.; 58 x 39 cm
Source Unknown, 0000.183

27

28. Textile Fragment

◆

Iran
Qajar period, 18th or 19th century
Silk and metal-wrapped silk thread
Brocaded plain weave; discontinuous
supplementary weft patterning
12 x 8.5 in.; 30.5 x 21.8 cm
Source Unknown, 0000.173

28

29. Textile Fragment

◆

Iran
Qajar period, 19th century
Cotton, ink, and pigments (also dye?)
Plain weave, printed and painted
13 x 9 in.; 33 x 23 cm
Source Unknown, 0000.2381

29

30. Kilim (detail)

✦

Iran (Zarand, near Kermānshāh)
Qajar period, 19th century
Wool weft, cotton warp
Tapestry weave
168 x 68 in.; 426.8 x 172.8 cm
The William Bridges Thayer Memorial,
1928.820

30

31. Carpet

Iran (Senna)
Qajar period, 19th century
Wool on cotton warp
Knotted pile on striped warp
66.5 x 53 in.; 169 x 134.5 cm
Source Unknown, 0000.2021

32. Carpet

Iran (Tābriz)
Qajar period, 19th century
Silk pile on cotton warp and weft
Knotted pile
70 x 51 in.; 177.8 x 129.5 cm
Source Unknown, 0000.2022

32

33. Carpet (detail)
✦

Iran (Heriz)
Qajar period, late 19th century
Wool pile on cotton warp and weft
Knotted pile, symmetrical knot
176 x 140 in.; 447 x 355.5 cm
Source Unknown, 0000.2423

33

Fifteenth-Century

34. Textile Fragment, Timurid style

✦

Iran or Central Asia
15th century
Silk
Satin lampas (satin weave with supplementary
weft-faced twill; one selvage)
13 x 10 in.; 33 x 25.5 cm
Source Unknown, 0000.683

"Satin lampas" refers to a figured weave in which the pattern is created by the addition of a warp and weft that are supplementary to the foundation weave. Many of the most important figured Safavid silks, using many colors, are woven in a lampas technique, with a satin foundation and supplementary twill weave. The Safavid examples have pictorial compositions, with themes drawn from literary works and historical episodes. Although the origins of this technique are at present unknown, this fragment, with its stark geometric pattern of circular medallions and its bright primary colors of red and blue with white, suggests a direct relationship to arts of the Timurid court. The utilization of the red satin warps to add touches of color in the lampas pattern shows an extremely sophisticated understanding of weaving technology. This textile thus represents a very high level of technical accomplishment prior to the industrial age, and may be an early indication that this technique was known prior to the Safavid achievement in textile arts.

34

CHINA

Contents

Chronology

Major Dynasties and Periods:

Xia	21st–16th century BCE
Shang	16th century–ca. 1045 BCE
Zhou	ca. 1050–256 BCE
Spring and Autumn period	722–481 BCE
Warring States period	481–221 BCE
Qin	221–206 BCE
Han	206 BCE–220 CE
Three Kingdoms	220–265
Jin	265–420
Northern and Southern dynasties	386–589
Sui	581–618
Tang	618–907
Five Dynasties	907–960
Liao	907–1125
Song	960–1279
Northern Song	960–1127
Southern Song	1127–1279
Jin	1115–1234
Yuan	1279–1368
Ming	1368–1644
Qing	1644–1911
Republic	1912–1949
People's Republic	1949–

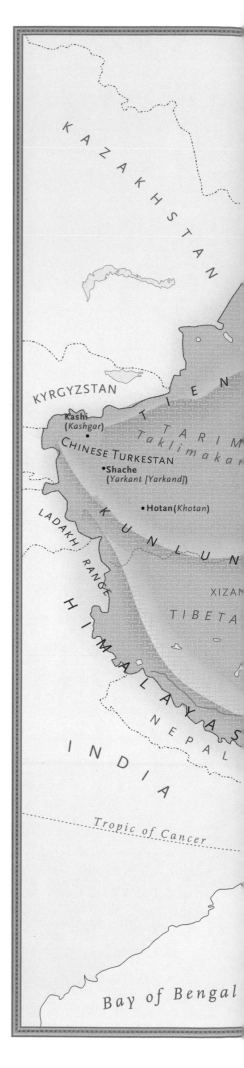

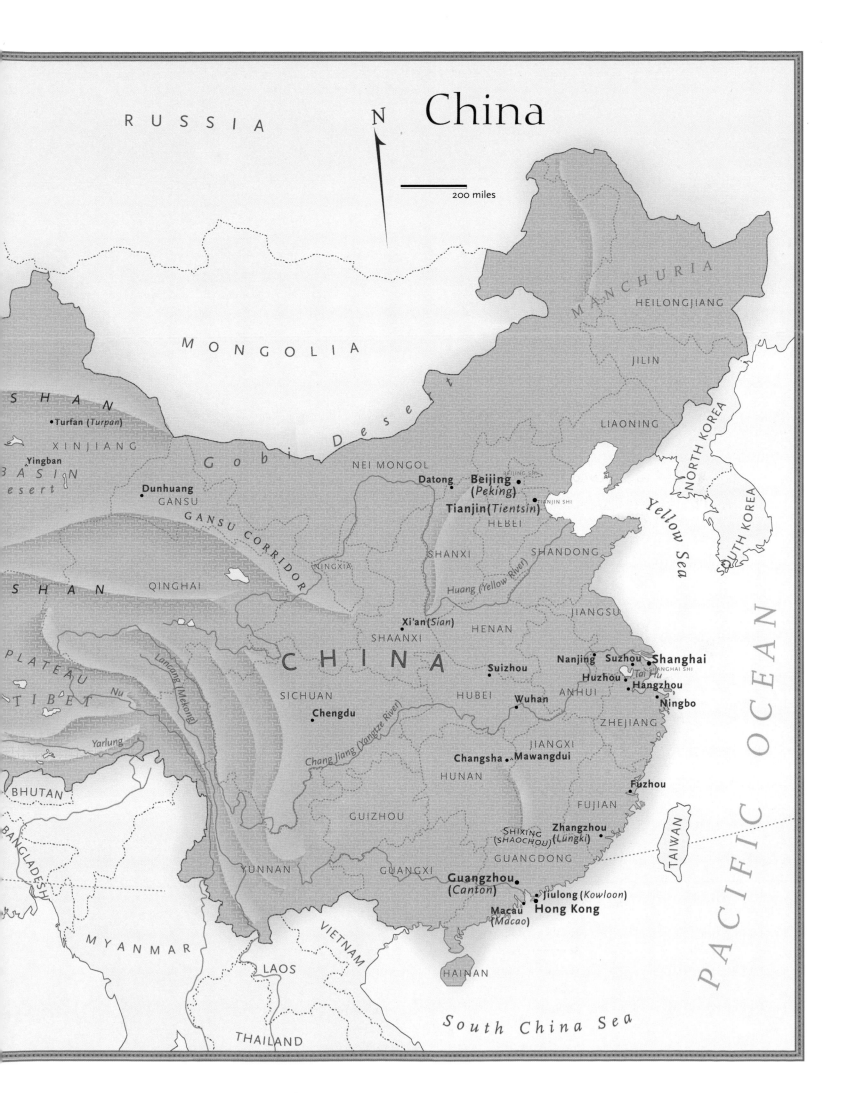

China

200 miles

RUSSIA

MONGOLIA

MANCHURIA

HEILONGJIANG

JILIN

SHAN

Turfan (*Turpan*)

XINJIANG

Yingban

BASIN
esert

Gobi Desert

NEI MONGOL

LIAONING

NORTH KOREA

Dunhuang

GANSU

GANSU CORRIDOR

Datong

Beijing
(*Peking*)

BEIJING SHI

Tianjin(*Tientsin*)

TIANJIN SHI

SOUTH KOREA

Yellow
Sea

NINGXIA

SHANXI

HEBEI

SHANDONG

QINGHAI

SHAN

Huang (*Yellow River*)

JIANGSU

Xi'an(*Sian*)

HENAN

SHAANXI

CHINA

Nanjing Suzhou **Shanghai**

SHANGHAI SHI

PLATEAU

Suizhou

Huzhou *Tai Hu* Hangzhou

TIBET

Nu

Lancang (Mekong)

SICHUAN

HUBEI

Wuhan

ANHUI

Ningbo

ZHEJIANG

Chengdu

Yarlung

Chang Jiang (Yangtze River)

Changsha Mawangdui

JIANGXI

BHUTAN

HUNAN

Fuzhou

FUJIAN

BANGLADESH

GUIZHOU

TAIWAN

SHIXING
(*SHAOCHOU*)

Zhangzhou
(*Lungki*)

GUANGDONG

MYANMAR

YUNNAN

GUANGXI

Guangzhou
(*Canton*)

Jiulong (*Kowloon*)

Macau **Hong Kong**
(*Macao*)

PACIFIC OCEAN

VIETNAM

LAOS

HAINAN

THAILAND

South China Sea

Introduction

The Chinese textile collection at the Spencer Museum of Art includes 138 official and informal garments, household furnishings, theatrical garments, accessories, armor, a Daoist priest's robe, and fragments or sections of larger works. Except for one Ming rank badge dating from the late fifteenth or early sixteenth century, all are products of the Qing dynasty (1644–1911).

In 1644 China was conquered by the Manchus, whose armies of skilled horsemen and formidable archers were legendary. The Manchus were a group of Jurchen peoples whose semi-nomadic ancestors originally came from the mountainous forests of the Russian maritime province and what was later known as Manchuria. In the early seventeenth century, they were consolidated into a powerful state by a succession of strong leaders. Considered "barbarians" by the native (Han) Chinese, the differences between the Manchu and native Chinese cultures created a dynamic tension throughout the Qing dynasty, affecting all aspects of life, including dress.

The core of the Spencer Museum's Qing dynasty textile collection, and some of its finest works, was part of Sallie Casey Thayer's original gift to the museum.[1] Mrs. Thayer was not alone in her interest in Chinese textiles, particularly court robes. Western collectors in the late nineteenth and early twentieth centuries—Europeans and Americans alike—were intrigued by these intricately woven and embroidered garments with their elaborate imagery and layered symbolic meanings. The complex iconography of the formal *chao fu* and official *long pao*, or "dragon robe," provided a synopsis of Chinese cosmology and was intended to indicate the owner's social and political place within it. Owning a court robe or even a beautifully embroidered pair of women's sleeve bands enabled an affluent middle-class Westerner to participate vicariously in an exotic world, where the virtue of a secluded "Son of Heaven" was thought to hold the cosmological, geophysical, and social forces of the universe in delicate harmony. There was a disconnection, of course, between this idealized view of the Chinese empire and descriptions of the realities of nineteenth-century China by Western observers, a disconnection similar to the nineteenth-century praise for an idealized "noble savage" with concomitant scorn for the persons and lifestyles of actual members of particular tribal groups.

The *chao fu* and two of the six *long pao* in the Spencer Museum collection, although listed as "source unknown," were almost certainly part of the original Sallie Casey Thayer gift of 1917. Throughout the twentieth century, Chinese court costume continued to enter the museum as the original collectors died and their collections were donated to the museum. The most recent addition to this group of textiles is a finely woven *kesi* (tapestry) *long pao* meant for a small boy. The gift was given in memory of James H. Walker, Jr. by his family in 1993 (see Plate 39).

Western collectors used their Chinese costume in a variety of ways. Some British civil servants assigned to China simply adopted Chinese official dress as their own, and appeared for their administrative duties dressed with Chinese symbols of rank. In Europe, affluent men adopted dragon robes for evening "at home" wear, in the manner of a smoking jacket. A few decades later, these splendid costumes were sometimes used for "dress up." The small boy's *long pao* shows signs of having been in a Western child's costume chest, and the Spencer Museum owns a photograph of a prominent member of the museum clowning around at a members' party in the late 1970s, wearing one of the Spencer dragon robes. In the 1970s, few non-textile objects in the museum's collection would have been handled in such a lighthearted manner. The incident reflects the comparative lack of appreciation of the textile arts in a majority of American museums throughout much of the twentieth century. Today, partly because of the extraordinary finds of Chinese archaeologists in the last several decades, there is a new appreciation of China's magnificent textile heritage, which is reflected in major exhibitions, catalogues, and scholarly research.

Qing Court Costume

COURT COSTUME AND THE POLITY

Throughout most of the twentieth century, Western scholars focused their studies of Qing dynasty textiles on official dress—its iconography, function, and lineage. The histories of the *chao fu* (audience robe) and *long pao* (dragon robe) have relevance beyond the development of these specific garments. Historically, official dress in China was intricately related to the philosophical basis and functioning of the polity. Changes in official costume reflected changes in the idea of the state, the heritage of the rulers, and their relationship to the people they governed. The costumes chosen by the founders of most dynasties included forms, materials, and iconography that carried weighty associations with the past, thereby underscoring the legitimacy of their rule. Official dynastic costume was used to identify a regional overlord or government functionary with the ruling dynasty, serving both to enhance his local authority by association with the distant court and to demonstrate visually his loyalty to that court. A passage in the *Shujing* (*Book of History*), compiled during the Zhou dynasty (ca. 1050–256 BCE), notes that one of the most serious offenses a local ruler could commit was failure to wear the prescribed costume. Such a failure was considered a sign of rebellion, and was punished severely. Another passage implies that an intentional departure from the prescribed dress code was sometimes employed as a form of political protest.[2]

This chapter will focus on the *chao fu* and the *long pao*, exploring their historical development and describing the context within which Qing rulers developed and codified their formal attire. These two official garments, with their accompanying accoutrements, were important instruments of the Manchu polity. They distinguished the Manchus as a unique people of foreign origin, something that mattered to the founders of the dynasty, while incorporating important elements of traditional Chinese costume and symbolism that allowed for their acceptance by the Chinese people as legitimate rulers of the great "Middle Kingdom."

PROTOTYPES FOR THE DISTINCTIVE GARMENT SHAPES OF QING COURT COSTUME

The most formal article of Qing court costume was the *chao fu*, or audience robe. More familiar was the *long pao*, or dragon robe, worn as part of the official costume of scholar-officials at all levels of government, including the local magistrates known to Westerners as "mandarins." Both of these garments differ markedly from the ceremonial Ming garments seen in portraiture of the preceding Ming dynasty (1368–1644); in fact, early Manchu leaders wrote several edicts stressing the importance of maintaining their own traditions and costume. For these reasons, most Western scholars assumed that the *chao fu* and the *long pao* were derived from earlier Manchu prototypes; that they were constructed to accommodate the needs of horse-riding herdsmen and mounted archers; and that the odd-shaped pieces from which they were fashioned (as opposed to the straight lengths of unshaped cloth that made up Ming dynasty garments, for example) might point to an evolution from the skins worn by the nomadic, hunting ancestors of these northern peoples.[3]

In the last few decades, however, excavations of Ming dynasty tombs have brought to light a steady stream of garments that are quite similar to the *chao fu* in construction. Some of the first to be revealed were from the tomb of the Wanli emperor (r. 1572–1620), excavated by Chinese archaeologists in the late 1950s.[4] At the time, in the early years of the People's Republic, politics coupled with the archaeologists' modest presentation of their finds kept their work from a wide audience. No one in the Western world paid much attention to the significance of the garments found in the Wanli tomb when it was first excavated. These Ming dynasty *chao fu*–like garments are often embellished with woven or embroidered dragons, and are thus called "dragon robes" in the excavation reports. (These Ming "dragon robes" should not be confused with the dragon robes of the succeeding Qing dynasty, which refer instead to the *long pao*—a garment that is quite different in cut, construction, and function from the Qing *chao fu* or Ming *chao fu*–like "dragon robes.") Since the excavation of the Wanli tomb, *chao fu*–like "dragon robes" with fitted bodices, fastenings on the right side, and flared skirts have been

found in tombs of members of the Ming imperial family and government officials in many parts of the country, from Shandong and Jiangsu along the eastern coast, to Jiangxi in the south, Shaanxi toward the northwest, and Peking (Beijing), capital of the Ming after 1421.[5] Most have upper sleeves that are integral to the bodice, with a second section of cloth added to extend the sleeve. This is also a feature typical of later Qing dynasty *chao fu*, which have two sections of cloth added to an integral upper sleeve.

Among the Ming "dragon robes" is a deep yellow silk robe with a gathered, fitted bodice and a full, pleated skirt (Fig. 7). The sleeves, integral to the bodice, are long and loose. This magnificent garment was one of several "dragon robes" of similar cut and decoration excavated in 1970 from the tomb of Prince Zhu Tan in Shandong (ca. 1411). Published in the Chinese archaeological journal *Wenwu* in 1973, it was introduced to the English-speaking world by Verity Wilson in 1986.[6] These side-fastening robes with fitted bodices, gathered or pleated flared skirts, and integral sleeves with dragon decoration appear to be immediate forerunners of—and prototypes for—the Qing *chao fu*. They differ significantly in just one respect: sleeves on the Ming dynasty "dragon robes" range from loose to voluminous, and are quite different from the narrow, tapering sleeves of the Qing *chao fu* with its flaring "horse hoof" cuff.

Although the *chao fu* was the most formal garment in the Qing dynasty, this was not true of the *chao fu*–like "dragon robes" of the Ming. The "dragon robes" that appear in significant numbers in burials of members of the imperial family and government officials do not appear in formal portraiture during the Ming dynasty. Perhaps they were worn underneath the voluminous outer robes shown in the portraits, or for other, less formal occasions. Robert D. Jacobsen suggests that they were used to conduct everyday official business.[7] In that case, they would have held the function served by the *long pao* in the succeeding Qing dynasty.

Prototypes of both the *long pao* and the narrow tapering sleeve that is a distinctive characteristic of Qing official costume (seen in both the *chao fu* and the *long pao*) can be found in the Mongol-controlled Yuan dynasty (1279–1368), just preceding the Ming. Despite significant differences between the two groups, the Manchus, who ruled China from the seventeenth to the early twentieth century, and the Mongols, who ruled in the late thirteenth and fourteenth centuries, both came from the vast regions to the north of China, shared a remote Altaic ancestry, and were known as superb horsemen and archers. The Yuan dynasty tomb of Li Youan in Shandong Province, dated to 1350, was excavated in 1975. It contained fifty-five men's and women's garments, including a number of full-length robes, with fastenings on the right side and long, narrow, tapering sleeves, some with flared cuffs—a clear precedent for the sleeves on Qing *chao fu* and *long pao*, and quite different from the voluminous sleeves characteristic of

garments in the intervening Ming dynasty. These garments were comparatively tight fitting through the torso and arms, and flared outwards toward the hem, a style that appears again in the Qing *long pao* (Fig. 8).[8]

The archaeological record thus reveals a clear precedent for the Qing *chao fu* in the Ming "dragon robes" excavated from imperial and official tombs. At the same time, Yuan tombs have yielded garments similar in construction to the Qing *long pao*, and with the narrow tapering sleeves, sometimes flared, that appear again in the next "barbarian" dynasty—on the Qing *chao fu* and *long pao*. These Yuan dynasty garments, however, do not have the slits in the hem that are typical of Qing *long pao*.

Unlike the Yuan and Qing dynasties, which were ruled by peoples considered "barbarians" by the native Chinese, the Ming dynasty that fell between them was governed by emperors who were very conscious of their native, or Han Chinese, heritage, and of the fact that they had ousted a foreign regime. When the forces of Zhu Yuanzhang (1328–1398), the future Hongwu emperor, overthrew the Mongolian Yuan dynasty and established the Ming in 1368, Ming leaders sought to restore traditional Chinese custom and costume to governance and its ceremonies. They abolished the Mongol costume regulations of the Yuan, and sought prototypes for official Ming costume among garment constructions that were typical of important dynasties from the past—from the Han (206 BCE–220 CE), Tang (618–907), and Song (960–1279). Ming costume deliberately reflects previous styles; it is therefore not unreasonable to search for prototypes of the Qing *chao fu* that are even earlier than the recently excavated examples from Ming tombs.

More than thirty Tang dynasty *hanpi*, or "short coats," as they are known collectively today, have survived in the Shōsōin Repository of the temple Tōdaiji in Nara, Japan. Like most of the other objects in this treasury of Buddhist and secular goods, the *hanpi* were either imported from China or closely modeled on Tang dynasty Chinese prototypes; most date from the eighth century. In construction (although not in decoration), they are clearly related to the Ming "dragon robes" discussed above. The garments show some variation, but are distinguished by a straight or fitted bodice with an attached skirt that is often flared and usually made of a different material. The difference in materials between the bodice and skirt of the Shōsōin *hanpi* might support a hypothesis that the Qing *chao fu* originally developed from two separate garments.[9] The brocade bodice of one dance costume, for example, has a design of grapevine arabesques on a green ground, while the attached flared skirt is made of a thin plain silk patterned with an unusual dyeing process employing a set of two pattern blocks (*kyōkechi*, or "clamp resist").[10] Several have very short sleeves that are attached at the shoulder.[11] Two are fashioned like the *chao fu*, in that the sleeve (or, in the case of the *chao fu*, the first section of sleeve) is an integral part of a wide, loom-width piece of fabric that is then cut and tailored below the sleeve to fit the torso.[12] The skirt, or *ran*, of a *hanpi* exhibited in 1974 and 1992 at Nara National Museum has a very pronounced flair that is achieved partially by a single large pleat at center front. Like the Ming excavated garments, the Shōsōin *hanpi* have cross-over closures. All have small lapels, and most have a much smaller overflap than the Ming garments (Fig. 9).

The large number and variety of *hanpi* in the Shōsōin indicate that this was a common garment construction in the eighth century that probably developed from even earlier prototypes.[13] In fact, an interesting example of such a garment was found at a tomb in Yingban, an important city in Xinjiang on the branch of the Silk Road that skirted the Taklamakan Desert to the north, just south of the Tien Shan mountains. The Yingban tombs date from the Han to the Jin (265–420) dynasties. The excavation of tomb M15 in 1995 revealed a magnificently attired male mummy with a finely rendered miniature garment of this type placed on his chest. Another tomb in this desert cemetery contained a full-length garment with the shaped body and long, tapering sleeves reminiscent of Qing *long pao*.[14]

The eighth-century *hanpi* preserved in Japan, and related Ming garments excavated from fourteenth- to early-seventeenth-century tombs, demonstrate a clear and ongoing tradition within China of a garment with integral sleeves (sometimes elongated with a separate piece of cloth), a fitted bodice, and an attached flaring skirt that is often pleated or gathered. The Ming examples, while important enough to be buried with their owners, were not the preferred attire for formal portraiture, and are inconspicuous in other forms of Ming painting as well. Since few Ming costumes survived above ground, this style of garment was unknown before the recent explosion of archaeological exploration in China. At the present time, however, all of the evidence points to the fact that the Qing *chao fu* was developed from a long-lived tradition of garment construction in China, and not from a northern prototype invented by horse-riding peoples and brought to China in 1644 by the Manchu invaders (or even in 1279 by the Mongols).

The prototypes for the Qing *chao fu* excavated from Ming tombs, as well as the eighth-century *hanpi* in the Shōsōin Repository in Japan, neither support nor refute the larger question of the influence of northern nomadic horse-riders on the cut and construction of this somewhat unusual garment—or, for that matter, on other Chinese clothing styles. They merely push the question to a much earlier period of Chinese history. Various groups of northern "barbarians," many of them feared for their superb horsemanship and skill with the bow, had haunted China's borderlands and interacted with the Han Chinese for more than fifteen hundred years before the Manchus invaded China. Most of the earlier foreign dynasties were headed by one or another of these groups. The question of the origin and derivation of the Qing *chao fu* remains as a larger issue that must be studied within the context of Han Chinese and foreign cultural interchange over the whole course of Chinese history.

MANCHU LEADERS CODIFY QING FORMAL ATTIRE

Qing rulers, well aware that they formed a small and potentially vulnerable foreign minority within China, sought to maintain power by acknowledging and honoring both their Manchu heritage and their adopted Chinese legacy. They preserved the Chinese administrative structure, studied Chinese, translated the Chinese classics into Manchu, and adopted traditional Chinese religious symbols and ritual practices, through which they associated themselves with traditions of imperial authority. Through their study of the Chinese classics, they buttressed the legitimacy of their dynasty—their right to hold the Mandate of Heaven—by retrieving and reviving ancient Chinese ritual practices. For example, the ritual vessels that the Qing rulers commissioned were deliberately based even more closely on ancient prototypes than the sacrificial vessels used by their Ming predecessors.[15] They also adopted the twelve traditional Chinese symbols of imperial authority for use on imperial dress. These symbols are mentioned and illustrated in the mid-eighteenth-century *Illustrated Precedents for the Ritual Implements of the Imperial Court (Huangzhaoliqidushi)*, and appear on an extant court robe that belonged to the Qianlong emperor (r. 1736–1795).[16]

At the same time, early Qing emperors stressed the dangers of becoming completely sinicized. They attributed the fates of earlier foreign dynasties—the Northern Wei (386–535), the Liao (907–1125), the Jin (1115–1234), and the Yuan—to overenthusiastic sinification and a concurrent abandonment of ancestral traditions. In order to retain a distinct cultural identity, they insisted on the importance of maintaining the Manchu language, Manchu dress (which was strictly regulated), and skill in riding and archery. The Manchu language was used for some purposes at court until the end of the dynasty, and Western scholars have realized only recently that the primary and unexpurgated version of a given document is often in Manchu, not in Chinese.[17] As late as 1857 the six ecclesiastical and four lay members of the Russian mission in Peking found it advantageous to study both Manchu and Chinese.[18]

Riding and archery were essential components of the Manchus' identity. Although their conquest of China had been greatly facilitated by the canon and muskets that they captured from Chinese troops (and soon learned to manufacture themselves), as late as 1800 Manchu youths were admonished to study riding and shooting. An edict of that year demanded that garrison officers train talented boys in riding, shooting, administration, and the Manchu language. This marked a change after a period of emphasis on Chinese studies.[19] Manchus who sat for the government civil service examinations also had to prove their skill at archery, both on foot and on horseback, a test that became more difficult later in the dynasty.[20]

People of Manchu descent were forbidden to wear Chinese clothing, while Han Chinese who served the government were required to wear Manchu clothing for official purposes. Abandoning Manchu dress, early Qing rulers insisted, would constitute a failure to honor the Manchu ancestors and lead to a loss of cultural identity that would enervate the dynasty. Manchus formed only about two percent of the Chinese population;[21] continued cultural vigor was therefore essential if the small Manchu minority was to maintain its rule over the vast empire of China.

Hong Taiji (1592–1643), the strong Manchu leader who prepared the way for the Manchu invasion of northern China, issued two edicts warning his followers against adopting Chinese dress and language.[22] A century later his great-great-grandson, Emperor Qianlong, consciously linked the continued vigor of the dynasty to Manchu cultural identity, and insisted on the pivotal role of costume in embodying, expressing, and transmitting Manchu culture.

It has proved surprisingly difficult to find Manchu prototypes for official Qing costume, or indeed much evidence for Manchu clothing styles before the Manchu conquest of China in the mid-seventeenth century. Part of the reason for the lack of data is that the Manchus themselves deliberately eradicated any aspect of pre-Qing Manchu culture that did not affirm the image of themselves that they wanted to project. The Qianlong emperor, for example, ordered that the *Manzhoushilutu*, an illustrated history recording the Manchu rise to power, be rewritten and re-illustrated; this was accomplished in 1781. As a result, scenes illustrating sixteenth- and early-seventeenth-century events depict figures wearing eighteenth-century, mid-Qing-style clothing.[23]

The *Illustrated Precedents for the Ritual Implements of the Imperial Court*, commissioned by the Qianlong emperor in 1759, forges a strong connection between costume, cultural identity, and power. The introduction is written in the name of the emperor himself. It reviews the efforts of the Qing to revive ancient Chinese forms and to bring contemporary ritual practice in line with ancient prototypes. At the same time, the writer warns his readers not to offend their ancestors by abandoning Manchu dress.

> Previous dynasties used sacrificial vessels just to make up the required numbers, but we
> have changed [the vessels] in order to conform to the ancient traditions. As for robes and

FIG. 10

Portrait of a Nobleman

China
Qing dynasty, 18th century
Hanging scroll
Ink and color on silk
Painting: 76.5 x 31.4 in.; 194.3 x 79.7 cm
The George Crofts Collection, Royal Ontario
Museum, 921.1.156
With permission of the Royal Ontario Museum
© ROM

hats, however, each dynasty sets forth its own regulations. Anciently, the *shou* [-hats] of the Hsia, and the *hsu* [-hats] of the Yin were not passed down [to succeeding dynasties]. We, accordingly, have followed the old traditons of Our Dynasty, and have not dared to change them, fearing that later men would hold Us responsible for this, and criticize Us regarding the robes and hats; and thus We would offend Our ancestors. This We certainly should not do. Moreover, as for the Northern Wei, the Liao, and the Chin [dynasties] as well as the Yuan, all of which changed to Chinese robes and hats, they all died out within one generation [after abandoning their native dress]. Those of Our sons and grandsons who would take Our will as their will shall certainly not be deceived by idle talk. In this way, the continuing Mandate of our Dynasty will receive the protection of Heaven for ten thousand years. Do not change [our Manchu traditions] or reject them. Beware! Take warning![24]

It is clear that Manchu leaders felt that their dress was distinctive; that by keeping their traditional costume they honored and maintained their own cultural heritage; and that this was an important thing to do. How, then, did they define their dress? What, in their eyes, made it distinctive?

The first item mentioned in the introduction to the *Illustrated Precedents* is headgear. The author states that the headgear of each of two ancient dynasties, the Xia (21st–16th century BCE) and the Shang (16th century–ca. 1045 BCE), was distinctive. By arguing that there was an ancient precedent for each dynasty to have its own costume, the author justifies the use of Manchu costume as the official costume of the Qing. The author's emphasis on headgear is noteworthy. Qing official costume did indeed include distinctive headgear that played a major role in distinguishing rank.[25]

HEADGEAR, HAIRSTYLES, AND FOOTWEAR: MING AND QING

The most common formal headgear for officials during the early Ming dynasty was the *fu dou*. Derived from a Song prototype of the same name, the Ming *fu dou* had a rounded crown with a high oval form behind it and two sharply protruding ends. It was typically made of starched black silk gauze. Qing official headgear was quite different. The winter hat had a low, round crown with an upturned brim, trimmed with fur or velvet, and was covered with red silk cords or dyed yak's hair radiating from the center of the crown. The hat was topped by an ornament mounted on a decorative metal base, or insignia spike. One or more peacock or pheasant feathers might protrude from a tube fastened to the side of the crown. The type of fur, the insignia spike, and the ornament (a pearl, colored glass, precious metal, or semi-precious stone) denoted the rank of the wearer. The right to wear a feather plume was originally granted by the court as a mark of meritorious service, but by the end of the dynasty, like other rank markers, feathers were often purchased at will by those who could afford them. Although contemporary observers all agreed on the shape and construction of the winter hat, they described the materials quite differently: fur, leather, velvet, wool, silk, and cotton are all mentioned. In practice, the material probably varied depending on the geographical area and relative affluence of the official.

The summer hat, conical in shape, was made of rattan, split bamboo, or wheat stalks wrapped in silk. Like the winter hat, a cascade of red tassels or dyed horse or yak hair fell from the top, and an insignia spike surmounted by an ornament rose from the crown.[26] During the Yuan dynasty, Mongol men wore round or square hats made of rattan. Some of these hats were surmounted by an ornament.[27] It is possible that the Yuan Mongol hat and the Qing Manchu hat had a common ancestry, or that the former served, in some way, as a prototype for the latter.

The Manchu conquerors required all men, including Han Chinese, to shave the fronts of their heads from the forehead to the crown and gather the remaining hair at the back of the head in a queue, a Manchu style known as *ma soncoho*. Qing rulers used this hairstyle as a visible mark of loyalty to the new regime, a requirement that was bitterly resented by their conquered Chinese subjects in the immediate post-conquest period.[28] Manchu and Han women's hairstyles were unregulated. Originally different from one another, they gradually intermixed to form a variety of new styles.[29]

Boots have been excavated from Ming tombs, although Ming dignitaries wore the "cloud toe" or "court" shoe for the most formal occasions.[30] During the Qing dynasty, however, boots became the established footwear for even the most formal court ceremonies. A Manchu official's formal boots in the nineteenth century were typically made of black satin with high white soles. They cost the equivalent of a servant's yearly salary.[31]

DISTINCTIVE FEATURES OF THE *CHAO FU* AND THE *LONG PAO*

The *chao fu* (audience robe) and the *long pao* (dragon robe, also called a *qifu* or *jifu*, "auspicious robe") formed the core of official Manchu costume. As noted above, both had precedents in earlier Chinese costume. Prototypes of the *chao fu* can be traced back at least as far as the eighth century, and this form—with fitted bodice, side-fastening closure, integral sleeves (or upper sleeves), and flared skirt (often gathered or pleated)—should probably be considered a traditional Chinese garment type. The *long pao*, on the other hand, appears to be quite specifically related to a distinctive garment style in the Mongol-controlled Yuan dynasty that was quite different from the voluminous, untailored robes of the preceding Song and succeeding Ming dynasties. Its cut and construction, as well as the narrow, tapered sleeves with flaring cuffs (typical of both the Qing *chao fu* and *long pao*), may well have been derived from garment types developed on the northern steppes and used in China by the Mongols in the Yuan dynasty, and later by the Manchus during the Qing dynasty.

These Qing garments, and their accoutrements, have several distinctive features that are not found in earlier garments of related construction—or, indeed, in other pre-Qing Chinese garments. These may be listed as follows:

HEADGEAR
- shared features with Mongol Yuan hat
- quite different from Ming headgear

HAIRSTYLE
- distinctive Manchu *ma soncoho* style

CHOICE OF GARMENT TYPE/ACCOUTREMENTS
- elevation of the Ming *chao fu*–like "dragon robe" to most formal status, replacing the voluminous robe of Ming rulers
- choice of the *long pao*, with Yuan precedents, for scholar-official costume
- incorporation of the archer's thumb ring into court costume

MODIFICATIONS TO EARLIER PROTOTYPES OF THE *CHAO FU* AND *LONG PAO*
- consistent use of a tripartite sleeve with upper arm integral to the garment, an added section for the lower arm (generally a ribbed, dark blue silk), and the final addition of a separate, dramatically flaring "horse hoof" cuff *(ma ti xiu)*
- distinctive shaping of the right overflap
- use of loop and toggle (or, later, loop and button) closures
- deep slits in the hem of the *long pao*

FOOTWEAR
- boots as part of formal wear

Scholars have generally believed that the long, narrow sleeves and flared "horse hoof" cuffs that distinguish both the *chao fu* and the *long pao* developed to accommodate the needs of archers. The fitted sleeve would not impede the action of the bow, and the cuffs could cover and protect the hand or be folded back out of the way. This explanation makes sense, particularly since the sleeves depart so radically from those on Ming garments. The incorporation of such sleeves into Qing official costume can be seen to support the Manchu emperors' stated goals of affirming and maintaining their Manchu identity as skilled archers. Qing rulers also incorporated the archer's thumb ring into official court costume.

The deep vertical slits in the hem of the *long pao* appear to be a Manchu innovation. They are not found on earlier known garment types in China or the northern steppes. They would have enabled a Manchu man to ride actively while wearing the *long pao*, which would have been impossibly cumbersome to wear on horseback without the slits. The *long pao* generally has two slits: one in center front and one in center back for men; one on each side for women; and four, similarly placed, for the emperor, his family, and high-ranking nobles.[32]

On the basis of current research, it appears that the early Manchu rulers chose an important—but not the most formal—Ming costume, and elevated it to most formal status. They altered both the *chao fu* and the *long pao* in several distinctive ways and broke sharply with Ming precedent in other aspects of costuming, such as headgear, hairstyle, and footwear.

CHAO FU

35. *Chao fu*

✦

China
Qing dynasty, 19th century
Silk, gold-wrapped thread, and peacock feathers
Embroidery (satin, seed, couching) on plain weave ground
55 x 85.5 in.; 140 x 217 cm
Source Unknown, 0000.1045
Literature: *Handbook of the Collection, Helen Foresman Spencer Museum of Art*, 152 (ill.).
Catalogue of the Oriental Collection, 67–70.

The *chao fu*, or "audience robe," was the most formal court garment during the Qing dynasty. The Qianlong emperor (r. 1736–1795) wore the *chao fu* on the most important ceremonial occasions, such as the offerings at the winter solstice, the Sacrifices to Heaven and Earth, imperial weddings, and the palace examinations.[33] In an epic novel of upper-class life in the eighteenth century, completed circa 1760, the women of the ancient Jia family wear *chao fu* for a formal New Year's visit to the palace, to visit a Jia daughter who is an imperial concubine.[34] Because the *chao fu* was also used as a burial robe, it is the rarest of extant Qing court costumes today.[35]

Men wore the *chao fu* with a stiff, flaring collar, a hat with insignia signifying the wearer's rank, and ceremonial boots. Women used a similar flaring collar, with epaulettes extending beyond the court vest that was worn over the *chao fu*, and additional bands of decoration on the sleeves.[36]

The *Illustrated Precedents for the Ritual Implements of the Imperial Court* of 1759 includes detailed regulations about the materials and iconography appropriate for winter and summer *chao fu* worn by the emperor, his relatives, and other nobility; civil and military officials from the first to the seventh ranks; and imperial guardsmen from the first to the third ranks.[37] The *Illustrated Precedents* also includes separate but closely related regulations for *chao fu* worn by their wives, daughters, and consorts.[38]

Regulations in the *Illustrated Precedents* specify that five-clawed dragons were reserved for the emperor, empress, empress dowager, the emperor's consorts (first through fourth ranks), the heir apparent and his consort, the emperor's sons, and first- and second-degree princes with their wives and daughters. Third- and fourth-degree princes and imperial dukes could wear the five-clawed dragon only if the emblem was bestowed upon them; similarly, golden yellow was assigned to the emperor's sons, but first- and second-degree princes could wear it if specially permitted. The rule seems to be that a person might be granted the privilege of wearing a color or insignia of the rank above his own, but that it would be unlikely for the privilege to extend further down the ranks. In practice, however, the use of five-clawed dragons had become widespread by the nineteenth century. Ranks—with their attendant privileges—were bought and sold, even by the court officials,[39] and at times restricted iconography and colors were directly and boldly misappropriated.

The main rank insignia were the hat ornament and the pair of rank badges worn on the outer coat, but there were rank specifications pertaining to the *chao fu* as well. First- through third-rank officials and officers were entitled to wear a robe displaying nine five-clawed dragons, the ninth hidden under the left front overflap of the skirt. Officials from the fourth to the sixth

35

rank wore eight four-clawed dragons, while the robes of those in the seventh, eighth, and ninth ranks displayed five four-clawed dragons.[40] Qing imperial *chao fu* are distinguished from other high-ranking *chao fu* by the display of all twelve traditional symbols of authority.

This *chao fu* is embroidered with eight five-clawed dragons, one each at the chest and center back, one on each shoulder, and two each on the front and back waist panels. It would have been appropriate for an official of the fourth, fifth, or sixth rank to be granted the right to wear the five-clawed dragon, perhaps in recognition of meritorious service. It would also have been appropriate for his wife, widow, and unmarried daughters to be granted this right.

The dragons are arranged so that the pair that coils over the shoulders appears above and flanking both the large dragon at center front and his counterpart at center back. Five symmetrically arranged dragons thus appear on both the front and back of the garment, although there are eight dragons in total on the upper garment. Symmetry and numerology were important concepts underlying the design of Qing court robes; the number of items carried almost as much significance as the motifs themselves. Symmetry suggested a harmonious balance in the universe—the ideal as well as the mark of a wise, just, and enlightened sovereign. This and other *chao fu* are designed so that the major motifs are symmetrical from side to side and front to back, and add up to an auspicious and appropriate number; particularly important numbers were five, eight, and nine.

The *chao fu* is constructed of several distinct pieces of cloth. The jacket-like upper portion of the garment, tailored from three pieces of cloth, has short, wide sleeves that are extended by a narrow length of dark blue cloth with impressed sets of ribs. The sleeves are finished with the separate flared, decorated handcovering that is distinctive to Qing garments, known in both Chinese and English as "horse hoof cuffs," or *ma ti xiu*. The cuffs were worn folded back for practical use or turned down for ceremonial occasions. The lower portion of the garment is constructed from two pleated panels that are overlapped and stitched to a waistband that also serves to join the upper and lower halves of the garment. The separate *jen*, or flap, at the proper right side of the waist has no remembered function but is a standard feature of Qing dynasty *chao fu*.[41] Borders of the garment and many seam joins are finished with separate bands of gold brocade.

Motifs on this *chao fu* are embroidered with glossed, reeled silk thread with little twist. This thread shows colors to their best advantage; dye is readily absorbed into its soft, untwisted surface, and after it is woven or embroidered, the light reflected from its long, smooth surfaces imparts a lustrous sheen to the colorful motifs. Most of the embroidery is satin stitch, a stitch that floats over the surface of the fabric, taking advantage of the properties of this high-quality thread. A few motifs are worked in a knotted stitch sometimes called the "Peking knot" or the "forbidden stitch," a stitch that is closely related to the French knot. The preferred Chinese name for this knotted stitch is "seed stitch." The dragons and a few other areas are worked in metallic threads couched with silk thread.

The motifs on this *chao fu* are drawn primarily from two major categories of auspicious symbols—Buddhist icons and "Precious Things" (or *Ba Bao*)—as well as from a general vocabulary of auspicious objects. The motifs float freely and abundantly among the waves and clouds on the upper half of the garment, and are arranged in bilateral symmetry in the abbreviated cosmos depicted on the hem and waistband. Although the designer carefully selected representative motifs from each of several auspicious categories, there was no attempt to depict all eight motifs from each category. Apparently one or two motifs could recall the whole category of symbols.

Auspicious motifs dominate the abbreviated cosmos at the hem and waistband. Branches of red and pink coral rise from the water while pearls, a round gold ornament sometimes depicted as a coin (*sheng*), a square gold ornament (*fang sheng*), and rhinoceros horns lie in the troughs of the rolling waves. Giant peonies float on the surface, and bats fly among the auspicious five-colored clouds. Bats, which stand for happiness, are one of the most common of many Qing dynasty rebuses. (A rebus is a pictorial pun based on two nouns that sound alike but have different meanings.) Because the word for "bat" and the word for "happiness" are both pronounced *fu*, a picture of a bat can represent the abstract concept of happiness. Here the bats are embroidered in red and pink, colors that also connote joy. Above the waves a pair of dragons prances toward a central mountain, with claws outstretched toward a flaming pearl. The mountain itself, flanked by two companion mountains, rises above the roiling sea as huge waves break against it and are deflected back on either side.

A large flaming pearl, framed by a rampant dragon coiling around it, dominates the front and back of the upper garment and provides a focal point for the eight Buddhist motifs that surround it, four on the front and four on the back. On the back of the upper garment, the central dragon is flanked on the proper left with a single endless knot and a vase and, on the right, with a flaming wheel of the Law and ceremonial parasol. Surrounding the dragon on the front are the canopy and conch shell on the proper left, with the fish and, under the overflap, lotus on the right. In an unusual pairing, each of the Buddhist motifs appears with a large peony. Although most of the embroidery on this *chao fu* is satin stitch, seed stitch is used to set off the peonies and the eight Buddhist emblems.

The peony, an emblem of wealth and distinction, was symbolic of flowers in general—it was called the "queen of flowers"—and was emblematic of womanhood. It appears as a prominent symbol on numerous women's informal garments, including many in the Spencer collection. It is unusual for it to be depicted on a formal garment or to appear in close association with Buddhist iconography.

By the late eighteenth and the nineteenth centuries the motifs in the established sets of felicitous objects (Daoist, Buddhist and Precious Things) were used primarily as general auspicious motifs and should be interpreted on the literal level only with considerable caution.[42] However, the almost total absence of Daoist imagery in this garment—coupled with the use of a different and more labor-intensive embroidery technique to emphasize the carefully enunciated assemblage of Buddhist emblems as well as the unusual peony motif—suggest that, in this instance, the iconography was intentional.

This *chao fu* has several distinctive features that may provide clues to its ownership. The first is the conspicuous inclusion of peonies in the iconographic scheme. The second is the prominence of the eight Buddhist emblems assemblage. The third is that *Ba Bao* motifs, such as the *shang*, the *feng shang*, the fish and the rhinoceros horn, that almost invariably appear as closely related pairs, often interlocking pairs, are here depicted as single motifs. The unusual inclusion of peonies as a dominant motif on this *chao fu* strongly suggests that it belonged to a woman. The emphasis on Buddhist motifs points to a person of mature years. The surprising use of single rather than paired motifs (a common symbol of matrimony) suggests that the owner herself was single. The robe is beautifully executed with iconography appropriate for a person who had risen in the ranks. Perhaps this *chao fu* belonged to the widow of a distinguished scholar-official.

LONG PAO

The six *long pao* in the Spencer Museum reflect the diversity of late-eighteenth- and nineteenth-century non-imperial dragon robes. Four belonged to men, one to a woman, and one to a male child. One was executed in brocade, two in embroidery, and three in *kesi*, or silk tapestry weave. Within the narrowly defined parameters of appropriate pattern layout and iconography, several of these dragon robes display a surprising individuality.

All six dragon robes appear to have been associated with officials or members of the Chinese (as opposed to Manchu) nobility. They all have two slits in the skirt—front and back center for men's robes, and right and left sides for the woman's. The number of slits was determined by nationality and rank in the *Illustrated Precedents* of 1759. According to these regulations, the

116

FIG. 11

School of Spoilum
Portrait of the Silk Merchant Eshing,
ca. 1805

China
Qing dynasty, early 19th century
Oil on canvas
31.2 x 25.5 in.; 79.4 x 64.8 cm
Peabody Essex Museum, Salem, M364
[Courtesy of Peabody Essex Museum;
Photograph by Jeffrey Dykes 06/96]

imperial family and Manchu nobility wore four slits in their skirts, while Chinese nobles and all ranked officials (most of whom were Chinese) were permitted only two.[43]

It is difficult to identify ownership of the Spencer robes precisely, as all six display nine five-clawed dragons. Contrary to a great deal of published opinion that associates nine (as opposed to eight) dragons with the emperor or his immediate family, the *Illustrated Precedents* explicitly states that all Manchu and Chinese nobles, as well as officials in the first three ranks, could wear nine dragons.[44] There was no difference in appearance between an eight-dragon and a nine-dragon robe when it was being worn. Both had a front-facing dragon at chest and back, two coiling dragons over the shoulders, and two pairs at the hems. The ninth dragon was hidden on the obverse side of the proper right front panel of the robe, covered by the left overflap. The placement and description of the ninth dragon is similar on the non-imperial late-eighteenth- and nineteenth-century Spencer *long pao,* and on two eighteenth-century imperial *long pao* in the Metropolitan Museum.[45]

Unlike the use of a ninth dragon, the *long* or five-clawed dragon was a status marker inappropriate for ranked officials and members of the Chinese nobility. According to the *Illustrated Precedents,* the five-clawed dragon was reserved for the emperor, heir apparent, imperial princes, and first- and second-degree (Manchu) princes, along with certain wives, daughters, and consorts of the above. Lower-ranking Manchu nobility, Chinese nobility, and all officials were restricted to four-clawed dragons (*mang*), unless they were explicitly granted permission to wear the additional claw. Qing dynastic records, however, record a long history of flagrant violations of costume regulations. Officials often usurped insignia of ranks higher than their own, and were admonished for this practice in edicts issued in 1662, 1687, 1723, 1730, and 1800.[46] Five-clawed dragons are found in abundance on non-imperial nineteenth-century Qing garments in many Western collections. All six of the *long pao* in the Spencer Museum sport five-clawed dragons.

Other sumptuary laws were also disregarded, though not always without consequence. In Cao Xueqin's *The Story of the Stone,* when government troops raided one of the Jia family homes, they found three sets of cushion covers and arm rest covers in imperial yellow satin, a color reserved for imperial use in the 1759 regulations.[47] The owner, Jia Zheng, was not charged for this offense only because he was related to an imperial concubine, and so might have had the textiles in his home for later contribution to her household.[48]

Any strict correspondence between scholarly achievement, an appropriate government post, and official regalia was also disrupted by the Qing practice of bartering rank and its financial rewards for support of the Manchu regime. As early as 1635, nine years before the Manchus took over China, a high-ranking Manchu official responded to a famine in Manchuria by offering to trade grain for a declaration that the donor was qualified to hold government office.[49] Beginning in the late eighteenth century, the sale of ranks became commonplace. A man could purchase rank with office for himself or his father—or, for a more modest sum, a rank without office. In either case, he had the right to wear the costume and all of the pertinent insignia of the rank purchased. The Qianlong emperor has been praised for his patronage of literature and learning, and his support of the examination system. He has been described as functioning "at the pinnacle of education and the examination system to keep alive the great tradition of China's cultural superiority as the center of civilization from ancient times."[50] It was during the Qianlong emperor's reign, however, that the court established and actually published price lists for purchasing the various ranks.[51]

An early-nineteenth-century portrait of the silk merchant Eshing in the Peabody Essex Museum in Salem, Massachusetts depicts that merchant wearing the outer robe, rank badge, and cap of a scholar-official (Fig. 11). This portrait was among several images of wealthy Canton merchants in official dress that were included in an exhibition on the China trade at the Metropolitan Museum of Art in 1941.[52] A watercolor portrait of Wu Bingjian (1769–1843) in the Victoria and Albert Museum depicts this other wealthy Canton merchant dressed even more luxuriously in a dragon robe and an expensive fur-lined overrobe with insignia badges and long beads, a scholar-official's costume never intended for merchants.[53]

At the same time that wealthy merchants were able to purchase rank, poor scholars who had passed the difficult civil examinations and were legitimately qualified to hold rank might be barred from accepting government positions by their lack of funds. In the late nineteenth century, the young scholar-official Li Ciming had to borrow a set of official robes from his employer in order to take his first government position after passing the civil service examinations. He was too poor to purchase the robes.[54] Others, with neither money nor a financial backer, had to decline positions they had spent their youth and young manhood studying to achieve.[55]

Scholar-officials and merchants were not the only ones purchasing *long pao* in the nineteenth and early twentieth centuries. Western merchants, diplomats, soldiers, missionaries, teachers, and travelers collected official costume along with many other objects of Chinese material culture. A number of Western men serving in official or semi-official positions were granted rank by the Qing government, and regularly wore Chinese official dress.[56] Others purchased this costume for its exotic interest. Liberty and Co. of London, for example, imported dragon robes and advertised them in a Christmas catalogue for the winter of 1895–1896; some of these were used as dressing gowns.[57] Sallie Casey Thayer, whose early-twentieth-century gifts to the University of Kansas formed the basis of the Spencer Museum's Asian textile collection, bought a number of these textiles from Marshall Field's in Chicago. By this time, *long pao* were comparatively easy to come by, and could be purchased ready-made or in second-hand stores in China.[58]

The *long pao* in the Spencer Museum quite likely reflect their owners' financial resources as much as their earned official status. One or another might have belonged to a well-to-do merchant who purchased his rank without studying for an examination and had no intention of taking a government job. Others might have been bought ready-made by a Western collector, or a Chinese for sale to a Western enthusiast. Others might be simply what they seem: the principal garment of a first- through third-rank scholar-official or member of the Chinese nobility, someone who appropriated the five-clawed dragon improperly but in a manner consistent with contemporary usage.

36. *Long pao*

◆

China
Qing dynasty, 19th century
Silk and gold-wrapped thread
Brocade (supplementary weft on plain weave
ground)
54 x 85 in.; 137.2 x 216 cm
Source Unknown, 0000.1030
Literature: *Catalogue of the Oriental Collection*,
66–70.

This dragon robe appears austere in comparison with most other Qing *long pao*, but would have been costly to produce. Except for the white silk eyes of the dragons, the patterning is achieved entirely by brocaded gold-wrapped thread on a dull red ground. Under magnification, the gold leaf is seen to adhere to red paper, which gives a subtle reddish cast to the gold and prevents a discordant note where the gold leaf has worn away. The gold-wrapped threads used to form the pattern run the full width of the cloth, hidden on the reverse beneath unpatterned areas.

Eight main dragons with flaming pearls dominate the garment, with a ninth on the right panel beneath the front overflap. Except for a few bats among the clouds and inconspicuous pearls in the waves at the hem, the primary iconography is divided between Buddhist and Daoist imagery, and *shou* (the Chinese character meaning "long life"). Motifs are balanced and well spaced. A pair of cranes, the mounts of Daoist Immortals, flank the central mountain at the hem and appear again on the sleeve bands. Daoist pavilions rise above the waves further toward the sides. A Buddhist canopy occupies the focal position just below the central dragon. It is flanked by a pair of *shou*. Other *shou* symbols, a pair of fish (Buddhist), a basket (Daoist) with *ruyi* scepter, and a few other motifs drawn from Buddhist and Daoist imagery complete the iconography.

The restrained elegance of this robe is unusual among extant Qing *long pao*, and suggests an owner of discriminating taste. Although many scholars warn that the Buddhist and Daoist motifs used on Qing garments should be thought of primarily as general auspicious symbols, the choice of motifs in this garment appears deliberate.[59] The emphasis on—and careful balance between—Buddhist and Daoist imagery, the unusual exclusion of most Precious Things motifs, and the concern for long life and immortality represented in the carefully depicted pavilions of the Immortals in the waves at the hem and sleeves (and in the repetition of *shou* symbols), suggest a mature man of a serious bent, endowed with the philosophical balance typical of an educated Chinese gentleman.

37. Man's Embroidered *Long pao*

◆

China
Qing dynasty, 19th century
Silk and gold-wrapped thread
Embroidery (satin, seed, couching) on blue
plain weave ground
54 x 88 in.; 137 x 223.5 cm
Source Unknown, 0000.1035
Literature: *Catalogue of the Oriental Collection*,
66–70.
Conserved in 1996 by Sharon Shore, Caring for
Textiles

This man's embroidered dragon robe is densely and intricately patterned with motifs that appear to be layered one over the other. The background is worked with a squared interlocking lattice pattern, inhabited alternately by an abstracted swastika and a lotus flower. Elongated scrolling clouds and auspicious symbols appear to float over the surface of the lattice, giving a strong feeling of three-dimensionality to the patterning. This effect was achieved by careful planning. In fact, no motif is superimposed on any other or on the lattice, but the interruptions of the background fret are worked so carefully that they must be examined very closely to determine that the ground pattern does not actually continue underneath these elements.

The Eight Buddhist Emblems are featured on this robe. They are prominently displayed around the central dragon on the front and back of the robe, worked in intricate knots that contrast with the satin and couching stitches used in the rest of the garment. A large and elaborate canopy occupies the focal position just under the central dragon on both the front and the back. Somewhat smaller versions of the canopy, flaming pearl, umbrella, fish, lotus, endless knot, vase, and conch shell appear in pairs surrounding the dragon, four pairs on the front and four on the back.

The hem pattern is executed in couched gold thread. Although pairs of felicitous symbols, most from the category of Eight Precious Things, surround the central mountains, they are inconspicuous against the waves. Above the meandering diagonal lines representing the deep ocean, giant breakers crash into the central mountains from a sea of rolling billows, four huge spirals of water, and little cloud-like curlicue waves.

This robe, like the other five in the collection, has nine five-clawed dragons. The ninth dragon, on the right underflap, is well articulated to match the dragons on the front, but appears isolated against the unpatterned blue twill ground.

36

37

38. Woman's *Long pao*

✦

China
Qing dynasty, 19th century
Silk and gold- and silver-wrapped thread
Kesi (silk tapestry) and embroidery (satin,
couching) on red ground
57.3 x 87 in.; 145.5 x 221 cm
Gift of Mrs. Ethyl C. Wellman, Topeka, 1968.13
Literature: *Catalogue of the Oriental Collection*,
66–70.

Women also wore a variety of *long pao*–like garments, derived from the dragon robe but with variations in construction—particularly sleeve width—and decoration.[60] With no official duties outside the household, women had more latitude in dress styles than their husbands. Wilson has suggested that Han Chinese women were more likely to wear a skirt under a shortened, comparatively wide-sleeved *long pao*, while Manchu women wore full length *long pao*, some with an extra decorated band on the sleeves.[61] Both Manchu and Han Chinese women wore a long, decorated vest over the *long pao* that replaced the plain overgarment with rank insignia worn by men (Plate 43). These vests might or might not display appropriate rank badges on front and back. Wives of Chinese officials and of Chinese and Manchu nobles were entitled to wear status garments commensurate with their husbands' ranks; unmarried daughters dressed in accordance with their father's rank.

An eighteenth-century portrait in the Victoria and Albert Museum illustrates what Wilson has defined as the Manchu style of women's formal dress. The wife of an official named Lu Ming wears a long dragon robe with a full-length vest decorated with cosmic landscape motifs and dragons. A large detachable collar covers her shoulders. She is wearing two strings of beads, a winter ceremonial hat with mounted ornament (presumably representing her husband's rank), and earrings.[62]

The Han Chinese style of wearing the *long pao* is depicted in a nineteenth-century portrait, also in the Victoria and Albert Museum, that shows an anonymous woman in a different formal assemblage. She wears a fully decorated skirt arranged in receding rectangles under a short, wide-sleeved dragon robe. Over this she has layered a vest with rank badges, and a cloud collar. She wears an elaborate headdress with dangling metallic ornaments and earrings.[63]

This *long pao* is identifiable as a woman's by the long slits at the left and right sides of the garment, and the lack of slits at the front and back. It is slightly longer than any of the male dragon robes in the collection, suggesting both that the owner was tall and that she might have been Manchu. This dragon robe was obviously designed to be the undermost visible layer in the assemblage. Although its owner would have worn either a skirt or a pair of trousers under the robe, they would not have been inconspicuous. There was considerable variation among women's *long pao*; this example, except for the side slits, accords in all particulars of construction and pattern layout with a man's.[64]

Gradated shades of red, purple, yellow, blue, and green form deep diagonal stripes at the lower border. Well-articulated Buddhist motifs intermingle with the waves. All eight are depicted, carefully paired on either side of the central mountain. The assemblage of Precious Things so often seen in this section of a *long pao* is represented only by pearls.

Unlike most other dragon robes in the collection, the body of this garment does not feature a carefully arranged sequence of motifs around the central dragon, and makes little use of Buddhist or Daoist iconography. Rather, the ground is filled with clouds and a few, often repeated, symbols representing wishes for a long and happy life. A small bat carrying peaches occupies the focal point underneath the central dragon. Other sets of bats with peaches (symbolizing happiness and longevity) and bats with swastikas (happiness, blessings, and long life) are scattered over the surface of the garment. The scene is punctuated at intervals by *shou* (the character for long life) woven with gold-wrapped threads.

As in several other garments in the collection, the gold leaf is adhered to red paper. The silver leaf, by contrast, is on plain paper. Both are wrapped around and couched with white silk. Although the ground appears to be a solid red, the warp is actually a very thin white, untwisted reeled silk that recedes visually under the slightly thicker red, polychrome, and metallic foil wefts. Five diagonal strips in each quadrant of the hem and the tips of several clouds in the body of the garment are woven with silk dyed with aniline purple. This highly prized purple pigment was imported to China from Europe beginning in the 1860s. Here it was used with great restraint to create vibrant elements of surprise in an already lively ground. The ninth dragon is depicted on the underflap in a fully described landscape.

39. Child's *Long pao*

◆

China
Qing dynasty, late 18th–early 19th century
Silk, gold- and silver-wrapped thread
Kesi (silk tapestry), embroidery (couching),
and painting
36 x 47 in.; 91.5 x 120 cm
Given in Memory of James H. Walker, Jr.
by his Family, 1993.351

This small boy's dragon robe, woven with meticulous attention to detail, is embedded with his family's blessings.

The meandering diagonals at the hem are woven in gradations of the five auspicious colors, red, blue, yellow, white, and black. Pearls, also depicted in the five colors, float in profusion in the troughs of the waves. Precious Things—rolls of tribute silk, a pair of wish-granting jewels, swastikas, and the popular round and square golden ornaments—appear to be tossed up by the billows.

A lotus occupies the focal point below the central dragon. Pink, white, and red lotus flowers and bats are interspersed among elongated blue and white clouds with polychrome tips. The dragons are lively; the two flanking the central mountain focus intently on the flaming pearls, which have branching flames that make them appear to rotate as they fly through the air.

Details on the robe are executed meticulously. The gold-wrapped thread, on red paper, is very fine. Tiny details on the wings of the bats are first described with white-on-white tapestry weave, and then further delineated with brushed pigment. Each wave is depicted with five or six gradations of color ranging from white to deep blue. Colored and white threads are plied together and then used as tapestry weft to add texture and visual interest to the rolls of tribute silk. A lotus pattern on the tiny toggles appears to be etched into the metal; under magnification, it is apparent that the lines are formed by tiny punch marks.

Later in its history, this robe appears to have been used by a second small child. The robe is soiled and watermarked. Both of these problems could have been caused by an accident or improper storage, but the frayed lining and heavy damage to several areas of the robe, coupled with roughly darned repairs, suggest a second life for this robe in the dress-up chest of a Western home.

RANK BADGES

During most of the Ming dynasty and all of the Qing, civil and military officials wore intricately woven or embroidered rank badges on their robes. Motifs on these badges—birds for civil officials and animals for military officers—indicated the rank of the owner. The practice of wearing rank badges was preceded by a custom of wearing decorative panels on the chest and back of formal robes, a custom that appears to have developed during the Mongol-controlled Yuan dynasty. Chinese woodblock prints from this period, as well as contemporary miniatures from Iran (also controlled by the Mongols), portray Mongol nobles wearing ornamental squares decorated with flowers, birds, and animals.[65]

The use of woven or embroidered insignia on discrete panels worn at the chest and back specifically to indicate rank dates from the late fourteenth century. In 1391, the newly established Ming dynasty promulgated detailed costume regulations. In general, these regulations inaugurated a return to earlier Chinese modes of formal court attire after the "barbarian" practices of the Mongol-ruled Yuan dynasty. The only significant addition to the formal costume of the Song dynasty, which preceded the Yuan, was the introduction of badges to indicate rank.

In the regulations of 1391, nobles and scholar-officials were instructed to wear Song-style loose robes of the Ming dynastic red, with a square plaque at chest and back to indicate the wearer's rank. The regulations specified a particular bird or animal for each of the nine civil and military ranks. These rank badges were generally woven or embroidered as discrete squares to enable their removal and replacement if the official were fortunate enough to be promoted. Portraits from the period show wives of Ming officials wearing rank badges identical to those of their husbands.

According to the costume regulations, the emperor wore a Song-style side-fastening yellow robe, with the addition of four roundels depicting coiled dragons worked in gold. The roundels were woven or embroidered directly on the chest, back, and shoulders of the imperial robe, and on the robes of the emperor's sons. Other male members of the imperial family wore the

39

mythical *qilin*, or unicorn; imperial women wore the phoenix. These figures were sometimes woven into or embroidered directly onto the robe.

During the Ming dynasty, festival costume was also embellished by the addition of discrete badges that could be sewn to a garment for a particular occasion. These patches, often elaborately woven or embroidered, displayed motifs appropriate to particular events, such as a gourd (symbol of abundance) for the New Year's holidays.

In the early Ming, birds or animals appeared in twos and threes on rank badges. By the end of the period, they often appeared alone. In the earliest badges, birds were usually shown in flight, but by the mid-Ming, one of the pair was often perched, with the other descending toward its mate, as in Plate 40. Iconography became more complex in the late Ming, although it remained simpler than that seen on Qing rank badges, with their multitudes of half-hidden auspicious objects. Late Ming badges also sometimes contain a red sun, an imperial symbol that is a standard focal point of most Qing badges. On these late Ming examples, a single bird or beast focuses on the sun, and the direction of energy, as in Qing badges, flows from the eyes of the creature diagonally up to the sun.

The Qing adopted the Ming system of rank badges with only minor changes. Qing costume regulations of 1759, promulgated under the reign of the Qianlong emperor, designated the use of rank badges for civilian and military officials as follows:

	CIVIL OFFICIALS	MILITARY OFFICIALS
First Rank	crane (*xianhe*)	"unicorn" (*qilin*)
Second Rank	golden pheasant (*jin ji*)	lion (*shizi*)
Third Rank	peacock (*kongque*)	leopard (*bao*)
Fourth Rank	wild goose (*yunyan*)	tiger (*hu*)
Fifth Rank	silver pheasant (*baixian*)	bear (*xiongba*)
Sixth Rank	egret (*lisi*)	panther (*biao*)
Seventh Rank	mandarin duck (*xichi*)	"rhinoceros" (*xiniu*)
Eighth Rank	quail (*anchun*)	"rhinoceros" (*xiniu*)
Ninth Rank	paradise flycatcher (*lianque*)	"sea horse" (*haima*)[66]
Unclassified officials	paradise flycatcher (*lianque*)	

Qing rank badges generally include an abbreviated cosmic diagram with an earth-mountain in the lower center, and a multitude of auspicious symbols filling the surrounding space. In the center, the animal or bird looks up at a prominent red sun, symbol of the emperor.

40. Phoenix Rank Badge
◆

China
Ming dynasty, late 15th–early 16th century
Silk and gold-wrapped thread
Kesi (silk tapestry)
13.3 x 14.5 in.; 33.5 x 37 cm
Museum Purchase: R. Charles and Mary Margaret Clevenger Fund, 1999.199

The phoenix was associated with the empress, just as the dragon was a symbol of the emperor. Here, the paired phoenixes identify the owner of this insignia badge as an imperial lady or high-ranking noblewoman. Luxurious materials and costly dyes enhance the fine workmanship of this *kesi* badge and support its identification as an imperial or aristocratic emblem.

One phoenix is perched on a rock over waves, an abbreviated reference to the deep sea/cosmic mountain motif that appears in a more developed form in Qing dynasty costuming. *Lingzhi* mushrooms of immortality grow near the rocks, the only minor symbolic motif on the badge. The perched bird turns its head towards its mate, who hovers above it in a cloud-filled sky. Three large peonies in full bloom, emblems of female beauty, separate the pair and complete the imagery. The badge has been trimmed at top and bottom.

Although one might expect the male phoenix, symbolic of the *yang* or active forces of the universe, to be in flight and the female phoenix, symbolic of the *yin* or passive forces of the universe, to be perched, on this badge (as on several others from the mid-Ming) the opposite is true. Here it is the female (identified by an even number of tail feathers) who is in flight, and the male (with an odd number of tail feathers) who is perched. (The perched male in this example has five tail feathers, while its swooping mate has four.) In a mid-Ming insignia badge with paired phoenixes in the Metropolitan Museum of Art, and a mid-Ming badge with paired mandarin ducks in the Cleveland Museum of Art, the females are also in flight, descending toward their perched mates.[67]

In this mid-Ming badge, the two long-tailed phoenixes focus on each other with intense energy, their curving forms spiraling that energy inward toward the center of the badge.

40

41. Egret Rank Badge (one of a pair)

✦

China
Qing dynasty, 19th century
Silk, ink, gold- and silver-wrapped thread
Kesi (silk tapestry) and painting on blue ground
11.8 x 11.5 in., 30 x 29.3 cm; 11.5 x 12 in., 29.3 x 30.5 cm
The William Bridges Thayer Memorial, 1928.48

42. Golden Pheasant Rank Badge (one of a pair)

✦

China
Qing dynasty, late 19th century
Silk, gold- and silver-wrapped thread
Embroidery (satin, couching) on blue-black satin ground
12.5 x 12.5 in.; 32 x 32 cm (each)
Gift of the Cooper Union through Oberlin College, 1954.347

These two sets of rank badges were designed to be displayed on a civil official's surcoat (*pufu*). The one-piece square was sewn to the back of the coat, and the bifurcated square covered the chest when the coat was closed with loops and toggles (see Fig. 11). Woven or embroidered insignia badges were one of the most conspicuous indicators of rank in the Qing dynasty, and are featured prominently in ancestor portraits and in late-nineteenth- and early-twentieth-century studio photographs (see Fig. 10). Both men and women wore rank badges, a woman's insignia indicating her husband's rank. From the mid-eighteenth century, wives of civil officials began to wear badges with the central figure reversed, so that when husband and wife sat side-by-side in formal attire (as depicted in paired ancestor portraits), the two birds or animals faced each other. As a woman sat to the right of her husband, her bird or animal figure faced to the left. There are earlier precedents for paired confronting figures designed for husbands and wives. A series of late Ming portraits depicted in the Li Family History shows the wives of noblemen wearing the same type of dragon robe as their husbands, but with the two coiling dragons reversed.[68]

The egret (*lisi*) represented in Plate 41 designated a civil official of the sixth rank. The golden pheasant (*jin ji*) depicted in Plate 42 designated a civil official of the second rank.

In the egret badge, the bird rests one foot on the cosmic mountain, spreading its wings for balance and looking up at the sun in the upper left corner. The sun disk appears consistently on civilian squares after the late seventeenth century. In design, it replaces a second bird that, in the late Ming, descended toward its perched mate (see Plate 40). That composition, in turn, developed from an early Ming convention of paired animals or birds (in flight). The sun represented heaven and, most specifically, the emperor, so this composition is a symbolic depiction of the scholar-official, with one foot firmly planted at the center of the cosmos, looking intently up at the emperor. The diagonal lines (*lishui*) below the waves at the base of the egret badge echo those that appear on contemporary dragon robes and represent the deep sea.

The border of the egret badge is a single enclosed row of connected swastikas. The swastika, one way of writing "ten thousand," signifies infinity and therefore conveys wishes for long life. The swastika can be combined with other auspicious symbols to signify a multiplication of blessings. Other auspicious symbols are worked into the key fret design and cloud background of the egret badge, some almost indecipherable within the complex background. Four auspicious emblems in each quadrant of the badge are taken from each of three major categories of auspicious motifs: the Eight Buddhist Emblems, the Emblems of the Eight Daoist Immortals, and the Eight Treasures. There are four Buddhist motifs in the lower left quadrant: a conch shell, an endless knot, a canopy, and a parasol. Motifs in the lower right quadrant, also predominantly Buddhist, include a flaming pearl or wheel of the Law, a vase, a lotus, and an unidentified motif. The motifs in the upper right quadrant are taken primarily from Daoist iconography and from the Eight Treasures: a pair of interlocking square golden ornaments, a pair of interlocking round golden ornaments (these often are represented as coins), a fan, and a flower basket. The upper left quadrant also contains Daoist and Eight Treasures motifs including a swastika combined with a *ruyi* scepter, a gourd, and a sword. The wish-fulfilling *ruyi* scepter becomes more powerful in combination with the swastika, and the assemblage can be read to mean "wishes fulfilled ten thousand times." The number and division of objects, their harmonious balance, and the fact that they represent the three major groupings of auspicious symbols all contribute to the conferral of good luck and blessings from the Buddhist, Daoist, and secular realms. Another layer of auspicious meaning is added by two descending bats that flank the cloud at top center.

The badge also incorporates references to the four seasons. A plum blossom, symbol of winter, appears regularly within the key fret pattern, and other seasonal flowers—the peony, lotus, and chrysanthemum—appear as discrete motifs within the clouds.

Auspicious plants grow on the jutting cliffs at each side of the badge. The tree peony on the left is paired with a peach tree on the right. The name of the peony is a rebus for attaining wealth and honor, and the peach is a symbol of immortality.

The egret badges show signs of wear, and have the remains of stitching threads at the borders. The badges appear to have been used for the purpose for which they were made before being detached from the surcoat and eventually finding their way into a Western collection.

The pheasant badge (Plate 42), by contrast, is in pristine condition. It displays no indication of wear, nor is there evidence that it was ever sewn to anything. The bifurcated square is attached to the full back square by what appears to be the original tacking at top center, and the two sides of the square are tacked together at top and bottom with similar thread.

The bright, almost garish colors date this pair of badges to a period after the introduction of aniline dyes from Europe in the 1870s. At the same time, the traditional iconography probably places them before 1898. In that year the young emperor Guangxu issued a series of edicts intended to modernize government, a short-lived endeavor known as the Hundred Days Reform. Rank badges produced after 1898 often display solely an animal or flying bird on a simple cloud-filled ground, sometimes with the Eight Buddhist Emblems in a circle around it.[69]

The pheasant badge is as packed with forms as the egret badge—in both badges every available space is filled with something—but the iconography is much simpler and easier to decipher. The Eight Buddhist Emblems—fish, vase, wheel of the Law, endless knot, parasol, lotus, conch shell, and canopy—are confidently, clearly, and colorfully depicted against a background of swirling clouds.

The pheasant stands in the traditional pose with wings outstretched and one leg raised, but seems more settled than the egret. Like the egret, the pheasant occupies the center of the badge, but in the pheasant badge the sun disk is low in the frame, so that the pheasant need hardly look up. Rather his red beak almost appears to pierce the identical red of the sun disk placed only slightly above him.

A border of alternating *shou* (long life) and *xi* (happiness) symbols worked with very fine gold- and silver-wrapped thread defines the edge of the badge.

41

42

43. Woman's Embroidered Vest with Rank Badges

✦

China
Qing dynasty, 19th century
Silk, gold- and silver-wrapped thread, and
metal bangles
Embroidery (satin, seed, couching, chain
stitch) on blue satin ground with applied
knotted net, tassels, and bangles
35.3 x 25 in.; 89.5 x 63.5 cm
The William Bridges Thayer Memorial,
0000.1033 (Thayer #2960)

This long embroidered vest was designed as the outermost garment of a woman's formal costume. With the addition of a headdress and long beads, it formed the assemblage that appears most often in Qing dynasty portraits of women.[70] The vest came in two basic formal styles. The *xiabei*, of which this is a good example, fell to mid-calf and had deeply cut, triangular hems embellished with heavy fringe or with knotted netting, tassels, and metal bangles. The *xiabei* generally was worn over a long skirt and wide-sleeved robe that also fell to mid-calf. A cloud collar often embellished the neck and shoulder areas of the vest, and a phoenix coronet of delicate metal filigree and beads completed the assemblage. The *xiabei* is a Han Chinese style; the Manchu-style vest, the *chaogua*, was longer and had straight hems with no embellishment. It generally was worn over a *long pao* with a court hat, a stiffened cape-like collar (*piling*), and beads.[71]

Despite the distinctions between Han- and Manchu-style vests as described above, Zhou Xun and Gao Chunming suggest that the Han-style tasseled vest was used at the Manchu court even by the empress and imperial concubines. While this might have been true for informal occasions, official portraits of empresses consistently depict the straight hemmed style, which appears as late as the early twentieth century in a standing photograph of Wan Rong (1906–1940), Emperor Xuantong's empress.[72]

The tasseled vest is depicted in a nineteenth-century portrait of an anonymous Han woman at the Victoria and Albert Museum.[73] The portrait shows a dignified elderly lady wearing a fringed vest over a long skirt and short robe with voluminous sleeves. Her panelled skirt is densely patterned with cosmic landscape motifs. *Lishui* diagonal lines and part of a central mountain decorate the border of her red dragon-patterned robe, just visible below the fringed vest. The vest itself is also profusely decorated with dragons in a cosmic landscape and a central rank medallion. It is similar to the Spencer vest seen here, except that the triangular cuts in the hem are not as deep, and are embellished simply with a dense fringe. The hem treatment of the vest in a portrait of a woman identified only as a Qing titled lady, however, closely resembles that of the Spencer vest. Its deeply cut triangular hem line is emphasized by a wide, densely patterned dark border and embellished with netting and tassels.[74]

This vest, like other formal vests of both styles, uses the same iconographical repertory as the *long pao*—dragons and auspicious symbols in a cosmic landscape—and displays the family rank badge on the front and back of the garment. The rank marker on this vest appears to be a crane, unless it is a sixth-rank egret woven to look like a first-rank crane. Rank birds were often portrayed in a deliberately ambiguous manner to make a lower-ranking bird look similar to one signifying a higher rank; short, stubby beaks were elongated, and colors often had more to do with design conventions than with any concern for verisimilitude. Even early in the dynasty this practice was so widespread that, in an edict of 1687, officials were warned not to wear rank badges with obscure patterns.[75]

Birds representing various ranks of the civil bureaucracy are arranged in pairs on the left and right edges of the vest, three pairs on the front and three on the back. In descending order these can be identified as cranes (first rank), peacocks (third rank), and silver pheasants (fifth rank) on the front, with golden pheasants (second rank), egrets (sixth rank), and an unidentified pair on the back. One might expect this final pair to represent the fourth-rank wild goose so that all of the top six ranks are included, but the birds look somewhat more like the ninth-rank paradise flycatcher.

Other tasseled vests have similar groupings of insignia birds. A Qing dynasty vest at the University of Oregon displays ten pairs of birds, five on the front and five on the back. They represent the nine civil ranks with one additional and unidentified pair.[76] This vest is almost identical to one illustrated by Zhou and Gao.[77] On both vests, the birds are arranged and described in a similar manner, and other elements of decoration and construction correspond closely. Only the rank badges differ significantly. The vest illustrated by Zhou and Gao was intended for the wife of a first-rank official, depicting a crane. The vest in Oregon displays a seventh-rank mandarin duck. These two vests suggest that there was a basic vest style and iconography appropriate for all women of civil-official rank, and that the badges were simply changed as the head of the household was promoted.

The disposition of rank birds around a rank badge on these women's vests probably is derived from the Ming dynasty "homage to the phoenix" pattern, in which eleven species of birds—including many familiar from later rank badges—encircle a phoenix.[78]

The insignia bird on the front badge of all three of these vests, as well as in the two portraits, looks to the viewer's right. It would face the left-facing insignia bird on the man's badge when husband and wife sat side by side in a formal setting.

43

Daoist Priest's Robe

44. Daoist Priest's Robe (*Jiangyi*)

◆

China
Qing dynasty, 18th or 19th century
Silk and gold-wrapped thread
Kesi (silk tapestry)
55.5 x 67.8 in.; 141 x 172 cm
Gift of Mrs. Elizabeth Ellis, 1946.28
Literature: *Catalogue of the Oriental Collection*, 70.

This *jiangyi*, or Daoist priest's Robe of Descent, was worn as the outermost layer of the costume of the highest-ranking priest during certain Daoist ceremonies. Rectangular in shape with a curved hem at the back, it is completely open at the sides and center front. The neck and front lapels are constructed from a separate piece of material that surrounds and protects the front opening, forming a handsome stand-up collar in back. The garment is voluminous, wide enough to cover the priest's wrists when standing with arms extended. It would have literally enveloped him in the signs and symbols of the Daoist cosmology, and dramatically accentuated his movements in the (often quite active) choreography of Daoist ritual. When the priest descended from the sacred space of the temple to enter the crowd, his robe and the images on it would have carried an aura of sanctity to the laity.[79]

The earliest extant *jiangyi* was excavated from a twelfth-century tomb near Datong in Shanxi Province. The main body of the *jiangyi* is unadorned; its borders are embellished with embroidered images of flying cranes. The tomb also contained a *daopao*, a coat-shaped Daoist priest's garment. Both types of garments continued in use throughout the Qing dynasty and into the modern era.[80]

On the back of the Spencer *jiangyi*, clearly defined Daoist images are set within an implied cosmological structure. The light pink ground, undoubtedly deeper in tone originally, recalls an alternate name for the garment, "Red Robe." The main body of the robe illustrates the heavens. At the center back is a golden pagoda, flanked by two golden dragons and surrounded by clouds. That central image, in turn, is surrounded by golden circles representing the Twenty-eight Lunar Mansions, stars situated along the moon's path of rotation around the earth that were used to track time and trace the movements of the planets. By the Six Dynasties period (420–589), these stars had been deified and incorporated into the Daoist pantheon.[81] Above the central motif to the left is a roundel representing the moon (a rabbit preparing the elixir of immortality), and to the right a roundel representing the sun (a rooster). The sun and moon are separated by three linked gold circles, which represent the abodes of the Three Pure Ones. These deities, the highest in the Daoist pantheon in the mid-Qing, were the Celestial Worthy of Primordial Beginning, the Celestial Worthy of Numinous Treasure, and the Celestial Worthy of the Way and Its Power. Their abodes, the three highest celestial realms identified with the Three Heavens, were those of Jade Purity, Highest Purity, and Great Purity. In simpler terms, these three stars may be called the gods of longevity, emolument, and good fortune.[82]

Five roundels with portraits of Daoist Immortals, each carefully depicted with his identifying attribute, surround the central pagoda in such a way that the collar behind the priest's neck marks the bottom of a sixth roundel, enclosing the priest's head. This was probably intentional, meant to indicate that the Grand Master wearing the robe participated in the realm of the Immortals and interceded there for the benefit of the populace. Containers of flowers and talismanic characters float between and around the roundels of the Immortals. The composition is filled with such elements, but not crowded.

The Eight Trigrams appear in gold tapestry on the side borders of the back of the robe. The trigrams alternate with containers of flowers or flowering plants, each different from the others. The Eight Trigrams are the most ancient imagery on this robe. Although they are now intimately associated with Daoism, they arose independently of it. This set of eight variations of three broken and unbroken lines can be traced back to the *Zhou yi*, or *Changes of the Zhou*, an ancient divination text with origins in the Western Zhou dynasty (ca. 1050–771 BCE). More fully developed in the *Yi jing*, or *Book of Changes*, the Eight Trigrams came to represent a philosophy, and to form the base for a system of divination. The two key trigrams are *kun*, composed of three broken lines and representing the female principle (*yin*), and *qian*, composed of three unbroken lines and representing the male principle (*yang*). Here *kun* is depicted at the top left of the back of the robe, and *qian* at the top right. The six other trigrams represent intermediary

44

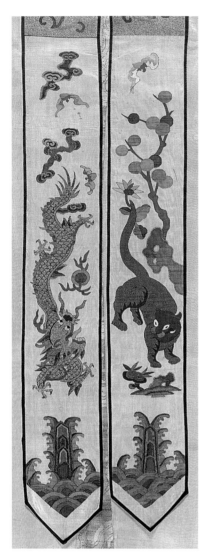

Detail of lapels from Daoist Priest's Robe (Plate 44)

stages in the repeating cycle of *yin* and *yang*. Stephen Little has noted that, because they represent cosmic flux, the Eight Trigrams "were easily adopted by Daoists to help explain cosmological principles of transformation." They were also a vital aid in alchemy, which "entailed manipulating the forces of *yin* and *yang* toward understanding and immortality."[83]

The deep sea is richly illustrated in the compressed lower borders, set off from the main body of the robe by a narrow gold band. A pair of cranes flies over the waves that break over half-hidden images of pagodas. At the center of the border on the back of the robe, in the spot reserved for the earth-mountain seen on the robes of secular officials, two huge branches burst from the water, borne up by breaking waves. The placement suggests Mount Kunlun, the mythical mountain sacred to Daoists. The branches spread symmetrically to either side, with peach blossoms and fully ripe peaches on the same branch. These represent the peaches of immortality that blossomed once every three thousand years on Mount Kunlun, home of the Queen Mother of the West. The peaches had the power to give immortality to those who ate them.

The front of the robe is comparatively plain. Against the simple pink ground, two cranes with *lingzhi* mushrooms in their beaks perch on rocks above waves at the bottom of the robe. Cranes, thought to be extremely long lived, are closely associated with Daoism, and believed to be couriers of the Immortals. One of the earliest recorded stories about a Daoist adept ascending to the heavens on a crane concerns Wang Ziqiao, a prince said to have lived during the Zhou dynasty (ca. 1050–256 BCE). Prince Wang imitated the songs of birds so realistically that a crane flew down and carried him to the land of the Immortals. Wang Ziqiao's story is recorded in a text from the later (or Eastern) Han dynasty (25–220 CE), the *Liexian zhuan* (*Biographies of the Assorted Immortals*), and on a stele near Mount Song in Henan Province dedicated to the cult of Wang Ziqiao in 165 CE.[84] Cranes are the only pictorial images on the twelfth-century *jiangyi* excavated at Datong.

The two front lapels are highly decorated and stand out against the soft pink of the unadorned front panels of the robe. The main image on the proper left lapel is a tiger, and on the proper right, a dragon. Tiger and dragon have been primary symbols of *yin* and *yang*, respectively, at least since the Zhou dynasty. They appear as paired images on a funerary shell sculpture dated to circa 3000 BCE (excavated in 1988).[85] Twenty-five hundred years later, they appear together on a red and black lacquer chest excavated in 1978 from the tomb of Marquis Yi of Zeng, who was buried circa 433 BCE near Suizhou in Hubei Province.[86] The paired images on the Spencer robe thus mark a tradition some five thousand years old. In Daoism, the tiger and dragon symbolize many of the most important concepts, elements, and dualities, including *yin* and *yang*, west and east, fire and metal, and two of the most important alchemical elements, lead and mercury.[87] Both appear above an abbreviated depiction of the earth-mountain and deep sea. The tops of the lapels have a gold ground with alternating flowers and ancient seal-script characters.

There are a considerable number of Daoist *jiangyi* in Western collections. The shape is quite consistent, but the imagery and composition vary greatly from robe to robe. Although the Spencer *jiangyi* incorporates a majority of the most important Daoist motifs, it is possible that the abundance and variety of the images of flower baskets spread over the garment indicate a particular connection to the Daoist Immortal Lan Caihe, patron of gardeners and minstrels, one of whose attributes was the flower basket.[88]

The steps of the hall and the stone foundations were covered with moss as delicate as embroidery.[89]

In China, embroidery was used to embellish garments, accessories, and household furnishings. In the Qing, women's garments, in particular, were ornamented with needlework. Embroidered inset panels, applied borders, edgings, and trim added layers of beauty to skirts and overgarments. Sometimes the whole garment was embroidered, but even then separate applied borders added visual interest.

In the nineteenth century embroidery was produced all over China. Professional workshops, including the imperial workshops, probably produced most of the embroidery that appeared on the market, including the weighty court robes embroidered with formal iconography. These garments required large frames that were strong enough to stretch and tension the heavy satin used as a base for embroidered *chao fu* and *long pao*. Professional workshops were staffed primarily by male artisans, a fact that surprised nineteenth-century Western observers.

Much of the decoration on women's less formal robes, however, as well as embroidered accessories such as women's shoes, fan cases, and men's bags, required only a simple frame and tools—short, round-eyed needles; a rainbow of silk embroidery floss; and scissors. In Qing China, as in eighteenth- and nineteenth-century Europe, the ability to embroider was considered the mark of a virtuous and talented woman. A young woman made many embroidered items for her dowry, including gifts for her new mother-in-law and other members of her husband's family.[90] A bride's character and talent were revealed to her new family in these first gifts.

Because embroidery required few tools and little space, and was practiced by genteel young women, it was considered a suitable occupation for women from aristocratic or scholarly families who had fallen on hard times, and for middle-class women who wanted to supplement their family's income. The work could be done at home (thus affording escape from the opprobrium attached to working in public), and was in high demand.[91]

AN 18TH-CENTURY EMBROIDERER

Chen Yun, from an impoverished eighteenth-century scholar-official family, used her skill at needlework throughout her life to augment family income, pay for goods and services, keep up family prestige, demonstrate her good character to a new mother-in-law, and enhance the beauty of her surroundings. As her future husband Shen Fu reports in his autobiographical *Six Records of a Floating Life*, Yun's father died when she was a young child, and at first, her small family was very poor. Yun, however, became a skilled needleworker as she grew, and before she turned thirteen, she was earning a living for her family and paying for her younger brother's education with her needle. She taught herself to read and write by studying her brother's books.

Yun married her cousin and friend Shen Fu in 1780, when they were both seventeen. They lived at first with Shen's family, but one summer, early in their marriage, the young couple spent a holiday in a small rented cottage away from the heat of Suzhou. They were supplied with fresh fish and vegetables by neighbors who refused pay. Yun thanked them for a summer's generosity with a pair of embroidered shoes. She and her husband dreamed of staying there, living the retired life that was the scholarly ideal.

> We could have servants plant melons and vegetables that would be enough to live on. What with your painting and my embroidery, it would give us enough to have a little to drink while we wrote poetry. We could live quite happily wearing cotton clothes and eating nothing but vegetables and rice. We would never have to leave here.[92]

Shen Fu, however, came from a scholar-official family very conscious of its heritage and civic duty. Scolding his son at one point, Shen's father admonished, "We are a family of robes and caps."[93] Despite his father's rebuke, Shen's career was hardly illustrious. He was often out of work and several of his business ventures failed. Throughout the years, Yun's embroidery brought in much-needed cash, enabling them to survive and to lead an enjoyable, if modest, existence. Yun also made and embroidered her husband's business and informal clothing, his "caps, collars and socks."[94]

In 1792, Shen Fu and Yun lived at a friend's villa for a time. Yun's embroidery brought in a bit of money, and her frugal but elegant housekeeping, as well as the couple's hospitality, made their house a meeting place for literary gatherings. A servant couple made clothes, and Shen himself kept the house clean. He remembered those days with nostalgia.[95] During this period, a relative invited him to go on a trading trip to Canton; among the items he took to trade were specialty foods and Yun's embroidery.[96]

Even when she was critically ill, Yun rallied to produce a major commission, an embroidery of the *Heart Sūtra* that she viewed at once as an offering and also as a significant source of income for her young family.[97]

Shen Fu's autobiography reveals the economic and social importance of embroidery for one family. Shen was a minor official, often out of work, and the family had few resources. Although it would have been a disgrace to Shen and his family for his wife to have earned money in almost any other way, Yun's accomplished embroidery was not only an acceptable means of income but brought honor to herself and to her household. Through it, Yun was able to contribute significantly to her family's economic well-being, to fulfill her social obligations by giving valued gifts to her in-laws and to others who helped the family, and to beautify her household. Many an aspiring scholar who passed the exams could not accept an official post due to lack of funds for the required costume. Yun's ability to provide her husband with suitable official garments enabled him to accept posts that he would not have been able to assume otherwise.

EMBROIDERIES IN THE SPENCER COLLECTION

In addition to complete garments, a man's *long pao*, and women's vests, coats, and skirts, the Spencer collection includes a variety of separate embroidered panels, such as sleeve bands and borders for women's garments, borders and edgings for formal robes, cushion covers, skirt panels, narrative and figural hangings, and some scraps of fresh embroidery on old fabric, the function of which is not immediately apparent. Some were made in professional studios, while others are more likely to have been embroidered within a household for personal use, as gifts, or for sale.

On many of the women's clothing items in the Spencer collection, there is no apparent relationship between the specific themes depicted on embroidered panels, borders, and edgings and the body of the garment. Major themes include birds, butterflies, and flowers; women in garden settings; women with young boys at play; and fragments of formal iconography. On the Spencer garments, embroidered panels applied to women's clothing seem to have been chosen from a ready-made supply, rather than produced for a specific garment. Embroidered panels were popular gifts, appropriate for many occasions, and could be purchased. Well-to-do families doubtless had a store to choose from when assembling a garment.

EMBROIDERED BORDERS

45. Embroidered Borders for a Garment

◆

China
Qing dynasty, 19th century
Silk and gold-wrapped thread
Embroidery (couching)
105 x 31 in.; 267.8 x 78.8 cm (backing cloth);
5.5 in.; 14 cm (approx. width of panels, varied lengths)
Gift of the Cooper Union through Oberlin College, 1954.351

Borders patterned entirely with couched gold on black or deep blue-black satin are seen most frequently as edgings on *chao fu* (see Plate 35), but appear on some other formal garments as well. Plate 45 closely resembles the borders on Plate 54, which were chosen, perhaps, to give dignity to a lively, but otherwise modest, woman's rental or theatrical wedding skirt. These borders, still not cut from the ground cloth, are composed entirely of an all-over fret pattern with interlocking swastikas in the interstices, faultlessly rendered in couched gold. Plate 45 would have required a comparatively large frame, possibly with rollers, to accommodate almost three yards of material. Its size and precision of execution suggest production in a professional workshop.

46. Embroidered Sleeve Borders (pair)

✦

China
Qing dynasty, 19th century
Silk
Embroidery (satin) on satin ground
39.5 x 3.3 in.; 100.5 x 8.3 cm (each)
Source Unknown, 0000.1074 and 0000.1088

On each of the sleeve borders pictured on the left a male peacock, perched on a rock under a tree, poses in full display for an interested female. The birds are depicted in a lush garden setting with butterflies, flowers, grasses, and prominent oversized peonies. The iridescent hues of the peacock and subtle shading of the peonies are rendered primarily in satin stitch with glossy silk floss. Light reflecting from the floss reveals even the slightest nuances of color shading, and enhances the brilliant sheen of the peacock feathers. In the Qing, these feathers were used as rank insignia and as a reward for meritorious service. Peacocks symbolized dignity and beauty, and were thought to ward off evil. They were familiar denizens of elegant gardens. The peony symbolizes wealth and distinction, feminine beauty, and love and affection. This microcosm of a Qing garden uses familiar and beloved flora and fauna to evoke ideas of beauty, dignity, distinction, prosperity, and conjugal bliss.

47. Embroidered Sleeve Borders (pair)

✦

China
Qing dynasty, 19th century
Silk
Embroidery (satin) on off-white patterned ground (supplementary weft floats on plain weave ground)
38 x 3.5 in.; 96.5 x 9 cm (each)
Source Unknown, 0000.1078 and 0000.1081

On the sleeve bands pictured in the center, the garden has been abstracted and compressed into an intricate assemblage of flora and fauna. Peonies and butterflies predominate among the motifs, and the whole is worked in subtle shades of indigo, ranging from almost white to deep blue. Green is used for the leaves, and shades of red and yellow highlight the butterflies flitting among a dense mass of flowering plants.

48. Embroidered Borders (pair)

✦

China
Qing dynasty, late 19th century
Silk
Embroidery (satin) on damask ground
43 x 3.5 in.; 110 x 9 cm (each)
Source Unknown, 0000.1077 and 0000.1080

The pair of borders on the right are similar to Plate 47 and also compresses butterflies, peonies, and other flora and fauna into a dense abstraction of a garden. In this pair, however, the embroidery is even denser, almost totally obscuring the ground fabric. The motifs appear thick and layered, as the butterflies flit between and dip behind flowers. The use of aniline purple adds to the stylistic evidence for a late-nineteenth-century date for these borders. The embroidery has a fresher appearance than the ground fabric, suggesting that an old piece of fine damask was recycled for this purpose.

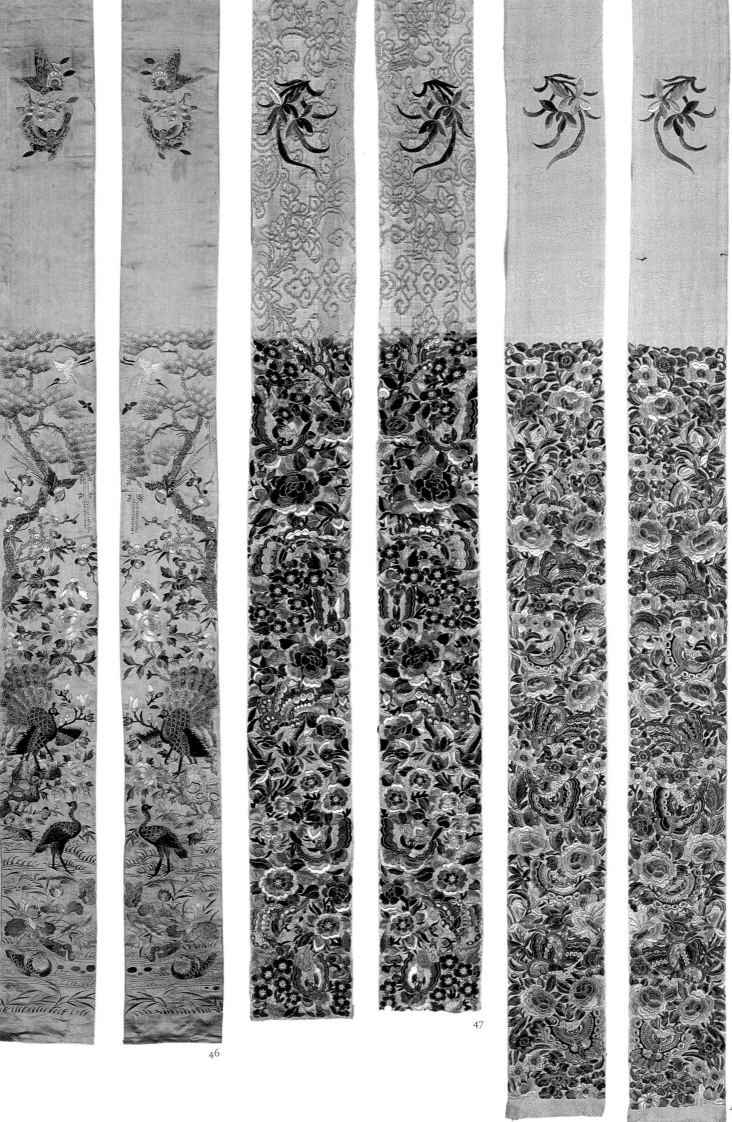

46

47

48

The wrapped skirt was an ancient and enduring part of Chinese women's costume. In some periods it was very long, tied under the armpits just below or above the bust. In the Qing dynasty, Han Chinese women wore a pair of pleated and embroidered apron-shaped skirts that overlapped and wrapped around the lower body. The skirts were fastened with a wide, undecorated waistband that extended beyond the skirt's width to form ties. Often made of a different and less expensive material, the waistband was hidden by a vest or by one of several styles of overgarments.

Wrapped skirts have been found in several Han dynasty tombs.[98] In the mid-eighth century, the widow of the Japanese Emperor Shōmu donated a lovely Chinese-style skirt to the temple Tōdaiji in Nara. The skirt, now kept in the south section of the Shōsōin Repository at that temple, is made of alternating strips of purple damask, red damask with wax-resist patterns, and stripes banded with various shades of green.[99]

Two wrapped skirts found in the Song dynasty tomb of Huang Shen in Fuzhou, Fijian Province, relate both to earlier prototypes and to later Qing skirts. The first is made of plain silk, with a wide reinforcing layer at the center, and narrow patterned borders on one side, the hem, and one side of the central panel. The disposition of the patterned borders suggests that the skirt was intended to be one of a pair. The second skirt is made of thin silk printed with an all-over pattern of large dots. The same material was used for the wide waistband, and for a narrow border that defines the edges of the skirt. The skirt is densely pleated except for two sections at either edge.[100]

A Ming dynasty skirt, now in the Zhenjiang Museum in Jiangsu Province, is made of red silk with an all-over pattern of small flowers broken by a wide band of patterning that would have fallen just below the knee. The skirt has two sections of deep, widely spaced tucks, probably designed to fall over the hips.[101]

Late Qing skirts, like many other garments, were heavier than their earlier prototypes. Weighted by embroidered panels and decorative borders, even gauze skirts had substantial heft. Skirts generally were worn in identical pairs. Each had a flat, decorated panel, usually at one edge of the skirt. The skirts were wrapped and overlapped so that a decorated panel hung at center front and back, flanked on both sides by pleated panels. In Plate 49, the pleating is narrow, deep, and even, hanging in meticulously regular, sharp folds from waist to hem. The pleated areas of the skirt (other than the hem) are undecorated except for the subtle damask pattern in the ground silk. In Plate 50, groups of narrow pleats appear as receding layers, set off by embroidered bands at the edge of each group. This idea is carried further in Plate 51, where the pleats are wide, and each is set off by an applied border.

There are three main subjects of decoration in the center panels of the six Spencer skirts illustrated here. Two skirts exhibit themes of beautiful women, gardens, and playful boys (the "hundred sons" motif) (Plates 49 and 50); two show flowers and butterflies (Plates 51 and 53); and two display references to Qing formal iconography (Plates 52 and 54).

These nineteenth-century Qing skirts are constructed of multiple discrete parts. A fine, often precisely pleated silk fabric forms the ground, generally damask for winter and gauze for summer. Multiple embroidered strips and panels, interspersed with ribbon or tiny edgings, are meticulously stitched to the ground, and to each other, to form layers of decoration. The placement of each border or edging affects not only the way the skirt looks, but also the way it moves. The trim stitched at regular intervals to the edge of each narrow pleat in Plate 51, for example, would cause the pleats to move independently, as opposed to the "ripple effect" caused by the pleats in skirts such as Plate 49.

49. Woman's Pleated Wedding Skirt

◆

China
Qing dynasty, 19th century
Silk, gold-wrapped thread, and applied ribbons
with cotton waistband
Embroidery (satin, couching) and appliqué on
white satin panels and borders of red pleated
skirt
L. 36.8 in.; 93.5 cm
The William Bridges Thayer Memorial,
0000.1032a,b (Thayer #2960)

49

50. Woman's Pleated Wedding Skirt

*

China
Qing dynasty, 19th century
Silk, gold-wrapped thread, and applied ribbons
with cotton waistband
Embroidery (satin, couching) and applique on
damask ground
H. 37 in.; 94 cm
Source Unknown, 0000.1047

49. Woman's Pleated Wedding Skirt

✦

China

Qing dynasty, 19th century

Silk, gold-wrapped thread, and applied ribbons
with cotton waistband

Embroidery (satin, couching) and appliqué on
white satin panels and borders of red pleated
skirt

L. 36.8 in.; 93.5 cm

The William Bridges Thayer Memorial,
0000.1032a,b (Thayer #2960)

49

50. Woman's Pleated Wedding Skirt

✱

China
Qing dynasty, 19th century
Silk, gold-wrapped thread, and applied ribbons
with cotton waistband
Embroidery (satin, couching) and applique on
damask ground
H. 37 in.; 94 cm
Source Unknown, 0000.1047

50

51. Woman's Pleated Skirt

✦

China
Qing dynasty, 19th century
Silk and applied ribbons with cotton waistband
Embroidery (satin, seed) on yellow damask
ground
L. 40 in.; 101 cm
The William Bridges Thayer Memorial,
0000.1050 (Thayer #29597)

51

148

52. Woman's Pleated Skirt

✦

China
Qing dynasty, 19th century
Silk, gold-wrapped thread, applied ribbons, and
sequins with cotton waistband
Embroidery (satin, couching) on red damask
ground
L. 38.8 in.; 98.5 cm
Gift of Mrs. Jacob Grant Strickler, 1946.31a,b

52

53. Woman's Skirt Panel
(detail)

◆

China
Qing dynasty, 19th century
Silk, gold-wrapped thread, and ribbons
Embroidery (satin, couching, seed) on yellow
satin ground
(waistbands missing)
30 x 44 in.; 76 x 112 cm
Gift of the Cooper Union through Oberlin
College, 1954.350a

WOMEN'S COATS AND ROBES

55. Woman's Embroidered Coat

◆

China
Qing dynasty, 19th century
Silk, gold-wrapped thread, and ribbons
Embroidery (satin, couching, seed, appliqué)
on red satin ground
45.5 x 48 in.; 115.8 x 122 cm
Gift of Dr. and Mrs. Alfred E. Farah, 1978.19
Literature: *The Register* 5, no. 6: 79 (ill.).

56. Woman's *Kesi* Robe

◆

China
Qing dynasty, 19th century
Silk and gold-wrapped thread
Kesi (silk tapestry), embroidery (couching,
seed), and painting
57 x 55 in.; 145 x 139.7 cm
The William Bridges Thayer Memorial,
0000.1044 (Thayer #2956)
Label: "Importer R. Bensanoth, Chicago"

The motifs on this Manchu-style woman's coat are organized symmetrically. A large peony dominates the central medallion; two flower baskets filled with peonies at lower right and left point diagonally toward the medallion; and other scattered blossoms appear in reflected symmetry on either side of a vertical axis bisecting the medallion. Stylized characters for *shuangxi*, or "double happiness," are couched in gold thread at regular intervals on the black satin border. The characters are separated by sprays of flowering plants. Peonies, auspicious symbols, and the "double happiness" motif embellish the sleeve bands. As on some of the formal court garments in the Spencer collection, seed stitch is used to distinguish the most important motifs; here, the peonies are worked in seed stitch, both on the body of the garment and on the separate sleeve bands. Background flowers and other motifs are embroidered in satin stitch and the palette is limited to shades of blue.

The formal symmetry, careful workmanship, and limited palette give this garment a stately appearance, quite different from the graceful elegance of many of the other women's garments in the collection.

Pairs of butterflies flit among paired blossoms on the brilliant red ground of this young woman's robe, evoking thoughts of springtime, young love, and conjugal happiness. The butterflies are rendered with the same attention to detail as seen in a scientific manual, and yet they appear to twist and turn with a spontaneity that belies the difficulty of the *kesi* (tapestry weave) technique. This was probably a wedding garment.

55

56

57. Woman's Bamboo-Patterned Robe

✦

China
Qing dynasty, late 19th or early 20th century
Silk, gold-wrapped thread, and applied ribbon
Embroidery (couching) on blue satin ground
with lavender borders
51.8 x 54.5 in.; 131.5 x 139 cm
Gift of Dr. and Mrs. Robert P. Woods, 1982.122

Tall bamboo stalks, rendered in couched gold on a deep blue ground, rise from ankle to shoulder, dominating the central field as if the garment were a painter's canvas. Related motifs of bamboo and *shou* (long life) symbols fill the borders and sleeve bands, rendered in gold on strong pink and white satin. A narrow gold ribbon defines the edge of the central field.

Unlike most women's informal garments in the collection, every detail of this unusual robe was conceived from the start to work together into a cohesive whole. Every border, band, and piece of trim, with the possible exception of the woven ribbon, had to be embroidered specifically for this garment. The bamboo stalks depicted in the central field and on the borders are closely related not only by theme, but by style. Details such as the veins of the bamboo leaves and joints on the stalks are rendered by negative spaces in the couching, which let the background color show through.

The idea of using the garment as a canvas had been thoroughly explored in Japan during the Edo period (1615–1868), and there are many *kosode* (forerunner of the modern kimono) patterned with a single motif sweeping from hem to shoulder. A late-seventeenth- or early-eighteenth-century *kosode* from the Nomura collection, now in the National Museum of Japanese History, features a flowering plum curving from left shoulder to right waist to left hem, a graceful form typical of the period. The painter Gion Nankai (1677–1751) is credited with painting a bamboo *kosode* now in the Metropolitan Museum of Art.

The depiction of the bamboo grove on this garment appears awkward and tentative when compared with the graceful plum or bold bamboo on these Japanese *kosode*, but it seems clear that the artist was looking at and responding to Japanese textile design when he or she designed this robe. Although this type of design remained rare for Chinese garments, a later man's jacquard-woven gown with a design of crane and pine tree shows a more graceful and confident use of space.[103]

After the Sino-Japanese war of 1894–1895, the Japanese began to exercise great influence in China. Businessmen settled in, Japanese sinologists traveled to China, and Japanese officials and scholars contributed to the Chinese discourse on governmental reform. Chinese students traveled in the other direction to study in Japan.[104] By the turn of the century, there was such a significant Japanese presence in China that Japanese travelers in that country could stay in Japanese inns and eat in Japanese restaurants, if they so desired.[105]

This robe probably was made between 1898 and 1914, a period when Japanese influence was at an early peak.[106]

57

Velvets, Furs, and Animal Skins

FURS AND
ANIMAL SKINS

European traders, travelers, and diplomats, not to mention Chinese writers, all attest to the widespread use of furs and animal skins in Ming and Qing China. Western collections, however, do not reflect the extent to which animal furs were used in Chinese costume. Perhaps because furs and skins are scarce in Western collections, they have not been studied by twentieth-century Western scholars, and their major role in Chinese costume has been largely ignored. In both the Ming and Qing dynasties, people throughout China in all social classes used furs and animal skins—from sable to rat—in their dress.

In the early sixteenth century, the Portuguese chronicler Damião de Góis included fur goods in a short list of Chinese textile products.[107] In 1569, when Father Luis Frois, S.J., met the Japanese warlord Oda Nobunaga, Frois was amazed at the variety and quantity of Nobunaga's treasures, which included feathered velvet caps from Portugal and Chinese furred robes.[108] The costume regulations of 1759 specify particular types of fur to be used for the facings and trim of winter court robes. The most prestigious court robe was faced (for men) or edged (for women) in sable; a more common type was trimmed in otter fur.[109] An English consul in Shanghai in 1872 published a description of a local mandarin's procession from his *yamen*, or office/residence. He noted that official sedan chairs were covered with broadcloth dyed the appropriate rank color, and "handsomely lined and fitted within, sometimes with expensive furs."[110]

Sir John Francis Davis, an English diplomat whose long career in China included service as Queen Victoria's plenipotentiary in China and governor of Hong Kong, wrote one of the first comprehensive descriptions of China in English. In his "A general description of that empire and its inhabitants, etc.," published in the mid-nineteenth century, Davis remarked on the wide variety of furs and animal skins that kept the populace warm in winter. These ranged from the skins of common rodents to exotic furs.

> The skins of all animals are converted into apparel for the winter. The lower orders use those of sheep, cats, dogs, goats, and squirrels. Even rat and mouse skins are sewn together for garments. The expensive fur dresses of the higher orders descend from father to son, and form sometimes no inconsiderable portion of the family inheritance.[111]

Davis reported that, in winter, men typically wore an outer jacket made of fur or lined with animal skins.

> Over a longer dress of silk or crape, which reaches to the ankles, they wear a large-sleeved spencer [short jacket], called *ma-kwa* (or riding coat), which does not descend below the hips. This is often entirely of fur, but sometimes of silk or broadcloth lined with skins.[112]

Official winter hats were made either of fur or black velvet.

One cold winter day, Davis attended an entertainment in Canton that took place in a large, unheated hall. The gracious host, he wrote, produced "handsome wide-sleeved spencers, all of the most costly furs" for his shivering European guests.[113]

Chinese writers have also left descriptions of furs and fur garments. In his autobiographical *Six Records of a Floating Life*, Shen Fu uses his family's lack of furs to describe their destitution in one particularly difficult period of their lives.

> I was weary and beset by hardships, and we often had no money. In the deepest winter I had no furs, but there was nothing to do but to be strong and bear the cold. Ching-chun [his daughter], too, shivered in an unlined dress, though she bravely denied being cold.[114]

In his eighteenth-century novel *The Story of the Stone*, Cao Xueqin included a detailed inventory of the personal possessions of Jia Zheng, head of the Jia family. The inventory includes a vast store of furs and animal skins:

18 black fox-furs

56 sables

44 russet fox-furs

44 white fox-furs

12 Mongolian lynx-skins

25 partly tailored Yunnan fox-skins

26 sea-otter skins

3 seal-skins

6 tiger-skins

3 brown-and-black striped fox-furs

28 otter-skins

40 red astrakhan-skins

63 black astrakhan-skins

20 partly tailored musquash-skins

24 squares of Mongolian suslik two hundred

63 grey squirrel-skins[115]

This portion of the inventory is interesting not only because of the astonishing number of furs and animal skins grouped with the textiles, but also because Jia Zheng's bolts of velvet are listed within the fur grouping rather than with other silks. Four rolls of "swansdown" velvet appear between the Mongolian suslik and the squirrel-skins, near the end of the grouping. Two categories of finished garments are listed together in the inventory. The first is "Sundry fur garments, one hundred and thirty-two." The second is "Various garments, padded, lined, unlined, gauze and silk—three hundred and forty." With the exception of eight sets of court costume, more than one-third of Jia's finished garments were made of fur.[116]

These passages, excerpted from the writings of late Ming and Qing European and Chinese authors, make it very clear that furs and animal skins—including whole skins pieced together—formed a major part of the winter costume of the Chinese populace. They were used in the south as well as in the north, by Chinese as well as by Manchu, by the emperor and by peasants. Recognition of the importance of furs and animal hides in China is necessary to an understanding of the development and range of Chinese costume.

VELVETS

The Chinese word for velvet, *rong*, refers to a fabric napped on either one or both sides. Although not true velvet in the technical sense, the earliest fabrics classified by Chinese scholars as *rong* date from the Han dynasty. Most Qing dynasty *rong*, however, were based on European models and manufactured using European technology. For simple unpatterned velvet, the pile was created by running an extra set (or sets) of warp threads over a series of fine metal rods inserted parallel to the weft threads every few picks. The rods were grooved on top to guide the sharp knife used to cut the loops. The weaver wove a small section of velvet, ran the knife along the grooves to cut the loops, removed the rods, and then reused them in the next section of weaving. Velvet looms needed two warp beams because the pile warp could be as much as fifteen times as long as the ground warp.[117]

Some Chinese velvets were woven with the rods left in. When these velvets were removed from the loom, they were stretched flat on a hard surface and the design was drawn on them with chalk. In a process known as "carving the pattern," the pile was then cut according to the chalk design, creating a pattern of cut velvet against uncut pile. Close examination of velvets produced in this manner generally reveals traces of the white marking chalk. No chalk traces have been found on any of the Spencer textiles, suggesting that they were woven in the customary European method of cutting the pile and removing the rods as the weaver progressed.

CHINESE PROTO-VELVETS IN THE HAN DYNASTY (206 BCE–220 CE)

Very fine silk pile fabrics with uncut loops have been excavated from Han dynasty tombs. One, from the first excavation at Mawangdui, has an astonishing ten thousand silk warps in a fifty-centimeter width. The textile historian Cheng Weiji has analyzed its intricate structure, and has proven that the draw loom was in use in the Han dynasty. In addition to the pile warp, which would have required its own warp beam, this "pile loop brocade" had two pattern warps and a ground warp. More than two thousand warp threads, both sets of pattern warps, and the pile warp had to be handled separately with string patterning heddles.

Despite the sophistication of the structure, the pile was created in a very cumbersome manner by inserting a heavy weft thread every few picks, and later picking these threads out from the woven cloth to leave fine, dense loops. The insertion of these threads would have been easy, but pulling or picking them out from a densely woven web would have proved cumbersome and time consuming. Perhaps it was this difficulty that discouraged Chinese weavers from producing pile silks after the Han dynasty.[118] The structure of this fabric also did not bind the pile tightly enough for the loops to have been cut.[119] Thus it would not have been possible to create cut pile, or to explore the patterning possibilities of "fast-pile velvet."[120] In this technique, as in all of the velvets in the Spencer collection, the pile warp is interwoven with the ground fabric in between loops, anchoring the pile to the fabric structure. This structural solidity makes it possible to cut the velvet loops without their falling out, and thus to juxtapose cut and uncut sections against one another to create free-form patterns in the cloth. For whatever reason, this Han dynasty forerunner of velvet was not developed further in China, and pile fabrics virtually disappeared from the Chinese weaver's repertory for almost a millennium.

LIMITED REEMERGENCE OF SILK PILE WEAVING IN THE SOUTHERN SONG (1127–1279)

Textile names from the Southern Song and Yuan dynasties suggest a limited reemergence of silk pile weaving beginning in the twelfth century. The name of one Southern Song textile suggests that it was brocade on the surface and pile on the reverse. The pile probably was woven and valued for its warmth and insulating properties, and would have been worn inside the garment, just like fur. Four centuries later, Emperor Shenzong (r. as the Wanli emperor 1573–1620) was buried in an unpatterned brown silk robe napped on both surfaces, with the inner pile hidden beneath a silk lining.[121]

Cheng Weiji proposes that the warmth and insulating properties of these Chinese velvets or proto-velvets were not accidental. He suggests that, in fact, the first dense silk pile textiles were woven in imitation of animal furs.[122] Cheng's view is supported not only by these early textiles—the inner pile of which would have served the function of a fur-lined garment—but by a continuing correspondence between velvet and fine fur, a correspondence that is seen, for example, in the aforementioned Jia family inventory.

The first known examples of patterned velvet in China date from the latter part of the Ming dynasty and probably were made using (or adapting) European technology. The Gushan collection at Fuzhou, for example, contains a deep red, patterned velvet dating from the Wanli reign period, with the designs formed by juxtaposing cut and uncut pile.[123]

CHINESE INTEREST IN EUROPEAN VELVET IN THE SIXTEENTH CENTURY

After Italian weavers developed the technology to produce fine silk patterned velvets in the fourteenth century, velvet quickly became a valuable trade item. Sixteenth-century Portuguese traders included the fabric in their China trade, noting the high quality and variety of Chinese silks and the absence of fine wools (camlets) and velvets there. The writings of these traders reveal Chinese interest in European velvet throughout the sixteenth century.[124]

In a lively account of his voyage to China, the Portuguese adventurer Fernão Mendes Pinto mentions a meeting with the Mandarin of "Nonday," a meeting that probably occurred in 1541.

The Mandarin was mounted on a good horse, with certain cuirasses of red velvet with gilt studs of ancient date, which we afterwards learned belonged to one Tomé Pires whom the king Dom Manoel sent as ambassador to China.[125]

Tomé Pires had headed the first Portuguese embassy to China in 1517, an overture that was not well received by Ming authorities. Some of the company were executed; others, including Pires, died in captivity.[126] Vasco Calvo, a member of the group, wrote hopefully from prison in Canton with recommendations for suitable gifts, should another embassy be attempted. The letter suggests large mirrors, coral, sandalwood, camlets, and velvets.[127]

In 1582, when a new viceroy in Kwangtung and Kwangsi threatened to rescind Portuguese trading privileges and evict them from Macao, he was mollified by gifts of European manufactured goods, including velvets, camlets, mirrors, and crystal.[128] A sixteen-year-old Dutchman, John Huyghen van Linschoten, traveled with a Portuguese East India fleet to Goa in 1583. Six years later he returned to Holland and published a compilation of his observations, along with those of other traders he had encountered. Unlike a number of other sixteenth-century chronicles based as much on fantasy as on fact, van Linschoten's *Navigatio ac itinerarium* proved to be an invaluable source of information for Dutch and English traders. Van Linschoten states that

Cloth made of Wool nor Velvet they cannot make in all China . . . The marchandises that the Portingals carrie to China, whereof they make most profite is Ryals of eight . . . some Wines both Portingal and Indian Wine, and some Oyle of Olives . . . Velvet, Cloth of Scarlet . . . Looking glasses, Ivorie bones, and all kinde of christall and Glasse, are well solde there.[129]

CHINESE PRODUCTION AND EXPORTATION OF VELVET IN THE SEVENTEENTH CENTURY

Chinese weavers appear to have learned European velvet techniques by the end of the sixteenth century. In 1592, Father Matteo Ricci, a Jesuit priest living in Shaochou (Guangdong Province), wrote to his father that "in the last few years they have been making velvet in this place and are now doing it very well."[130]

By the beginning of the seventeenth century, China was exporting plain velvet and velvet patterned with gold embroidery to the Philippines and to Japan. Antonio da Morga, in a report published in 1609, lists plain velvet and velvet embroidered with gold among the articles brought by Chinese ships for sale in Manila.[131] John Saris, a visitor to Japan in 1613, noted quantities of velvets and velvet hangings embroidered with gold brought by Chinese ships to Japan.[132]

At the same time as Chinese ships carried velvets to Manila and Japan, Emperor Shenzong, as noted above, was buried in an unpatterned robe napped on both surfaces. In the early seventeenth century, thus, the Chinese valued velvet sufficiently to bury an emperor in a plain double-faced velvet robe, and wove sufficient quantities of plain velvet to export. Although there is some evidence of a very small amount of cut-velvet patterning in the seventeenth century, it was not until the late eighteenth or nineteenth century that Chinese weavers produced significant quantities of patterned velvet. The large number of sophisticated cut-velvet garments in museum collections today, as well as paintings and photographs depicting Chinese men and women wearing patterned velvet over-garments, attest to the skill of Chinese velvet weavers and the popularity of cut-velvet garments in late Qing dynasty China. In 1878 Natalis Rondot, a representative of the Chamber of Commerce in Lyon, requested information about silk production in China from the Inspector General of Customs in Peking. In 1881, a full report arrived from China with a collection of samples (of which one set was placed in the Musée Historique des Tissus in Lyon). According to this report, velvet was woven in Nanjing, Hangzhou, Suzhou, Zhangzhou (which also produced velvet for the court), and Ningbo.[133]

58. Woman's Velvet Jacket

◆

China
Qing dynasty, 19th century
Silk
Cut velvet on satin ground
36.8 x 71 in.; 93 x 180 cm
The William Bridges Thayer Memorial,
0000.1034 (Thayer #2947, 1150)

The velvet seen here was planned and woven specifically for this piece. On a loom width of satin ground, velvet loops were pulled to conform to the size and shape of each piece that would be cut out of the fabric and sewn to form the garment. The loops were selectively cut by hand within this framework as the weaver progressed, in order to form the pattern. When the tailor or seamstress received the length of finished cloth, he or she would simply have cut around the outside edges of the garment shapes, leaving only enough of the background satin to stitch the pieces together.

This full jacket combines construction features that have their origins in both Manchu and Han dress styles. The wide, full sleeves derive from a Han-style model, whereas the shaped lapel and evidence of loop and toggle closures suggest Manchu prototypes.[134] Women, excluded from official responsibilities in the public domain, exercised more freedom of dress than did men. As noted previously, in the early years of the Qing dynasty, Han and Manchu women wore their hair very differently, but over time came to adopt features of each other's coiffure, creating a variety of new hairstyles.[135] The same interaction occurred with garment styles, underscoring the blurring of ethnic distinctions in dress conventions after nearly three hundred years of Manchu-Han interaction.

The motifs are purely Han Chinese. Several different species of butterflies, emblem of conjugal happiness, fill the body of the robe. Bats and the endless knot and small plant motifs fill an inner border. A tiny row of conventionalized upright flowers with tall, straight leaves marches around the outer edges of the inner border.

A wide outer border is filled with an abbreviated description of blossoming plants and trees. In each motif, the most relevant part of the plant is represented with only enough surrounding detail to enable clear identification. Thus plum blossoms are shown on a twig with only one or two leaves, and bamboo is represented by its leaves alone. Other motifs include chrysanthemums and an orchid. The assemblage is a conventionalized representation of the four seasons, although the plants depicted are not all typical of this grouping.

The designs on this robe are simple but subtle. The velvet appears to have been cut freehand, using the grooves on the velvet rods to guide the cutting knife, but not following a detailed pattern. Not only are several species of butterflies represented, but details vary slightly within the depiction of each species. The same subtle changes are found in the rendering of other motifs throughout the garment.

58

59. Velvet Vest

◆

China
Qing dynasty, late 19th or early 20th century
Silk
Cut velvet
32 x 30 in.; 81 x 76 cm
Source Unknown, 0000.1042

This black vest is constructed in classic Manchu style, with a shaped lapel and loop and toggle closures. A Western-style pocket on the right underpanel (hidden beneath the front right panel) shows knowledge and judicious use of a prominent feature of Western dress. The "Three Abundances" (peach, pomegranate, and "Buddha's hand" citrus fruit) fill the central front and back panels, and auspicious symbols, chosen primarily from the Daoist repertory, fill the borders. The wide sleeve openings suggest that it might have been a woman's vest, but in the late Qing men also wore ribbed silk or velvet vests such as this one over a plain robe, sometimes with a homburg hat and two-tone shoes.[136]

59

60. Woman's Velvet Jacket

◆

China
Qing dynasty, 19th century
Silk
Cut velvet
30.5 x 57.5 in.; 77.5 x 146.5 cm
The William Bridges Thayer Memorial, 1928.55

Dragon medallions fill the field of this short jacket patterned by contrasting cut and uncut velvet. Pairs of four-clawed dragons encircle a flaming pearl in each medallion. The field was planned so that the medallions appear complete over the panel closures. Differences of small details in similar motifs add visual interest to the design.

The distinctive lapel is called a *pipa*, or lute, fastening because of its resemblance to the shape of the upper surface of the *pipa*, a stringed instrument with a rounded soundbox.[137]

60

61. Woman's Cut Velvet Coat

✦

China

Qing dynasty, 19th century

Silk, gold-wrapped thread, and applied ribbons

Cut velvet on satin ground with embroidered

(satin, couching) satin borders and cuffs

47 x 55.5 in.; 119.5 x 141 cm

Gift of Dr. and Mrs. Robert P. Woods, 1982.121

Unlike other velvets in the Spencer collection, this velvet was not shaped on the loom. The motifs repeat in a regular order without regard for the shape of the garment. They are cut off at the edges, and do not meet at the seams.

In the main field, copper-colored cut velvet peonies, peaches, bats, and butterflies appear to float above a blue satin ground. Figures in garden settings interspersed with blossoms and scrolling vines decorate the outer border, central opening, collar, and sleeve bands. A woven ribbon is applied to the outer border of the velvet panel; the ribbon, in turn, is edged with blue satin.

This garment was assembled from several discrete textiles, including a large piece of regularly patterned cut velvet, embroidered borders, sleeve bands that do not match the borders, woven ribbon, and several plain silk fabrics used for edgings. Although it is likely that none of these textiles were created specifically for this garment, the motifs share a common vocabulary typical of women's garments and furnishings. The use of a two-color velvet and the fact that the cloth was not woven to shape suggest that this coat might have been constructed from furnishing fabric. Most velvet garments were monochrome or a combination of monochrome and black. The copper and blue combination was popular for furnishings, but quite unusual for a garment.[138] This coat may have been altered in China for a resident Westerner, or even produced specifically for the tourist trade.[139]

61

Iconography

Motifs on Qing Chinese textiles represent all aspects of the natural, mythical, and human worlds.[140] Many are ancient, appearing in the Chinese classics and on artifacts unearthed from prehistoric and early historic tombs. Over time, the meanings of symbols changed or multiplied. Symbols were grouped into categories, some of which were organized as late as the mid-Qing. Some motifs worked within two different sets of categories. Motifs could be paired to create new and sometimes very specific meanings based on the root meanings of the two motifs, or on some combination of their homophones, an important non-visual part of the symbolic language. A motif could carry a hidden secondary meaning (or meanings) that related more to homophonic wordplay than to the core meaning. Rebuses—pictorial puns based on homophones—became increasingly popular and more complex in the later Qing.

Of course, a robe might appear beautiful or interesting to an uneducated observer who understood the motifs on a purely visual level—a boy holding a lotus and a mouth organ in a garden setting, for example, may be appreciated for its aesthetic appeal. But on another level, appreciation of the imagery would be deepened by a knowledge of the meaning of each motif, a knowledge that was enhanced if the viewer was well read and knew something of the history of that motif in Chinese literature and visual culture. In the example above, an observer well versed in Chinese culture would think of the importance of a son, and the high hopes invested in him for family advancement through his scholarly achievements. The lotus blossom would bring to mind the precepts of Buddhism, the idea of purity, and the possibility of the extraordinary rising from the ordinary. The mouth or reed organ was an ancient instrument that called up associations with the role of music in a boy's classical education and in right governance of the state.

The rebus meanings of this simple scene would have added yet another dimension to its interpretation. These playful puns could be used and combined in infinite ways to send very specific literary messages through visual means. The scene of a boy holding a lotus (*lian*) in one hand and a mouth organ (*sheng*) in the other can be "read" to mean *lian sheng*, "uninterrupted social advancement," based on the meanings of homophones *lian*, "uninterrupted," and *sheng*, "social advancement." Likewise, a magpie (*xi*) picking seeds (*guo*) from a lotus (*lian*) can be read as "May you have the joy (*xi*) of passing one exam (*guo*) after another (*lian*)."[141]

Rebus meanings relied on phonetic resemblances, and could be comprehended only by those who spoke or understood the official Mandarin dialect. Other levels of meaning were available to all literate Chinese.

Symbols on Qing textiles should not be taken too literally, however. Many, if not most, Qing textiles used specific motifs not to convey a specific meaning, but simply to bring visual delight and appropriate auspicious wishes to their owners. Buddhist, Daoist, and Precious Things motifs are often mixed on a single garment. The meaning of each element is probably less important than the fact that the textile combines auspicious symbols from each of these three primary categories. Basic human desires for prosperity, happiness, long life, and progeny are expressed in a complex vocabulary of interrelated symbols.

In the *chao fu*, *long pao*, and other formal and semi-formal textiles, individual motifs work together to present a diagram of a cosmos ordered by a just, benevolent, and powerful emperor. This cosmos is most fully developed on the semi-formal *long pao*, or "dragon robe." The diagonal lines at the hem, *lishui*, represent the deep ocean thought to surround the earth. Above them, concentric half-circles represent waves. Auspicious symbols appear half-hidden in the troughs of the waves and thrown up on the shore, evidence of the abundance of the sea. At the center of the hem in front and back, a stylized series of peaks represents the earth-mountain. Associated both with the mythical Mount Meru sacred to Buddhists and the Daoist Kunlun Mountains of the Immortals, it functions as an *axis mundi* (axis of the world), connecting the deep ocean, the earth, and the heavens. Above the mountains dragons desport themselves with their flaming jewels in a heaven filled with clouds and auspicious symbols. The focus of the

Iconographic Details

DETAIL 1
Daoist Priest's Robe (Plate 44)
Rabbit (moon), stars, and rooster (sun)

DETAIL 2
Daoist Priest's Robe (Plate 44)
Peaches of Immortality

DETAIL 3
Woman's *Kesi* Robe (Plate 56)
Pairs of butterflies with blossoms of the four
seasons (clockwise from upper left: chrysanthemums, lotus, plum blossoms, and peonies)

DETAIL 4
Rank Badge (Plate 42)
Eight Buddhist Symbols, clockwise from upper
left: parasol, endless knot, flaming and beribboned wheel of the Law, royal canopy, lotus,
fish, conch shell/sea slug, and vase

DETAIL 5
Rank Badge (Plate 41)
Fan with interlocking round- and square-
shaped golden ornaments, the latter with
central swastika patterns

DETAIL 6
Rank Badge (Plate 41)
Sword with sun and clouds; interlocking
swastika border

DETAIL 7
Daoist Priest's Robe (Plate 44)
Daoist Immortal with gourd

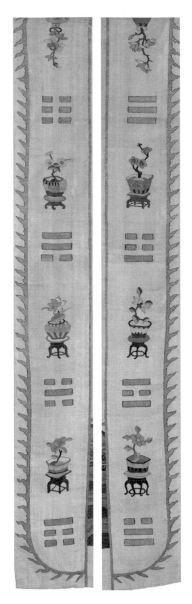

DETAIL 8
Daoist Priest's Robe (Plate 44)
Eight trigrams and flower baskets

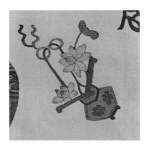

DETAIL 9
Daoist Priest's Robe (Plate 44)
Lotus in vase

DETAIL 10
Chao-fu (Plate 35)
Earth mountain bordered by square-shaped golden ornaments with pearls, red coral, and interlocking pairs of round-shaped golden ornaments in the waves of the cosmic ocean, with five-colored clouds and bats above

DETAIL 11
Child's *Long pao* (Plate 39)
Bolt of silk and beribboned *lingzhi* mushroom

DETAIL 12
Chao-fu (Plate 35)
Rhinoceros horns and bats. Also a dragon with flaming orb; five-colored clouds and bats over the waves of the cosmic ocean with red coral, square-shaped golden ornaments, and pearls.

DETAIL 13
Rank Badge (Plate 41)
Ruyi scepter and swastika. *Ruyi* can be translated as "whatever you want"; the swastika is one representation of "ten thousand." The two motifs combined, therefore, convey the blessing of ten thousand wishes granted.

DETAIL 14
Daoist Priest's Robe (Plate 44)
Crane

DETAIL 15
Chao-fu (Plate 35)
Five-clawed dragon with flaming orb

DETAIL 16
Phoenix Rank Badge (Plate 40)
Pair of phoenixes with peonies and five-colored clouds

DETAIL 17
Rank Badge (Plate 42)
Border design of alternating rounded *shou* (long life) and *xi* (happiness) characters

DETAIL 18
Woman's Skirt (Plate 51)
Blossoms of the four seasons with butterflies

DETAIL 19
Woman's Embroidered Robe (Plate 55)
Flower basket with plum blossoms (winter), peonies (spring, summer), and chrysanthemums (fall)

elaborate imagery is the rampant dragon at center front and back, curled around a flaming orb. Some or all of this cosmic landscape is usually repeated in miniature on borders and cuffs.

Numbers were important in the Chinese cosmological system, and auspicious objects were grouped together into categories of certain meaningful numbers. For example, there are the Four Friends of Winter and Blossoms of the Four Seasons; the Five Classics and Five Elements; the Eight Buddhist, Daoist, and secular Precious Things, and the Eight Trigrams; and the Twelve Symbols of Authority.

DETAIL 1   (SUN, MOON, STARS): The oldest set of symbols is the Twelve Symbols of Authority. Together they represent the emperor's rulership of the universe, his relationship to the cosmic forces of sun, moon, and stars, and to the earth (mountains) and sea (water weed). His power to administer justice is represented by the ax and by the *fu* symbol, a doubled mirror-image representing the dualistic principle of the universe. A pair of sacrificial cups represents his central role in the ritual life of the nation, and his responsibility to provide for the welfare of the people is represented by grain (millet). The dragon is a symbol of imperial authority, and the flowery fowl symbolizes the world of feathered creatures, and by extension, the natural world. In combination, mountains, bronze cups, water weed, fire, and grain represent the Five Elements of earth, metal, water, fire, and wood.

Over time, these symbols accrued further layers of meaning, mostly related to the qualities of a good ruler. The sun, for example, became a symbol of intellectual enlightenment; the water weed, of purity; the "flowery fowl" (represented by a pheasant in Qing times), of literary refinement; the sacrificial cups, of filial piety; the dragon, of the power of adaptability through transformation and renewal; and the fire, of a brilliant intellect. The *fu* symbol, called the "symbol of distinction" in the *Shujing* (*Book of History*), compiled in the mid- to late Zhou dynasty (ca. 900–481 BCE), was later associated with happiness.[142]

In a passage in the *Shujing*, the emperor instructs his ministers to place these symbols appropriately on the sacrificial robes. His reference to them as "the emblematic symbols of the ancients" implies that they were already well-established symbols in the mid-Zhou.

> I wish to see the emblematic figures of the ancients,—the sun, the moon, the stars, the mountain, the dragon, and the flowery fowl, which are depicted on the upper garment;—the temple cup, the aquatic grass, the flames,—the grains of rice, the hatchet, and the symbol of distinction, which are embroidered on the lower garment:—I wish to see all these displayed with the five colours so as to form the official robes; it is yours to adjust them clearly.[143]

The Twelve Symbols appear on the ceremonial robes of the rulers depicted in the *Scroll of the Emperors* attributed to Yan Liben (d. 673) in the Museum of Fine Arts, Boston. With the development of dragon robes in the fifteenth century, the Twelve Symbols were incorporated into the main body of a type of robe that featured large dragon medallions. The *Portrait of Emperor Shizong [Jiajing] of the Ming Dynasty* (r. 1522–1566) shows the symbols in two prominent vertical lines flanking a row of large dragon medallions.[144] When the Manchus conquered China in 1644, at first they did not use Ming imperial garments. In 1651, Shunzhi, the first Manchu ruler of China, forcefully rejected a Chinese official's suggestion that he use Chinese ceremonial robes to perform the annual sacrifices.[145] Chinese robes are included, however, in the regulations of 1759 promulgated under the Qianlong emperor, and Qing emperors used the Twelve Symbols from the mid-eighteenth century until the end of the dynasty. Ceremonial robes with the Twelve Symbols were last worn in China in 1914, when Yuan Shikai, first President of the Chinese Republic, wore them for a ceremony at the Altar of Heaven.[146]

Although other marks of rank, such as the five-clawed dragon and rank badges, were wrongly appropriated by people without the proper rank to wear them, the imperial symbols seem to have been respected. Only the emperor used all twelve, although certain other members of his family were entitled to use a few of them. The Spencer collection is replete with misappropriated five-clawed dragons, but there is not a single example of the misuse of the Twelve Symbols of Authority.

Commonly seen, however, are elements from three other sets of meaningful objects. These sets were generally conceived in groups of eight, although more than eight motifs might at one time or another be included in the group. Two of the three most common groupings are the Eight Buddhist Symbols and the Eight Daoist Symbols. The third group is composed of a somewhat amorphous set of auspicious objects, often referred to as the Eight Precious Things, but also known as the eight symbols of the scholar and as eight treasures of Confucius. Although meaning (or meanings) are ascribed to each element in these three sets, in general each refers to its category and is used primarily as an auspicious symbol. Unlike the Twelve Symbols of Authority, motifs from the Buddhist, Daoist, and Precious Things categories appear with great frequency on textiles in the Spencer collection, recurring like so many themes with variations.

Following is an abbreviated list of the sets and individual symbolic motifs seen most commonly in Chinese textiles of the Qing dynasty.

DETAIL 2   **PEACHES OF IMMORTALITY AND THREE ABUNDANCES:** peach, pomegranate, and "Buddha's hand" citrus fruit; symbolize longevity, fertility, and happiness. The peach is a widely used longevity and immortality symbol, derived from the legend of miraculous peach trees that grew deep in the Kunlun Mountains in the garden of the Queen Mother of the West. These Peaches of Immortality ripened only once every thousand (or three, or nine thousand) years, and conferred immortality on any creature that ate them. The peach sometimes appears as one unit in a trifold motif showing three fruits emerging from a single source. The other two fruits are the pomegranate and the "Buddha's hand." Due to its multitude of seeds, the pomegranate is a fertility symbol. The citrus fruit called "Buddha's hand" is a rebus for "abundant happiness."

THREE FRIENDS OF WINTER: pine, bamboo, and plum; represent the virtue of the worthy scholar-official. The pine, which holds its leaves and remains green throughout the winter, represents steadfastness. The bamboo, which bends in a storm but does not break, symbolizes resilience. The plum, which produces pure and beautiful blossoms even in bitter surroundings and at a venerable age, represents perseverance. All three trees have a long history of representation in Chinese poetry and painting.

DETAILS 3, 18, 19   **BLOSSOMS OF THE FOUR SEASONS:** the peony (associated with spring), the lotus (summer), the chrysanthemum (autumn), and the plum blossom (winter); alternately the magnolia may be used to represent spring, and the peony can replace the lotus for summer; bamboo may also represent winter. The peony is an emblem of wealth and distinction. The lotus is a symbol of purity, and also a rebus for marriage or "continuous harmony."[147] The chrysanthemum is an emblem of long life and friendship. Because it flowers in the cold of late winter, the plum blossom was extolled by poets and painters for its beauty and fortitude. Taken together, the Blossoms of the Four Seasons are a common motif on women's costume and furnishings.

DETAIL 4   **EIGHT BUDDHIST SYMBOLS:** represent the spiritual attributes of the Enlightened Buddha.

- wheel of the Law (or wheel of learning): symbol of the Buddhist teaching
- royal canopy: symbol of victory, and protection of all living creatures
- parasol: symbol of nobility that sheds the heat of desire; also stands for just government
- lotus: symbol of divine purity
- vase: probably a reference to purification; a rebus for "peace" (*bing*). Sometimes the vase is depicted filled with flowers or branches chosen for their rebus meanings.

- endless (or mystic) knot: symbol of the infinite mercy of the Buddha; associated with longevity; also called the entrails of the Buddha. The endless knot is probably derived ultimately from the mystic mark on the belly of the Hindu god Vishnu, but some scholars suggest derivation from the swastika.

- twin fish: symbol of the union of happiness and utility; also the symbol of yin and yang (see below); a rebus for "plenty" (*yu*)

- conch shell (or sea slug): symbol of victory; called the sign of the "blessedness of turning to right." A conch shell was originally used to call the faithful to prayer.

EIGHT DAOIST SYMBOLS: associated with the Eight Daoist Immortals, who, by their nature, are associated with longevity and immortality.

DETAIL 5
- fan: symbol of Zhongli Quan, patron saint of the military; can bring people back to life

DETAIL 6
- sword: symbol of Lu Dongbin, a scholar-warrior and patron of barbers; used by Lu to slay demons

DETAIL 7
- gourd: often shown in combination with the crutch needed by the lame Li Tieguai, patron saint of the sick. A gourd was part of the paraphernalia of the Daoist magician, who used it to carry magic potions or as a supposed hiding place.

- castanets: symbol of Cao Guoqiu, patron saint of actors and uncle of an emperor, who always appears in court dress holding an official scepter or castanets

DETAIL 8
- flower basket: symbol of Lan Caihe, patron of minstrels and of gardeners, who is sometimes regarded as male, sometimes as female, and sometimes as a hermaphrodite

- bamboo cane or tube and rods: symbol of Zhang Guolao, patron saint of artists and calligraphers

- flute: symbol of Han Xiangzi, patron of musicians

DETAIL 9
- lotus: symbol of He Xian'gu, female patron of housewives

EIGHT PRECIOUS THINGS (*BA BAO*): also known as the eight symbols of the scholar and as eight treasures of Confucius; sometimes reduced to four or multiplied to fourteen. Most refer more specifically to worldly success than the motifs in the Buddhist and Daoist sets, although, depending on the particular combinations chosen, they may also refer to scholarship, a love of learning, and artistic accomplishment.

The following are some of the most commonly found motifs incorporated into the set.

DETAILS 12, 15
- pearl: believed to grant wishes

DETAILS 5, 10, 12
- square-shaped golden ornament: symbol of wealth; the open lozenge is a symbol of victory. Often depicted as an interlocking pair of square ornaments.

DETAILS 5, 10
- round-shaped golden ornament: symbol of wealth. Often depicted as an interlocking pair of round ornaments, and/or as a coin with a central hole.

DETAIL 11
- bolt of silk: symbol of prosperity. Sometimes rendered as scroll books or scroll paintings, a reference to the scholarly life.

- musical stone: symbol of musical accomplishment; an ancient musical instrument

DETAIL 12
- pair of rhinoceros horns: symbol of health; valued for medicinal purposes, and also an expensive aphrodisiac

- artemisia leaf: for prevention of disease; also a general good omen

DETAILS 10, 12
- red coral: emblem of longevity and of official promotion. Coral was a highly valued item imported from Iran and Ceylon, and was associated by legend with a mythical tree that grew on the ocean floor and bloomed only once each century.

DETAIL 13 • gold or silver ingot: symbol of wealth

DETAIL 13 • *ruyi* scepter: composed of a staff and a head resembling a lingzhi mushroom, symbol of long life, the combination fulfills wishes. *Ruyi* may be translated as "whatever you want." A finely carved wood or jade scepter was a valued gift on important occasions, and conveyed the desire that all of the recipient's wishes would be fulfilled. Although resembling the imperial scepter in shape, the *ruyi* was not the insignia of a ruler.

DETAILS 5, 6, 13 • swastika: symbol of longevity (see below); one of the ways of writing *wan*, or "ten thousand"

DETAIL 8 THE EIGHT TRIGRAMS: mystic symbols composed of sets of three broken and/or unbroken lines in various configurations. The Trigrams form the base of a system of divination and philosophy derived from the *Yijing* (*Book of Changes*). They often appear in conjunction with the *yin/yang* symbol.

MISCELLANEOUS FLORA AND FAUNA:

DETAILS 10, 12 • bat (*pianfu*): derives its primary meaning as a rebus for *fu*—blessings, happiness, or good fortune; red bats are particularly auspicious, as red (*hong*) is a homophone for "majestic" or "sublime," and the color red wards off demons. Bats are a very common motif in Qing textiles. They appear among clouds on the majority of Qing court robes, and with butterflies and flowers on women's informal robes. A group of five bats may symbolize the Five Blessings: long life, prosperity, health, love of virtue, and a natural death. Bats often appear in conjunction with other objects; a bat with a musical stone, for example, would be read as *fu qing*, which also means "happiness and prosperity." Likewise, a bat with a swastika (*wan fu*) represents "ten thousand times happiness."[148] An upside-down bat means "happiness has arrived," because the word for "upside-down" (*dao*) is itself a pun on the word for "arrived."[149]

DETAILS 3, 18 • butterfly (*hudie*): symbol of happy marriages; closely associated with women and with lovers. The recurring image of a butterfly amidst flowers has erotic overtones, as the butterfly (lover) sips nectar from the calyx of a flower (a female symbol). The butterfly can also represent women; the soul of a deceased woman may reappear as a butterfly. As a rebus, *hudie* suggests "seventy to eighty years old" or length of days (*die*), and is an emblem of long life. On the Spencer textiles, the butterfly appears most frequently on women's garments, where it likely is used for its association with happy marriages.

DETAIL 14 • crane (*he*): symbol of longevity; aerial courser of the Immortals, thought to live to a fabulous age. The figure of a crane was sometimes depicted on the center of a coffin. It was supposed to carry the soul of the deceased to the Western Paradise. The crane is often depicted with other symbols of longevity, such as a pine tree and a rock or a tortoise.

• mandarin duck (*xichi*): symbol of faithfulness and conjugal happiness. Mandarin ducks were thought to mate for life. All pairs of motifs, by extension, might include the meaning of marital happiness.

DETAIL 11 • sacred fungus (*lingzhi*): symbol of long life and immortality; an ingredient in Daoist elixirs of immortality. The *Polyporus lucidus* is a woody fungus that grows on the roots of trees.[150] It also appears as part of other motifs. The head of the *ruyi* wish-granting scepter is in the shape of a *lingzhi* mushroom; the curls at the edges of stylized clouds are also in this shape.

MYTHOLOGICAL CREATURES:

DETAILS 12, 15 • dragon: symbol of the emperor and imperial authority; a masculine (*yang*) symbol associated with clouds, rain, thunder, and lightning; has the power to control the weather. The dragon can change size at will, transform itself into other creatures, and become visible or invisible. It lives among the clouds (the *lung* dragon), under the sea (the *li* dragon), and in marshes (the *jiao* dragon). There are many manifestations of dragons in Chinese culture, from regional Dragon Kings inhabiting and responsible for local rivers, to the mythological dragons of high culture that were understood more as abstract philosophical concepts than as concrete entities.

The dragon is one of the most ancient Chinese motifs. A dragon made of shells, radiocarbon dated to about 4000 BCE, was excavated from a Yangshao tomb in Henan Province in 1987. A jade dragon ornament was unearthed from a tomb in Inner Mongolia dating from the Shang dynasty.[151]

The dragon was closely associated with the emperor and with imperial authority from very early times. The mythical Yellow Emperor won a decisive battle aided by a dragon who created a flood that drowned his rival. Legend has it that the dragon then descended from the clouds to meet the emperor, and carried him and his retinue to the heavens. A number of emperors have claimed descent from dragons. The first was Han Gaozu, founder of the Han dynasty, who was from a peasant background; as Qiguang Zhao has said, Han Gaozu "needed a dragon father badly," since his rival for the throne was from a distinguished aristocratic family. After he founded the prosperous and expansive Han dynasty in 206 BCE, Han Gaozu adopted the dragon as his emblem, as all life was dependent upon the rains that it controlled.[152]

The dragon has the highest status among the Five Sacred Animals, a group that also includes the *qilin* (unicorn), *fenghuang* (phoenix), *he* (crane), and *gui* (tortoise). (The crane is sometimes omitted from this group, which then becomes the Four Mythological Animals.) It is also one of the Four Directional Animals. In cosmological diagrams, the dragon stands in the east, opposite the white tiger in the west, with the black serpent or tortoise to the north and the red phoenix to the south.

Standard depictions of the dragon have changed comparatively little since the Han dynasty. At that time, the dragon was said to possess attributes belonging to many other creatures: the horns of a stag, the skull of a camel, eyes like a demon, a neck like a snake, the belly of a sea monster, the scales of a fish, claws of an eagle, and the paws of a tiger.[153] The list of likenesses varies but always numbers nine; the broader significance of this plethora of attributes is that the dragon incorporates within itself the particular abilities associated with birds, animals, reptiles, and fish. Qing dragons have horns, a mane, prominent whiskers, and carp-like scales. The carp and the dragon, which are closely associated, can metamorphose into one another.

From the Shang to the Five Dynasties period (907–960), most dragons had three claws. A fourth claw was added to some dragons during the Song, and in the Yuan, a fifth claw was added as an imperial emblem. The number of claws appropriate to dragons in the insignia of different ranks was specified in the Qing regulations of 1759, but by the end of the dynasty (as discussed above), five-clawed dragons adorned the costumes and accessories of many lowly officials as well.

The dragon is the dominant image on Qing court costume. Closely associated with the emperor, it appeared on many objects used by the imperial court. The emperor was carried up the "dragon path" into the palace, where he sat on the "dragon throne." Dragons adorned the emperor's throne, utensils, architecture, furnishings, and clothing, along with those of his courtiers.

DETAIL 16

• phoenix (*fenghuang*): symbol of the empress; represents goodness and benevolence; the messenger of the Daoist Immortals. Dragon and phoenix together represent the emperor and empress. A pair of phoenixes—*feng*, the male, and *huang*, the female—represents the male and female principles. This mythical bird appears in the earliest Chinese texts;[154] in ancient China, the phoenix was thought to appear only when the land was governed by a just and wise ruler. A phoenix was often incorporated into women's wedding attire, as the bride was considered empress for a day.

FEATURES OF THE NATURAL LANDSCAPE:

DETAILS 4–7, 10–16
- clouds: symbol of good fortune and happiness, particularly when colorful; represent heaven (in water-earth-heaven group), and union of dual principles of *yin* and *yang* (see below). Stylized clouds appear as an omnipresent background motif in formal iconography. Five-colored clouds are seen on many of the Spencer textiles, where they serve as a harbinger of "five-fold happiness." The edges of some clouds are shaped like *lingzhi* fungus, a reference to longevity.

DETAIL 10
- mountains: sacred spaces; home of the Daoist Immortals, local gods, and Buddhist retreats; represent earth (in water-earth-heaven group). The Kunlun Mountains to the west, like Mount Sumeru of Indian legend, were thought to be the source of water, and the home of Taiyi (the "Supreme One" or "Supreme Unity") and the Queen Mother of the West. *Yin* and *yang* alternated with each other in the depths of that monumental range, the source of the "ten thousand things" (i.e., all things). Stephen Little has called Mount Kunlun a "cosmic pivot connecting Heaven and Earth."[155] In Qing textiles, stylized mountains represent earth in the water-earth-heaven assemblage of formal iconography, and suggest the Kunlun Mountains or Mount Sumeru. Young Y. Chung suggests that their use as a textile motif originated with the pictorial capabilities of *kesi* (tapestry weave), and therefore does not predate the Song dynasty.[156]

ABSTRACT MOTIFS AND CHARACTERS:

- *ji*: a character meaning "luck"

DETAIL 17
- *shou*: a character meaning "long life"; generally represented in one of a number of archaic forms. Sometimes the swastika is integrated into the character, augmenting the meaning of longevity.

DETAILS 5, 6, 13
- swastika: represents "ten thousand" (*wan*), symbolizing infinity; also represents longevity. One of the oldest symbols in Asia, the swastika was carried east across the Bering Strait about 25,000 BCE; it appears, much later, in Native American design. It was the emblem of the Hindu gods Vishnu and Shiva in India, and is found in the Indus culture of Mohenjo-Daro (2500–1500 BCE). Chung suggests that it was derived from prehistoric shamanist rituals.[157] The swastika probably entered China in conjunction with Buddhism. Angled to the right, it is the first of the sixty-five signs on the footprint of the Buddha; angled to the left, it is the fourth. Placed on the heart of the historical Buddha (śākyamuni in Sanskrit), it represents the Buddha's heart and mind. From about 700 CE, it was used in China to mean "ten thousand"; in Qing dynasty textiles and other objects, it refers to longevity, and in combination with other objects, to a multiplication of blessings.

- thunder line: represents "thunder/lightning." Another ancient symbol, the thunder line appears on Shang dynasty bronzes. Its form is derived from an ancient form of the character for thunder. In the Qing, it was used mainly as a background or border motif, appearing as conjoined squared or rounded spiral shapes, or as a series of S-curves. Similar key styles appear in Middle Eastern and Greek decorative motifs.

- *wan*: a character meaning "ten thousand"

DETAIL 17
- *xi*: a character meaning "happiness" or "joy"; also represented in a stylized archaic form. Sometimes it is doubled, a form often used on wedding textiles. "Double happiness" can refer both to happiness and to longevity.

- *yin/yang*: represents the duality of the universe. Four of its core dualities are female/male, dark/light, moon/sun, and water/fire. The symbol is a circle bisected by an S-curved line. Half of the circle is dark, the other half light; each half has an eye-like dot of the opposite color at its center, symbolizing the inseparability and interpenetration of the dual principles.

DETAILS 12, 15   • flaming orb: may represent pearl of wisdom, an allusion to Buddhist enlightenment; sometimes called a flaming jewel or flaming pearl. On Qing textiles, the flaming orb appears alone and in conjunction with dragons. The center contains an ancient emblem for thunder (an elongated, backward S-curve), a predecessor of the Qing thunder line pattern described above. The flames surrounding the pearl conjured up thunder and lightning, reflecting and augmenting the awesome power of the dragons.

DETAILS 12, 15   • flames: symbol of fire, lightning, and the aura emanating from a concentrated energy source. Stylized flames surround dragons and other potent creatures on Qing court robes, rank badges, and in Buddhist art.

DETAILS 4, 11   • ribbons: represent pieces of red cloth that were tied around objects thought to possess the efficacy of charms. Many auspicious objects are depicted festooned with ribbons. These ribbons represent the aura of the charm in much the same way that a halo represents the aura of a divinity.[158]

Manufacture

THE SILK INDUSTRY

Throughout most of the Qing dynasty, textiles for imperial use were manufactured in official workshops known as Imperial Silkworks, or in private workshops sub-contracted to one of the official workshops. The Imperial Silkworks produced imperial robes, textiles for use in the palace and as official gifts, and silk prepared for use as a trading currency. At the height of the Qing, government demand for silk textiles was enormous; in 1768, for example, more than twelve thousand bolts of silk were traded for horses and other livestock in Xinjiang alone. The palace and the central government silkworks in Peking (Beijing) contained storage facilities for an immense number of textiles. Nearly one hundred years after the fall of the Qing, there are still reported to be some ten thousand robes of various descriptions in the palace collection in Beijing.[159]

The Qing government established a Court Weaving and Dyeing Office, the Zhi ran ju, in the mid-seventeenth century.[160] Qing rulers also took advantage of established silk weaving centers located in the lower Yangtze valley, reauthorizing three official Ming Imperial Silkworks in Suzhou, Hangzhou, and Nanjing as Zhi zao ju (Weaving Offices). The Court Weaving and Dyeing Office in Peking and the three subsidiary Imperial Silkworks were organized under the administration of the Office of the Imperial Household. The Imperial Silkworks were imposing affairs. The one at Suzhou covered about ten acres, and included a building used as a temporary palace by both the Kangxi and Qianlong emperors on their southern inspection tours.[161] At the height of the Qing, these silkworks operated about two thousand looms and employed more than seven thousand workers.[162] They produced most of the complex textiles required by the court, such as material for dragon robes, brocades, satins, and gauzes.

The production of an imperially commissioned textile was a complex and lengthy affair, often requiring considerably more than a year to complete. Once each year the Board of Rites and the emperor approved designs drawn by artisans attached to the Office of the Imperial Household. The approved designs were sent to one of the Imperial Silkworks. Using these designs, skilled weavers produced the cloth, which was then sent back to the palace for tailoring.[163] The cloth was plotted so that when the variously shaped segments were cut out and constructed, the larger units of design carried across seams, while smaller segments—such as rounded collars and "horse hoof" cuffs—formed discrete and complete design units in themselves (see Plate 45).

Private workshops also played a significant role in government production. Acting under the auspices of the Imperial Silkworks, "government-registered" private workshops produced most of the ordinary silk textiles required by the court, with silk thread provided by the Imperial Silkworks. The finished textile was brought to the Silkworks, where it was inspected and sent on to Peking. If it did not pass inspection in Peking, the official in charge was considered responsible.

Alternately, instead of producing the textile in their own facilities, these private workshops occasionally sent skilled weavers to the Imperial Silkworks to weave a particular order.[164] Some private workshops became known for specialty textiles, and apparently received direct court orders for the finest products of their looms. In 1881 the Inspector General of the European-staffed Imperial Maritime Customs published an extensive report on silk production. The report indicated that luxury textiles, including those specifically commissioned by the court, were produced not just in Peking and the lower Yangtze valley, but in some surprisingly remote parts of the country as well. The report specifically mentions luxury silks coming from Sichuan, Zhangzhou (velvet), and Shanxi.[165]

One would expect to find identifying marks on some of the luxury textiles and court garments produced in the Imperial Silkworks and in the more specialized "government-registered" private workshops. To date, however, no such mark—not even an inspector's seal—has been noted in Western collections.[166] Perhaps identifying marks, if they existed, were placed at the end of a bolt of fabric, as they often are even today in Japan and India. In this case, the marks would have been cut off and separated from the cloth when it was made up.

During the Qing, the silk industry was complex in organization, with many different modes of production existing at the same time. Although some villagers tended mulberry groves, raised silkworms, reeled the cocoons, and wove and sold the cloth, most of the silk produced in the eighteenth and nineteenth centuries passed through many hands before it reached the consumer. A lively market in mulberry leaves—including price speculation—suggests that, even at the initial level of raising cocoons, production was split between mulberry grove owners and cocoon raisers, and financed in part by outside investors. This type of differentiation existed at each level of production.

There were three basic groups of silk weavers. The first were self-employed. The wealthiest of this group hired other weavers, concerning themselves only with quality control and business matters. The poorest were barely self-sufficient, often relying on loans from the middlemen who sold the silk for them. The second category of weavers took work on consignment with materials provided by entrepreneurs, just as the government's registered private workshops took work and the requisite materials from one of the Imperial Silkworks. In this case, the financier might be a merchant who dealt in silk textiles. This system was common in the lower Yangtze-Lake Tai region. The silk merchant was crucial to these two categories of producers. It was the local silk merchant who was the first link in the chain that moved silk from the workshop of a skilled artisan to the consumer, who might be in an entirely different part of China. An eighteenth-century study of the silk weaving town of Puyuan in the Huzhou area of the lower Yangtze-Lake Tai region states that wealthy entrepreneurs bought the wide variety of silks available at the local market, and held them for sale to traveling buyers from Peking and the provincial capitals.[167]

The third category of weavers was comprised of skilled artisans who worked for hire. Some artisans were employed on a regular basis by one of the Imperial Silkworks or a private workshop. They were either paid by the piece, or earned a daily or monthly salary, often supplemented by a food allowance paid in kind. Some positions were hereditary, such as those of the regular weavers at the Imperial Silkworks in Suzhou.[168] Less fortunate artisans worked only when the Imperial Silkworks or one of the private workshops needed extra help. A gazetteer of Suzhou Province vividly describes the plight of these highly specialized workers in the late seventeenth and eighteenth centuries:

> The weavers without regular employers go to the bridges at dawn each day to await the calls. Satin weavers stand on Flower Bridge, damask weavers on Kuang-hua Temple Bridge, and spinners who make silk yarn at Lin-hsi Ward. They congregate by the score and by the hundred, scanning around expectantly with outstretched necks, resembling groups of famine refugees. They will stay until after the breakfast hour. If work should be curtailed at the silk textile establishments, these workers would be without a living.[169]

Officials and others entitled to wear *chao fu* and *long pao* bought or commissioned the appropriate cloth and then had it tailored to their specifications. Within the parameters of the basic design features and appropriate rank signifiers of official dress, the patron's pocketbook, occasion for wear, and personal taste dictated the specific imagery and relative elegance of his attire. The imperial workshops were free to handle private orders, so long as these orders did not interfere with their work for the court. Toward the end of the dynasty, at least, court robes could also be bought pre-tailored or even second-hand.[170]

Brocades, damasks, and velvets required huge draw looms with the capacity to manipulate hundreds of warp threads in complex arrangements. To produce such fabrics, a master weaver worked with a drawboy perched high above him who pulled the required pattern threads. The *Diangongkaiwu*, a Ming text describing various industries, states that the looms necessary for weaving dragon robes were even larger, with fifteen-foot pattern towers that required two skilled drawboys as well as a master weaver.[171]

Kesi, or tapestry weave, did not require complex equipment, but many hours of painstaking labor as each weft thread was manipulated into position by hand on tiny shuttles. Producing *kesi* was rather like embroidering directly on the warp, except that each tiny passage of thread formed part of the structure of the cloth.

In a series of edicts regulating textile production in 1652, the Imperial Silkworks were ordered to send one yellow *kesi* robe in the spring and one blue *kesi* robe in the fall to the palace storehouse. The Silkworks were also forbidden to weave any other *kesi* textiles. Thus in the early Qing, *kesi* was reserved for imperial use.[172] There are no *kesi* textiles listed in the lengthy inventory of luxury textiles belonging to Jia Zheng, a senior member of the Jia family, in Cao Xueqin's mid-eighteenth-century novel, *The Story of the Stone*, although the list includes other proscribed textiles.[173] In the nineteenth century, however, *kesi* garments were apparently worn by those who could afford them, although they were never as common as brocade or embroidered robes. The Spencer has several *kesi* garments that do not have imperial connections, including men's, women's, and children's clothing and household furnishings. Illustrated in the present volume are a woman's *long pao* (Plate 38), a male child's *long pao* (Plate 39), and a woman's informal robe (Plate 56).

Much of the embroidery for the palace was done by professional embroiderers working within the palace precincts. Some orders were filled by the Imperial Silkworks in Suzhou, which was famous for its embroidery.[174] The cloth to be embroidered was stretched on a frame. The artisan worked with both hands, one above and one below the cloth; the many long, smooth filaments of glossed silk that formed a single thread had to be handled with great care in order not to ruffle them in the embroidery process.

Professional embroidery houses owned stencils of the most popular motifs. A powder of ground oyster shells was pounced, or dusted, through the stencil. Then a solution made of this powder and water was painted in a fine line over the dusted design.[175]

Embroidery was done throughout China by both men and women. A number of European men, who did not have access to women's quarters, noted with surprise that the business of embroidery was "generally performed by men."[176] By the late nineteenth century, Europeans had become more aware of women's roles in professional embroidery as women became more visible in public, entering workshops instead of working in seclusion at home. A report by the European customs commissioners issued in 1881 states that most of the 1,050 embroiderers in Suzhou were women and young girls.[177] Throughout the Qing dynasty, however, a great deal of embroidery, particularly on small items, was done by women working at home for the use of their own households or to supplement family income.[178]

DYES

TRADITIONAL DYES

Most of our information on traditional dyes used during the Ming and Qing comes from two Ming texts: the aforementioned *Diangongkaiwu*, a book about basic industries written by Song Yingxing in 1637; and the *Bencaogangmu*, a text on useful plants and animals.[179]

The *Diangongkaiwu* includes a section on the composition and production of the major dye materials used for court robes in the Ming dynasty. Most of these were materials that had been used in earlier times and continued in use during the Qing, until some were supplanted by European aniline dyes in the second half of the nineteenth century.

Yellow was an imperial color in both the Ming and the Qing, an important rank signifier for the emperor and members of the upper nobility. The particular shade and type of yellow dye differed in the two dynasties. The *Diangongkaiwu* cautions dyers to be careful in dyeing imperial yellow (*zhehuang*), because if the threads are not dyed properly, the finished textile will look like a more common yellow after it is woven. The document refrains from describing the process for producing Ming imperial yellow, merely noting, "Manufacture not explained." The *Bencaogangmu* explains that the Ming imperial reddish yellow was made from the wood of a *zhe* tree related to the mulberry (*Cudrania triloba*). The same text says that the buds of the *huai* or Japan Pagoda tree (*Sophora japanica*) produce a very bright yellow. Cammann suggests that this might be the source of the Qing imperial yellow (*ming huang*), a much brighter yellow than the Ming imperial reddish yellow. The golden yellow (*jin huang*) used for the robes of Qing imperial princes was dyed with wood chips from a sumac tree, *huang lu* or *lu mu* (*Rhus cotinus*), with potash made from hemp straw as a mordant. Other yellow dyes commonly employed on official garments included those made from gardenia hulls (*Gardenia florida*) and the inner bark of the Amur cork tree (*Phellodendron amurense*).

The most common sources of red dye used on official costume were the thistle-like petals of the safflower (*Carthamus tinctorius*), madder roots (*Rubia cordifolia*), and the inner bark of the sappanwood tree (*Caesalpinia sappan*) imported from peninsular southeast Asia (present-day Thailand and Malaysia). A deep crimson—used for the dragon robes of Ming officials—was made by adding alum and gall nuts to a boiled decoction of sappanwood.

Blue came from a variety of plants, including woad (*Isatis tinctoria*), a member of the mustard family that was also a traditional source for blue dye in Europe, and indigo (*Polygonum tinctorium*). Cultivated in north China and Manchuria, indigo produced the finest blues, and was probably the most common blue dye used on silk textiles. The *Bencaogangmu* states that sappanwood was added to the indigo to make very dark shades of blue. This may have been the method used to produce the exceedingly dark blue-black found on many Qing official robes.

Black dyes were made from gall nuts and from acorns from the chestnut oak (*Quecus serrata*). The particular black used for Ming ceremonial robes was made with indigo, the bark of the wax myrtle, and sumac wood, with copperas or ferrous sulphate (iron) and gall nuts.

Green was usually produced by overdyeing a yellow with indigo. Purple came from the roots of the gromwell (*Lithospermum officinale*), or was produced alternately by overdyeing a red with indigo. Brown, according to the *Bencaogangmu*, was made from the bark of the wax myrtle with ferrous sulphate as a mordant; however, there are many plants that yield good browns, and it is unlikely that the dyers restricted themselves to this source.

Although the *Bencaogangmu* and the *Diangongkaiwu* provide a great deal of information about the composition of dyes used on official garments in the Ming and Qing dynasties, neither text gives specific information on dyeing procedures. Such information was treated as a trade secret, and transmitted orally within families of dyers from generation to generation. As a result, a great deal of information was lost during tumultuous times.

CHEMICAL DYES:
DEVELOPMENT IN EUROPE
AND EXPORT TO CHINA

From the late eighteenth century, European chemists and dyers had studied the chemistry of coloration. The Royal Society in London and the Académie in Paris offered prizes for new colors. Much of this interest was spurred by an attempt to reproduce, commercially and inexpensively, the clear, vibrant colors seen on imported Indian calicos and chintzes, and the popular near Eastern "Turkey Red," a strong, fast red produced in a lengthy process involving madder roots, oil, and cow dung.

The first synthetic dye was created in 1856 by a young chemistry student at the Royal College of Chemistry in London. William Henry Perkin (1838–1907) was attempting to synthesize quinine when the combination of potassium bichromate and aniline that he was using accidentally dyed a piece of silk bright purple. At the time, aniline had to be extracted in very small quantities from benzene, itself a rare chemical. Although the scarcity of aniline was a serious detriment to commercial production, Perkin immediately patented his findings and left the Royal College to manufacture his purple commercially. Despite its initial high cost (ninety English pounds per kilo), "Perkin's Purple" was very popular, and Perkin was later knighted for this and subsequent discoveries.

The cost of aniline was drastically reduced a few years later with the discovery that aniline could be extracted from coal tar, a by-product of the coal industry. Perkin's professor, August Wilhelm Hofmann (1818–1892), produced an aniline red in the late 1850s, and other aniline colors followed quickly. These new brilliant colors were a huge success at the 1862 International Exhibition in London.[180] Soon aniline dyes from coal tar were being exported from Europe in considerable quantities.

In 1871 China imported eight tons of aniline dyes. Two and a half tons entered Shanghai, destined primarily for the silkworks in the lower Yangtze valley, while five and a half entered the country through Tientsin, the port city for the capital of Peking.[181] Customs reports from this period also note a steady importation of European silk thread.

METALLIC THREAD

Gold and silver foil, and foil-wrapped threads, added a sumptuous magnificence to many Qing garments. This thread was made by adhering metallic leaf to a sheet of paper, burnishing the leaf, cutting the paper into thin strips, and either inserting the strips directly into the web or winding them around strands of silk thread. On well-made garments, the edges of each tiny strip of metallic foil touch as the foil spirals around a thin strand of thread. The foil is wrapped so closely that, even under magnification, it is sometimes difficult to see the core thread. On less costly garments, the foil is often wrapped more loosely; on close inspection, it is easy to see the core thread. Although this is not immediately apparent to the naked eye, there is less gold visible overall, and the garment may appear tawdry rather than opulent.

On some Qing garments, the gold leaf is adhered to red paper, which imparts a subtle reddish cast to the gold, an effect that increases with time as the gold leaf wears away. Under magnification, the red shows clearly at the edges of the foil and in areas where the gold leaf has worn. See, for example, the man's gold brocade *long pao* on dull red ground (Plate 36) and the man's embroidered *long pao* (Plate 37).

In 1875, a Western observer, John Henry Gray (1828–1890), described the manufacture of gold- and silver-wrapped thread as follows:

> Several long, and narrow sheets of paper having been coated with a mixture of earth (well pounded) and glue are, in the next instance, covered either with gold, or silver leaf. In order that a bright glossy appearance may be imparted to these sheets of paper, which, with gold, or silver leaf have been covered, men rub them, heavily, from one end to the other, with pieces of crystal, which, for this purpose, are, to the ends of the bamboo rods, attached. This polishing process having been accomplished, the gilded, or silvered sheets of paper are, now, cut, by means of large knives, into very thin strips, which strips, are, then, by a twirling process, carefully entwined round ordinary threads of silk.[182]

The gold and silver leaf to which Gray refers were alloys made from several different metals. Some alloys had a high percentage of gold or silver with only traces of other metals, while others were made primarily of less expensive materials. Tests done on a variety of metallic threads from Qing textiles in the Victoria and Albert Museum show a combination of gold with iron, lead, copper, and sometimes silver. Although the color of the foils varied considerably from silver to reddish to yellow, the metallic make-up of the foils differed very little in the samples tested.[183]

An analysis of thirteen types of metallic thread found on seven late-eighteenth- and nineteenth-century Chinese textiles in the Indianapolis Museum of Art revealed somewhat different results. Silver, copper, and gold, in that order, were the primary metals. Although eight of the thirteen samples taken from the textiles appeared gold in color to the naked eye, gold was the primary metal in only three. In the rest, silver, copper, and gold appeared in combination with each other and with silicone, calcium, magnesium, iron, and aluminum. Iron, a main element in the Victoria and Albert textiles, appeared in only one sample, where it was only one of a group of seven trace elements. Lead did not appear at all.

The two simplest samples in the Indianapolis analysis contained only silver, with copper as a secondary element. One appeared gold in color; the other, copper. The most complex sample was gold with eight trace elements.[184]

Europeans admired Chinese gold and silver threads, and sought to discover the secrets of their manufacture in order to improve the quality of those produced in Europe. Sir George Staunton's account of Lord Macartney's embassy to China in 1793–1794, for example, said that he was accompanied by an English manufacturer named Eades who hoped to discover the secret of keeping gold and silver threads from tarnishing. Apparently Eades died on the journey before he was able to study the process.[185]

In the late Qing, with much of its silk industry destroyed, China imported large quantities of both real and imitation gold and silver thread (some of it smuggled) as well as silk thread, bolts of dyed silk, and aniline dyes.[186]

Textiles in the Late Qing

With the economic and political dislocations of the nineteenth century, the court was hard pressed to support the silk industry. The Court Weaving and Dyeing Office closed in 1843, and none of the Imperial Silkworks survived to the end of the century. A widespread and destructive series of rebellions in the third quarter of the nineteenth century challenged the Qing government, wreaked havoc in the regions affected, and crippled the silk industry. One of the most famous—and most devastating to the silk industry—was the Taiping Rebellion of 1850–1863.

In 1853 the Taiping rebels invaded the Yangtze valley and scourged the countryside. The population of the important silk-producing province of Zhejiang dropped by almost two thirds from 1850 to 1898, while the number of silk weavers in the provincial capital of Hangzhou fell from a pre-rebellion high of sixty thousand to about twenty thousand at the end of the dynasty.[187] Travelling after the rebels were defeated, Baron von Richthofen observed a vacant and neglected countryside, where "plantations of old mulberry trees, half of them decayed from want of care, tell of one of the chief industries of the former inhabitants. . . ."[188] The three Imperial Silkworks in the Yangtze valley survived the Taiping Rebellion, but were phased out in the 1890s.[189]

Despite the difficult circumstances and the undeniable existence of inferior work, production of some fine traditional textiles continued throughout the nineteenth century; at the same time, established textile traditions continued to change and evolve. The words "decay" and "decline" have often been associated with the late Qing, coupled with the idea of an unchecked downward slide toward the end of the dynasty. As Schuyler Cammann has stated,

> Later Ch'ing dragon robes are interesting chiefly as examples of decline in technique, reflecting political and economic decay. For specimens of textile skill and real beauty, it is necessary to go back to the satin dragon robes of Early Ch'ing, or the fine *k'o-ssu* [*kesi*] robes and the richly embroidered ones of the Ch'ien-lung [Qianlong] period.[190]

Extant textiles, however, belie these words, and reveal an enthusiastic response to new ideas and materials that suggests a vibrant, if subdued, industry. The European aniline dyes, for example, which are considered garish by many twentieth-century Western scholars, were classified as *yi pin*, or "first-class colors," by the Chinese.[191] They were enjoyed for their brilliance, imported in huge quantities, and rapidly incorporated into even the most conservative court costumes.[192] It is easy to forget that Europeans also responded with great enthusiasm to these vibrant, fast colors when they were first discovered.

Some late Qing textiles are different from their earlier prototypes. Their makers played with the possibilities of the brilliant aniline dyes, tucked Western pockets deep under the flaps of traditional Chinese women's jackets, and responded to foreign conceptions of space and design. Rather than dismissing all deviations from a mid-Qing norm as evidence of decline, these late Qing textiles should be viewed as innovative and experimental.

1. Several of the Spencer's finest Chinese textiles are listed as "source unknown." These were almost certainly part of Mrs. Thayer's gift. The "oooo" prefix assigned to their Spencer accession numbers, as with several other objects in her gift, was almost certainly due to incomplete cataloging at the time of the gift. A number of Chinese textiles with "oooo" prefixes also have Thayer tags attached—tags with their identifying numbers within Mrs. Thayer's personal collection.

2. James Legge, trans., *Li Chi Book of Rites*, 2 vols., ed. Ch'u Chai and Winberg Chai (New Hyde Park, New York: University Books, 1967), 1:216–217, 2:11.

3. See the work of Schuyler Cammann, *China's Dragon Robes* (New York: The Ronald Press, 1952); and John Vollmer, *In the Presence of the Dragon Throne* (Toronto: Royal Ontario Museum, 1977), *Five Colours of the Universe* (Edmonton: The Edmonton Art Gallery, 1980), "Manchu Style and Ethnic Identity," in *Secret Splendors of the Chinese Court*, ed. Imelda Gatton Degraw (Denver: Denver Art Museum, 1981), and *Decoding Dragons* (Eugene, Oregon: Museum of Art, University of Oregon, 1983). See also Dorothy Burnham, *Cut My Cote* (Toronto: Royal Ontario Museum, 1973) for an exposition of the theory that nomadic hunting (and herding) cultures in circumpolar regions of the globe developed fitted garments (such as the Chinese *chao fu* and *long pao*) that were ultimately based on joining together odd-shaped animal skins, while sedentary agricultural societies developed unfitted garments (such as the Roman toga, Indian sari, Japanese kimono, and Ming dynasty formal outer robe) derived from long, comparatively narrow lengths of woven cloth. Burnham and Vollmer (Burnham's colleague at the Royal Ontario Museum) analyzed the cut of a number of garments in the ROM collection, calculating how the pieces could have been made on the original loom-width of cloth. Their work showed that many traditional garments were based on geometric cuts (horizontal, vertical, and diagonal) and designed to utilize every scrap of fabric. Their analysis also included a number of European garments, the elaborate appearance of which belie their simple cut and efficient use of material. The Chinese *chao fu* and *long pao*, however, cannot be cut efficiently from a loom-width of cloth; in fact, the cut of the garments is quite wasteful. For this reason, Burnham suggested that the Qing *long pao* was "closer to the ancient skin cuts" than to the cloth tradition (*Cut My Cote*, 33).

4. See *Wenwu*, 1964, no. 11: pl. 6, no. 3; and Robert D. Jacobsen, *Imperial Silks: Ch'ing Dynasty Textiles in The Minneapolis Institute of Arts* (Minneapolis: The Minneapolis Institute of Arts, 2000), 36, fig. 47.

5. Zhou Xun and Gao Chunming, *5000 Years of Chinese Costumes* (San Francisco: China Books and Periodicals, 1987), 152.

6. *Wenwu*, 1973, no. 5: figs. 19, 35; Verity Wilson, *Chinese Dress* (London: Victoria and Albert Museum, 1986), figs. 21, 35. For a larger photograph, see Jacobsen, *Imperial Silks*, 37, fig. 48.

7. Jacobsen, *Imperial Silks*, 38.

8. See ibid., 34–35 and 36, fig. 46.

9. See Cammann, *China's Dragon Robes*, 138–139.

10. See Kaneo Matsumoto, *Jōdaigire: 7th and 8th Century Textiles in Japan from the Shōsōin and Hōryūji* (Kyoto: Shikosha, 1984), cat. 129.

11. In addition to the *hanpi* just noted, see the following examples from exhibition catalogues of the annual Shōsōin exhibition at Nara National Museum: *Shōsōin-ten* (Nara: Nara National Museum, 1991), cat. 28; *Shōsōin-ten* (Nara: Nara National Museum, 1989), cats. 28, 29; and *Shōsōin-ten* (Nara: Nara National Museum, 1974), cat. 26.

12. *Shōsōin-ten* (Nara: Nara National Museum, 1992), cat. 26. This same *hanpi* was exhibited also in 1974 as cat. 28. See also *Shōsōin-ten* (Nara: Nara National Museum, 1978), cat. 25.

13. The difference in materials between the bodice and skirt of the Shōsōin *hanpi* might support a hypothesis that the Qing *chao fu* originally developed from two separate garments. Verity Wilson has questioned this theory, stating that the only evidence to support it is an anomalous seventeenth-century skirt (which looks like the skirt of a *chao fu*) in the Victoria and Albert Museum. According to Wilson, if the *hanpi* do point to a two-piece prototype, that prototype is much earlier in history than Cammann has suggested. See Cammann, *China's Dragon Robes*, 138–139; Vollmer, *Five Colours of the Universe*, 30 n. 1; and Wilson, *Chinese Dress*, 33.

14. See Wang Binghua et al., *The Ancient Corpses of Xinjiang and their Culture (Xinjiang gu shi: gu dai Xinjiang ju min ji qi wen hua)* (in Chinese and English), trans. Victor H. Mair (Ürümqi, Xinjiang: Xinjiang ren min chu ban she, 2002), 149–155; and Li Wunying, "Section Three: Yingpan Burial Ground," trans. Edith Cheung, in *Recent Excavations of Textiles in China*, ed. Zhao Feng (Hong Kong: ISAT/Costume Squad Ltd., 2002), 40, 58.

15. Cammann, *China's Dragon Robes*, 50.

16. Wilson, *Chinese Dress*, 29 ff. This robe is now in the Victoria and Albert Museum in London.

17. See Pamela Kyle Crossley, *The Manchus* (Cambridge, Mass. and Oxford: Blackwell Publishers, 1997), 10–11; and Edwin O. Reischauer and John K. Fairbank, *East Asia: The Great Tradition* (Boston: Houghton Mifflin, 1960), 364, 369.

18. Sir John Francis Davis, *China: A General Description of That Empire and Its Inhabitants* (London: John Murray, 1857), 1:32. The author was governor of Hong Kong and the English plenipotentiary in China.

19. Crossley, *The Manchus*, 129.

20. Mark C. Elliott, *The Manchu Way* (Stanford: Stanford University Press, 2001), 204.

21. Reishchauer and Fairbank, *East Asia: The Great Tradition*, 364.

22. Hong Taiji was mistakenly referred to in older histories as "Abahai," and in some Chinese references as Huang Taiji. See Elliott, *The Manchu Way*, 396 n. 71. The edicts are found in *Donghua lu, chongde* 1.19b ff, 2.8b ff; and *Taizong wenhuangdi shilu* 32.8 ff, 34.26b ff. Cited in Cammann, *China's Dragon Robes*, 20.

23. Cammann, *China's Dragon Robes*, 24 n. 7.

24. "Introduction," in *Huang-ch'ao li-ch'i t'u-shih [Huangchaoliqitushi]* 5.6; quoted in Cammann, *China's Dragon Robes*, 50.

25. See Wilson, *Chinese Dress*, 27.

26. See Elliott, *The Manchu Way*, 704–709; Wilson, *Chinese Dress*, 27–28; and Zhou and Gao, *5000 Years*, 172.

27. Zhou and Gao, *5000 Years*, 140.

28. See Elliott, *The Manchu Way*, 400 n. 104; Reischauer and Fairbank, *East Asia: The Great Tradition*, 364; and Cammann, *China's Dragon Robes*, 21.

29. Zhou and Gao, *5000 Years*, 172–173.

30. Ibid., 147 and 160, pl. 275.

31. Wilson, *Chinese Dress*, 29; citing Zhang Dechang, *Qing ji yige jing guan de shenghuo* (The life of a capital official in the late Qing) (Hong Kong, 1970), 16. See also Zhou and Gao, *5000 Years*, 173.

32. Cammann, *China's Dragon Robes*, 193.

33. Wilson, *Chinese Dress*, 29, citing the Chinese textile historian Chen Juanjuan.

34. Cao Xueqin, *The Story of the Stone*, 5 vols., trans. David Hawkes and John Minford (Bloomington, Indiana: Indiana University Press, 1973–1987), 2:567; quoted in Wilson, *Chinese Dress*, 29. Wilson is quoting from a different edition than that listed in the bibliography in the present publication.

35. Vollmer, *In the Presence*, 31; quoting Helen Fernald, *Chinese Court Costumes* (Toronto: Royal Ontario Museum of Archaeology, 1946), 14.

36. Cammann, *China's Dragon Robes*, Appendices D and E.

37. Margaret Medley, *The "Illustrated Regulations for Ceremonial Paraphernalia of the Ch'ing Dynasty"* (London: Han-Shan Tan, 1982), 1. Reprinted from *Transactions of the Oriental Ceramic Society* 31 (1958–1959): 95–104.

38. Cammann, *China's Dragon Robes*, Appendix D.

39. Wilson, *Chinese Dress*, 17.

40. Zhou and Gao, *5000 Years*, 182.

41. Verity Wilson suggests that it might be a vestigial scabbard slide (*Chinese Dress*, 36).

42. Cammann, *China's Dragon Robes*, 97; and Wilson, *Chinese Dress*, 18.

43. Cammann, *China's Dragon Robes*, 193.

44. Ibid.

45. Metropolitan Museum of Art, 35.84.8 and 32.2.3.

46. See the Chia-ch'ing edition of the *Hui-tien shih-li [Huidian shili]*, p. 262.20, p. 263.15b, p. 263.18b, p. 263.21b, 22, and p. 263.30b. Cited in Schuyler Cammann, "The Development of the Mandarin Square," *Harvard Journal of Asiatic Studies* 8 (1944–1945): 86–87.

47. Cao, *The Story of the Stone*, 5:120.

48. Ibid., 5:117.

49. P. C. Hsieh, *The Government of China, 1644–1911* (Baltimore, 1925), 106–107; cited in Cammann, "The Development of the Mandarin Square," 87 n. 47.

50. John King Fairbank, Edwin O. Reischauer, and Albert M. Craig, *East Asia: The Modern Transformation* (Boston: Houghton Mifflin, 1965), 88.

51. Cammann, "The Development of the Mandarin Square," 87.

52. See the exhibition catalogue *The China Trade and its Influences* (New York: Harbor Press, 1941), pl. 92, 93, 98. I am grateful to Joyce Denney for calling my attention to this catalogue.

53. Wilson, *Chinese Dress*, 17, fig. 6.

54. Wilson, *Chinese Dress*, 17, fig. 6; and citing Zhang Dechang, *Qing ji yige jing guan de shenghuo*.

55. Lady Hosie, *Two Gentlemen of China* (London, 1924), 83; cited in Wilson, *Chinese Dress*, 17.

56. See, for example, the early-twentieth-century portrait of Edward Brenan in the Victoria and Albert Museum. Brenan was a Deputy Commissioner in the Imperial Chinese Maritime Customs. The portrait is reproduced in Wilson, *Chinese Dress*, 13.

57. Wilson, *Chinese Dress*, 12 and n. 2.

58. Verity Wilson, "Studio and Soirée: The Use and Misuse of Chinese Textiles in a European Setting," in *Textiles in Trade*, Proceedings of the Textile Society of America (Los Angeles: Textile Society of America, 1990), 217; and Wilson, *Chinese Dress*, 100, citing A. S. Roe, *China As I Saw It: A Woman's Letters from the Celestial Empire* (London, 1910), 88, and John Henry Gray, *Walks in the City of Canton* (1875; reprint, San Francisco, 1974), 468.

59. Cammann, *China's Dragon Robes*, 97.

60. See Wilson, *Chinese Dress*, 50–51, pl. 32, 33.

61. Ibid., 47. See portrait of a Qing empress in Zhou and Gao, *5000 Years*, pl. 301.

62. Illustrated in Wilson, *Chinese Dress*, 47 and pl. 27.

63. Illustrated in ibid., pl. 35.

64. Verity Wilson has questioned whether this might be a man's *long pao*, despite the side slits. Written communication, October 2001.

65. Beverley Jackson and David Hugus, *Ladder to the Clouds: Intrigue and Tradition in Chinese Rank* (Berkeley: Ten Speed Press, 1999), 102; and Valery M. Garrett, *Mandarin Squares* (Oxford: Oxford University Press, 1990), 33.

66. Names in quotation marks are Robert Thorp's translations of mythical or semi-mythical animals. There is a great deal of variation in the ways that these creatures are portrayed. The "unicorn" often has two horns, the "rhinoceros" sometimes looks like a goat, and the "sea horse" may resemble a horse. Robert L. Thorp, *Son of Heaven: Imperial Arts of China* (Seattle: Son of Heaven Press, 1988), 82–85.

67. Illustrated in Jackson and Hugus, *Ladder to the Clouds*, 105–106.

68. See Cammann, *China's Dragon Robes*, 18.

69. Garrett, *Mandarin Squares*, 37.

70. See Zhou and Gao, *5000 Years*, 194, fig. 343 (Qing titled lady); and Wilson, *Chinese Dress*, 48, fig. 35.

71. See Vollmer, *Decoding Dragons*, 24, 30, fig. 5; and Wilson, *Chinese Dress*, 48.

72. The photograph of Wan Rong (1906–1940), Emperor Xuantong's empress, is illustrated in *De Verboden Stad: Hofcultuur van de Chinese keizers (1644–1911) (The Forbidden City: Court Culture of the Chinese Emperors [1644–1911])* (Rotterdam: Museum Boymans-van Beuningen, 1990), 88. See also Zhou and Gao, *5000 Years*, fig. 301; and "Portrait of Empress Xiaoxian" (1712–1748), ink and color on silk, hanging scroll, Palace Museum, Beijing, illus-

trated in *De Verboden Stad*, 123, pl. 2, and also in Thorp, *Son of Heaven*, 87 (as "Portrait of the Empress Xiaoxianchun").

73. Wilson, *Chinese Dress*, 48, fig. 35.

74. Zhou and Gao, *5000 Years*, 194, fig. 343.

75. Cammann, "The Development of the Mandarin Square," 86–87.

76. Illustrated in Vollmer, *Decoding Dragons*, pl. 19.

77. Illustrated in Zhou and Gao, *5000 Years*, 194, fig. 345.

78. In a Ming dynasty *kesi* (tapestry-woven) panel in the Metropolitan Museum of Art, the phoenix stands on one foot on a rock at the bottom center of the panel, surrounded by a silver pheasant, a paradise flycatcher, a crane, a goose, a peacock, a golden pheasant, a parrot, a kingfisher, a mandarin duck, and two unidentified birds. James C. Y. Watt and Joyce Denney, "Tapestry-Woven Panel," in "Recent Acquisitions: A Selection: 1994–1995," *Bulletin of the Metropolitan Museum of Art* (Fall 1995): 77.

79. See Verity Wilson, "Cosmic Raiment: Daoist Traditions of Liturgical Clothing," *Orientations* (May 1995): 42–49.

80. *Wenwu*, 1978, no. 4. Discussed in Wilson, "Cosmic Raiment," 44 and figs. 6a, 6b.

81. Stephen Little, entry for Cat. 8, in Stephen Little with Shawn Eichman, *Taoism and the Arts of China* (Chicago: The Art Institute of Chicago in association with University of California Press, 2000), 128.

82. Shawn Eichman, entries for Cats. 65–67, in ibid., 228–229; and Little, entries for Cats. 117, 118, in ibid., 321.

83. Little, entry for Cat. 14, in ibid., 139. Little is following Isabelle Robinet, *Daoism: Growth of a Religion*, trans. Phyllis Brooks (Stanford: Stanford University Press, 1997), 234–236.

84. Kristofer Schipper, "Taoism: The Story of the Way," in Little and Eichman, *Taosim and the Arts of China*, 40; Eichman, entry for Cat. 22, in same, 151; and Little, entries for Cats. 46–51, in same, 195.

85. Little, entry for Cat. 10, in Little and Eichman, *Taosim and the Arts of China*, 130.

86. Little, entry for Cat. 8, in ibid., 128.

87. Little, entry for Cat. 10, in ibid., 130.

88. C. A. S. Williams, *Outlines of Chinese Symbols and Art Motifs* (Rutland, Vermont and Tokyo: Charles E. Tuttle, 1974), 192.

89. Shen Fu, *Six Records of a Floating Life*, trans. Leonard Pratt and Chiang Su-hui (London: Penguin Books, 1983), 131.

90. Young Y. Chung, *The Art of Oriental Embroidery: History, Aesthetics, and Techniques* (New York: Charles Scribner's Sons, 1983), 28.

91. Francesca Bray, *Technology and Gender: Fabrics of Power in Late Imperial China* (Berkeley, Los Angeles, and London: University of California Press, 1997), 259–260, 267.

92. Shen Fu, *Six Records of a Floating Life*, 45.

93. Ibid., 78.

94. Ibid., 68.

95. Ibid., 64.

96. Ibid., 116.

97. Ibid., 77.

98. Mozuizi in Wuwei County, Gansu Province, and Mawangdui in Changsha, Hunan Province. See Zhou and Gao, *5000 Years*, 44 and fig. 67.

99. See Nara National Museum, *Shōsōin-ten* (Nara: Nara National Museum, 1992), pl. 27.

100. See Zhou and Gao, *5000 Years*, figs. 217, 218.

101. See ibid., figs. 282, 287 (reproduction of a Ming lady from the picture album, *Leisurely Pursuits*).

102. Dale Gluckman, written communication, December 2001.

103. Illustrated in Zhou and Gao, *5000 Years*, 216, fig. 379.

104. Joshua Fogel, "Kangaku Travellers," in *The Literature of Travel in the Japanese Rediscovery of China: 1862–1945* (Stanford: Stanford University Press, 1996), 66–125. See also Fairbank, Reischauer, and Craig, *East Asia: The Modern Transformation*, 382–384.

105. Fogel, "Kangaku Travellers," 66.

106. Fairbank, Reischauer, and Craig, *East Asia: The Modern Transformation*, 631.

107. Harold Burnham, *Chinese Velvets* (Toronto: University of Toronto Press, 1959), 9.

108. Ibid., 11.

109. Cammann, *China's Dragon Robes*, 194–195.

110. W. H. Medhurst, *The Foreigner in Far Cathay* (1872; reprint, San Francisco: Chinese Materials Center, 1977), 79.

111. Davis, *China: A General Description*, 1:390.

112. Ibid., 1:388.

113. Ibid., 1:390.

114. Shen Fu, *Six Records of a Floating Life*, 77.

115. From a larger inventory of the Jia family goods. Cao, *The Story of the Stone*, 5:120.

116. Ibid., 2:567, 5:120.

117. Lotus Stack, *The Pile Thread* (Minneapolis: Minneapolis Museum of Art, 1991), 5.

118. Cheng Weiji, *History of Textile Technology of Ancient China* (New York: Science Press, 1992), 260–261.

119. Stack, *The Pile Thread*, 14.

120. H. Burnham, *Chinese Velvets*, 17.

121. The robe was excavated from the Dingling imperial tomb in Beijing (during 1956–1958). See Cheng, *History of Textile Technology*, 425–426.

122. Ibid., 425.

123. Gao Hanyu, *Chinese Textile Designs*, tr. Rosemary Scott and Susan Whitfield (London: Viking, 1992), 20. First published in Chinese as *Zhongguo lidai zhi ran xiu tulu* (Hong Kong: The Commercial Press, 1986).

124. See H. Burnham, *Chinese Velvets*, 9 ff, for a review of this literature.

125. Ibid., 11; citing the sixteenth-century travelogue, *Perigrinacam*, by the self-confessed adventurer Fernão Mendes Pinto.

126. H. Burnham, *Chinese Velvets*, 5.

127. Donald Ferguson, "Letters from Portuguese Captives in Canton" (written in 1534 and 1536 [or possibly 1524]), *The Indian Antiquary* 30, 31 (1901–02): 64; cited in H. Burnham, *Chinese Velvets*, 11.

128. T'ien-tse Chang, *Sino-Portuguese Trade from 1514–1644* (Leyden, 1934), 98–99; Henri Bernard, S.J., *Aux Portes de la Chine* (Tientsin, 1933), 165; and Montalto de Jesu, *Historic Macao* (Hong Kong, 1902), 35. Cited in H. Burnham, *Chinese Velvets*, 13.

129. *The Voyage of Jan Hughyen van Lonschoten to the East Indies*, Hakluyt Society, series 1, nos. 70, 71 (London, 1885), 1:136, 150; see also 1:147–148. Cited in H. Burnham, *Chinese Velvets*, 14–15.

130. Pasquale M. d'Elia, S. M., *Fonti Ricciane* (Rome, 1942–49), 1:20 n. 7; and Tacchi Venturi, *Opere Storiche del Matteo Ricci* (Macerata, 1913), 2:98. Cited in H. Burnham, *Chinese Velvets*, 15.

131. Antonio da Morga, *Sucesos de las Islas Filipinas* (Mexico, 1609), 161; cited in H. Burnham, *Chinese Velvets*, 15.

132. *The Voyage of John Saris to Japan, 1613*, ed. Sir Ernest M. Satowl, K. C. M. G., Hakluyt Society, series 2, no. 5 (London, 1900), 216, 227; cited in H. Burnham, *Chinese Velvets*, 15.

133. H. Burnham, *Chinese Velvets*, 20–21.

134. See Vollmer, *Decoding Dragons*, 18–19. Dale Gluckman has pointed out that by the late Qing, the loop and toggle was used throughout Chinese dress, and had lost its specific association with the Manchus (written communication, December 2001).

135. Zhou and Gao, *5000 Years*, 172.

136. Verity Wilson raised the possibility that this might be a man's vest (written communication, June 2001).

137. *De Verboden Stad*, 197.

138. Verity Wilson, written communication, June 2001.

139. Dale Gluckman and Verity Wilson have both made this suggestion, although both agree that the garment could have been worn by a Chinese woman as well. Gluckman, oral communication, December 2001; Wilson, written communication, June 2001.

140. References for this section include Cammann, *China's Dragon Robes*, 77–107; Chung, *The Art of Oriental Embroidery*, 163–173; *De Verboden Stad*, 102–117; Wolfram Eberhard, *A Dictionary of Chinese Symbols*, trans. G. L. Campbell (London and New York: Routledge and Kegan Paul, 1986); Mae Anna Pang, *Dragon Emperor: Treasures from the Forbidden City* (Melbourne: National Gallery of Victoria, 1988), 42–52; Vollmer, *Decoding Dragons*, 58–164; Vollmer, *Five Colours of the Universe*, 46–47, 63, 65–66; Williams, *Outlines of Chinese Symbols and Art Motifs*; Qiguang Zhao, "Dragon: The Symbol of China," *Oriental Art* (Summer 1991): 72–80; Terese Tse Bartholomew, *Myths and Rebuses in Chinese Art* (San Francisco: Asian Art Museum of San Francisco, 1988); Terese Tse Bartholomew, *The Hundred Flowers: Botanical Motifs in Chinese Art* (San Francisco: Asian Art Museum of San Francisco, 1985); and Jacobsen, *Imperial Silks*, 1169–1177.

141. Eberhard, *A Dictionary of Chinese Symbols*, 168–169.

142. Cheng, *History of Textile Technology*, 164.

143. James Legge, trans., *The Shoo King or The Book of Historical Documents* [*Shujing*] (1865; reprint, Taipei: Southern Materials Center, 1985), 79–80.

144. See Chung, *The Art of Oriental Embroidery*, 45, figs. 3–7.

145. Cammann, *China's Dragon Robes*, 87. In 1651 Kuang Lanzhao, a censor, wrote a memorial to the emperor suggesting that he wear traditional Chinese ceremonial garments (including robes with the Twelve Symbols) to conduct the annual sacrifices. The memorial was rejected at the time. It is included in the *Shizu zhang huangdi shilu* 54.18b.

146. Cammann, *China's Dragon Robes*, 86.

147. The lotus is variously named *hehua* and *lianhua*. *He* means harmony, and *lian*, continuous. Bartholomew, *Myths and Rebuses*, unpaginated.

148. *De Verboden Stad*, 114.

149 Bartholomew, *Myths and Rebuses*, unpaginated.

150. Bartholomew, *The Hundred Flowers*, 2.

151. Qiguang Zhao, "Dragon: The Symbol of China," 72–73.

152. Ibid., 77.

153. This description is attributed to Wang Fu, a writer of the Later Han dynasty. See *Eryayi* 28.1b, noted in Cammann, *China's Dragon Robes*, 77–78. See also *De Verboden Stad*, 107.

154. Eberhard, *A Dictionary of Chinese Symbols*, 234.

155. Ibid., 194–195; and Little, entry for Cat. 25, in Little and Eichman, *Taosim and the Arts of China*, 155.

156. Chung, *The Art of Oriental Embroidery*, 170.

157. Ibid., 168.

158. Williams, *Outlines of Chinese Symbols and Art Motifs*, 157.

159. Thorp, *Son of Heaven*, 73.

160. Wilson states that the office was established by the Kangxi emperor (1654–1722), while Cammann states that it was set up a few years earlier, in 1652, in conjunction with a series of textile-related regulations. Wilson, *Chinese Dress*, 97; Cammann, *China's Dragon Robes*, 116.

161. Wilson, *Chinese Dress*, 98.

162. E-tu Zen Sun, "Sericulture and Silk Textile Production in Ch'ing China," in *Economic Organization in Chinese Society*, ed. W. E. Willmott, Studies in Chinese Society (Stanford: Stanford University Press, 1972), 100. Citing Shih Min-hsiung, *Ch'ing tai ssu chih kung yeh ti fa chan* (The development of the silk textile industry in the Ch'ing period) (Taipei: Commercial Press, 1968), 14; and "K'ao kung-tien" (Section on industries), ch. 10 ("Textile production"), in *K'u chin t'u shu chi ch'eng* (The great compendium of published works in China since ancient times) (reprint, Taipei: Wen Hsing shu tien, 1964).

163. Wilson, *Chinese Dress*, 97 ff.

164. Sun, "Sericulture and Silk Textile Production," 99–101.

165. Wilson, *Chinese Dress*, 98–99; and citing *Silk: Replies from Commissioners of Customs . . .*, Maritime Customs 2, Special Series, no. 3 (1881;

reprint, Shanghai, 1917), 33, 36, 63–64, 83–84, 143. See also Sun, "Sericulture and Silk Textile Production," 79–80, for comments on Shanxi.

166. Wilson states that "no silk has been found in any western collection which bears the mark of [the official in charge of the Zhi ran ju] or the establishment under his charge" (*Chinese Dress*, 97).

167. Sun, "Sericulture and Silk Textile Production," 95.

168. Ibid., 98.

169. "K'ao kung-tien" (Section on industries), ch. 10 ("Textile production"), in *K'u chin t'u shu chi ch'eng (Ku jin tu shu ji cheng)*; quoted by Sun, who states that Shih Min-hsiung reports similar conditions for Nanjing ("Sericulture and Silk Textile Production," 96). See Shih Min-hsiung, *Ch'ing tai ssu chih kung yeh ti fa chan (Qing dai si zhi gong ye di fa zhan)*, 1977.

170. Wilson, "Studio and Soirée," 217–222, and Wilson, *Chinese Dress*, 100, citing Roe, *China As I Saw It*, 88, and Gray, *Walks in the City of Canton*, 468.

171. Cammann, *China's Dragon Robes*, 110; with information from Ying-hsing Sung [Song Yingxing], *T'ien-kung k'ai-wu [Diangongkaiwu]* 2.12 (1637), a work on basic industries, and one of the few works in the Ming to describe the production of "dragon robes."

172. *Ta Ch'ing hui-tien [Daqinghuidian]* (Qing dynastic statues), K'ang-hsi edition, 136; cited in Cammann, *China's Dragon Robes*, 117.

173. Cao, *The Story of the Stone*, 5:119–121.

174. Wilson, *Chinese Dress*, 98; *Chinese Repository* (August 1835): 185.

175. Garrett, *Mandarin Squares*, 57.

176. Wilson, *Chinese Dress*, 105; citing a note on the back of a watercolor of a woman embroidering (ca. 1790, Victoria and Albert Museum).

177. Ibid., 106; citing *Silk: Replies from Commissioners of Customs . . .*, 75.

178. Shen Fu, *Six Records of a Floating Life*, 25. See also Lucy Soothill, *A Passport to China* (London, 1931), 181–182; cited in Wilson, *Chinese Dress*, 105.

179. Information in this section is from these two texts as compiled in Cammann, *China's Dragon Robes*, 112–115.

180. Joyce Store, *The Thames and Hudson Manual of Dyes and Fabrics* (London: Thames and Hudson, 1978), 73–74.

181. See *Catalogue of the Shanghai Customs Collection* (Shanghai, 1873), 46–47; and *Returns of Trade at the Treaty Ports in China for the Year 1871* (Shanghai, 1872), 153 for records of the importation of aniline dyes. Noted in Cammann, *China's Dragon Robes*, 63 n. 17.

182. Gray, *Walks in the City of Canton*; quoted in Garrett, *Mandarin Squares*, 54.

183. Wilson, *Chinese Dress*, 109; and Gray, *Walks in the City of Canton*, 290.

184. L. P. Stodulski, D. Nauman, and M. Kennedy, "Technical Appendix: Analysis of Precious Metal Threads," in Peggy Gilfoy, *Fabrics in Celebration from the Collection* (Indianapolis: Indianapolis Museum of Art, 1983), 373–374.

185. Garrett, *Mandarin Squares*, 53–54.

186. S. W. Williams, *Chinese Commercial Guide*, 5th ed. (Hong Kong, 1863), 93; cited in Cammann, *China's Dragon Robes*, 124.

187. Sun, "Sericulture and Silk Textile Production," 104; citing Ch'uan Han-sheng and U. C. Wang, "Ch'ing tai jen k'ou ti pien tung" (Population changes in China during the Ch'ing dynasty), *Bulletin of the Institute of History and Philology*, 32 (1961): 156, table 4.

188. Ping-ti Ho, *Studies on the Population of China: 1368–1953* (Cambridge, Mass.: Harvard University Press, 1959), 243; cited in Sun, "Sericulture and Silk Textile Production," 104.

189. Wilson, *Chinese Dress*, 98; Sun, "Sericulture and Silk Textile Production," 107.

190. Cammann, *China's Dragon Robes*, 124.

191. In the *Catalogue of the Shanghai Customs Collection*, published in Vienna in 1873, the Chinese referred to aniline dyes as "first rank colors," or *yipinse*. See Cammann, *China's Dragon Robes*, 124 and n. 38.

192. Cammann, *China's Dragon Robes*, 123–124.

JAPAN

Contents

Chronology

Jōmon	ca. 10,000–ca. 300 BCE
Yayoi	ca. 300 BCE–ca. 300 CE
Kofun	ca. 300–552
Asuka	552–645
Hakuhō	645–710
Nara	710–794
Heian	794–1185
Kamakura	1185–1336
Nanbokuchō	1336–1392
Muromachi	1392–1573
Momoyama	1573–1615
Edo	1615–1868
Modern period	1868–

Meiji	1868–1912
Taishō	1912–1926
Shōwa	1926–1989
Heisei	1989–

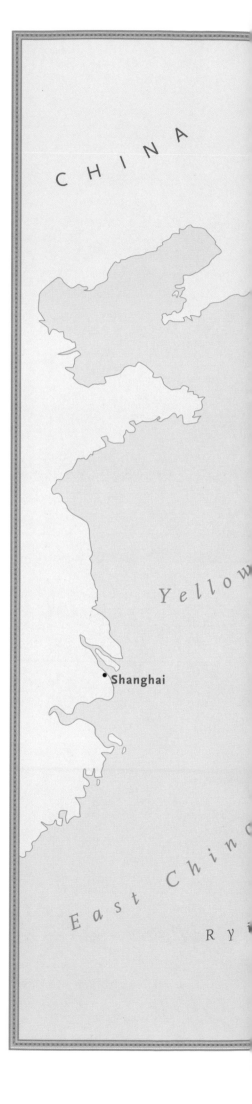

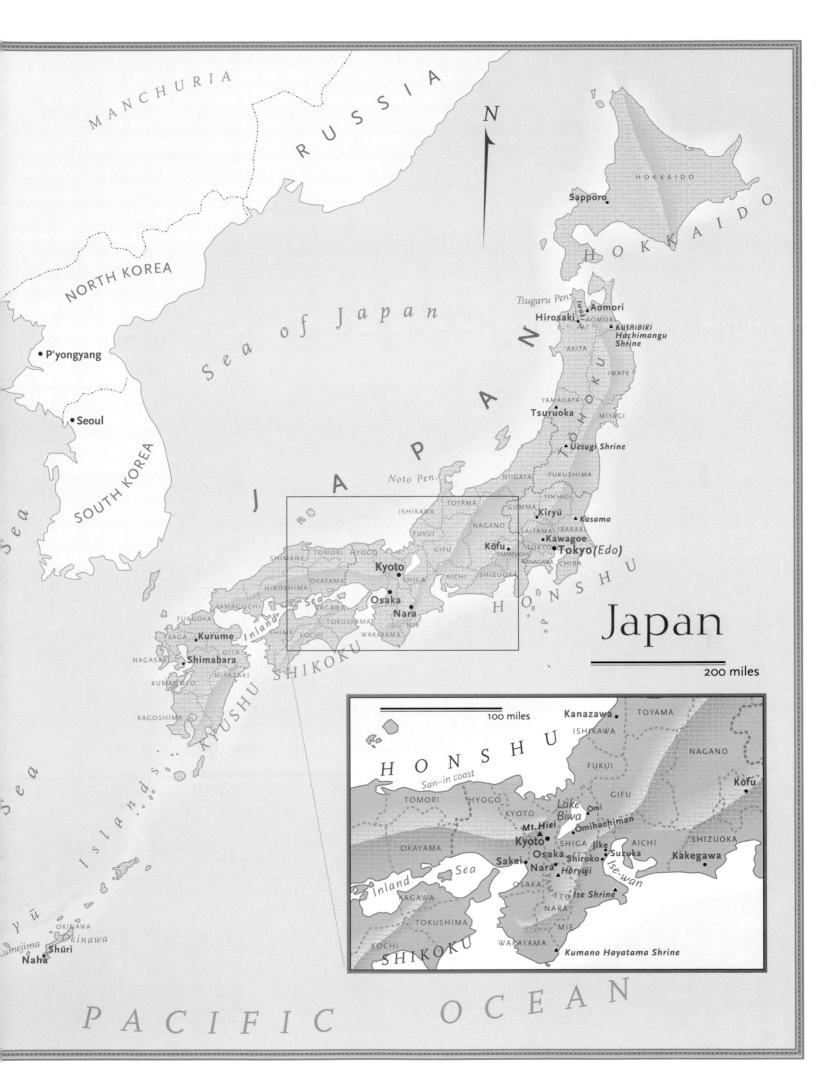

Japan

200 miles

Inset map

100 miles

HONSHU

San–in coast

TOMORI · HYOGO · KYOTO · Lake Biwa · Omi · GIFU · FUKUI · NAGANO

Kanazawa · ISHIKAWA · TOYAMA

Kōfu

Mt. Hiei · SHIGA · Omihachiman · AICHI · SHIZUOKA

Kyoto · Jike · Suzuka · Kakegawa

Osaka · Shiroko

OKAYAMA · Sakai · Nara · Hōryūji · Ise-wan

Inland Sea · KAGAWA · OSAKA · YAMATO · Ise Shrine

TOKUSHIMA · NARA · MIE

KOCHI · WAKAYAMA · Kumano Hayatama Shrine

SHIKOKU

Main map

MANCHURIA

RUSSIA

N

NORTH KOREA

• P'yongyang

• Seoul

SOUTH KOREA

East Sea

Sea of Japan

J A P A N

HOKKAIDO

Sapporo •

Tsugaru Pen.

Iwaki · **Aomori**
Hirosaki · AOMORI · Kushibiki Hachimangu Shrine

AKITA

IWATE

YAMAGATA · MIYAGI

Tsuruoka

▲ Uesugi Shrine

T O H O K U

Noto Pen.

NIIGATA · FUKUSHIMA

ISHIKAWA · TOYAMA

GUMMA

NAGANO · **Kiryū** · ▲ Kasama

FUKUI

SHIMANE · TOMORI · HYOGO · GIFU · SAITAMA · IBARAKI

Kōfu · YAMANASHI · TOKYO · **Kawagoe**
Kyoto · SHIGA · AICHI · SHIZUOKA · KANAGAWA · CHIBA

Tokyo (Edo)

HIROSHIMA · OKAYAMA

Osaka
Nara · MIE

H O N S H U

YAMAGUCHI · Inland Sea · KAGAWA · WAKAYAMA

FUKUOKA · EHIME · TOKUSHIMA

SAGA · KOCHI

Kurume · OITA

NAGASAKI

Shimabara · MIYAZAKI

KUMAMOTO

KAGOSHIMA

K Y U S H U

S H I K O K U

S E A

R y ū k y ū I s l a n d s

OKINAWA · umejima · Okinawa

Shūri

Naha

P A C I F I C   O C E A N

Introduction

Collectors change, as do their tastes. Museum curators and directors focus on different things in different times. In the late nineteenth and early twentieth centuries, many Western collectors, as well as curators, were fascinated by superb drawloom and jacquard-woven silks such as those from Nishijin in Kyoto, and by magnificent embroideries in soft, glossy silks and rich colors. After the Second World War, many Westerners were drawn to simpler textiles—to plain woven cottons and hemp—patterned in the weaving with stripes, checks, or *kasuri* designs, or on the cloth with stencil-dyed or painted patterns. If the Japanese textile collections of the early twentieth century were characterized by rich colors and glossy silks, it may be said that many collections of the last decades were dominated by deep indigo blue with reserved white patterns (and occasional bold splashes of red) on plain woven cottons, hemp, and ramie. Sometimes collectors deliberately sought coarse materials and uneven, rough workmanship, shunning the elegant silks and virtuosic skill that had entranced their forebears earlier in the century.

Part of this shift on behalf of Western collectors may be attributed to the work of the Japan Folkcraft Movement, and to the attention drawn by British potter Bernard Leach (1887–1979) to Japan's rich heritage of crafts designed for everyday use. The Japan Folkcraft Movement (Nihon Mingei Kyōkai—literally, "Japan People's Art/Craft Association") was founded in 1926 by the potters Hamada Shōjiro, Kawai Kanjirō, and Tomimoto Kenkichi, and their colleague, the art historian Yanagi Sōetsu (1889–1961). Yanagi was a close friend of Bernard Leach, who introduced the Japanese art historian to the work of William Morris and the British Arts and Crafts Movement. Espousing the beauty of ordinary, functional objects, these men traveled the country collecting rural textiles, lacquer, and ceramics. Drawing both from ideas associated with the British Arts and Crafts Movement and from Japan's tradition of honoring rustic simplicity within the arts of tea (or the "tea ceremony"), Yanagi began championing the beauty of "folk" objects in his extensive writings. In 1931 Yanagi and his colleagues established a publication; its successor, *Mingei*, continues today. In 1936, with growing public support, he completed work on the building that is now the Japan Folk Craft Museum (Nihon Mingeikan) in Komaba, Tokyo, home to the association and repository for the collections made by its founders.

In 1972, Leach and Hamada introduced a small collection of Yanagi's extensive writings to Western audiences as *The Unknown Craftsman: A Japanese Insight into Beauty.*[1] This book helped spark Western interest in Japan's "folk" heritage and the philosophical web that Hamada, Kawai, Yanagi, and Leach had woven around it. Although the term "folk" or "folkcraft" (*mingei*) is misleading—encompassing, as it does, a wide range of textiles from Okinawan (Ryūkyūan) royal costume, to the output of professional urban workshops, to roughly stitched work vests from the mountains of Tōhoku, far to the north of Tokyo—the term has stuck in both languages, apparently striking a chord in the late-twentieth-century industrialized nations of Japan, Europe, and North America. Most collections of Japanese folk textiles in the West were assembled after the Second World War, and several important collections not until the last decades of the twentieth century, a period that has seen increasing dealer specialization in Japanese folk textiles, as well as major museum exhibitions that feature the strong, vibrant patterns, bold designs, and simple, sturdy construction of these nineteenth- and early-twentieth-century works.

The Spencer Museum collection of seventy-seven Japanese textiles reflects the changing tastes of collectors from the late nineteenth century to the end of the twentieth. Although only three small fragments are specifically connected to Sallie Casey Thayer's founding gift in 1917 (with a first accession date of 1928), many of the Japanese textiles (almost half of the collection) that are listed as "source unknown" were actually gifts from her (as evidenced by the large number of these textiles bearing Thayer tags). The largest group of textiles without provenance is a group of kimono and *obi* fragments dating from the late nineteenth and early twentieth centuries. These were joined in 1995 by five sample books that the museum received by transfer from the Cincinnati Museum of Art. Assembled when they entered the Cincinnati Museum

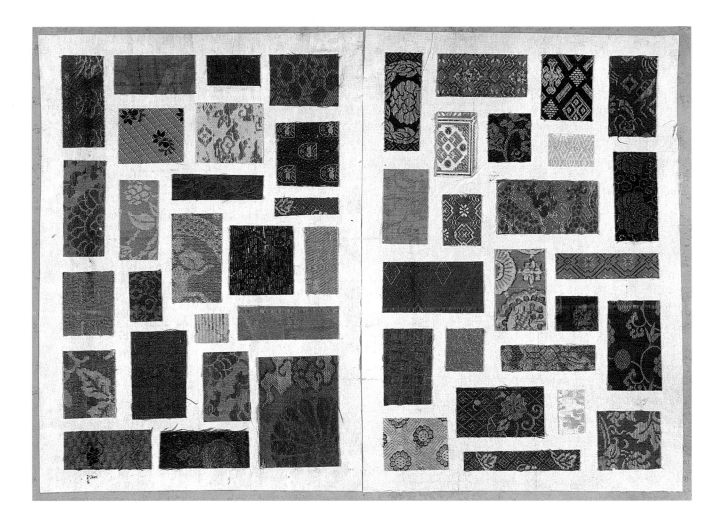

FIG. 12a

Pages from a sample book

Japan
Edo or Meiji period, 19th century
Silk, gold- and silver-wrapped thread,
and paper-backed gold and silver foil
on paper
Complex woven silks, some
embroidered
14.5 x 24 in.; 37 x 56 cm
Transfer from Cincinnati Museum of
Art, 1995.32

FIG. 12b

Page from a sample book

Japan
Edo or Meiji period, 19th century
Cotton on paper
Katazome (stencil and paste-resist
dyeing)
16 x 12 in.; 41.8 x 30.5 cm
Transfer from the Cincinnati Museum
of Art, 1995.33

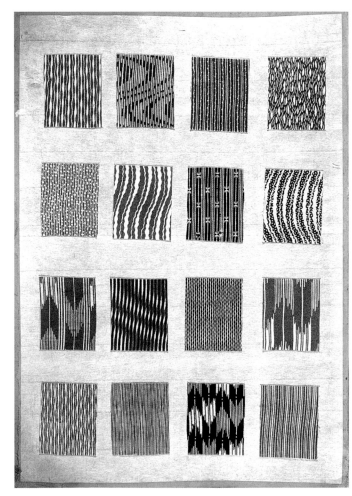

FIG. 13

Woman's Outer Kimono (*Uchikake*)

Japan
ca. 1953
Silk with gold- and silver-wrapped thread
Embroidery (couching, satin) on blue satin
ground
68 x 48.5 in.; 175.8 x 123 cm
Gift of Mrs. John Manwaring in memory of
Mr. and Mrs. Russell Gordon Smith, 1995.38

in the nineteenth or very early twentieth century, the books contain fragments of eighteenth- and nineteenth-century drawloom and jacquard-woven cloth (Fig. 12a), as well as swatches of stencil-dyed textiles (Fig. 12b). Also listed as "source unknown" are two splendid Meiji period (1868–1912) embroidered panels depicting red-crowned cranes among iris (Plates 90 and 91). It is difficult not to associate the crane and iris panels with Sallie Casey Thayer. It is unlikely that two such magnificent works should have entered the museum after the confusion of the initial years without a careful notation of their provenance, although to date, no evidence has been found to support a connection. Another textile that entered the United States in the early years of the twentieth century (but was not acquired by the museum until 1995) is a seventeenth-century *kesa*, or priest's robe, that had been part of the collections of the Traphagen School of Design in New York, founded by fashion designer Ethel Traphagen (1882–1963) (Plate 87).

The Japanese textile collection lay dormant for many years. After the 1928 accession date of the three Thayer fragments, no other documented textile entered the museum until the 1960s, when five textiles were given to the collection, including an eighteenth-century Buddhist

FIG. 14

Noh Robe Fragment (detail)

Japan
Edo period, 18th or early 19th century
Silk and gold-wrapped thread
Brocade on gold-patterned twill against
dangawari ground
Given in Memory of James H. Walker, Jr.
by his Family, 1993.349

priest's arm stole, or *ohi*, given by Rose K. Auerbach (Plate 89). Again there was a hiatus until the early 1990s, when the collection was augmented by several gifts of formal garments and other textiles including a twentieth-century wedding kimono and *obi* given by Mrs. David W. Isaac (Plate 86); and an *uchikake*, or outer kimono, given by Mrs. John Manwaring, who said that it had been presented to her parents, Mr. and Mrs. Russell Smith, when they arrived in Japan in the early 1950s to set up the Bank of America. The *uchikake* (Fig. 13), which was probably commissioned for the occasion, was presented with a lacquer stand and storage box. In 1993, as part of a larger gift, the family of James H. Walker, Jr. gave the museum fragments of an eighteenth- or early-nineteenth-century Noh robe (Fig. 14) and several embroidered gift covers (*fukusa*) (Plates 82–84).

In the 1990s, the Spencer actively acquired several significant Japanese textiles, including the Traphagen *kesa* and a collection of folk textiles dating from the nineteenth and early twentieth centuries (see Plates 67–73, and 78–81). An American collector working with a dealer who specialized in Japanese folk textiles—an unheard-of specialization earlier in the century when Sallie Casey Thayer was collecting—acquired most of this collection in Japan in the late 1970s and 1980s. As a group, these textiles exemplify the qualities that were admired by Yanagi Sōetsu and other founders of the Japan Folkcraft Movement, and represent a variety of techniques, materials, functions, and geographical sources. Most of these museum purchases were made possible by the generosity of the family of Barbara Benton Wescoe, which established a general acquisitions fund in her name.

Katazome and Tsutsugaki

KATAZOME (STENCIL AND PASTE-RESIST DYEING): HISTORICAL OVERVIEW

The use of stencils (*katagami*) to pattern textiles and other objects has a long history in Japan. The Shōsōin Repository of Imperial Treasures at the temple Tōdaiji in Nara contains seventeen examples of stenciled paper dating from the eighth century. The patterns on these *fuki-e* (blown pattern) papers were made by spraying pigment around cutouts placed on the paper, producing a reserved pattern against a background of scattered pigment. Stencils were used in the Heian period (794–1185) to decorate sutra (Buddhist scripture) papers with plant and animal motifs, a tradition seen again in a late-fourteenth-century set of decorated papers owned by the Kumano Hayatama Shrine in Wakayama Prefecture. In these *tatōgami* (pocket papers), the motifs, mostly graceful plants, are rendered in gold and silver foil attached to an adhesive base. Beginning in the Heian period, armor was also decorated with stenciled designs; the stencil—often made of sheet metal—was stamped into the soft deerskin, and the pattern brushed through it. A Kamakura period (1185–1336) suit of *ōyoroi* (great armor) owned by the Kushibiki Hachiman Shrine in Aomori Prefecture, for example, has a leather breastplate with an elaborate design of *shishi* (mythical lion-like creatures) and peonies on a foliated ground. As in many other examples of armor with stencil-dyed leather, the design was executed in blue and red against the soft brown of the hide. In all of these examples, no resist technique was used; the dyes were applied directly through openings in the stencil.[2]

Stencils and paste were used together to pattern Chinese Ming dynasty (1368–1644) textiles with gold and silver foil by applying an adhesive (probably soybean based) through a stencil, and then affixing gold or silver foil to the adhesive. Imported into and imitated in Japan, these luxurious *surihaku* textiles, as they were known, were fashionable among Japan's warrior elite in the Momoyama period (1573–1615), and were adapted for use within the stately Noh dance/drama. As in the examples cited above, *surihaku* stencils were used to create a positive pattern; i.e., the openings in the stencil became the pattern on the finished textile.

At this writing, the earliest extant example of stencil dyeing with a resist process is a pair of gauntlets from the Kamakura period with small, scattered wisteria roundels reserved in white against a light indigo-blue hemp ground, owned by the Kasuga Taisha Shrine in Nara.[3] Late Heian and Kamakura picture scrolls, however, depict *bushi* (warriors) and commoners wearing what appear to be stencil- and paste-resist-dyed clothing. The many varieties of patterns suggest that some form of stencil and paste-resist dyeing was known by the late twelfth century, and became fairly widespread by the fourteenth.[4]

A sixteenth-century *katabira* is the earliest of a group of superb late Muromachi (1392–1573) and Momoyama period stencil- and paste-resist-dyed garments associated with three great feudal warlords—Uesugi Kenshin (1530–1578), Oda Nobunaga (1534–1582), and Tokugawa Ieyasu (1542–1616)—and the warrior-sponsored Komparu Noh family. A *katabira* is an elegant unlined summer *kosode* (precursor to the modern kimono) usually made of very high quality hemp or ramie. This *katabira*, traditionally associated with Uesugi Kenshin and preserved in the Uesugi Shrine in Yamagata Prefecture, is decorated with a *komon*, or "small pattern," design of tiny all-over floral motifs, and a handsome set of paulownia crests.

The production of this *katabira* required exceptional materials, consummate skill, and a sophisticated understanding of the properties of paste and dye. The stencil paper had to be thin enough to permit the cutting of intricate patterns, totally waterproof, flexible, and yet tough enough to allow for the meticulously cut patterns to maintain their crisp edges through multiple uses. The paste had to be malleable enough to fill each small perforation in the stencil, hard enough not to spread and blur the crisp edges of the tiny patterns, soft enough not to crack when it dried, and dense enough to resist penetration by the dye. Whatever materials had been used for stencils and resist paste before this time, most scholars agree that by the late Muromachi period, craftsmen were using persimmon-soaked mulberry paper stencils with a rice-paste resist, making and handling these materials with great skill.[5]

There are several sets of paintings from the seventeenth and eighteenth centuries that

FIG. 15
Kunichika Toyohara
(1835–1900)
Clear Breeze by Ryōgoku Bridge
From *Eight Views of Edo*

Japan
Edo or Meiji period, 19th century
Color woodblock print (triptych)
a. 13.6 x 9.3 in.; 34.7 x 23.7 cm
b. 13.6 x 9.3 in.; 34.5 x 23.5 cm
c. 13.6 x 9.3 in.; 34.7 x 23.5 cm
Gift of Dr. and Mrs. George A. Colom,
1994.83a-c

depict craftsmen's workshops in Kyoto. The earliest extant set is a six-panel screen belonging to Kita-in, a temple in Kawagoe City, Saitama Prefecture, and painted by Kanō Yoshinobu (1552–1640), probably in the early seventeenth century. The screen depicts twelve commercial establishments including a *katazome* (literally, "stencil-dyeing") workshop, a workshop that specialized in producing stencil- and paste-resist-dyed textiles. The main figure in the painting is a craftsman using a bamboo spatula to apply paste to a stencil, which is placed on a length of fabric laid flat on a long board, much as the process is done today. A tub of paste sits at his feet. At the right, a woman immerses a length of cloth in a half-sunken dye vat. This image has often been cited by scholars as evidence that indigo dyers were using a heated vat of fermented indigo by the late sixteenth or early seventeenth century.[6] In the foreground, a young apprentice stretches out a length of finished *komon* fabric.

Tiny all-over *komon* patterns remained popular throughout the Edo period (1615–1868). Associated primarily (though not exclusively) with the warrior class, *komon* were used to pattern *kamishimo*, the stiffened formal costume of the samurai consisting of a vest with protruding shoulders and wide, pleated pants. Daimyo (provincial lords) reserved certain *komon* patterns exclusively for themselves or their retainers; thus, a lord's retainers could be identified by the pattern on their garments. The stencil cutter Nambu Yoshimatsu (1894–1976) stated that until the Genroku era (1688–1704), most stencils produced in workshops in the Ise region were *komon* patterns carved on order for daimyo.[7] Beginning in the mid-Edo period, *katazome* dyers worked for a wider clientele, developing a rich repertoire of geometric and painterly designs, including renditions of designs primarily associated with other techniques (such as woven stripes, *kasuri,* and interpretations of the popular Indian block-printed designs). *Katazome* dyers also patterned *kosode* with stenciled imitations of the tiny, hand-tied *shibori* dots (*hitta*) that had been outlawed to commoners—albeit not entirely effectively—in the sumptuary laws of the Tenna era (1681–1684).[8] Although certainly not visually ostentatious, *hitta shibori kosode* were outlawed to commoners because they were very costly, due to the months of highly skilled labor required for their production. Since the value of a *hitta* garment was well known to the public, wearing one was an effective display of wealth.

As might be expected, the finest stencil- and paste-resist-dyed fabric was produced in and around the ancient capital of Kyoto, where a centuries-old textile and dyeing industry continued to cater to a wealthy and sophisticated clientele, even after the Tokugawa shogunate moved the de facto government to Edo (present-day Tokyo) in the seventeenth century. A note in a miscellany entitled *Kebukigusa*, published during the Kan'ei era (1624–1644), refers to *Horikawa kongata*, or Horikawa dye stencils, and mentions that dye shops (*konya*; literally, "indigo shops") were clustered near the intersection of Nijō street and Horikawa boulevard.[9] Undoubtedly dyers washed the paste off their fabrics in the narrow, man-made Horikawa river. Their descendants continued to use Kyoto's waterways until the early 1970s, when the city forbade dyers to use the rivers in order to prevent excess chemical dyes from polluting the water.

Kyoto dyers excelled at *yūzen*, a type of dyeing technique that became prominent in the Genroku era. This technique made it possible to create *kosode* with freely executed painterly designs in an array of sumptuous colors.[10] *Yūzen* dyers worked with silk, often a fine damask, treating each garment as if it were a painting. They applied the resist paste free-hand, originally with a small stick and later with a tube made of stencil paper, which was often fitted with one of a series of tips like a cake-decorating tool. They did not dye the cloth in vats, but applied the dyes and pigments with brushes, some wide and flat for coloring large areas and creating gradated washes of color (*hikizashi*), others small enough to paint minute details of the design (*irozashi*).

During the Edo period, the use of stencil and free-hand paste-resist techniques to pattern a wide variety of clothing and household articles spread throughout much of the country. Three factors contributed to this spread:

1. The warlord Toyotomi Hideyoshi (1536–1598) actively promoted the expansion of cotton cultivation throughout the country. Cotton was softer, warmer, and considerably quicker to process than *asa* (hemp or ramie), the only domesticated fiber available to farmers and other common folk before the introduction of cotton.

2. Professional indigo workshops proliferated with the expansion of cotton cultivation. Cotton dyes well in indigo, which is comparatively colorfast and has insect-repellent properties. Indigo strengthens the cloth, and its smell was believed to repel the poisonous snakes that lurked in wet rice fields. It was also among the few colors permitted to commoners in the Edo period, and by far the most widely used.

3. The relative speed of producing cotton cloth meant that women were able to make more than they needed for their own use. Cotton textiles dyed in the local indigo workshop became a commercial commodity. There was a lively interest in these textiles in the cities, where the demands of a prosperous urban merchant class, prohibited by sumptuary laws from wearing fine pattern-woven silks and bright colors, fostered the development of a large and ever-expanding vocabulary of striped, checked, and *kasuri* (thread-resist) woven patterns, as well as *katazome* and *tsutsugaki* (tube-drawn paste-resist) designs, many of them dyed in indigo.

Some indication of the presence and importance of indigo workshops can be gained from local records. In 1707, for example, there were 1,213 households in the town of Shimabara, Hizen Province (present-day Nagasaki Prefecture). Of these, 115 were artisans' shops, of which thirty, the largest number, were dyers. Dyers also constituted the greatest number of artisan households in Kofu, Kai Province (present-day Yamanashi Prefecture), in records dating from the period 1804–1817.[11]

A detailed record describing the servant and shophand population in the castle town of Kasama in Hitachi Province (present-day Ibaraki Prefecture) suggests that the seven dye households in that town maintained busy and prosperous workshops. The *Machikata kenbetsu aratame-chō* (*Townspeople's House-Frontage Registry*), compiled in 1705, records a commoner population of 1,800 in Kasama, composed of 483 households.[12] The largest group registered was cultivators (113 households), followed by rice-wine (*sake*) dealers (20), fish shops (15), carpenters (11), and bean-curd dealers (8). These were followed by seven households each of dyers, blacksmiths, and rice-wine shops. The seven dye households employed a total of thirteen assistants, or approximately 1.8 per household, more than double the average. The town's dye workshops were supported by a cotton dealer—probably a shop that sold bolts of handspun cotton ready for dyeing—and three households selling ginned cotton (cotton with the seeds removed, ready for spinning). With four and five servants, respectively, these two types of merchants (who may well have produced some of the ginned cotton and cotton cloth they sold) also employed an unusually large number of assistants. Unfortunately the document does not differentiate between household servants and workshop employees, although in artisan households where the shophands lived with the family, tasks were often mixed. Specific figures for each household within a group also are not given; we do not know whether the dye workshops were more or less the same size, employing one or two assistants each, or whether most of the assistants were employed in a single workshop. In any case, the figures do suggest that dye workshops were comparatively numerous in Kasama, and that, as a group, they prospered.

Indigo dyers were taxed on the number of vats in their workshops, at a rate of 200 *monme* per vat.[13] In 1719 this was approximately equivalent to the value of three *koku*, or about fifteen bushels of rice, and equalled the annual cash wages paid to a high-class manservant (or almost double that paid to an unskilled chambermaid) in the early nineteenth century.[14] The tax seems rather high, considering that indigo dyers kept a number of vats—four to eight for a modest establishment, sixteen to thirty-two for a larger one.

Local lords encouraged the development of crafts within their territories. Their patronage could take a variety of forms, including active purchasing of the craft product and reduced taxes for producers and merchants. The craft, in turn, brought increased income to the domain, especially if the product made a name for itself throughout the country. The Kii Tokugawa family encouraged and supported the stencil carvers and merchants in their district of Ise; the lords of Awa (present-day Tokushima Prefecture) on the island of Shikoku spurred the development of indigo production; and the Maeda family, overlords of Kaga (present-day Kanazawa Prefecture) on the Sea of Japan, were renowned for the high quality of ceramics and textiles produced in their domain. In fact, free-hand paste-resist dyeing (*yūzen*) developed in the Maeda family's castle town of Kanazawa at the same time—or perhaps even earlier—as in Kyoto. Today there are several *yūzen* dyers in Kaga who have been designated Living National Treasures by the Japanese government for their skill in *Kaga yūzen*.

Although materials, functions, and subject matter differed, the *yūzen* technique is basically the same as that termed *tsutsugaki* (literally, "drawing with a tube"). *Tsutsugaki* was done on a hemp or cotton ground for a variety of functional everyday textiles, such as the strips of cloth that hung in the open doorways of shops and restaurants, and work jackets with insignia that identified the wearer as belonging to a particular shop or guild. *Tsutsugaki* was also employed to decorate festival banners such as the Boys' Day Banner (Plate 71) in the Spencer collection, and (particularly in rural areas) the bridal textiles that formed an important part of a young woman's dowry, such as the Spencer's *yogi* (kimono-shaped coverlet) (Plate 72).

By the mid-eighteenth century, Edo had become the primary market for stencil- and paste-resist-dyed patterned fabric, and a thriving community of stencil merchants, carvers, dyers, and indigo workshops grew up there. Edo indigo dyers formed a guild in 1721 that included 552 registered indigo workshops by 1854.[15] It was Edo craftsmen who, in 1695, pioneered the production of informal *katazome* cotton kimono with white patterns reserved on a dark indigo ground. These *yukata* (literally, "bath wear") were originally used in the evenings for going to and from the public baths, but they soon were adopted by both men and women, young and old, as informal summer costume.[16] Edo townsmen, affluent and sophisticated, had money to spend on fashionable clothing, but were constrained by stringent sumptuary laws from flaunting their wealth in brocades, damasks, fine silken embroideries, and bright colors. The famous woodblock print artist Hiroshige (1797–1858) depicted the indigo dyers' district in one part of Edo

in a print entitled *Kanda konya machi (Indigo Dyers' District in Kanda)*. The print was published in 1857 as Number 75 of the series *Meisho Edo hyakkei (One Hundred Views of Edo)* (Fig. 16).

Stencils were supplied primarily by a specialized group of stencil cutters in the towns of Shiroko and Jike near Suzuka on the Bay of Ise in Kii Province (present-day Mie Prefecture), and by emigrant craftsmen from those towns working in Edo. In the late eighteenth and early nineteenth centuries, emigrant merchants from Ise established twelve stencil shops in Edo. The Kishū or Kii Tokugawa family had stimulated the development of a center of stencil production in their domain from the earliest days of the Tokugawa shogunate in the seventeenth century. In 1622, Tokugawa Yorinobu reduced the packhorse tax required of Kii stencil merchants and peddlers from the standard merchant rate of 239 *mon* to the samurai rate of 100 *mon*. After a subsequent Kii daimyo, Tokugawa Yoshimune (1684–1751), became the eighth

Tokugawa shogun in 1716, the Ise stencil merchants were given the right to travel with complete freedom and at significantly reduced costs throughout the country. Ise stencil merchants thus enjoyed unrivaled freedom to travel at considerably less expense than their competitors. They had the protection of both the shogunate and their well-organized guild of 138 registered stencil dealers. They also sold a fine product. Ise stencils were skillfully carved, and the designs were fresh and interesting. It is no wonder that Ise stencils were widely used throughout the country; Sugihara Nobuhiko has noted that the majority of Edo period stencils surviving in collections throughout Japan today were handled by dealers from Ise.[17] Kyoto—and the five "home" provinces surrounding it—were exceptions to this rule. Dyers in the capital bought few stencils from Ise, relying instead on the products of their own carvers. This preference was apparently justified as daimyo, samurai, and wealthy Edo townsmen continued to order their finest garments from Kyoto.[18]

In the Meiji period (1868–1912), traditional *katazome* craftsmen were faced with changing styles of dress influenced by Western fashions, as well as chemical dyes and newly invented and introduced technologies that enabled the efficient and inexpensive mass production of polychrome fabrics. But surprisingly, demand for traditionally patterned *katazome yukata* actually increased during the Meiji period, and Tokyo *yukata* dyers continued a lively trade in fabrics with both traditional and innovative designs until the early Taishō period (1912–1926). Business was already falling off when the 1923 earthquake and fire demolished most *katazome* workshops in Tokyo and destroyed priceless collections of old stencils. Only a few workshops were rebuilt, but from these came craftsmen who were among the first to be designated Living National Treasures.[19]

In 1950 the Japanese government enacted the Bunkazai Hogo-hō (Law for the Protection of Cultural Properties), and established a commission—forerunner of the Agency of Cultural Affairs (Bunkachō)—to designate, preserve, and protect Japan's cultural treasures. The commission recognized certain traditional skills as Important Intangible Cultural Properties (Jūyō Mukei Bunkazai), and designated certain objects as National Treasures (Kokuhō) or Important Cultural Properties (Jūyō Bunkazai). On February 15, 1955, the commission named nineteen craftsmen as Holders of Important Intangible Cultural Properties (popularly known as Ningen Kokuhō—literally, "Human National Treasures"—but usually translated as Living National Treasures); on May 12 the commission made another eleven designations. Craftsmen have been added to this list almost every year since then. Nine artisans in the first group of nineteen were highly skilled in one or another aspect of *katazome* dyeing. These included one dyer of Edo *komon*, two *yukata* dyers (of *nagaita chūgata*—literally, "long board, middle-size pattern"), five stencil carvers from Ise, and one artisan (the only woman in the first group) who specialized in making and securing the slender silk mesh necessary to support and strengthen the most delicate stencils (*itoire*). Of the eleven artisans honored in May of that year, five were *yūzen* dyers and one, Chiba Ayano (1889–1980), was honored for preserving a method of indigo dyeing particular to the Tōhoku region of northern Honshu, the main Japanese island.[20]

Chiba Ayano also exemplified another tradition of *katazome* dyeing. Mrs. Chiba raised her own hemp, prepared the thread, wove the cloth on a traditional back-tensioned loom, chose a stencil (from a stack of old stencils she had received from a professional dyer), made a resist paste (using flour from locally grown wheat instead of rice), stenciled the fabric, harvested indigo she had grown herself, made a vat of fermented indigo, and finally dyed the cloth. In an interview with Barbara Adachi, Mrs. Chiba said that when she was young, farm women in her area performed all of these tasks themselves; she asserted that she was not unusual, but just the last one left.[21] Although in more affluent rural areas many women might not have done quite so much of the process themselves, many extant *katazome* fabrics were produced under similar circumstances, albeit perhaps with the help of a local professional indigo dyer. The stenciled woman's work jacket with bark fiber lining (Plate 70) is an example of this type of rural *katazome*.

PRODUCTION

MAKING THE STENCIL PAPER

Each step in the production of a stencil is a specialized skill. Stencil paper is made from the inner bark of the paper mulberry tree (*kōzo; Broussonetia kazinoki sieb*). Two or three sheets of paper are laid at right angles to each other (much like plywood), and laminated together with aged persimmon tannin (*kakishibu*). Persimmon tannin has good adhesive properties; it also serves to strengthen the paper and make it water resistant. Generally for stencils, tannin aged for five years is combined with tannin aged for about a year. Even the process of brushing the laminated sheets on the drying boards affects the quality of the paper. After the paper has dried in the sun, it is either put away and aged for several years, or smoked for several days over burning sawdust in a tightly sealed smokehouse. The former process is preferred, but the latter—which is much quicker—has been the more common method since the beginning of the Meiji period. The aging (or smoking) process turns the persimmon-soaked paper a deep, rich brown.

Stencil paper is made in various thicknesses for different purposes. For example, two thin sheets are lacquered together to make stencil paper for carving *komon* patterns. A somewhat thicker paper is required for stripes, while *chūgata* (mid-sized patterns, usually with geometric or pictorial motifs) need even sturdier paper.[22] The demands on stencil paper are high. It must be resilient, durable, and tough enough for even the most minutely carved designs to withstand multiple applications of spatula-applied paste. Stencil paper is wetted before use and kept damp with the application of the moist paste. It is essential that the paper have the inner stability to return to its exact, original dimensions when dry, without warping or shrinking.

CARVING THE STENCIL

A carver, traditionally male, sits on the floor with the stencil on a slanted desk in front of him. He generally cuts between five and ten stencils at once. The stencils are placed in a stack with the backs slightly oiled to facilitate carving, held tightly together with a bit of twisted paper threaded through small holes at the edges. There are several basic carving techniques, each a specialty.

In *kiribori* (awl carving), the tool resembles an awl or chisel with a small, semi-cylindrical blade. The carver holds the tool in his left hand, perpendicular to the paper. Securing the awl with his right hand, he pushes it through the paper while rotating it in a 180-degree arc to complete the circle. *Kiribori* is used to make tiny round holes that, when executed properly, can be built up to create tiny, all-over patterns (*komon*) such as undulating waves. The most intricate *kiribori*-carved *komon* stencils have as many as nine hundred perforations per 3.3 square centimeters.[23] *Kiribori* is one of the oldest methods of cutting stencils, and the one used to pattern the *katabira* garment in the Uesugi Shrine cited above. *Kiribori* was used to outline some of the quatrefoils in the water chestnut quatrefoil stencil (Plate 64), and to create the interior veins of the paulownia leaves in the chrysanthemum stencil (Plate 63).

Tsukibori is another old technique. The carver pushes a flat triangular blade away from him with his left hand, as his right hand moves the blade up and down to perforate the layers of stencil paper. The stencils are placed on a board made of paulownia wood with a hole in the center. The carver works over the hole, moving the stencil paper as he works. *Tsukibori* probably was used to carve the major motifs in the water chestnut stencil (Plate 64), the paulownia leaves in the chrysanthemum stencil (Plate 63), and the swallows in the net and swallows stencil (Plate 62). All of these motifs also could have been carved with the *hikibori* technique and tools.

Hikibori utilizes a similar blade, but the carver pulls the knife towards him. This method is used primarily to cut patterns with fine stripes, and developed in association with the vogue for stripes during the Edo period. It was probably used to create the narrow stripes in the chrysanthemum (Plate 63) and water chestnut (Plate 64) stencils, and the net pattern in the net and swallows stencil (Plate 62).

In the *ichimaizuki* technique, carvers use one of a series of flat, arched, or wavy blades to shape multiples of tiny *komon* patterns of geometric or floral motifs by hand. *Dōgubori*, a later technique, enables the carver to create these *komon* patterns more quickly by employing a punch in the shape of the specific motif. The earliest extant examples of *dōgubori*-carved stencils date from the early eighteenth century, but this quicker technique was not commonly used until the late Edo period, when popular demand for *komon* patterns fostered the development of a less time-consuming (and hence less costly) method of stencil carving. *Dōgubori* was used to create the checkerboard patterns within some of the quatrefoils on the water chestnut stencil (Plate 64), the knots joining strands of the net in the net and swallows stencil (Plate 62), and the entire design on the *komon* stencil (Plate 66). *Ichimaizuki* produced cleaner, sharper edges than *dōgubori*, and continued to be used for carving the highest-quality *komon* stencils.

It would be impossible to cut with such precision without very sharp tools, and preparing to cut a stencil could take longer than the carving itself. Kodama Hiroshi (1909–1992; designated a Living National Treasure in 1955), honored for his interpretations of narrow striped patterns (*shimabori*), which included meticulously rendered narrow stripes and fine interlocking lines, spent two or three days selecting and sharpening his tools before beginning to carve a new stencil. Once prepared, he worked with intense concentration from dawn to dark (or beyond), stopping only for a cup of tea or to resharpen a tool.[24]

Many carvers specialized in a single technique, and the Agency of Cultural Affairs honors carvers for a particular skill. It is evident from the Spencer stencils, however, that by the Meiji period, stencils designed to produce popular *yukata* fabric had become quite complex, each requiring a variety of specialized tools and carving techniques. Some complex patterns required the use of two stencils: a primary stencil (*omogata*) for the main image with a secondary stencil for intricate details (*keshigata*).

STABILIZING THE DESIGN: ITOIRE

As designs became increasingly complex and painterly, perhaps imitating the more costly *yūzen* fabrics, Edo carvers devised a method of stabilizing hair-breadth lines and designs that had large areas of open space. *Itoire*, or "putting in the thread," is a process of lacquering a network of fine silk threads to the back of a stencil to stabilize it. In the most traditional method, silk threads are laced over pegs on a frame in a pattern appropriate for the stencil, with square, rectangular, or triangular openings in the mesh. The stencil layers are then separated, the edges of the bottom layer pasted to a board, and the entire surface of the stencil brushed with persimmon tannin. The silk mesh, in its frame, is then fitted over the wet bottom stencil, and the top stencil is carefully positioned over it so that the patterns are aligned. After the two layers have been joined and the top layer brushed with persimmon tannin, each tiny element of the design is adjusted with a needle so top and bottom layers of the stencil match perfectly. The edges of the silk webbing are then cut from the frame, the frame is removed, and excess persimmon tannin is blown from the surface and perforations of the stencil. It is an exacting task, sometimes performed by a member of the carver's family, and sometimes by a separate workshop.[25] In 1955 Jōnokuchi Mie (1917–) was designated a Living National Treasure for her skill in *itoire*.[26] All of the stencils illustrated here have a hand-laced silk web sandwiched between the layers of paper.

After the carver has cut away any small connecting strips of paper that were left to stabilize the pattern, the stencil is put away to mellow. Kodama let his stencils mature for three years before they left his workshop, an amount of time he felt was necessary for persimmon tannin, paper, and silk web to form a single, cohesive unit.[27]

Some carvers prefer to use a woven silk gauze—an intertwined web of silk fibers— made for the purpose in the old weaving district of Nishijin in Kyoto. This fine woven gauze is inserted between the stencil layers as in the hand-laced method described above. Less expensive stencils, however, were often simply backed by a woven gauze or even a widely spaced plain weave fabric, the web lacquered to the back of the stencil rather than sandwiched between its layers.

In the Edo period and into the twentieth century, a stencil carved in Ise was handled first by a merchant/peddler from Ise. From there it might go to a wholesaler in Edo, and perhaps pass through one or more additional hands before it reached the craftsman who stenciled the cloth. Today that network has been simplified. There are still shops that specialize in selling stencils, but there is a closer connection between stencilers and carvers.

In his workshop, the stenciler lightly pastes half a length of cloth to a fir board. The board for cotton *yukata* fabric is approximately six and a half meters long and forty-five centimeters wide, long enough to accommodate the fabric to make one *yukata* when both sides of the board are used. The stencil is laid down at one end of the cloth, and the paste spread evenly over it. It is then moved in regular intervals along the cloth, using small registration marks to position it properly. Early Edo illustrations of *katazome* workshops depict the use of a bamboo spatula to spread the paste, but by the time the Spencer stencils were carved in the nineteenth or twentieth century, the bamboo spatula was largely replaced by the curved wooden spatula used today. After the first side of the cloth is stenciled once, the board with the cloth still attached is placed outside to dry. Cloth stretched on boards leaning against the sides of buildings was a picturesque site in Edo Japan, and was illustrated in a number of woodblock prints.[28]

If the cloth requires a second stenciling to add detail, this is applied next, again using registration marks to position the stencil exactly over the first pattern. Some stencilers add a fugitive color to the first paste as a guide in applying the second. After the paste has dried, the board is turned over, the second half of the cloth unrolled and pasted onto it, and the process repeated. After the whole cloth has been stenciled on one side, the cloth is removed from the board, turned over, and stenciled on the back. This process requires meticulous attention to detail, as front and back patterns must match exactly. If the back is not stenciled, the pattern will only appear clearly on one side of the cloth. It was important for good quality *yukata* to be patterned on both sides, as the underside shows at the hem and sleeve openings.

Some stencilers make their own paste; others buy it from commercial workshops that specialize exclusively in making the resist paste. Traditionally the paste is composed primarily of cooked and kneaded glutinous rice, rice bran, and lime. Proportions vary according to weather conditions, the type of stencil pattern, and the nature of the cloth (fiber, structure, and density).

In the Edo period, indigo-dyeing workshops (*konya*) were established throughout the country, serving rural communities as well as urban townsfolk. Most dyers purchased some or all of their indigo from places that specialized in growing and processing the plant. The most famous was Awa Province in Shikoku, where conditions were favorable for growing indigo, and where the local lord encouraged its production as a commercial enterprise. There the harvested leaves were composted and compressed into bricks of highly concentrated indigo that could be transported easily throughout the country.

In the workshop, the dyer combined indigo with bran, lime, and water that had been filtered through ash (to raise the pH) in a large conical ceramic jar buried in the floor. These vats, about one and a half meters deep, were arranged in sets of four, with a firebox set in the ground between them. A bolt of long, narrow fabric was folded in accordion fashion and secured by dyeing ribs, thin skewers of bamboo with needle-sharp ends that were placed end to end along one edge of the cloth. Holding the cloth by the bow of these ribs, the dyer immersed the fabric in the first vat, which held a weak solution of indigo, and then removed it to air. Airing permitted the dye to oxidize, turning the cloth from a greenish yellow to the characteristic indigo blue. This process, using vats with solutions of varying intensities, was repeated many times. Indigo provides a deep, lasting color if it is handled correctly, but knowledgeable attention is required to maintain the correct balance of ingredients in each vat.

Today, as in the Edo period, indigo dyers use multiple vats both to preserve the correct balance in each and to build up the dye slowly on the cloth. Dyers believe that the color will be deeper, more lasting, and more colorfast when applied in this manner than if the cloth were dipped fewer times in a more intense dyebath. As the rice resist paste is water soluble, *katazome* fabrics require a series of immersions with time for the paste to stabilize in the intervals. If the cloth is immersed for too long, the paste will start to disintegrate in the vat.

When dyeing is complete, the dyer, an apprentice, or a family member washes the paste from the cloth, preferably in naturally flowing water. The paste comes off fairly easily under these conditions, often helped by nibbling fish.

TIME FRAME

In the *katazome* process, as in many other Japanese arts, time is an important part of the process, an essential tool of the craft. To make a high-quality stencil, the persimmon tannin must be mature and the finished stencil paper either aged or cured. The *itoire* process also requires several intervals of drying and resting. The best carvers put their stencils away for several years before they are used or sold. A good stenciler must be able to determine the proper drying time for the paste after each successive application; the weather, the type of paste used, and the particularities of the stencil pattern all affect the drying rate. Shimizu Kotarō (1897–1988), who was designated a Living National Treasure in 1955 for *nagaita chūgata yukata* dyeing, generally let his stenciled fabric rest for about a month before he sent it to the dyer. He noted that if the paste dried for too long, it would crack; if it was not dried long enough, it would run.[29] Even the finished cloth was given time to age. Chiba Ayano liked to put her indigo-dyed cloth away for as much as six years, saying that the color improved and continued to deepen during that period.[30]

62. Stencil for *Yukata*, Swallows in Flight Against Net Pattern

◆

Japan
Edo period, ca. 1826–1834
Stencil paper with silk mesh
Hikibori, dōgubori, tsukibori
21.5 x 16.5 in.; 54.8 x 42 cm
Source Unknown, 0000.2959

A pattern such as this, in which most of the ground is formed by resist, is called *jishiro*, or white ground. *Jishiro* patterns with scattered motifs on a striped ground were popular between about 1826 and 1834. Here swallows fly against a net pattern, with intersections fashioned of meticulously cut knot motifs. For his striped patterns, particularly his execution of thin, wavy lines such as these, the carver Kodama Hiroshi (1909–1992) was designated Holder of an Important Intangible Cultural Property (Living National Treasure) in 1955.[31]

This stencil would have been appropriate for a young woman's summer *yukata* (unlined cotton kimono).

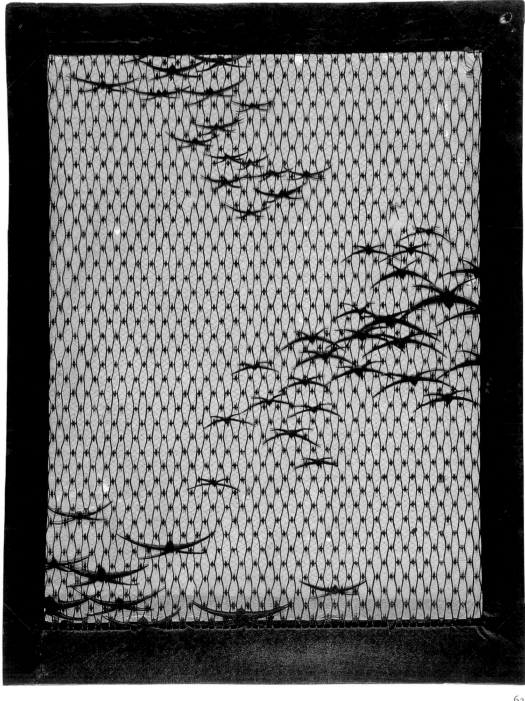

62

63. Stencil for *Yukata*, Chrysanthemums and Insect-Eaten Paulownia (?) Leaves on Striped Ground

◆

Japan
Meiji or early Taishō period, late 19th–early 20th century
Stencil paper with silk mesh
Tsukibori, hikibori, kiribori
21 x 16.8 in.; 54.3 x 42.5 cm
Source Unknown, 0000.2961

A pair of stencils—a primary (or *omogata*) stencil and a secondary (*keshigata*) stencil—in the collection of the Kyoto National Museum, dated to the Meiji period, depicts several different varieties of chrysanthemum blossoms floating on an abstracted lattice ground.[32]

This single stencil, probably less costly, crowds more images onto a simpler ground of narrow stripes, but the artist displays a similar interest in combining realistic depiction with abstraction. The insect-eaten leaves, rendered with an eye for detail, appear layered over the chrysanthemum blossoms, creating a sense of three-dimensional space. As in the Kyoto National Museum stencils, though, the motifs appear to float above a geometric ground, and here the blossoms—depicted with dots—resemble a pattern more than actual chrysanthemums.

This stencil probably also dates from the Meiji period, perhaps toward its end in the early twentieth century.

63

64. Stencil for *Yukata*, Water
Chestnut Quatrefoils on
Striped Ground

◆

Japan
Late Meiji or early Taishō period, early 20th
century
Stencil paper with silk mesh
Tsukibori, hikibori, kiribori, dōgubori
21.5 x 16.5 in.; 54.8 x 42 cm
Source Unknown, 0000.2960

64

65. Stencil for *Yukata*, Bows and Birds

◆

Japan
Taishō period (1912–1926)
Stencil paper with silk mesh
Tsukibori, hikibori with applied dots
21.8 x 16.8 in.; 55 x 42.8 cm
Source Unknown, 0000.2962

The shadow images—wavy lines formed by a series of unevenly spaced dots that seem to float over and between the straight lines of the ground—in this stencil of bows and birds would have been extremely difficult to carve as part of the main stencil. The dotted lines are so casually executed, however, that it seems unlikely that the stencil was a technical tour de force, or that two stencils were used. Probably the dots were applied to the back of the stencil after carving was completed. The twentieth-century carver Nambu Yoshimatsu used such a technique to add the central dots to stenciled imitations of tie-dyed *kanoko shibori* (*shibori* composed of tiny, all-over resist-dyed squares with pinpoints of color in the centers). To make this imitation *shibori*, Nambu first carved a stencil of interlocking squares, and finished the stencil with a backing (or insertion) of gauze. He cut the pinpoint dots that would form the centers of the squares from stencil paper, and pasted them in exact position on a piece of paper. He then pressed this paper to the freshly lacquered back of the stencil, taking care that each pinpoint dot fell in the center of its corresponding square. After the lacquer dried, he wet the paper backing and peeled it off.

65

The dots, firmly lacquered to the gauze, became part of the stencil. Nambu's imitation *kanoko* was done with such precision that it is extremely difficult to tell that the fabric was not tie-dyed. His son has noted that one of the most difficult aspects of the process is choosing the right drying times for both the paper and the lacquer, so that the paper will peel off easily but leave each dot in its proper place on the stencil.[33]

In this stencil, the dots are not regularly dispersed between or on the lines, and are unevenly spaced. Both factors suggest that they were applied to the stencil rather than carved from it, but in a more casual, free-hand manner than outlined above. Either they were placed on the paper in a very uneven manner, or the craftsman did not have (or use) the skill to make the dots adhere properly to the stencil; perhaps both were true. As it is, the casualness with which the carver has drawn the images conveys a carefree charm that is very fitting for a young girl's *yukata*. It would have appeared cool and delightful on a hot summer's evening.

66. Stencil, *Komon* Pattern (detail)

✦

Japan
Meiji or Taishō period, late 19th–early 20th century
Stencil paper
Dōgubori
7.8 x 16.5 in.; 19.5 x 42 cm
Gift of Elizabeth Sherbon, Professor of Dance 1961–75, 2000.182

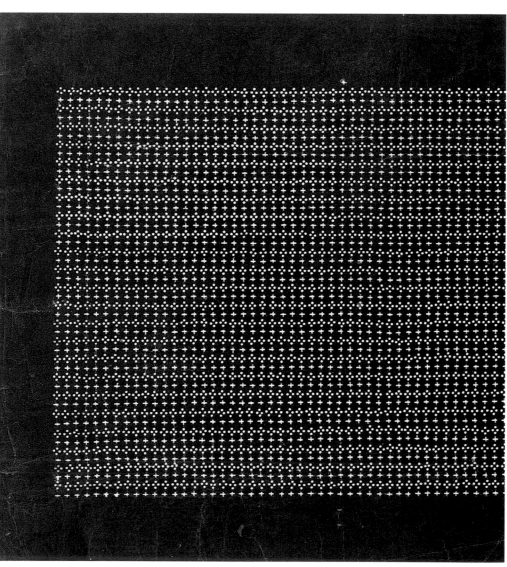

66

KATAZOME TEXTILES

67. *Katazome Futonji* Fragment with Design of Chrysanthemums and *Karakusa* Scrolls
✦

Japan
19th-20th century
Cotton
Katazome on indigo plain weave ground
61 x 12.5 in.; 155 x 31.7 cm
Museum Purchase, 1992.82

68. *Katazome Futonji* Fragment with Design of Carp, Waves, and Floating Chrysanthemum Blossoms
✦

Japan
19th-20th century
Cotton warp, bast fiber and cotton wefts
Katazome on indigo weft-faced plain weave ground
56 x 12.5 in.; 142 x 31.4 cm
Museum Purchase, 1992.83

These panels come from covers for *futon*, Japanese bedding. *Futon* covers (*futonji*) were composed of long panels of fabric of similar design that formed an envelope around a padding of raw cotton. *Futon* came into use toward the end of the seventeenth century in the capital area (Kyoto, Osaka, and environs), and from there spread throughout Japan. Their use developed in conjunction with the availability of cotton. Before *futon*, wealthy Japanese slept under layers of clothing or, from the sixteenth century, warmly padded *yogi* (quilted, kimono-shaped bed coverings). Commoners wrapped themselves in old clothing or straw; in fact, poor townsmen and farmers slept without *futon* well into the twentieth century.[34] Dr. Engelbert Kaempfer (1651–1716), physician to the Dutch mission in the seventeenth century, noted the absence of any bedding in inns even along the well-traveled Tōkaidō highway between Osaka and Edo. Innkeepers provided a hard wooden block for a pillow, but travelers carried their own bedding or did without.[35]

Chrysanthemums are a common motif on *futonji*, and are found in many variations. On the chrysanthemum and *karakusa futonji* (Plate 67), chrysanthemum blossoms form an abstract pattern against a background of scrolling vines (*karakusa*; literally, "Chinese grass"). The chrysanthemum plant, along with an associated set of beliefs and legends, was imported to Japan from China during the Tang dynasty (618–907). With orchid, bamboo, and plum, the chrysanthemum was among the "four princes" celebrated by Chinese painters. The entire middle section of the seventeenth-century Chinese *Mustard Seed Garden* manual of painting is devoted to four books, one for each of these four plants. Chrysanthemums were considered by the literati to be noble, pure, "defiant of frost and triumphant in autumn," and to have a lingering fragrance.[36] In an abstract rendition, as here, the chrysanthemum motif resembles the sun; in Japan it was known also as "sun splendor" (*nikka*) and "sun spirit" (*nissei*).[37] Perhaps because of the association of the Japanese imperial line with the sun goddess Amaterasu Ōmikami, the motif was popular with the aristocracy during the Heian period. At the end of the twelfth century, Emperor Gotoba (r. 1184–1198) adopted the sixteen-petalled chrysanthemum for the imperial crest.

Another sobriquet for the chrysanthemum is *ennenso*, or "longevity plant." The association with longevity is derived from Chinese legends about a group of exceptionally long-lived mountain hermits who subsisted solely on a diet of chrysanthemums. In both China and Japan, the ninth day of the ninth month is the Chrysanthemum Festival, a festival that, in China, dates back to the Han dynasty (206 BCE-220 CE). In China, chrysanthemums were brewed as a medicinal tea for this occasion; in Japan, observance of the festival included the drinking of a specially brewed chrysanthemum wine believed to increase longevity.[38]

Chrysanthemums were also enjoyed in Japan for their sheer beauty. Over the centuries, the Japanese have developed more than five thousand varieties of chrysanthemums, which are featured in flower arrangements and chrysanthemum competitions, depicted in painting, and used as a design motif in many media.[39] Chrysanthemums were a popular *katazome* motif, and they appear often and in many variations on *futonji*.

The design of carp, waves, and floating chrysanthemum blossoms (Plate 68) links two sets of imagery through a common motif of running water. Wild carp, like salmon, spawn on the upper reaches of rivers, scaling rapids and waterfalls to reach their goal. They are symbols of perseverance and success in China and Japan, especially for students struggling to pass important examinations. In China, passing a series of difficult examinations, like scaling a waterfall, was the single most critical step in a young person's career. A successful result qualified him for appointment to a position in the imperial civil service, which, in turn, provided him with social prestige and at least a measure of financial security. The higher the level of examination the student passed, the better position he could expect to hold in the government hierarchy. In Japan, too, examinations are crucially important in allowing students access to the best schools and the most rewarding jobs. While carp signify success, the floating chrysanthemum blossoms in this design remind the viewer of the tale of a mountain village where multitudes of chrysanthemums habitually dropped their blossoms in the stream. The villagers, who drank the water, all lived for

68

a century.[40] On this bedding, carp and floating blossoms are emblems for success and longevity, with a reminder of the importance of perseverance. Water, one of the Five Elements, was associated with night, the *yin* principle (see p. 177), and sexual activity.[41]

This *futon* material has an unusual texture. It is slightly thicker and less pliable than most cotton *futonji*, and the indigo appears streaked with lighter lines in the weft. Close examination reveals that the weft is composed of alternating single strands of bast fiber and handspun cotton laid side by side. The bast fiber appears flat, smooth, and lustrous, and at first glance could be mistaken for raw silk. Natural lengths of the fiber are laid in the weft. The bast fiber has not been joined into thread, but overlapped with cotton; it has not absorbed the dye as deeply as the cotton, accounting for the striations seen in the weft. The appearance of the fiber and the fact that the natural lengths of fiber have not been joined suggest that it is *kuzu* (kudzu or arrowroot), a wild bast fiber capable of being split into fine, glossy filaments with such a lustrous, even texture that, unlike other wild bast fibers, it has always been considered a luxury fiber. Traditionally it was associated with the military class and used for formal samurai wear.

In Japan, bast fibers traditionally were not spun as linen was spun in the West, but instead joined end to tip by hand. The process varied from fiber to fiber, but usually involved applying a "Z" twist to the separate fibers, held between thumb and first finger, by rolling the two separate fibers toward the tip of the finger with the thumb and then, with a quick counter motion, joining them into a single thread while rolling them back toward the base of the finger. These motions result in two "S" spun fibers joined in a "Z" ply. (The terms "S" and "Z" refer to the direction of twist in a single strand of fiber as it is spun into thread, or the direction of ply when two threads are twisted together. The reference is to the direction of the center stroke of the letter.) *Kuzu*, however, is difficult to process in this way, and even for luxury goods was often used just in the weft, as here, where the fibers could be simply overlapped.[42]

The town of Kakegawa, on the old Tōkaidō highway joining Osaka and Edo, was famous for producing and marketing fine *kuzu* cloth, and with the support and protection of the local daimyo, the town had a virtual monopoly on the production of luxury *kuzu* fabrics. Demand fell off sharply with the abolition of warrior domains in 1871 (following the return of the emperor to power in the Meiji Restoration of 1868), and many dealers went out of business. Others searched for new uses for their product. The most successful was the export of "grass cloth" to Europe and the United States until about 1960, when Korean producers took over the market. Perhaps this textile was produced somewhere around Kakegawa in present-day Shizuoka Prefecture.

69. *Katazome Yukata* Fragment with Design of Flowering Gourds

◆

Japan
19th–20th century
Cotton
Katazome on indigo plain weave ground
27.5 x 12 in.; 69.9 x 30.8 cm
Museum Purchase, 1992.84

This *katazome* fragment with a design of scattered flowering gourds is stenciled to resemble a *shibori* textile. The blossoms resemble motifs dyed in this technique, in which the cloth is pinched and thread wrapped around the pinched section to reserve the area from the dye. The leaves and tendrils are dyed to resemble *hitta shibori*, tiny points resist-dyed by pinching only a minute section of cloth. The outlines of the gourds imitate the uneven markings characteristic of a pattern that has been dyed in a stitch-resist technique. In that process, the shape is outlined in running stitches, which are pulled taut before the fabric is dipped in the dye bath. The method creates a white outline with characteristic white lines radiating from it.

Katazome stencil carvers were capable of producing imitations of *shibori* textiles so exact that only the sharpest eye could tell the difference. That was not the attempt here. There was no effort, for example, to reproduce the tiny points of dye that appear in the center of *shibori hitta* dots. Rather, the dots have been rendered as typical *katazome kiribori* dots. *Shibori*-like designs such as this rendered in *katazome* were quicker to produce and less costly than if they were actually stitched and tied in the *shibori* technique, making these patterns available to a wide clientele. Here the casually rendered reproduction does not suggest an attempt to fool the observer, but rather to play with the idea of rendering a pattern typical of one technique in another.

70. Woman's *Katazome* Jacket with Striped Tree-Bast Fiber Lining

◆

Japan
Late 19th or 20th century
Hemp, cotton, and tree-bast fiber
Katazome on indigo plain weave ground
37 x 23 in.; 92.5 x 58 cm
Museum Purchase: The Barbara Benton
Wescoe Fund, 1993.10

This heavy jacket from northern Japan was designed to be worn over a kimono, indoors and out, in the cold winter months. The jacket was probably made by an older woman for her own use. The small scale of the motifs suggests the age of the owner; a younger woman would normally have worn larger motifs. The use of hemp, lined with a tree-bast fiber, for a winter garment suggests a provenance in a region too far north to grow cotton, which is much warmer than hemp and other bast fibers. Although the repetition of the stenciled motifs is well done, the indistinct edges of some of the patterns suggest two things: that the stencil was worn; and that the stenciler was not a professional, and therefore did not have access to the quality of resist paste available in commercial workshops.

The jacket is made of *katazome*-patterned hemp, lined and faced with three different materials, all probably recycled from other garments. The *eri* (collar band) and bindings at sleeves and hem, sections of a garment that wore out and were commonly replaced, are probably made from the same piece of indigo-dyed handspun cotton. The lining is made of a rough tree-bast fiber; too short for the jacket, it was lengthened with a 4.5–centimeter piece of brown cotton. The primary sewing thread is a single strand of indigo-dyed hemp. The lining is sewn with long basting stitches to the hemp garment, with horizontal rows of stitching placed approximately every 5 centimeters.

The jacket is patterned with an all-over floral motif with crossed lines that suggest a lattice ground. The motifs are light blue against a dark indigo ground. Normally fabrics with designs in lighter and darker indigo were dyed to the lighter color first, before the motifs were reserved. Sometimes old or soiled garments that originally sported white motifs against a dark blue ground were dipped in indigo instead of (or in addition to) being washed, a process that turned the dirty white motifs to a pleasing light blue, and freshened the deep blue of the ground. In this garment, however, it appears that the motifs were reserved before the multiple dips in the indigo vat. A few remnants of white within the light blue motifs suggest that the fabric was given a final dipping after the paste was removed; the white remnants indicate areas where a few scattered bits of paste clung stubbornly to the fabric after the first washing. Perhaps the process was planned that way. Throughout Japan there were many customs particular to local areas, such as Chiba Ayano's use of a flour resist paste instead of the standard rice paste. Alternately, the owner may have looked at the finished garment and decided that it would look better with pale blue instead of sharp white motifs.

This is the only Japanese textile in the Spencer collection that incorporates a fabric woven entirely of tree-bast fiber.[43] Rural farmers throughout the main islands of Japan traditionally made use of fiber from the inner bark of locally available plants, including wisteria vines (*fuji*), mulberry (*kōzo* and *kajunoki*), nettles (*irakusa*), and linden (*shina*). The Ainu, an indigenous people on the northern island of Hokkaido, used the inner bark of elm trees (*ohyō*).[44] Fibers coaxed from wild trees, vines, and plants are tough. Most make excellent cordage, grain sacks, and work clothing, but they are difficult to process, generally rough, and not particularly warm.[45] They were not a choice for use as a lining material if other fabrics were available, and by the mid-nineteenth century, cotton was available throughout most of the country. Everyone who had access to cotton preferred it to hemp for winter use. After a visit to the mountain district of Iya (in present-day Tokushima Prefecture) in the fall of 1842, for example, a local scholar reported that elderly people whom he had seen in summer and winter wearing clothing made from mulberry fiber ("thick cloth," or *tafu*) were now wearing cotton garments.[46] The use of tree-bast cloth in this garment, which likely dates from the early twentieth century, suggests that it was made in a poor region of northern Honshu, where residents could neither grow cotton nor afford to buy it. The fabric is probably made of either wisteria or linden fibers.

The tree-bast lining of this jacket has been patterned with vertical warp stripes of dark brown against the natural tan of the fiber. The bark, nuts, or gall nuts of a number of trees growing in Japan's forests produce a brown dye. The lining was probably recycled from a work jacket.

70

71. Hekizan
(artist's dates unknown)

✦

Boys' Day Banner
Japan
Edo period, late 18th–19th century
Cotton with dyes and pigments
Tsutsugaki and painting
165 x 72 in.; 419.1 x 182 cm
Museum Purchase: The Barbara Benton
Wescoe Fund, 1993.12

This fourteen-foot banner, or *nobori*, was designed to fly from a pole planted in the ground on the annual Boys' Day Festival, which was celebrated on the fifth day of the fifth month. Erected near the front door of the house, a long *nobori* flapping in the wind celebrated the presence of sons in the family, and served to ward off evil. The custom persists today, although the holiday is now officially called Children's Day.

The fifth day of the fifth lunar month had been a festival day in Japan (as it was in China) since ancient times, but was not originally associated specifically with boys, and the practice of erecting banners honoring male children was a much later addition. Originally this day was a festival designed to ward off the evil spirits that were thought to be particularly dangerous during the fifth month, a liminal period between winter and summer. One of the oldest practices, dating at least as far back as the Heian period, was the aristocratic custom of gathering irises (*shōbu*), which were then placed on the roofs of houses and infused into a beverage, both practices designed to ward off evil and promote good health.[47] The word *shōbu* can also be read to refer to the military arts, a reading that provided a link between the military culture of Japan's rulers in the Edo period, classical Heian court culture, and this ancient festival of exorcism and protection.

During the Edo period, the feudal government officially designated the fifth day of the fifth month as Boys' Day. Competitions among boys at this festival included mock sword fights using *shōbu* as weapons. During his two-year stay in Japan from 1690 to 1692, Englebert Kaempfer noted the observance of a festival honoring boys on the fifth day of the fifth lunar month, a day on which people also placed medicinal herbs on the roofs of houses and drank infusions made of them. He further noted a practice of flying *nobori* on the seventh day of the seventh month (during the Tanabata Festival). On that day, boys affixed examples of their best calligraphy to tall bamboo poles to celebrate their scholarly progress. In Kaempfer's discussion, there was no association of *nobori* with the Boys' Day Festival.[48] This association came later, probably sometime in the mid- to late eighteenth century.[49]

Many scholars believe that the practice of flying tall banners to celebrate Boys' Day began among the samurai class.[50] Such banners, emblazoned with a family crest, had served as identification and rallying points during the wars that preceded the Edo period. Perhaps the first Boys' Day banners were simply *nobori* proudly depicting the family crest and planted outside the door on the fifth day of the fifth month to announce the presence of a boy child in the family, to protect him from harm, and to encourage him in the ways of his samurai family.

This banner depicts the Chinese folk deity Zhong Kui, a Confucian scholar who was best known for his loyalty to the emperor and his prowess as a demon queller.[51] Images of Zhong Kui are derived from a Tang dynasty legend. One night, Emperor Xuanzong (r. 712–756) dreamed that he saw a small demon stealing his jade flute and a beloved consort's embroidered perfume bag. The imp then mischievously danced around the palace grounds with his loot. The emperor confronted him and was about to call the palace guards when a huge, ferocious-looking demon appeared, caught the thief, gouged out his eyes, tore him into pieces, and ate him. Upon the emperor's query, the demon queller introduced himself as Zhong Kui, a Confucian scholar who had committed suicide by bashing his head against the palace steps a century earlier, mortified at his failure to pass the next stage of examinations. After Zhong Kui's death, Emperor Gaozu (r. 618–626) honored him with burial as a court official of the green-robe rank, and Zhong Kui then vowed to rid the world of demons, such as the pest that had stolen Xuanzong's flute and bag. (Green robes designated officials of the sixth and seventh of the nine official ranks.)[52] When Emperor Xuanzong woke from his dream, he summoned the famous court painter Wu Daozu and asked him to paint a portrait of Zhong Kui. The painter's rendition was so close to the emperor's recollection that Xuanzong declared, "You and I must have had a similar vision," and, as the story goes, he rewarded Wu Daozu handsomely.[53]

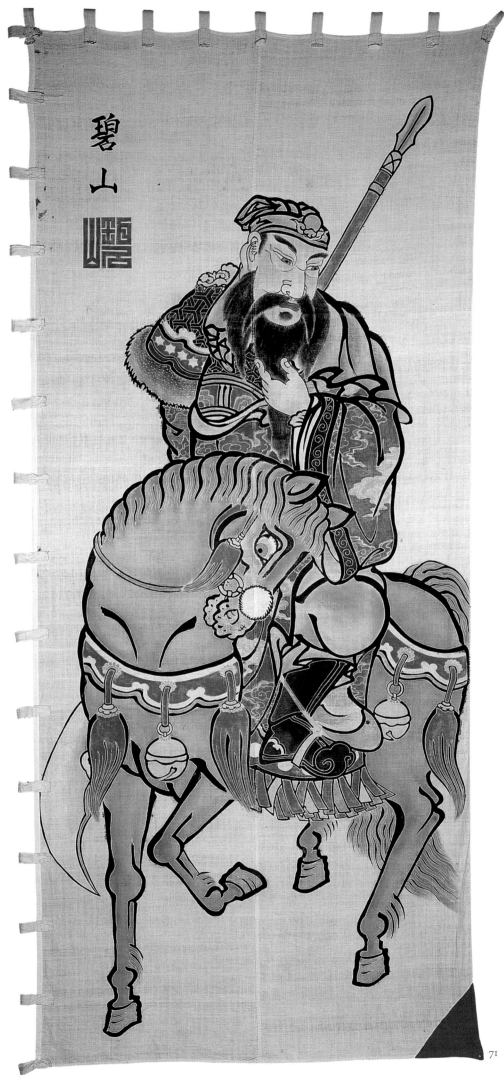

碧山

71

Shortly after this time, painters in the Hanlin Imperial Painting Academy began to produce portraits of Zhong Kui for the emperor to distribute to his courtiers at the beginning of each new year, probably to function as door guardians.[54] Although Zhong Kui was a newcomer to the pantheon in the Tang dynasty, his image was incorporated into the set of protective deities displayed on house doors and renewed at the New Year.[55] By the twelfth century, Zhong Kui had become a standard subject for portraits. Images of the demon queller were listed as one of the established categories of religious painting in the *Xuanhe huapu* (*Catalogue of the imperial painting collection during the Xuanhe era*), which has a preface dated to 1120; and there are records of Zhong Kui painting competitions in the *I zhou ming hualu* (*A record of the famous painters of I zhou* [present-day Sichuan]), with a preface dated to 1006).[56]

Extant Yuan dynasty (1279–1368) paintings of Zhong Kui depict the demon queller not as a giant demon but as a Confucian scholar, often with tame demon retainers, but still with his characteristic heavy black beard, boots, and Tang official robes. Story and iconography changed over time. By the late Ming, Zhong Kui had become a popular hero-god who had committed suicide after the emperor denied him the first place in the examinations only because he was so ugly (i.e., his ferocious aspect and barbarian features).

Two early Qing dynasty (1644–1911) portraits of Zhong Kui attributed to Emperor Shunzhi (r. 1644–1661) depict the demon queller standing alone, against a blank background, in scholar's robes, boots, a heavy beard, and with ferocious eyes.[57] These depictions became prototypes for later Qing portraits of Zhong Kui. The painter of this banner also followed the Qing convention of removing the figure from any indication of place or setting, but chose to render the image in a detailed and precise manner rather than employing the quick ink sketches typical of Emperor Shunzhi's portraits and of many later Qing dynasty and Edo period depictions of the demon queller.

The earliest depiction of Zhong Kui in Japan is found in the *Jigoku zōshi*, illustrations of the Buddhist hells usually dated to the late twelfth century.[58] In this picture scroll, Zhong Kui clutches a demon and gouges out his eyes, an almost literal interpretation of the original Tang dynasty legend. In subsequent centuries, paintings and sketches of Zhong Kui by major artists such as Sesshū Tōyō (1420–1506) and Kanō Tanyū (1602–1674) were issued as woodblock prints, so that by the mid-Edo period images of the demon queller, known as Shōki in Japan, had entered the popular vocabulary. The popularity of Shōki imagery reached a peak in the late Edo period with portraits that are often quickly sketched and somewhat humorous. The demon queller sometimes appears, for example, as an authoritative figure who is bettered by his impish retainers, a theme (as Matthew Welch suggests) that might have been intended as a parody of the weakening Tokugawa government.[59] This theme is fully explored in the humorous master-servant interplays that provide so much of the material for the comic *kyōgen* interludes during Noh performances. Nineteenth-century Japanese depictions of Shōki often exhibit an interest in the grotesque, humorous, and macabre.

Extant Boys' Day *nobori* are usually made of one or two lengths of kimono-width cotton material, each approximately thirteen inches wide. The designs are executed in the *tsutsugaki* technique—the edges of the patterns drawn with rice paste squeezed through a tube, and the image painted with pigments, dyes, and ink. Themes are martial, ranging from the simple depiction of a samurai helmet to complex scenes from famous medieval battles. Sometimes a family's crest is boldly displayed above the image.

This banner is constructed of two panels, each approximately three feet wide (91.5 cm), or more than double the standard width. Cloth width was regulated during the Edo period, and most people were prohibited from using cloth of this size. Furthermore, Edo period looms were built efficiently to perform one or more specific tasks, with the vast majority of looms designed to weave narrow, kimono-width cloth, a width used—in multiples, if necessary—for most other products as well. Very few looms could have accommodated cloth of this width. The unusual width of these panels of finely woven cotton suggests association with a fairly high-ranking member of the military class or ruling shogunate.

The association of this *nobori* with the upper levels of the samurai class is supported by the style, materials, and other features of the banner. At a time when many depictions of Shōki treated the subject playfully, here the demon queller is depicted in a conservative style. The brushwork is finely detailed. Red was considered a protective color, and a number of Shōki images that were probably used in association with Boys' Day depict the figure as red.[60] Here the red dye is from safflower, a regulated dye material that was prohibited to commoners. The extensive use of this coveted, regulated, and very expensive dye also points to a well-to-do samurai household. Finally, the banner is signed; the signature and seal at upper left read "Hekizan" (literally, "blue mountain"). Although the artist is not otherwise known (at least by this sobriquet), the quality of his work and the fact that he signed and sealed the image suggest an unusually careful production.

This depiction of Zhong Kui follows the Ming dynasty interpretation of a respected scholar-official, while retaining the iconic heavy beard and high boots, and adding impressive weaponry. The demon queller is mounted on a finely caparisoned prancing horse, and carries a double-headed spear or lance. His horse is not confined by the boundaries of the picture plane and would have seemed even more lively as the banner fluttered in the wind. Zhong Kui sits calmly astride his lively steed, thoughtful but prepared for action, wearing a combination of Chinese scholar's robes and armor.

In combining the robes and mien of a Confucian scholar with the accoutrements of battle, Zhong Kui serves in this banner both as a protective guardian of male children and as a model of loyalty, scholarship, strength, and courage—all core samurai values.

72. *Yogi*

◆

Japan (western region)
Late 19th-early 20th century
Cotton with dyes and pigments
Tsutsugaki and painting
65 x 32 in.; 162.5 x 80 cm
Museum Purchase: The Barbara Benton
Wescoe Fund, 1993.13

A *yogi* ("night garment") is a heavily padded, kimono-shaped bedcovering, a form that developed from the practice of using an extra garment as a bedcover. *Yogi* can be seen in medieval picture scrolls, such as the *Kasuga gongen genki-e*, an illustrated religious history of the Kasuga Shrine in Nara produced in 1309; in Edo period screens; and even—albeit rarely—in nineteenth-century photographs.[61]

Extant *yogi* generally are woven of cotton and padded with cotton batting. Often, as here, triangular gussets under the arms give a small measure of flexibility to the cumbersome sleeves, and increase the area of the textile. Most are considerably larger than a standard garment, in both length and width. The extra width is achieved by inserting an additional panel, about half the width of a standard panel, between the two back panels of the garment. Household looms were narrow, designed to produce a plain woven cotton or bast fiber cloth of standard width (approximately 13 inches). Women used this standard width, singly or in multiples, to make all of the household garments, bedding, carrying cloths, and other necessities of daily life.

By the time this *yogi* was made, most Japanese, including villagers, slept on *futon*, rectangular mats made from and padded with cotton, with a *shikibuton* ("under *futon*") or heavily padded mat underneath, and a more lightly stuffed *kakebuton* ("cover *futon*") on top. *Yogi* had evolved into ceremonial textiles, commissioned particularly for weddings. In rural Japan they were often patterned with *tsutsugaki*. They formed part of the bride's dowry and were paraded through the village—along with her other household furnishings and textiles—in a festive bridal procession from the bride's house to the groom's. Bride and groom slept under the *yogi* for the first nights after the wedding. After that, the *yogi* was brought out only on special occasions, such as the visit of an honored guest. The pristine condition of this *yogi* suggests such a history. It was probably used very little after the newlyweds' first nights of marriage.

Wedding *yogi* were decorated with time-honored auspicious motifs suitable to the occasion. Here a mythical phoenix (*hōō*) prepares to alight on a paulownia tree (*kiri*) with small bamboo

72

(*take*) growing at its base. The *kiri-take-hōō* motif, derived from Chinese mythology, had a long history in Japan. First associated with imperial and aristocratic garments in the Heian and Kamakura periods, the paulownia-bamboo-phoenix motif became popular with commoners in the Edo period as well. Rural craftsmen usually interpreted the motif in a bold, vigorous style, often (as here) executed free-hand with a rice-paste resist, dyes, and pigments—a style that contrasted markedly with the formal, repetitive patterns woven into imperial and aristocratic garments of the same period. The Taishō emperor (r. 1912–1926), for example, owned a formal garment (*hō*) with a stylized, repeating pattern of descending phoenix, paulownia, and bamboo. On this imperial garment, the *kiri-take-hōō* motif appears elegant, orderly, and restrained, totally different from the dynamic interpretation of the motif in nineteenth- and early-twentieth-century rural wedding *yogi* such as this example.

Paulownia leaves were associated with the emperor and the upper aristocracy until the fourteenth century. In the Muromachi and Momoyama periods, successive emperors occasionally granted the use of the paulownia for a family crest as a mark of imperial esteem. The shogun Ashikaga Takauji (1305–1358), for example, was granted the use of the paulownia, as was the military ruler Toyotomi Hideyoshi.[62] In the Edo period, however, the paulownia leaf motif became popular with all classes. Bamboo—due to its ability to bend but not break under heavy snows or in wild storms—symbolizes resilience, the strength to survive adversity, and the ability to conform to varying circumstances without losing one's fundamental principles. The motif became very popular in the Yuan dynasty among Confucian scholar-officials estranged from an alien (Mongolian) government. In Japan, it had become part of a popular vocabulary for imagery long before this *yogi* was made.

In East Asia, the mythical phoenix was believed to appear in times of enlightened rule that brought peace and prosperity to the realm. It alighted only on paulownia trees, and fed only on bamboo seeds. The phoenix lived to a very old age and mated for life. Its tail feathers represented the traditional virtues of truthfulness, propriety, righteousness, benevolence, and sincerity. As they lay together through the first nights of marriage, the young couple would have been covered with these familiar and time-honored symbols, wishes for prosperity, harmony, virtue, and a long, happy marriage.

Most *yogi* in Western collections have had their padding and linings removed, as they are heavy and cumbersome in their original form. This example retains its original padding and lining. The green lining, made by an overdye of indigo with a common yellow dye such as bark from the Amur cork tree (*kihada*) or miscanthus grass (*kariyasu*), extends beyond the sleeves and hem, further increasing the size of the *yogi*.

The phoenix dominates the upper portion of the back of the *yogi*, his tail feathers swirling around him and over the shoulders of the textile to form a handsome pattern on the front. He descends, eyes intent and beak open, toward the stump of an old paulownia tree whose large leaves reveal its age. The paulownia is just beginning to bloom; a pair of blossoms, surely another reference to the human couple, graces the bottom of each stalk, with a myriad of buds above, suggesting children yet to come.

Tsutsugaki textiles were popular throughout rural Japan, and were made in many cotton-producing areas. The bright colors of this *yogi* suggest that it was made on the island of Kyushu or Shikoku.[63]

Front view (Plate 72)

Kasuri

The patterns of *kasuri* textiles are made by tying off, or otherwise compressing, sections of the threads to be used in the warp and/or weft before they are dyed, so that the tied areas remain white (or the original color) while the rest of the thread is dyed. The sections to be tied must be measured exactly, and the threads handled with meticulous care throughout preparation, loom set-up, and weaving. *Kasuri* weaving is slow and requires precise attention to detail. The final thread-by-thread alignment of the warp as it is tied on the loom alone can take several hours, and some patterns require that *kasuri* weft threads also be adjusted one by one as they are inserted in the web.

The word *kasuri* refers specifically to Japanese "thread-resist" textiles (textiles where the pattern has been reserved on the threads before weaving). It most often refers to plain-woven textiles made of cotton or *asa* (hemp, ramie) with white patterns reserved on an indigo-blue ground. The Malay-Indonesian word *ikat* is used widely to refer generically to this thread-resist technique.

The earliest extant *ikat* textiles in Japan date from the seventh and eighth centuries, and were undoubtedly among the many textiles and other objects imported to Japan from Korea, China, and Southeast Asia. These *ikat* textiles are all fragments of elaborate polychrome silk banners that were used for Buddhist ceremonies. Today they are preserved in the Hōryūji Hōmotsukan (a treasury of objects from the ancient temple Hōryūji housed at the Tokyo National Museum) and in the Shōsōin Repository of the temple Tōdaiji in Nara. The patterns of linked curved lines in the warp are somewhat reminiscent of later Central Asian and Southeast Asian *ikat* patterns of linked human figures.[64]

There is no evidence that Japanese craftsmen ever produced warp *ikat* patterns derived from the banners imported in the seventh and eighth centuries. Beginning in the Heian period, however, they began to use a simple *ikat* technique to change the ground color of wide, flat-plaited sashes (*hirao*) that were used in Japanese court costume. At least by the Muromachi period, weavers had adapted this technique to change the ground color of fashionable silk garments with complex weave structures. From the Edo period to the present, this use of the *ikat* technique to effect changes in ground color in different sections of the garment has been reserved primarily for use in costumes for the Noh theater, where it is known as *dangawari* (rung-patterning). (See Fig. 14.)

The origins of *kasuri* weaving are somewhat obscure. It seems clear only that *kasuri* weaving as it is known today is a product of the Edo period, when the demands of a thriving urban economy spurred developments in rural textile production. It is also apparent that there was a lively interplay between developments in *kasuri* weaving in various parts of Japan, and between Japan and the Ryūkyū islands (present-day Okinawa).

The popularity of *kasuri* textiles in the marketplace spurred the development of new patterns, and in the late nineteenth and early twentieth centuries, of new techniques designed to increase the range of possible patterns and to speed production.[65]

73. Kasuri Furisode

Japan
Early 20th century
Indigo-dyed ramie
Warp and weft *kasuri* on plain weave ground
37 x 12 in.; 92.5 x 30 cm
Museum Purchase: The Barbara Benton
Wescoe Fund, 1993.11

74. Kasuri Futonji (detail)

Japan
19th or 20th century
Indigo-dyed cotton
Warp and weft *kasuri*, plain and "log cabin"
weaves
60.5 x 39 in.; 153.6 x 99 cm
Museum Purchase, 1992.78

75. Kasuri Futonji (detail)

Japan
19th or 20th century
Indigo-dyed cotton
Warp and weft *kasuri* on plain weave ground
56.5 x 13 in.; 143.6 x 33 cm
Museum Purchase, 1992.79

76. Kasuri Futonji (detail)

Japan
19th or 20th century
Indigo-dyed cotton
Warp and weft *kasuri* (hand tying and *e-dai*) on
plain weave ground
61 x 12.8 in.; 155 x 32.4 cm
Museum Purchase, 1992.80

77. Kasuri Futonji (detail)

Japan
19th or 20th century
Indigo-dyed cotton
Weft *kasuri* on plain weave ground
61 x 12.8 in.; 155 x 32.4 cm
Museum Purchase, 1992.81

The child's formal kimono (Plate 73) and four lengths of cotton bedding material (*futonji*) (Plates 74–77) are patterned by selectively resisting sections of the warp and weft yarns from the dye before they are set on the loom. At its most basic, as in Plate 74, *kasuri* requires few tools or materials beyond those necessary to dye and weave a simple, plain-woven fabric, of the type produced in households throughout rural Japan.[66]

In the nineteenth century, Japanese weavers developed a variety of tools and techniques designed to increase the complexity of patterning and to speed textile production. Two of these methods are represented here. The *e-dai*, or "picture stand," represented by two *futonji* lengths (Plates 76 and 77), was used to produce cotton *kasuri* along the San'in coast facing the Inland Sea, in areas of Iyo and Bingo Provinces (present-day Ehime and Hiroshima Prefectures, respectively), and in Kurume in northern Kyushu. The *itajime* (board-pressed) technique was used to produce both *asa* and cotton *kasuri* textiles in the Yamato district near Nara, Ōmi in present-day Shiga Prefecture, the Noto peninsula, and Kurume. *Itajime* was used in the child's kimono (Plate 73).

The simplest of the *futonji* patterns is seen in Plate 75, with horizontal and vertical stripes and a *kasuri* "well" pattern at alternating intersections. To make this *futonji*, the warp threads were counted, measured, and stretched out in three groups of the same length. One group was comprised of the threads to remain white. After these warp threads were wound, they were taken from the warping board, formed into a loose chain to keep them from getting tangled, and set aside. Threads to be dyed a solid, deep blue comprised the second group. These also were removed from the warping board and set aside. The threads of the third group were stretched out, and the sections to be reserved from the dye were measured and bound off. Binding materials varied depending on the type of fiber, length of the resisted section, preference of the individual weaver or workshop, and common practice in that part of the country. The simplest method was to wind a thick thread tightly around the bunched warp yarns. Often, though, for long resisted sections such as those seen here, something like a piece of paper the length of the resisted section was wound around the warp threads first to help the resist. After these warp threads were tied, they too were loosely chained and set aside.

After the warp threads were tied, the *kasuri*-patterned weft yarns had to be measured and tied. These were wound around two pegs (or some other device) to make a small skein slightly wider than the projected width of the finished cloth. The extra width allowed for the movement of the weft over and under the warp threads. With the skein still stretched on the pegs, the sections to be resisted from the dye were measured and bound. When tying was complete, all of the bundles of warp and weft threads to be dyed were taken to a local indigo shop. After they were dyed, the warp threads were stretched on the loom. Two people often worked together to wind a *kasuri*-patterned warp, one monitoring the white reserved sections to keep them from slipping as the other wound the warp on the back beam of the loom. In this *futon* cover (Plate 75), the warp threads that had been bound in order to form tight rectangles slid considerably as they were placed on the loom, giving a hazy edge to the pattern, a feathering that is characteristic of *kasuri*-woven textiles.

After the loom was set up, the weft was wound on bobbins on a wheel with a spindle shaft. If the reserved sections of the weft threads were tied accurately, the weaver had more control over the weft than the warp, as the threads could be adjusted slightly at the selvages during weaving. Many Japanese *kasuri* textiles have slightly uneven selvages as a result of this adjustment. Although the weaver of this *futonji* probably could have made a precise rectangular pattern if she had chosen to do so, instead she chose not to adjust the weft threads at the selvages, allowing the pattern to feather in the horizontal as well as the vertical direction. The warp and weft *kasuri* bars appear as half-tones, like the stripes in the warp and weft, except at the corners of the "well," where warp *kasuri* and weft *kasuri* come together to create sharp white squares. This *futonji* was probably made by a woman working at home to produce a handsome bedding fabric for her

73

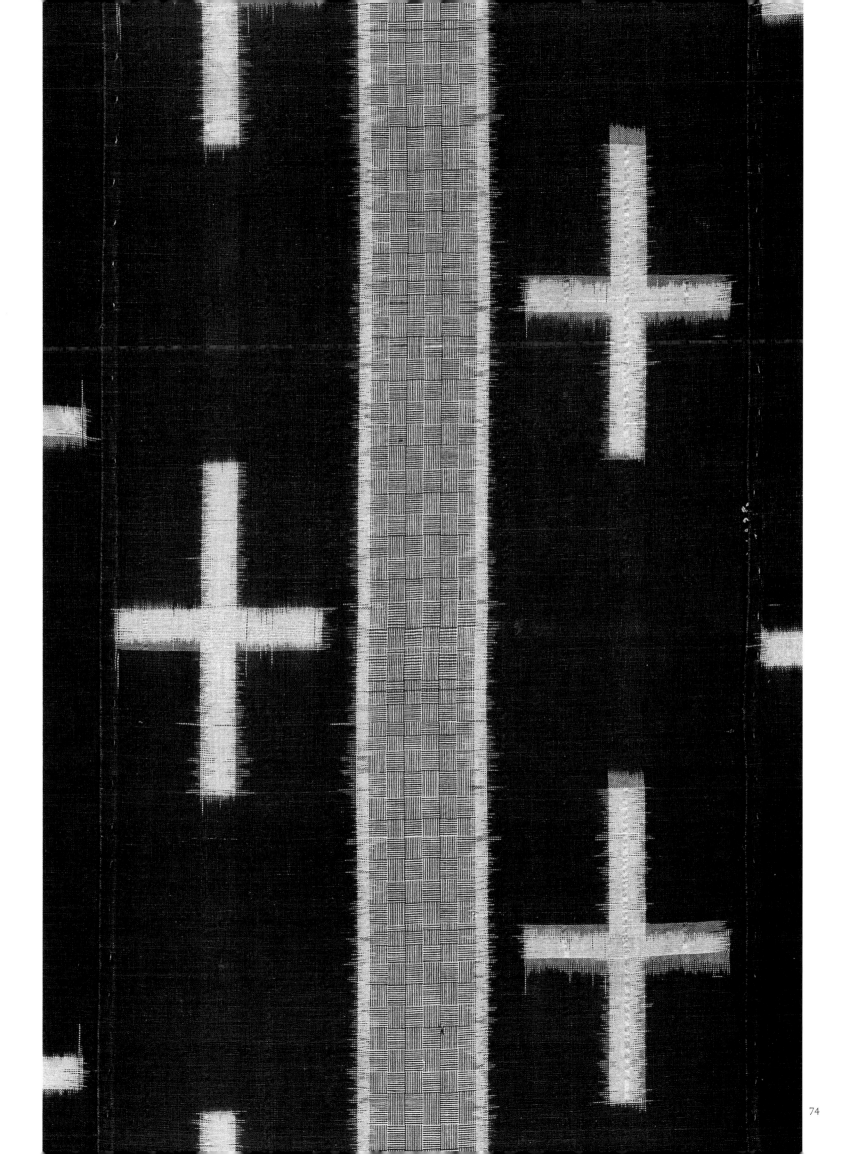

234

household. By allowing the edges of the simple bands of white to feather, she would have been able to weave the cloth quickly. The feathering also adds a pleasing element of irregularity to the otherwise regular grid of warp and weft stripes. The pattern is simple but effective.

The patterning of Plate 74 is both more precise and more complex. Although the edges of the crosses are slightly feathered, the feathering does not extend markedly beyond the cross, except for a single errant warp thread here or there. The checkerboard band is unusual. It was created by alternating white and indigo threads in that section of the warp and weaving, alternately, a white and an indigo weft. Both of these weft threads had to be tied: the weft threads that were to remain white through the checkerboard were tied the width of the band, and the weft threads that were to appear blue in the checkerboard were given two small ties to create the narrow, pure white vertical edges of the checkerboard band. This fabric, too, was probably woven at home, perhaps in the San'in district of Honshu on the Inland Sea.

Both Plates 76 and 77 are typical of *kasuri* from the San'in coast, and likely are products of local workshops. The free-form patterns of octopus and decorated fan, both created entirely with weft yarns, were made with the aid of an *e-dai* (also called an *osa-dai, ezu-dai, tane ito dai*, and *sumi ito dai*), a rectangular wooden frame with an open-topped reed fastened to the two longest sides. The distance between the reeds was equal to the projected width of the finished cloth, plus the necessary "take-up" (the extra width needed to account for the movement of the weft threads over and under the warp as they pass from selvage to selvage). To pattern wefts using an *e-dai*, a thick thread was wound back and forth between the openings of the reeds to simulate the passage of weft. When enough had been wound for one repeat of the design, the pattern was drawn or stenciled onto this guide thread, or *tane ito*, usually with sumi ink. The *tane ito* was then taken off the *e-dai* and stretched out on a large frame, such as a warping frame. Finally, the pattern weft threads were wound next to the *tane ito* and tied at the appropriate points, as indicated by the ink marks on the guide thread.

All of the patterning in Plate 77 is in the weft. The fan pattern in Plate 76 was created with an *e-dai* and *tane ito*, but the interlocking squares required both warp and weft ties and were formed in the manner outlined above for Plates 74 and 75. The warp and weft threads in unpatterned sections of the cloth are a deeper blue than the rest of the fabric, indicating that they were dyed separately. These darker lines form a shadow grid in the cloth, adding subtle interest to the ground. The use of the *e-dai* and precision of the patterning suggest that these two lengths of *futon* material were produced in a small commercial workshop.

The little girl's formal kimono, or *furisode* (swinging sleeves), (Plate 73) was made in the Ōmi district of present-day Shiga Prefecture, across Lake Biwa from Kyoto. Ōmi was famous for its fine ramie cloth and complex *kasuri* patterning (*Ōmi jōfu*). The intricate designs of chrysanthemums, waves, and butterflies among well and rice field motifs on this small robe were carefully planned and meticulously rendered. Many *kasuri*-patterned children's garments were made of cloth recycled from adults' clothing. The small scale and fine proportions of the patterns on this *furisode*, however, suggest that this textile was designed and woven specifically for a child.

The primary patterning is in the weft, as in the two *e-dai futonji* discussed above. Here the weft motifs were reserved by a process akin to printing. The *itajime* technique was used in the Yamato and Ōmi districts to create complex, precise free-form motifs in the cloth.[67] Local records suggest that textile production using this technique began in both regions during the second quarter of the nineteenth century (1837 in Yamato, and 1850 in Ōmi).[68] *Itajime* required the use of two boards carved in a manner similar to the woodblocks carved for paper prints. Either ground or motif could be reserved. Yamato *kasuri* motifs generally appear in blue against a white ground, while Ōmi *kasuri* looks more similar to the blue and white *kasuri* produced in other parts of rural Japan, with motifs that appear white against an indigo-blue ground.

In the *itajime* process in Ōmi, the ground around the motifs on pairs of boards was carved away, leaving the motifs raised. One board was a mirror image of the other. Holes were carved through to the surface of the boards for each area to be dyed. The weft threads were stretched, in order, between the boards, which were then aligned exactly and clamped together. They were then either immersed in the dye, or dye was poured in through the holes. The process made it easy to produce precise, free-form patterns faster and more efficiently than if the threads had been hand tied. Many *itajime* patterns resemble contemporary *kasuri* (or *katazome*) patterns. Here the carver has deliberately feathered the edges of the short horizontal bands in the weft of this child's garment to simulate the effects of hand tying (a more labor-intensive process resulting in a more costly textile). In the *itajime* process, it actually would have been easier to make the edges of the bands precisely even.

Like the *e-dai*, the *itajime* process was developed for use in commercial workshops to make it possible to create complex patterns. The *e-dai* used stencils; *itajime*, carved woodblocks. The *e-dai*, however, still required artisans to hand-tie the weft threads. *Itajime* eliminated this time-consuming step, speeding up production almost by a factor of three.[69]

Although the weft patterning in this young girl's *furisode* is complex, the warp patterning is minimal. It consists only of simple sets of three narrow, vertical lines. The lines are quite ragged at top and bottom, as if little attention had been paid to producing a straight edge. This might have been intentional. One characteristic of *itajime* is the crisp edges of the weft patterning, which make it possible to produce small, intricate patterns that fill the field. The feathering of the simple lines of warp *kasuri* softens and offsets the overall hard-edged precision and complexity of the weft patterning. The feathered lines also create layers of tonality, yielding a convincing sense of three-dimensionality, an illusion of depth.

Kasuri was the height of fashion in the late eighteenth and early nineteenth centuries. Courtesans and the wives of wealthy merchants alike appear in contemporary woodblock prints clad in handsome hand-tied *kasuri* garments. A century later, old photographs show an entire populace clad in stripes, *katazome*, and *kasuri* attire. Although *kasuri* garments were no longer the rage that they were around 1800, fashionable women and the artists who portrayed them still occasionally chose a fine *kasuri* kimono, such as the one seen here.

Textiles from Okinawa

78. *Bashō* Garment

◆

Japan (Okinawa)
20th century, before 1945
Bashō (banana fiber) with cotton stripes
Plain weave
42.5 x 22.5 in.; 106.3 x 56.3 cm
Museum Purchase: The Barbara Benton
Wescoe Fund, 1993.14

This garment of *bashōfu* (banana fiber cloth), patterned with simple vertical stripes, is a fine example of traditional Ryūkyūan commoners' attire. It is cut to reach half-way between knee and ankle, and constructed with a very long neckband. The tubular sleeves are sewn completely to the body of the garment. This garment does not show the influence of Japanese kimono construction, which appears in many late-nineteenth- and twentieth-century Okinawan garments intended for fashion-conscious gentry or for export to other Japanese prefectures.

The garment is made of *bashō*, fiber from a species of banana (the thread-banana plant; *Musa liukiuensis* [Matsumura], Makino). *Bashō* was used on the Ryūkyū islands (present-day Okinawa Prefecture) to weave garments for people in all strata of society, as well as for tax payments to the Ryūkyūan court in Shuri and tribute payments to China and Satsuma Province (present-day Kagoshima Prefecture) in Japan.[70] *Bashō* was not native to the Ryūkyūan archipelago and may have been introduced in the first half of the sixteenth century, when references to banana fiber cloth can be identified clearly in written records for the first time.

A 1546 account by a group of shipwrecked Korean sailors includes a record of *bashō* processing. The sailors noted that *bashō* fibers were split into three different grades, and likened the highest quality to the smooth, white skin of a beautiful woman:

[T]he finest grade is white as snow, smooth and flawless as a beautiful woman's skin.[71]

Bashōfu appears on lists of tribute goods beginning in 1587.[72] By the late sixteenth century, the Ryūkyūan court was sending high quality *bashō* fabric to the Ming court in China as tribute. In 1610 bolts of *bashōfu* were included in the submission gifts that King Shō Nei presented to retired shogun Tokugawa Ieyasu and his son, the ruling shogun Hidetada, following the invasion of Ryūkyū by the daimyo of Satsuma Province.[73] By 1638 the domain of Satsuma was selling imported *bashōfu* in Kyoto as one of its own "famous products;" the cloth was included that year in the *Kebukigusa*, a publication that listed the numerous regional products available in the Japanese capital.[74]

The "stalk" of the thread-banana plant is composed of tight concentric layers of "leaf sheaths" that open to "leaves" at the top of the plant. Fibers pulled from the innermost layers of the vertical leaf sheaths can be split into hair-like threads to make fabric as fine as silk. Fiber from the outer leaf sheaths, by contrast, is so coarse that it was reserved for cordage.[75] Formal robes worn at the Ryūkyūan court were made of the finest *bashōfu*, dyed in brilliant colors that were rank specific.[76] Garments made from middle-grade *bashō*, such as this example, clothed commoners.[77]

Even the *bashō* used for this handsome but practical garment, designed for everyday wear, has a lustrous sheen, which is created as light strikes the smooth, flat, and almost untwisted fibers. The natural rich tan of the banana fibers is set off by brown, light (indigo) blue, and natural white cotton stripes in the warp. Well into the twentieth century, many women gathered and prepared the fibers, dyed them, and wove the material that their households required. The weaver of this *bashōfu* garment probably purchased only the small amount of cotton thread needed for the warp patterning.

A special feature of this garment is the addition of tiny diagonal lines, made by plying together white and indigo-dyed cotton threads, to add subtle visual interest to the stripes. This plying technique, which was called *mūdei* in and around the Naha and Shuri districts on the main island of Okinawa, is particular to Okinawan textiles.[78]

Mūdei—or *moku ito*, as it is known to some Japanese weavers[79]—is not seen in textiles produced on the main Japanese islands, except for those deliberately inspired by Okinawan textiles.[80] Tanaka Toshio and Reiko, a husband and wife team whose extensive research in Okinawa provided the first comprehensive study of Okinawan woven textiles, found the *mūdei* technique throughout the Ryūkyūs in the mid-twentieth century.[81] Among extant historical textiles with assigned provenance, however, the technique seems to appear most in textiles from Shuri and Naha, and from Kumejima Island, which supplied cloth for the court in Shuri.

78

To date, *mūdei* has been almost completely overlooked by scholars studying Okinawan textiles. The Tanakas are unusual even in naming and noting it, although they only note its use in a few of the textiles they illustrate that employ the technique. Research into this simple but effective technique, or even an inventory of extant textiles in which it appears, might add a small but significant bit of knowledge to the history of Okinawan textiles, and perhaps aid in the often difficult task of dating and classifying textiles from the archipelago.

The oldest extant examples of Okinawan textiles with two-color plied-thread patterning are fragments from three aristocratic *dōsui* (generally equivalent to the Japanese *kosode*, forerunner of the kimono) that the Tanakas have dated to the early nineteenth century. Although the patterns and colors are quite different, all have silk warps and cotton wefts with stripes in each, along with *kasuri* patterns and *mūdei* plied threads in the weft. *Mūdei* is featured in a mid-nineteenth-century fragment associated with the royal family. This polychrome *tsumugi* (spun silk) garment fragment from Kumejima is patterned exclusively by stripes—plain, *kasuri*, and *mūdei*. A cotton fragment from a garment probably used by a member of the gentry in the castle town of Shuri has white *kasuri* patterns on an indigo ground in the warp and weft, with a wide stripe of light blue, white, and dark indigo in the warp setting off two bold interior *mūdei* stripes. The Tanakas also illustrated a deep indigo cotton clothing fragment from the mid-twentieth century with a blue and white *mūdei*-patterned band in the center of each regularly placed, plain light blue stripe, a pattern that they found throughout Okinawa.[82]

From the small group of textiles reviewed here, it appears that *mūdei* two-color plied threads were a patterning device first associated with the aristocracy and royal family. In most of these textiles, *mūdei* was used as a minor design element in a multicolored textile that included a variety of patterning techniques, including checks, stripes, and *kasuri*. Later, in simpler cotton and *bashōfu* garments for the gentry and for popular use, two-color plied threads played a larger role in adding visual interest to a basic striped pattern in indigo and white.

In this garment, the *mūdei* technique has been used to great effect. It adds liveliness to the unassuming striped pattern through an unexpected shift in the strict vertical and horizontal directionality of the threads, and provides the shimmering effect of tiny, irregular color shifts.

79. Fragment of *Bingata*
◆

Japan (Okinawa)
Second half of 19th century
Ramie, dyes, and pigments
Bingata on plain weave ground
25.3 x 14 in.; 63 x 35 cm
Museum Purchase: The Barbara Benton
Wescoe Fund, 1993.15

The term *bingata* refers to polychrome textiles with dyed patterns associated with the royal court, aristocracy, and wealthy gentry in the kingdom of Ryūkyū. Most scholars believe that these textiles reached their present form in the eighteenth century.[83] All *bingata* production seems to have been located in and around Shuri and the nearby commercial centers of Tomari and Naha (on the main island of Okinawa). There is no evidence of production in any other part of the kingdom.

Bingata dyeing involved several distinct processes, including the use of multiple stencils, paste-resist techniques, immersion dyeing, and the application of dyes and pigments with brushes. The largest and boldest patterns and most brilliant colors were reserved for the royal family and court nobility. The light blue ground and small, overall patterns—worked identically on both sides of a fine ramie fabric—identify Plate 79 as part of the summer garment of an affluent gentry woman who probably lived in the castle town of Shuri.

One of the distinguishing characteristics of *bingata* is a clear, brilliant palette with colors that many visitors to the archipelago have likened to the hues of the sea, sky, forests, dazzling coral reefs, and bright flowers seen there. Ryūkyūans used these clear, bright colors as rank markers. Number Five in a list of Eleven Great Achievements of the Age, inscribed in 1509 on the front balustrade of the Momourasoe Hall, the main palace of King Shō Shin, notes that the king had appointed "one thousand officials" to court ranks and "one hundred officials" to posts. Furthermore, the noble and the mean, the high and the low, their ranks are regulated by the yellow and red colors of their caps and the gold and silver pins in their hair. . . . This is the model . . . for men of later generations.[84]

Foreign observers commented on the beauty of Ryūkyūan dyed textiles and the high quality of the dyes and pigments. The following appeared in a report written in 1802 by Li Dongyuan, Chinese envoy to the court of Shō En:

> The people of this country are very skillful in the stamping of flowers of many kinds. They make paper stencils, apply the stencil to the fabric, and paint it with ash [ash lye used as a mordant]. If the fabric is washed after having been dyed and the ash is washed out, the flowers emerge in very brilliant colors. These colors do not fade, even if the garment is in tatters. They must be in possession of a production secret that they do not reveal to others. For this reason the *dongyang huabu* [flowered cloth from the Eastern Ocean] is highly valued.[85]

Although Li Dongyuan viewed *bingata* textiles with admiration and suggested that Ryūkyūan dyers held secrets that others did not possess, Kamakura Yoshitarō (1898–1983), a *bingata* scholar and dyer who was designated a Living National Treasure in 1973, pointed out the close historical connection between Fujian in southern China and the Ryūkyūan kingdom.[86] Kamakura suggested that dyeing and painting techniques, materials, and styles from Fujian played a major role in the development of *bingata* dyeing. The following discussion is based largely on Kamakura's research.[87]

Kamakura believed that Ryūkyūan court painters trained in Fujian profoundly influenced the patterns and styles of *bingata* textiles. During the reign of King Shō Kei (1713–1751), for example, the court painter Yamaguchi Sokei introduced Fujian-style Chinese bird and flower motifs into *bingata* design, radically changing the appearance of the textile. Fujian was also the source of new techniques and essential materials. In 1766, a Chinin Chikudun Pēchin returned from a trip to Fujian, where he had learned to make high-quality stencil paper. On his return, Pēchin founded the main line of Shuri *bingata* dyers. *Bingata* is probably named for *bin*, or lac (*Coccus lacci*; *enji* in Japanese), a brilliant red dye imported from Fujian. *Bin* came from a scale insect related to the *Coccus cacti* (cochineal) of the Western hemisphere. The word *bin* refers to lac specifically, to red more broadly, and also to color in general; *bingata* means scarlet stencil or pattern.

Bingata was closely associated with the royal court in the castle town of Shuri, and textiles dyed for royal or aristocratic use were strictly supervised. Dyers were organized under the Tax Revenue Office. Orders for official garments were given to a magistrate in charge of the dyers who coordinated the collection of the requisite materials and distributed them to the various dye workshops. Court painters, organized under the shell-processing office (responsible for producing mother-of-pearl, a lucrative export item), provided designs for the stencils. Lac came directly from the Tax Revenue Office, which controlled and stored imported raw materials. Other necessary materials—including stencil paper, fabric, ingredients for sizing the cloth and making the resist, and firewood—were supplied by magistrates from the appropriate outlying areas, the shell-processing office, and the Royal Household Agency.

Only the highest-quality *bingata* textiles were reserved exclusively for the royal family and aristocracy. Materials were provided to dyers from government stores for textiles commissioned for official use, but non-official commissions even from the royal family were treated as private accounts. In this case, dyers procured and paid for the materials themselves, and were reimbursed from their clients' personal funds. Court dyers also worked for affluent commoners, producing fine textiles in smaller patterns with non-restricted colors for wealthy clients in Shuri.

The Spencer *bingata* fragment was probably such a privately commissioned textile. Its light blue ground, *miji'iruji*, was specifically designated for general use. Other *bingata* workshops

79

located in the nearby port cities of Tomari and Naha produced simpler and less colorful textiles for a wider clientele.

Along with other craftsmen in Shuri, Tomari, and Naha, *bingata* dyers were required to pay cash taxes. In 1715 dyers contributed one sixth of all taxes raised from artisans. Although it is not clear whether this figure represents tax paid on all of their production or only on private commissions, it is apparent that dyers provided a significant source of income for the government.[88]

Little research has been done on the role of *bingata* in international trade, although two small pieces of evidence suggest that it was known and traded outside the kingdom, at least in southern China. Li Dongyuan, the Chinese envoy quoted above, had heard of this "flowered cloth from the Eastern Ocean" before he went to the Ryūkyūs, and he spoke of it as a "highly valued" textile. In marketplaces in Fujian, a Ryūkyūan cloth of the same name (*dongyang huabu*) was a "famed trade commodity."[89]

Ryūkyū was a maritime kingdom at the confluence of several major ocean currents that formed the spine of a network of ancient trade routes. Ryūkyūan ships plied the waters from northern Japan and Korea to China, and sailed the waterways surrounding the peninsulas and islands of Southeast Asia. Foreign ships stopped at the kingdom's ports. Lists of tribute goods suggest that textiles formed an important part of international trade throughout the region. Ryūkyūans were undoubtedly familiar with pattern-dyed cloth from Southeast Asia and India (as well as from Japan), but no research to date has been able to unravel the intricacies of influences from other textile traditions on the development of *bingata*, or vice versa.

One intriguing question is the possible relationship between the development of *bingata* in and around Shuri in Okinawa, and *yūzen* in Kyoto and Kanazawa in Japan. Observers have drawn obvious parallels between these two dyeing traditions, both of which use a combination of stencils, paste resist, and hand-painting. Visual resemblances are particularly strong between *bingata* and *Kaga yūzen* (*yūzen* produced in the Kaga domain of the Maeda family, who ruled from the castle town of Kanazawa). At present, however, there is no substantial evidence linking the two traditions.

Textiles From Tōhoku

80. *Nizuri*

Japan (Tsuruoka district, Yamagata Prefecture)
Early 20th century
Cotton
Sashiko on plain weave cloth
22.5 x 12.5 in.; 57 x 31.8 cm
Museum Purchase: The Barbara Benton
Wescoe Fund, 1993.8

81. *Kogin* Overgarment

◆

Japan (Tsugaru peninsula, Aomori Prefecture)
Late 19th century
Cotton and bast fiber (*asa*)
Kogin on plain weave *asa* ground
37 x 21 in.; 94 x 53.3 cm
Museum Purchase: The Barbara Benton
Wescoe Fund, 1993.9

In many parts of Japan, vulnerable sections of a garment were covered with heavy cotton stitching to strengthen the fabric and prolong its life. In Tōhoku, a general name for the cold and mountainous region of northern Honshu (Japan's main island), this stitching became a highly developed form of artistic expression. In the *nizuri* vest (Plate 80), dense lines of vertical stitching protect the shoulders from abrasion. The back and front of the vest are also strengthened with stitching, but in a carefully figured tessellated pattern of nesting diamonds. In the *kogin* garment (Plate 81), the dense, counted-thread patterning primarily added warmth and beauty.

Tōhoku was isolated from the economic and cultural centers of Edo (present-day Tokyo), Kyoto, and Osaka, and its residents developed distinct garment types, designs, and stitching techniques. Until the late nineteenth century, the region could be reached only by ship or over rugged mountain passes. Rice was the main crop, and in good years Tōhoku exported shiploads of rice to other parts of Japan. The climate was harsh, however, and rice yields were often severely compromised. Poor harvests coupled with heavy land taxes kept many farmers at a bare subsistence level throughout the Edo period.[90] Conditions improved for Tōhoku farming communities in the late nineteenth century. The Meiji government reduced land taxes in 1876, and inflation further reduced the real impact of the remaining taxes. The railroad reached Aomori in 1892 and Hirosaki in 1895, greatly increasing access to goods including cotton thread and cloth, neither of which was produced locally.

Cloth for household use was woven at home primarily from locally grown bast fibers (*asa*), both hemp and ramie. Cotton, the warmest material permitted to farmers, could not be cultivated successfully in this northern climate and had to be imported. In a period when most farm families in other parts of Japan wore padded cotton garments insulated with cotton batting in winter, peasants in Tōhoku put on layers of *asa* garments to keep warm, or quilted two or three layers of *asa* cloth together to form a thicker material. The geographer Furukawa Koshōken (1725/6–1807), writing in 1788 during a trip to Tōhoku, noted the absence of padded garments and the use of layers of hemp: "The farmers of below average means do not wear padded cotton garments. They stitch *asa* fabric and layer three such garments for warmth during the winter."[91]

Originally hemp or ramie thread (on a hemp or ramie ground) was used for embroidered patterning on Tōhoku garments. After cotton became more readily available in the late nineteenth century, women used thick, soft cotton thread imported from regions further south to pattern their bast fiber garments. Cotton was softer and whiter than bast fiber; it made the fabric warmer and created denser and more conspicuous patterns.

Tōhoku had several distinctive garment types, stitches, and stitching patterns. Besides the women's wood-hauling vests (*nizuri*; see Plate 80) and *kogin* garments (see Plate 81), there were sled-pulling vests for men (*sorihiki banten*) with broad bands that lay diagonally across the chest. The *nizuri* is an unshaped vest designed specifically to protect a woman's back from the heavy wooden frame that was used to carry firewood down from the mountains. It is typically patterned with the running stitch (*sashiko*) used by women throughout Japan for quilting, embroidering, and strengthening fabric. Although the garment was designed for heavy toil, young women and their female relatives stitched intricate patterns into the *nizuri* that brides brought with them to their new homes.

The maker of this *nizuri* chose a cotton fabric with a narrow vertical stripe, a fabric that would have been reserved for a man's or elderly woman's kimono in much of Japan. Such a subdued pattern of dark, narrow stripes would not have been considered desirable or appropriate for a younger woman. The regularity of the stripes, however, aids in the difficult task of creating an even and balanced pattern of nesting and tessellated diamonds, and once the stitched pattern was complete, the striped ground fabric was only barely visible under the prominent design. Like most finely worked *nizuri*, this one was probably made as part of a dowry. The pattern of nesting diamonds is typical of the Tsuruoka district of Yamagata Prefecture.

The term *kogin* is derived from *koginu* (literally, "small garment"). This woman's *kogin* garment is decorated with finely executed counted-thread embroidery (alternately called *kogin* and *sashikogin*) on indigo-dyed bast fiber panels that can be removed, reused, and replaced as needed. *Kogin* patterns are made by inserting the embroidery thread in the interstices of warp and weft threads to create a pattern based on the grid of the plain weave fabric. Geometric patterns are built up using either an odd or an even number of threads as a basic unit, depending on the region of Tōhoku in which the garment was produced. *Kogin* garments made on the Tsugaru peninsula at the far northern tip of the main island of Honshu were characteristically worked on a grid with an odd number of threads. In southeastern Aomori, *Nanbu hishizashi* garments were worked in a related counted-thread technique on a less versatile even-numbered grid. Edo period travelers to Tōhoku noted both stitched indigo patterning on a natural white ground, and white designs on a deep blue ground. *Kogin* garments created in and after the late nineteenth century are generally stitched with undyed cotton on an indigo-dyed hemp or ramie ground.

This *kogin* garment represents a narrowly localized tradition centered on the Tsugaru peninsula. Each geographical area on the peninsula had a distinctive type of patterning, although all were based on an odd-numbered grid. Within that pattern type, each maker chose or created specific motifs. The large-scale, overall patterning of this *kogin* garment is typical of the region east of the Iwaki River, while the snowflake-like motifs set into the overall pattern of interconnected diamonds was specifically chosen (or created) by its producer. Patterns traditionally were handed down from mother to daughter, recorded in the cloth.

Most scholars believe that the embroidered embellishment typical of many Tōhoku garments is derived from stitching used for practical purposes, such as reinforcing vulnerable parts of a garment, repairing or replacing worn fabric, stitching layers of fabric together to make a stronger and warmer cloth, or strengthening a new garment that would be subject to hard wear. In the case of the *nizuri* work vest, this seems quite probable; the many examples of used *nizuri*, heavily worn and abraded, attest to the abuse that the garment routinely endured. There are also extant examples of *nizuri* work vests that were stitched for strength with no apparent decorative intent.

It is more difficult to decipher the history of the unusual counted-thread patterning that was used to decorate *kogin* garments. Certainly this type of embroidery added a certain degree of warmth to the garment, but particularly before the availability of cotton, this result could be achieved by means simpler, quicker, and more efficient than the laborious counted-thread process. *Kogin* panels on extant garments are often considerably older than the rest of the garment, and even then, they are usually in fairly good condition. Rather than stitching a worn garment to strengthen it, extant examples indicate that beautifully decorated *kogin* panels were carefully moved from worn-out garments to new ones, suggesting that the *kogin* panel was the most valuable part of the garment. Perhaps this time-consuming technique was used primarily for its decorative potential.

The earliest descriptions of *kogin* garments date from the late eighteenth century, although the term appears in records of the Tsugaru clan written in 1685.[92] Both the geographer Furukawa Koshōken (quoted above) and a vassal of the local lord of Tsugaru wrote about the manners and customs of the people of the region in 1788. Furukawa noted the lovely clothing worn by Tsugaru women during Obon, an annual summer festival honoring ancestors: ". . . eight women out of ten are dressed in white kimono embroidered with dark blue thread in various designs."[93] He did not comment on the type of stitching used to embellish these garments, and may not have been aware that technically, as well as visually, he was seeing distinctively patterned attire. The Tsugaru clan vassal Hirano Sadahiko, however, was more knowledgeable in this subject, referring specifically to the counted-stitch technique (if one can assume that the terms had the same meaning in the late eighteenth century that they do today). Hirano noted,

> As for *sashikogin*, it is [used] to embroider a fabric in various designs and it is quite beautiful. Both men and women wear [such clothing]. Many are dark blue garments stitched with white thread.[94]

80

81

Of the several distinctive garment shapes in Tōhoku, the most intriguing in cut and construction is the *kogin*. Both the women's *nizuri* and men's *sorihiki banten* were simple work garments designed for specific tasks, with structures closely related to their functions. The *kogin*, however, was the most visible and common everyday and festival garment worn in the region. In some old photographs, it appears unbelted or loosely belted as an overcoat; in others, it is worn like a kimono, with the left flap folded over the right and belted.

Because the *kogin* was the main garment type in the region, it is particularly intriguing that these garments do not follow the basic Japanese model for garment construction: two panels, seamed at the back and sides, that pass from the back hem up over the shoulders to the front hem. Instead, the body of the *kogin* was constructed of six panels, two for the bodice and four below, joined at the back and side seams and at the waist. In some examples (including this one), the *kogin* (counted-thread) panels are the bodice panels. In others, the *kogin* panels are applied to unpatterned bodice panels. Many *kogin* garments, such as the one seen here, have a distinctive gathering at the waist where the bottom panels join the bodice. This gathering would occur naturally if the heavy embroidery on the top panels narrowed the width of these panels (during the embroidery stage or through shrinking in subsequent washings), but this could be—and sometimes was—compensated for by slightly deepening the side hems of the bottom panels. On this garment, the puckering is even, carefully considered and executed. The slight gathering must have been considered desirable.

Extant *kogin* appear in several styles, including some, like this one, with relatively narrow sleeves and large gussets—a shape modeled roughly on that of a work jacket. Others have kimono-like sleeves, and still others have wide, flowing sleeves that resemble those of a *furisode*. All *kogin* garments examined by the present author, however, are constructed of separate bodice and skirt panels.

To date, little research has been done on the construction of Tōhoku *kogin* garment types. There are no immediate and obvious prototypes for the *kogin*'s construction of separate bodice and skirt panels joined at the waist. There are, however, many eighth-century examples in the Shōsōin Repository of the temple Tōdaiji in Nara of both sleeved and sleeveless garments with separate bodice and skirt panels joined at the waist with gathers or pleats. These garments are either Chinese or based on Chinese prototypes. (See Fig. 9, page 105.) Although the garment type was inconspicuous in Japan after the Nara period, it survived in several conservative clothing traditions, usually as an undergarment. Parallels can be drawn, for example, between several eighth-century garments of this basic construction and the *kasane hanpi* (layered vest), a sleeveless vest with a very short skirt that was worn just under an aristocratic man's formal court robe (*hō*). The *kasane hanpi* was also preserved in costuming for the courtly Bugaku dance.[95] The *dōfuku*,[96] used from the early Muromachi period by high-ranking aristocrats for informal attire at home, had a comparatively long flared or pleated skirt attached to a kimono-like bodice, and very wide sleeves open at the ends. Although it was designed for informal wear, the *dōfuku* was made of the finest materials: damask or figured twill in winter, and figured gauze in summer.[97] In the Edo period, Buddhist priests wore similar garments (called *jikitotsu* and *dōfuku*) made of simpler materials and subdued colors. These garments are not usually visible in illustrations, but may be spotted through the front opening of a longer, fuller outer robe.[98] Itinerant priests—and other travelers as well—used the *dōfuku* (literally, "road garment") as an outer layer to protect their other garments while on the road.[99]

It seems improbable that the Tōhoku *kogin* had a direct relationship to any of the garments mentioned above. It is more likely that much earlier forms of clothing construction were retained separately by both the conservative garment traditions of the court and Buddhist establishment on the one hand, and by peoples in an isolated and remote part of the islands on the other. The subject bears further research.

Wedding Textiles

FUKUSA

82. *Fukusa*

Japan
Edo period, late 18th or 19th century
Silk and gold-wrapped thread
Embroidery (couching, satin, stem) on blue
satin with red crepe lining
35.3 x 27.3 in.; 89.5 x 69.2 cm
Given in Memory of James H. Walker, Jr. by his
Family, 1993.353

83. *Fukusa*

Japan
Edo period, late 18th or 19th century
Silk and gold-wrapped thread
Embroidery (couching, satin, stem) on dark
blue satin with red crepe lining
33.3 x 27.3 in.; 84.5 x 69.2 cm
Given in Memory of James H. Walker, Jr. by his
Family, 1993.354

84. *Fukusa*

Japan
Edo period, late 18th or 19th century
Silk and gold-wrapped thread
Embroidery (couching, chain) on blue satin
ground with red crepe lining
29 x 28 in.; 73.8 x 71.3 cm
Given in Memory of James H. Walker, Jr. by his
Family, 1993.355

Fukusa are padded and lined silk cloths used in Japan as coverings for formal gifts. Most are elaborately decorated with subjects symbolically appropriate for a particular significant event (e.g., a wedding), or with a motif such as a family crest that could be used for any occasion throughout the year. Most *fukusa* designed for celebratory occasions, including these examples, originally had decorative tassels at each corner.

Each of these *fukusa* was part of a bride's trousseau, and was made for her use in the extensive formal gift-giving that surrounded her wedding. The gift, perhaps something given in return for a wedding gift received, was set on a lacquer tray and covered with a *fukusa* for presentation to the recipient. Later the *fukusa* and tray were returned to the bride with a small gift tucked beneath the covering. Although customs in Kyoto, Edo, and the countryside differed slightly and changed over time, a small table or tray and *fukusa* have remained the primary accoutrements of formal gift-giving since the early eighteenth century.[100]

The first two *fukusa* (Plates 82 and 83) depict a shell-matching game (*kai awase*), a game that originated in the twelfth century during the late Heian period. The interior sections of both halves of a clam shell were covered with gold leaf and then painted with miniature scenes from popular fiction, often taken from the early-eleventh-century courtly romance, the *Tale of Genji* (*Genji monogatari*). In the game, the "ground shells" (*jigai*) were drawn from their hexagonal or octagonal bucket (*kai oke*) and placed, face up, in a circle. The players then drew a "drawing shell" (*dashigai*) from the companion box, and attempted to find its match. The player who matched the most shells won the game. The number of shell halves in the game—360—equalled the number of days in a lunar year. During the Heian period, the game, called *kaiōi* at the time, was played by young noblewomen on the Girls' Festival (third day of the third month) and the Chrysanthemum Festival (ninth day of the ninth month). Today, the game is most commonly enjoyed as part of traditional New Year's celebrations.

Boxes to hold the clam shells were beautifully decorated with felicitous motifs executed in lacquer, gold leaf, and mother-of-pearl. Thick, tasseled silk cords, dyed a celebratory red, secured the lids, and were tied in two types of elaborate knots that distinguished the box holding the *jigai* from that holding the *dashigai*.

Because the markings on the two halves of a clam's shell are identical and unique to each clam, clams signified conjugal felicity and faithfulness. As the symbolism developed, the ground shells signified the male (or *yang*) principle and the drawing shells, the female (or *yin*) principle. By the Edo period, the *kai awase* game had become associated with weddings, and was one of the most important gifts that a bride brought with her to her new home. *Fukusa* decorated with *kai awase* motifs were fitting accoutrements for the gift ensembles that were a prominent feature of marriage ceremonies.

Plate 82 depicts a pair of *kai awase* boxes and some scattered ground shells. The bride's family crest is prominently displayed on the lid at lower right. Cranes and pine trees, common emblems of longevity, decorate the side panels of the boxes. Cranes are monogamous and mate for life, and so also serve as symbols of marital fidelity. These two images combine to convey wishes for a long life of conjugal happiness.

Plate 83 has several layers of meaning. To the theme of the *kai awase* game is added a visual and phonetic pun. Images of pine (*matsu*, with a homophone meaning "wait") and plum (*ume*, with homophone "birth") combine to convey auspicious wishes for the birth of children to the newlyweds. The tiny reference to bamboo, only half visible in the shell at lower right, would have been enough to complete the imagery of the Three Friends of Winter (pine, bamboo, and plum), suggesting the time-honored Confucian virtues of steadfastness, resilience, and perseverance (see p. 173).

In the context of a wedding *fukusa*, the pair of lobsters depicted in Plate 84 represents the primordial couple, the ancient Japanese deities Izanagi-no-mikoto and Izanami-no-mikoto, whose union produced the islands of Japan.[101] The bent back of the lobster also suggests extreme old age and thus conveys wishes for a long life.

82

84

OBI

85. Wedding *Obi*

Japan
Meiji period (1868–1912)
Silk and silver-wrapped thread
Jacquard weave
27.5 x 89.5 in.; 70 x 227.3 cm
Source Unknown, 0000.1107

86. Wedding *Obi*

Japan
Mid-20th century
Silk with paper-backed gold and silver foil and
silver-wrapped thread
Jacquard, supplementary weft with simple
gauze
162 x 12.5 in.; 412 x 32 cm
Gift of Mrs. David W. Isaac, 1990.27

Both of these *obi* (the wide, folded belt worn with traditional Japanese dress), woven about fifty years apart, were designed as part of a woman's formal wedding attire. Both are products of the Nishijin weaving district in Kyoto, an area still famous today for the quality of its silk woven products.

Nishijin was founded in the sixteenth century as Kyoto was rebuilt after the devastating Ōnin war (1467–1477), during which much of the city was destroyed, including the weavers' workshops and large, complex drawlooms. As their houses burned, weavers fled the capital; many went to the port city of Sakai (near present-day Osaka), where they mingled with Chinese weavers fleeing from the disorder of the late Ming period. As peace was restored, Kyoto weavers began to return to their home city. They settled in the northwestern part of the city on the site of what had been the western camp (*nishi jin*) of one of the factions in the civil wars. The weaving families returned with new knowledge gained from Chinese weavers in Sakai, including an understanding of how to weave many of the coveted Ming silks. They had learned, for example, to make gold and silver thread by lacquering foil on a thin sheet of paper and wrapping it around a core of silk, which allowed them to imitate and then develop the prized Ming gold and silver brocade fabrics (*kinran* and *ginran*, respectively). These *obi* make use of such gold and silver-wrapped threads.

The preeminence of the Nishijin district was challenged during the Edo period by the defection of weavers (bearing important trade secrets) to newly established weaving centers in other parts of the country.[102] In 1720 some of the most skilled weavers were brought to Edo to work for the Tokugawa shogunate, and in 1738 others moved to Kiryū in present-day Tochigi Prefecture, where the quality and efficiency of their work soon posed a formidable threat to the Nishijin weavers. Nishijin also suffered from the severe inflation of the early eighteenth century, and two devastating fires in 1730 and 1788. After the Meiji Restoration of 1868, however, when the government realized that the quality of Japan's silk industry was one of its most valuable assets (and a potential source of income from foreign exchange), the new Meiji government turned to Nishijin.

For their part, Nishijin weavers established an association to modernize the industry in 1869. They secured a loan from the new government in that same year to send three of their most highly skilled weavers to Lyon, France, to study the great silk weaving tradition there as well as new European textile technology. In 1873 they imported their first jacquard loom.

The jacquard loom, invented in Lyon in the late eighteenth century by Joseph Marie Jacquard, revolutionized the weaving industry in Europe in the early nineteenth century, and in Japan in the years immediately following the Meiji Restoration (about seventy years later). The traditional drawloom, used in both Japan and Europe, required a drawboy to sit high in the beams on top of the loom, pulling the pattern cords by hand. The master weaver, on the weaver's bench below, worked the treadles with his feet to raise and lower the appropriate groups of warp threads to form the ground pattern. Meanwhile, his hands threw the shuttles that inserted the weft threads, one or more shuttles for each color, to create a complex structure with ground and pattern securely interwoven. The jacquard loom replaced the drawboy with a set of punched cards that moved automatically as the master weaver worked, making it easier to design more complex patterns, and permitting quicker, more efficient, and more accurate weaving. Resistance to the new technology might have been expected, especially from Kyoto weavers. It displaced workers (or, at least, required them to learn different skills), made existing looms obsolete, and required costly modifications and new equipment. The new looms were also noisy. But despite these factors, weavers in the old capital were at the forefront of experimentation with new techniques, materials, and equipment at the beginning of the Meiji period.

Plate 85 comprises one half of what once formed a single wedding *obi*. The center fold line indicates where the *obi* was folded when it was worn. The original *obi* was probably cut into two pieces after it entered a Western collection, likely to function as a household decoration, perhaps a table runner or hanging. This *obi* reveals the pleasure that master weavers in Nishijin took in their newfound ability to design and weave complex, pictorial patterns on the jacquard loom, as well as their interest in Western painterly techniques of shading and the representation of three-dimensional space. The weaver of this *obi* had a thorough technical understanding of the jacquard loom and its possibilities: a variety of weave structures adds texture and dimensionality to the design; transitions from one structure to another are smooth; and the cloth is solid, each thread well secured in the web of the fabric.

Horizontally and vertically repeated sets of paired phoenixes dominate the space. They are separated by smaller assemblages of pine trees and plum blossoms set into an abbreviated landscape of mountains and waves. The mythical phoenix is a symbol of conjugal happiness, as the bird is believed to be monogamous and to mate for life. Pine and plum are often represented together with bamboo, symbolizing the virtues of fortitude, courage, and resilience (see p. 173). Here the fleetingly lovely plum blossom is juxtaposed with the long-lived pine, a visual metaphor for a long and harmonious marital life encompassing both the fragile loveliness of youth and the constancy of old age, and pursued with courage and perseverance. The male phoenix is resplendent with outspread wings and open beak. On the verge of flight, he appears self-confident and full of energy and power. The female phoenix is comparatively inconspicuous, half-hidden under her mate's outstretched left wing. Somber in color, with wings furled and beak closed, she looks in the same direction as the male, the gaze of the pair sharing the same focus.

By the mid-twentieth century, Nishijin weavers had attained complete control of their looms and had thoroughly explored its capabilities. Competition was fierce as they vied with one another to produce stunning and original products for the luxury market. In Plate 86, the weaver used his masterful control of the weaving process to produce an elegant and understated design of pampas grass set against a background of other autumn grasses. He also employed an unusual combination of flat, paper-backed gold and silver foil (the usual choice of Nishijin weavers) with silver foil wrapped around silk thread (used more generally for couched-thread embroidery) to heighten the interest of the design. The contrast of silver-wrapped thread with flat foil creates an effective difference in texture that is one of the most distinctive features of this lovely design. Autumn grasses have been a theme of poetry and painting since the Heian period, and situate this *obi* in a classical heritage that gives authority and allusive beauty to this important part of the wedding ensemble.

Buddhist Textiles

The *kesa* (*kaśāya* in Sanskrit), a large rectangle of patched cloth, is the oldest and most important Buddhist garment, and the prototype for other Buddhist textiles. In Japan, it was normally worn draped over the left shoulder and under the right arm.

The monk Dōgen (1200–1253), a brilliant scholar and founder of the Sōtō sect of Zen Buddhism in Japan, wrote a treatise on the *kesa* in which he emphasized its crucial role in the practice of Buddhism. In his *Kesa kudoku* (*The Merit of the Kaśāya*), Dōgen wrote that the garment "is the very essence of those who have realized enlightenment."[103] Imbued with the spiritual power of a great master, the *kaśāya* was an important emblem of the transmission of authority from master to chosen disciple. Dōgen illustrated this with the example of a *kaśāya* enshrined in the Baolin mountain monastery in China, a *kaśāya* that had originally belonged to an Indian patriarch who had passed it to his Chinese disciple. Since that time, the Baolin *kaśāya* had been passed down further through generations of Chinese Buddhist prelates. Because of the spiritual power that this robe had accrued in its long history, Dōgen wrote that "successive emperors respectfully asked that it be brought to court, where, while bowing, they made venerative offerings to it."[104]

Such *kaśāya* were a visible sign of the legitimacy of a particular Buddhist sect and its head priest. The Japanese monks Saichō (767–822) and Kūkai (774–835) returned from study in China to found the Tendai and Shingon sects, respectively. Both had been given *kaśāya* by their Chinese masters, and these robes have been preserved to this day as treasures of two temples closely associated with them. Saichō's *kesa* has been preserved by Enryakuji, located on Mt. Hiei northwest of Kyoto, and Kūkai's by Kyōōgokokuji or Tōji, located to the east of the main south gate of the capital. The *kaśāya* was such an important symbol of legitimacy that Dōgen, writing in the *Kesa kudoku*, challenged the transmission of authority from the twenty-seventh Indian patriarch to the Chinese monk Sengzhao (d. 414) because "there was . . . no correct transmission of a *kaśāya* between them."[105] In the *Vinaya* (the rules of conduct for the monastic community), *kaśāya* were also credited with miraculous powers:

> My disciple! Unfold a *kaśāya* as if it were a *stūpa* [funerary or relic mound],
> For it gives good fortune, extinguishes crimes, and saves both human and Celestial beings
> . . .
> The *kaśāya* is endowed with miraculous power,
> For it is able to plant the seeds of Bodhi-practice [meditation leading to enlightenment] . . .
> If a dragon wears even a single thread of one,
> He will be saved from being devoured by a garuda.
> If one wears a *kaśāya* in crossing the sea,
> There is no need to fear dragon-fish or demons.[106]

The form of the *kaśāya* can be traced back more than two millennia to ancient India, where simple rectangles of handwoven cloth were worn wrapped, wound, or draped around the body, similar to how the sari is worn today. The *Vinaya* contains detailed instructions for constructing, handling, and even washing a *kaśāya*. According to this ancient document, as explicated by Dōgen, the ideal *kaśāya* was known as a *pāmsūla* (*funzō-e* in Japanese), which means, literally, "excreta-sweeping robe." It was to be constructed of "discarded cloth" of ten types:

> (1) cloth munched by oxen, (2) cloth gnawed by mice, (3) cloth burned by fire, (4) cloth soiled by menstrual blood, (5) cloth soiled by the blood of childbirth, (6) cloth discarded at shrines, (7) cloth discarded in a cemetery, (8) cloth presented as an offering, (9) cloth discarded by government officials, and (10) cloth used to cover the dead.[107]

Monks were instructed to gather these scraps of soiled cloth with their left hands (the hand reserved in traditional Indian society for impure tasks), tear off any irrevocably stained portions, wash the rest, and then construct a *kaśāya* from these fragments. The Buddhist scriptures emphasize that these discarded scraps are not only the most appropriate, but are also, in fact, the purest and cleanest materials for the purpose. Like the pure white lotus blossom that rises from the muck of a muddy pond, the impure fragments of cloth are transformed through the process of construction into a sacred garment. This is a powerful metaphor for the transformation and resolution of apparent opposites associated with the experience of enlightenment.

Despite these regulations, extant *kesa* do not include examples of cloth picked up from the streets or soiled by childbirth or menstruation. In fact, most extant *kesa* are made of luxurious fabrics. The list in the *Vinaya* can be interpreted to leave room for these luxurious *kesa*. The meaning of cloth "discarded" at shrines and by government officials, and "presented" as an offering, could be stretched to include gifts of handsome fabrics; the "offering" could be money that was then used to purchase fine materials. Even the most luxurious *kesa*, however, bear traces of the idea of a patched cloth made from discarded fragments. Most *kesa* are actually patched, even if a single piece of fabric is cut up and put back together again, as in the Spencer *kesa* (Plate 87). The use of scraps of cloth patched together—though the scraps be made of gold brocade—symbolizes the Buddhist vow of poverty, a reminder that poverty and frugality are necessary companions in the search for ultimate truth.

The *Vinaya* ascribes many of the regulations concerning the construction, handling, and use of the *kaśāya* to the Buddha Śākyamuni (the historical Buddha, ca. 560–ca. 480 BCE) himself, who instructed his disciple Ānanda to construct a rectangular garment based on the divisions of rice fields and levees, and to teach this construction to the other monks. In addition to numerous other regulations concerning the structure of the garment, Śākyamuni even specified the type of stitch to be used: "The Buddha Śākyamuni has said, 'The *kaśāya* of all the Buddhas in the three stages of time should . . . be made by backstitching.'"[108]

According to the *Vinaya*, the Buddha admonished his disciples to own only three robes, all to be constructed of scraps of discarded fabric. The first, a small five-column robe, was wrapped as a skirt (much like the Indonesian sarong) and worn when the monk performed menial physical tasks around the monastery. The second, a medium-sized, seven-column *kaśāya*, was layered over the first for religious gatherings within the monastery. The third and largest of the three garments was constructed of nine columns, a number that later increased to as many as twenty-five. This large mantle was worn over the other two robes for preaching, teaching, and other public appearances. The three *kaśāya* could also be worn in layers for protection against the cold. When Buddhism spread to Central Asia and China at the beginning of the Common Era, the *kaśāya* went with it. In the colder climate of these northern countries, it came to be worn over indigenous clothing, and thus took on a primarily symbolic function.

Kaśāya are traditionally constructed of an uneven number of columns of patched fabrics. The number of columns—three, five, nine, or more—was related originally to the size of the garment, and indirectly to the occasions upon which it was worn, as detailed above. Later, in China and Japan, the number came to indicate the relative status of the owner; generally, the larger the number of columns, the higher the status of the priest.

The earliest extant *kaśāya* are of the *pāmsūla* (*funzō-e*) type. They are constructed of a variety of odd-shaped miscellaneous fabrics pieced and stitched together, or woven in such a manner as to imitate the visual effect of such construction. The British Museum owns a Tang dynasty *kaśāya* discovered in Cave 17 of the ancient temple complex at Dunhuang on the Silk Road. It is constructed of irregular pieces of various sizes and shapes, an encyclopedia of colorful figured silks, embroidery, and resist-dyeing. The high quality of the silk fragments suggests that the *kaśāya* belonged to a high-ranking priest. The fragments were probably votive offerings to the temple.[109]

Funzō-e are also well represented among the earliest extant *kesa* in Japan. The robes brought back from China by Saichō and Kūkai were both *funzō-e*. Shōtoku Taishi (Prince Shōtoku, 574–622) and Emperor Shōmu (701–756), two of the most important early patrons of Buddhism in Japan, both owned *funzō-e* that have been preserved by the primary temples associated with them (Hōryūji and Tōdaiji, respectively).[110] Saichō's *funzō-e*, two owned by Shōtoku, and one owned by Shōmu were made of multiple layers of small fragments of silk or *asa* held together by closely-spaced vertical rows of fine quilting (*shinō*). Kūkai's *kesa* and a second one attributed to Emperor Shōmu are considered to be *funzō-e*, but actually represent woven imitations of their pieced and stitched prototypes.

Over time, as Japanese Buddhist temples became ever more firmly entrenched in the fabric of society, the patched *kesa* became, oddly, a symbol of the prestige, power, and wealth of the clergy. *Kesa* were constructed from luxurious Chinese fabrics woven in complex new techniques, and from specially commissioned brocades and damasks with Buddhist motifs (such as the lotus) woven into rich surfaces. Occasionally they were made from (or, more often, lined with) stylish garments donated by powerful patrons. These materials were cut up and then pieced back together, usually within a lattice framework of cloth strips made from another opulent fabric. The basic idea of an uneven number of columns pieced together was never abandoned, even if it was represented only minimally.

As rules for the construction of the *kesa* were codified and additional layers of symbolism accrued, four small corner patches, seen on all of the Spencer Museum Buddhist textiles (and perhaps originally used to reinforce ties),[111] came to represent the Shitennō, or Four Celestial Monarchs. These Four Guardian Kings, as they are often called, guard just and virtuous rulers, protect the state, defend the Buddhist Law, and stand sentinel at the cardinal points of the universe.[112] The Four Guardian Kings appear very early at Buddhist sites in India; they guard such major monuments as the four gates of the *stūpa* (relic mound) at Sanchi, constructed between the third century BCE and the early first century CE. The Four Guardian Kings were also among the earliest Buddhist figures to receive recognition in Japan, along with Shaka (Śākyamuni in Sanskrit), the historical Buddha; Yakushi (Bhaishajyaguru), the Buddha of Healing; Miroku (Maitreya), the Buddha of the Future; and the compassionate bodhisattva Kannon (Avalokiteśvara).[113]

The earliest Buddhist temple built in Japan of which visible evidence remains is Shitennōji in present-day Osaka. Tradition holds that this temple was built by Shōtoku Taishi in 593 in gratitude to the Four Guardian Kings after a decisive victory in 587 that led to the adoption of Buddhism as the state religion. Since that time, Buddhism and its pantheon of deities were used to protect and legitimize the rule of the imperial house as it forged a unified state from a group of contending clans. Shitennōji provided a prototype for temples built in the provinces dedicated to the Four Guardian Kings, temples established to protect the flanks of the emerging state and introduce the new Sino-Buddhist culture that was such an important part of its authority.[114] In Buddhist paintings, sculpture, ritual objects, and textiles, the figures of the Four Guardian Kings appear both together and in isolated pairs. The guardian of the north, known as Tamonten or Bishamonten in Japan (Vaiśravana in Sanskrit), assumed a position of prominence among the Four Kings in Japanese belief and became a figure of independent worship.[115]

Reference to corner patches on *kaśāya* does not appear in the *Vinaya*, at least as quoted and interpreted by Dōgen. The patches also do not appear on the earliest extant *kaśāya*, such as the Tang dynasty example from Cave 17 at Dunhuang and the eighth-century *kesa* preserved in the Shōsōin Repository at Tōdaiji in Nara.[116] Corner patches do appear, however, on an eighth-century *kesa* preserved at Enryakuji and Kyoto National Museum, but the patches, as well as the matching lattice, could be a later reconstruction.[117] If this is the case, the later addition of corner squares may suggest that when the *kesa* was repaired and reassembled, corner patches were considered more important than historical accuracy. The corner squares appear to be original, however, on two nine-column fourteenth-century *kaśāya*, one associated with the émigré Chinese monk Qingchou Zhengcheng (known in Japan as Seisetsu Shōchō, 1274–1339) and one with Kūkoku Myōō (1328–1407).[118] By the second half of the seventeenth century, when the Spencer Museum *kesa* was constructed, corner patches had probably become the norm. They

FIG. 17

*Portrait of the Zen Master Wuzhun
Shifan* (J: Bujun Shiban; 1177–1249)
With an inscription by the master for
Enni Ben'en (1202–1280)

China
Southern Song dynasty, inscription dated to
1238
Hanging scroll
Ink and color on silk
49.1 x 21.7 in.; 124.8 x 55.2 cm
Tōfukuji (temple), Kyoto, Japan
National Treasure
[Reproduced with permission from Tōfukuji]

After his apprenticeship with Wuzhun Shifan,
prelate of Mount Jing (west of Hangzhou),
Enni Ben'en returned to Japan in 1241, and
founded Tōfukuji in 1255. The portrait has been
in the temple's possession since that time.[119]

appear as a standard feature in an Edo period block-printed manual on *kesa* published for Buddhist clerics in 1806, and in Kyūma Keichō's comprehensive study of *kesa* in 1967, which includes detailed instructions for the construction of the corner squares and their application to the *kesa* ground.[120]

Corner patches were often made from a distinct material, different from the rest of the *kesa*. Sometimes this material was an older or more valuable textile (an imported Chinese fabric, for example) added to a *kesa* that was otherwise constructed of one or more Japanese textiles. Occasionally, as in the Spencer example, the patches have different and increased wear patterns, suggesting that they were recycled, perhaps from the worn *kesa* of a former distinguished prelate. According to the textile historian, collector, and dealer Nomura Shōjirō, the corner patches and the two patches flanking the center of the back (also associated with Buddhist deities) were the sacred part of the robe. Relics were sometimes hidden in the pouch formed between the corner patch and the ground fabric beneath, just as they were hidden within Buddhist sculptures.[121] According to this interpretation, these "guardian" patches held the spiritual power of the *kesa*. There are examples of *kesa* and other Japanese Buddhist textiles in American collections that have had the corner patches removed or replaced, presumably to desanctify the *kesa* before it left the temple, and to save these valuable corner fragments and any relics they might have enclosed for future use within the temple. Most *kesa*, however, appear to have their original corner patches intact. The only obvious example of replaced corner patches on textiles in the Spencer Museum collection is the priest's stole, or *ohi* (Plate 89).

87. Kesa

◆

Japan
Edo period, second half of 17th century
Silk and metallic foil on flat paper strips
(in corner patches)
Brocaded satin and patchwork
45 x 89 in.; 114.5 x 226 cm
Museum Purchase: The Barbara Benton
Wescoe Fund, 1995.13

In this *kesa*, the corner patches, located in the four corners of the main ground just inside the outer border of the garment, are older than the main textile. They were probably woven in Ming dynasty China in the sixteenth century. The main fabric dates from the second half of the seventeenth century, about the time the *kesa* was constructed. The patches at the four corners, as well as the two flanking the center back, show more wear than the rest of the *kesa*, and the wear patterns are inconsistent with their use as part of this garment. It is therefore probable that they were recycled from an older *kesa*. This garment has recently been conserved, and no evidence of relics under the corner patches was found.[122]

The main field of the *kesa* is constructed of brocaded satin with long, glossy silk floats defining a pattern of abstracted chrysanthemums and hollyhocks, both embedded with stylized Chinese pears (*nashi*). These motifs are set into a tessellated ground with smaller, twelve-petalled oblong figures, which have indentations on the sides enclosing another variant of the *nashi* motif.

The kesa has seven panels (*jo*), defined by lattice work constructed of the same fabric. There has been no attempt to align the patterns as in many later *kesa*. Here the play of regular, symmetrically disposed geometric shapes is enlivened by a deliberate breaking of the symmetry where the fabric was cut and pieced.

The *kesa* probably left Japan in the Meiji period, a time when government persecution of the Buddhist establishment and resultant poverty forced many temples to sell their treasures. At one point the garment was in the collection of the Traphagen School of Design in New York, founded by fashion designer Ethel Traphagen (1882–1963) in the early 1920s. A label on the reverse of the *kesa* typed on cotton bias tape reads "J-11–3 Japanese/Traphagen School."

87

88. Ohi

◆

Japan
Edo period, 18th–19th century
Silk and metallic foil on flat paper strips
Compound weave with multiple warps and
wefts, plain weave structure; supplementary
weft on twill ground (for corner patches); and
patchwork
61.3 x 12.3 in.; 155.8 x 31.8 cm
Given in Memory of James H. Walker, Jr. by his
Family, 1993.347

An *ohi* is a long, narrow stole worn by a Buddhist priest on formal occasions. It is worn draped over the forearm that is not encumbered by the folds of the *kesa*. Since the *kesa* usually covers a priest's left shoulder, the *ohi* is generally hung over the right forearm.

The pattern on this *ohi* is unusual. Motifs on the main field represent the Buddhist flaming pearl of wisdom, and branches of coral associated with the Daoist Immortals. Both are motifs found commonly on Qing dynasty textiles, where the ubiquitous dragon is usually seen in conjunction with a flaming pearl, and coral appears both as an isolated element and in the sea that forms part of the cosmic landscape depicted on official robes and regalia. Both motifs appear rarely in Japan, except on textiles imported from China. Here, however, the flaming pearl is set within a *segaiha*, or wave motif, while the branches of coral are disposed to break the rhythm of the pattern. The *segaiha* pattern and the skillful play between symmetry and assymetry are typical features of Japanese design of the period.

The patching has been arranged to maintain the original design as much as possible. The fact that this is not achieved more exactly suggests that this *ohi* was constructed from used fabric, perhaps a worn *kesa* or a votive offering of a garment or other textile from the family of a deceased patron or parishioner.

On this *ohi* the Shitennō are interpreted literally as they define the four corners of the interior field. One figure can be identified as Bishamonten, Guardian of the North, by the characteristic reliquary held in his left hand and lance in his right. (See figure at left below.) All four figures wear armor and stand on rocky ground representing Mount Meru (or Sumeru), abode of the Shitennō. The rocks also emphasize the unshakable resolution of these Four Guardian Kings.[123]

Detail of Plate 88

88

89. *Ohi* (detail)

Japan
Edo period, 18th century
Central panel: Muromachi or Momoyama
period, 16th century with late-19th-century
replacement corner patches
Silk with gold and silver foil on flat paper strips
Brocaded twill, figured twill, and patchwork
48 x 12 in.; 122 x 30.5 cm
Gift of Rose K. Auerbach, 1967.49

The fabrics that compose this modest textile date variously from the sixteenth to the nineteenth century. The oldest is the sixteenth-century center panel, with a sparse central field dominated by eight imperial sixteen-petal chrysanthemums with radiating spirals, depicted in silver against an orange-red safflower ground.[124] This panel is set into a primarily green, polychrome textile with a design of unevenly disposed half rosettes, which set off the formal regularity of the main field. This outer panel probably dates from the eighteenth century. The corner patches are nineteenth-century replacements.

The use of the imperial sixteen-petal chrysanthemum, the luxurious materials (such as safflower dye and high-quality gold and silver thread), the quality of the weaving, and the distinguished design suggest that the center panel might have belonged to an imperial prince. A number of royal relatives served as abbots of temples that had connections to the court or imperial family. The green fabric is less distinctive and more difficult to date, as Buddhist textiles were conservative and the repertory of patterns changed slowly. It was chosen carefully, however, to complement the center panel. By contrast, the gold and white corner patches are uneven in size and shape, and placed so that they cut into the chrysanthemums on the ends.

This *ohi* is fragile and shows signs of significant wear. The new corner patches appear startlingly bright. Their newness, uneven sizing, and sloppy placement suggest that they were hasty replacements for the original patches when the *ohi* was sold.

89

Textiles for Export: Meiji Period

90. Panel with Crane and Irises

Japan
Meiji period (1868–1912)
Silk and gold-wrapped thread
Embroidery (satin with couching, running, and seed stitches) on damask ground
56 x 39 in.; 143.6 x 97.5 cm
Source Unknown, 0000.2432

91. Panel with Cranes and Irises

Japan
Meiji period (1868–1912)
Silk and gold-wrapped thread
Embroidery (satin with couching, running, and seed stitches) on damask ground
53 x 65 in.; 134.6 x 166.1 cm
Source Unknown, 0000.1111
Literature: *Catalogue of the Oriental Collection*, 71.

Sir Oliver Impey, discussing the collection of Meiji decorative arts in the Ashmolean Museum at Oxford, wrote,

> Purely in terms of skill, the art/crafts of Meiji . . . and Taishō Japan have rarely been equalled, even by Fabergé. Nor has it been generally realised that the majority of the finest of Japanese decorative art of these periods was made for export.[125]

One of the key works that Impey discussed was "a magnificent needlework hanging" depicting a group of cranes in various poses set in a landscape of grasses and wisteria. The subject and style of the Ashmolean hanging is very close to the two Spencer Museum panels depicted here.

These two large embroidered hangings of red-crowned cranes in an iris marsh were made for export to a Western audience fascinated with the beauty of traditional Japanese craftsmanship. They exhibit the skill of Japan's professional embroiderers and the high quality of hand-reeled, lustrous silk embroidery floss. They were the product of a superb needlework tradition that can be traced back to the eighth century.[126] At the same time, these panels show many of the same concerns as contemporary painting, such as an interest in realistic depiction (including naturalistic representation of flora and fauna), experimentation with Western notions of shading, and a believable description of three-dimensional space.

The cranes are depicted in careful detail with breast feathers, wing caps, and primary and secondary wing feathers skillfully and minutely rendered in a variety of embroidery stitches. The primary stitch is satin, a long stitch used to fill a given space. Satin stitch is well designed to show off the luxurious, glossy embroidery floss and reveal subtle colors to best advantage. Different textural effects can be achieved just with satin stitch by varying the length and direction of the stitches (see, for example, the breast and wing feathers of the single standing crane in Plate 90). For additional textural effects, the artisan employed other stitches including couching, running, and seed stitches. In couching a heavy thread is laid over the surface of the fabric and secured with small, inconspicuous stitches that encircle the couched thread. Here, couched threads, layered on top of a satin stitch ground, are used to define the veins of leaves. Seed stitch is a term used to describe a variety of knotting techniques, especially the "Peking knot," a variant of a "French knot." The hard, tight, three-dimensional surface of the seed stitch provides a strong contrast to the lush softness of the satin stitch. Densely packed groups of seed stitches are used here to define the crowns of the cranes. They draw attention to those single points of bright red that identify this species as the red-crowned crane, one of three species of cranes indigenous to Japan.[127]

The ground and framing fabrics of both hangings exhibit patterns associated with the Buddhist establishment. The framing fabrics are considerably older than the images, and the fragile condition of the ground fabrics suggests that they may have been recycled as well. It is puzzling that fragile ground materials should have been chosen for these finely worked embroideries. There would have been no particular meaning attached to the use of old Buddhist fabrics in a secular image created for a Western market. The answer may lie instead in the circumstances surrounding the manufacture of these panels.

In the early years of the Meiji period, Buddhism was attacked by ascendant nativist forces that declared the primacy of Shinto, Japan's indigenous ancient religion. They advocated the division of the closely intertwined Shinto and Buddhist establishments, the persecution of Buddhist temples, and the total separation of Buddhism from the state.[128] The difficulties of these years had a devastating impact on the financial stability of many Buddhist temples, on their position within society, and even on the priests' own evaluation of their heritage. Temples that did not lose their sculpture, paintings, textiles, and furnishings often sold them. In 1876, for example, the ancient temple Hōryūji donated a portion of its seventh- and eighth-century treasures to the Imperial Household in exchange for money for seriously needed repairs. Many

Buddhist artifacts found their way into foreign collections as well. In 1878 Ernest Fenollosa, a young Harvard graduate, accepted a post in philosophy at Tokyo University, where he stayed until 1886. During the first six years of his eight-year stay, Fenollosa made the acquisitions that would form the basis of the Japanese collection at the Museum of Fine Arts, Boston. Not without a conscience, Fenollosa wrote to Edward Morse, probably in 1884, that he was ambivalent about bringing some of Japan's "greatest treasures" out of the country.[128] Many of these "treasures" were Buddhist artifacts, acquired from temples that were desperate for funds and from priests who undervalued their artistic legacy of statues, paintings, scrolls, and textiles. Fenollosa could not have assembled the same collection if he had started even a decade later. Partly as a result of his advocacy, the Meiji government promulgated the first law requiring registration of all important works of art as Kokuhō, or National Treasures, in 1886, the same year that Fenollosa's collection entered the museum.

In the Meiji period, temple treasures (including *kesa* and other Buddhist textiles) as well as old secular paintings, woodblock prints, screens, ceramics, Noh costumes, *kosode*, kimono, accessories (such as *netsuke* and *inrō*), and contemporary crafts found their way into Western collections. European and American collectors were intrigued by the wonders and mystery that they perceived in the Orient, and justly aware of the quality and beauty of many of the works of secular and religious art that they were able to purchase. The Meiji government, always in need of foreign currency, was eager to promote contemporary arts and crafts (a distinction that Japan adopted from the West), and facilitated their exhibition at international fairs in Europe and the United States, where these beautiful objects received wide recognition.

Although it has not proved possible to trace the history of these two Spencer hangings, it seems likely that the choice of fragile, probably recycled, Buddhist textiles for the ground fabrics is related to the impoverished circumstances of Buddhist temples in the Meiji period. But whether a temple sold the textiles to a professional workshop that may have bought them because they were less expensive than new cloth; whether an atelier associated with a temple, monastery, or convent produced the embroideries to raise funds for the institution; or whether there is a completely different explanation for this unusual choice of ground fabric is, at present, unclear.

These two embroidered images of two icons of Japanese art, the crane and the iris, are closely related and were probably made in the same workshop, perhaps as part of a series. It is possible that the hanging in the Ashmolean Museum is also from that workshop. All three hangings are closely related in theme, style, subject matter, and presentation.

1. Yanagi Sōetsu, *The Unknown Craftsman: A Japanese Insight into Beauty*, adapted by Bernard Leach, with foreword by Hamada Shōji (Tokyo: Kodansha, 1972). In 1906 Okakura Kakuzō, curator at the Museum of Fine Arts, Boston, had published *The Book of Tea*, introducing his small circle of museum patrons to the aesthetics of Japanese tea practice (the "tea ceremony"). This surprisingly popular and enduring little book laid the foundation for an understanding and appreciation of Yanagi's thinking in the United States and Great Britain. See Okakura Kakuzō, *The Book of Tea* (Rutland, Vermont: Charles E. Tuttle, 1956).

2. Later, leather was sometimes patterned with resist paste using a stencil, and smoked to darken the unresisted areas of the material. A late Muromachi period leather *dōboku* (a short jacket worn by high-ranking samurai in the late sixteenth and early seventeenth centuries) owned by the Ueda Municipal Museum in Nagano Prefecture and designated an Important Cultural Property, for example, is patterned with a fine geometric *komon* (small pattern) motif.

3. According to Sugihara Nobuhiko, this fabric was originally an inner layer of the gauntlets. When the badly damaged outer brocade was removed during repair in the mid-Edo period, the conservator left the inner layer as the outer, and noted this in a memorandum to Arai Hakuseki (1657–1725). The memorandum is preserved in the archives of the Imperial Household Agency. Although some scholars have questioned whether or not this fabric is an Edo period replacement, Sugihara reports that, after he studied the gauntlets as part of a team of experts in 1974, the team concurred with the experts who had studied the metalwork on the gauntlets, and found that both cloth and metalwork date to the Kamakura period. Sugihara Nobuhiko, "Introduction," in *Nihon no Katazome*, ed. The National Museum of Modern Art (Tokyo: The National Museum of Modern Art, 1980), Section 4 (unpaginated).

4. See the late Heian period *Ban Dainagon ekotoba* (*Illustrated Narrative of Ban Dainagon*), and the Kamakura period *Mōko shūrai ekotoba* (*Illustrated Narrative of the Mongol Invasion*) and *Kasuga gongen genki* (*Miracles of the Deities of Kasuga Shrine*). See also Yamanobe Tomoyuki, *Some* (*Dyeing*), *Nihon no bijutsu* 7, no. 11 (1966): 44–46; and Dale Carolyn Gluckman and Sharon Sadako Takeda, *When Art Became Fashion:* Kosode *in Edo-Period Japan* (Los Angeles: Los Angeles County Museum of Art, 1992), 71. *Bushi* are shown with white family crests on dark blue ground in the *Mōko shūrai ekotoba*; commoners are seen in the *Kasuga gongen genki-e* with fairly detailed depictions of horses reserved on a very dark blue ground.

5. See, for example, Sugihara, *Nihon no katazome*, and "Some no katagami," in Kyoto National Museum, *Some no katagami* (Kyoto: Kyoto National Museum, 1968); and Yamanobe, *Some*, 55 ff.

6. See, for example, Reiko Mochinaga Brandon, *Country Textiles of Japan: The Art of* Tsutsugaki (New York and Tokyo: Weatherhill, 1986).

7. Nambu Yoshimatsu, designated a Living National Treasure in 1955 for his skill as a *tsukibori* carver, as quoted in Barbara Adachi, *The Living Treasures of Japan* (Tokyo, New York, and San Francisco: Kodansha International, 1973), 51. See also *Ningen Kokuhō jiten* (*Dictionary of Living National Treasures*), ed. Minami Kunio, Yanagibashi Makoto, and Ōtaki Mikio (Tokyo: Unsōdō, 1998), 91–92.

8. For a discussion of sumptuary laws, see Donald H. Shiveley, "Sumptuary Regulation and Status in Early Tokugawa Japan," *Harvard Journal of Asiatic Studies* 25 (1964–1965): 123–164. In 1683 the shogun Tokugawa Tsunayoshi (1646–1709) included *hitta shibori* in a list of items prohibited to *chonin*. Literally "householders," *chonin* generally referred to the urban merchant class. Shiveley points out that Tsunayoshi, although a lavish spender himself, issued many more sumptuary laws than his predecessors, including seven sets of regulations in 1683 alone.

9. Sugihara, "Some no Katagami," 9 and 16. The notes are found in the fourth fascicle.

10. *Yūzen* was named for the Kyoto fan-painter Miyazaki Yūzensai, active in the Genroku period (1688–1704), probably because of the popularity of his painterly designs for *kosode*. These designs were intended to be executed in the comparatively new techniques of free-hand paste-resist and brush dyeing. For a discussion in English, see Amanda Mayer Stinchecum, "Evolution of the Kosode," in Amanda Mayer Stinchecum, Kosode: *16th–19th Century Textiles from the Nomura Collection* (New York: Japan Society and Kodansha International, 1984), 35–38.

11. Brandon, *Country Textiles of Japan*, 47; citing Endō Motoo, *Nihonshokuninshi* (*A history of Japanese artisans*) (Tokyo: Yūzankaku, 1967), 201–203 and 213.

12. The information in this paragraph is from Gary P. Leupp, *Servants, Shophands, and Laborers in the Cities of Tokugawa Japan* (Princeton: Princeton University Press, 1992), 25–27.

13. Sugihara Nobuhiko, "Nihon no katazome ni tsuite," in *Nihon no katazome*, ed. The National Museum of Modern Art, Section 8.

14. In 1845 the mistress of the Numano household in Wakayama noted in a wage notebook that she had dismissed a thirty-three-year-old chambermaid for incompetence. The maid's salary had been set at 110 *monme* per year. See Leupp, *Servants, Shophands, and Laborers*, 102. Of course, cash wages were only part of a servant's (or shop assistant's) wages; they also received room, board, and some of their clothing.

15. Sugihara, "Nihon no katazome ni tsuite," Section 8.

16. Shimizu Kotaro, as quoted in Adachi, *The Living Treasures of Japan*, 55.

17. Sugihara, "Nihon no katazome ni tsuite," Section 6.

18. See Sugihara, "Some no katagami," 16, and ibid., Section 7.

19. One such rebuilt workshop belonged to the Shimizu family. Shimizu Kotaro's father opened a *katazome* workshop in Edo in the 1890s in response to increased demand for traditionally patterned *katazome yukata*. Shimizu learned the craft from his father, and in 1955, was one of the first craftspeople to receive the distinguished designation of Holder of an Important Intangible Cultural Property (or Living

National Treasure). Adachi, *The Living Treasures of Japan*, 53 ff.

20. *Ningen Kokuhō jiten*, 254.

21. Adachi, *The Living Treasures of Japan*, 16.

22. Sugihara, "Some no katagami," 18.

23. Jan Fontein, ed. *Living National Treasures of Japan: An Exhibition Organized by the Committee of the Exhibition of Living National Treasures of Japan* (1982?), 22.

24. Kodama stated that a stencil could take from four hours to two weeks to complete, depending on its complexity. Adachi, *The Living Treasures of Japan*, 30.

25. For a good description of this process, see Barbara Adachi's description of Mrs. Kodama's *itoire* process (ibid., 30 ff).

26. See *Ningen Kokuhō jiten*, 99–101.

27. See Adachi, *The Living Treasures of Japan*, 30.

28. Not only stenciled fabric was stretched on boards to dry. *Yukata* were disassembled before they were washed, and then spread on boards to flatten and dry before they were restitched.

29. See *Ningen Kokuhō jiten*, 89–90; and Adachi, *The Living Treasures of Japan*, 55.

30. See Adachi, *The Living Treasures of Japan*, 16, 31, and 55.

31. See *Ningen Kokuhō jiten*, 97–98; and ibid., 28 ff.

32. *Some no katagami*, pl. 402.

33. See Adachi, *The Living Treasures of Japan*, 52.

34. Michiyo Morioka and William Jay Rathbun, "Tsutsugaki and Katazome," in *Beyond the Tanabata Bridge*, ed. William Jay Rathbun (New York: Thames and Hudson in conjunction with the Seattle Art Museum, 1993), 131–132.

35. Engelbert Kaempfer, *Kaempfer's Japan: Tokugawa Culture Observed*, ed., trans., and annotated by Beatrice M. Bodart-Bailey (Honolulu: University of Hawai'i Press, 1999), 264.

36. "Book of the Chrysanthemum," in *The Mustard Seed Garden Manual of Painting: Chieh Tzŭ Yuan Hua Chuan, 1679–1701*, trans. and ed. Mai-mai Sze (Princeton: Bollingen Series, Princeton University Press, 1956), 435–436. This is a facsimile edition of the 1887–1888 Shanghai edition.

37. John W. Dower, *The Elements of Japanese Design: A Handbook of Family Crests, Heraldry and Symbolism* (New York and Tokyo: Walker/Weatherhill, 1971), 52. Dower notes that the chrysanthemum-sun motif is ancient, and found in many cultures.

38. Ibid., 52–53. Wolfram Eberhard suggests that a phonetic affiliation associates the word for chrysanthemum, *ju*, with the verb "to remain" (*ju*), while the word for "nine" (*jiu*) is associated with the word for "long time" (*jiu*). See Wolfram Eberhard, *A Dictionary of Chinese Symbols* (New York: Routledge and Kegan Paul, 1986), 63. These phonetic associations or wordplay, popular in the late Qing dynasty, reinforced earlier associations linking chrysanthemums with longevity.

39. See Frances Blakemore, *Japanese Design through Textile Patterns* (New York and Tokyo: Weatherhill, 1978), 242–243.

40. Dower, *The Elements of Japanese Design*, 52.

41. Eberhard, *A Dictionary of Chinese Symbols*, 309–310.

42. See Louise Allison Cort, "The Changing Fortunes of Three Archaic Japanese Textiles," in *Cloth and Human Experience*, ed. Annette B. Weiner and Jane Schneider (Washington and London: Smithsonian Institution Press, 1989), 391; and Nagano Gorō and Hiroi Nobuko, "Sashi Kuzuori" (Kudzu Weaving in Sashi), in *Orimono no genfūkei*. English title: *Base to Tip: Bast-Fiber Weaving in Japan and Its Neighboring Countries* (Kyoto: Shikosha, 1999), 217–224 and pl. 166–171 (in Japanese with English summary and caption headings). *Kuzu* vines grew throughout much of Japan, and the material could be processed roughly, given a heavy twist throughout its length, and used like other wild bast fibers. The villagers of Sashi, in Saga Prefecture, now use *kuzu* to make rougher household materials like openwork mesh used in food preparation.

43. For a definitive discussion of the processing and weaving of tree and grass bast fiber textiles in the late twentieth century, see Nagano and Hiroi, *Orimono no genfūkei*. See also Mary Dusenbury, Nobuko Hiroi, and Gorō Nagano, "Asa and Juhi," in *Textiles of Old Japan: Bast-Fiber Textiles and Old Kasuri* (San Francisco: San Francisco Craft and Folk Art Museum, 1986); and Takahashi Yōji, ed., "Nihon no nuno: genshi nuno tanbō" (Japanese cloth: an inquiry into primitive cloth), *Taiyō, Nihon no kokoro*, no. 67 (Autumn 1989). Although the processing of different types of tree-bast fibers is similar, there are differences in method, tools, and terminology particular to the type of fiber and location.

44. The stalk-like leaves of the fiber banana (*bashō*) in Okinawa produce cloth more akin to cultivated *asa* (hemp, ramie) than to cloth made from the tough inner bark of most other wild plants. Fiber from the *kuzu* (arrowroot vine), traditionally used for the formal *kamishimo* of samurai, can be split fine, resembles raw silk, and was always considered a luxury fiber.

45. For a description of processing *fuji* in the mountains of Kyoto Prefecture, see Mary Dusenbury, "Tree-bast Fiber Textiles of Japan," *Spin-Off* 10, no. 3 (Fall 1986): 35–39.

46. Cort, "Three Archaic Japanese Textiles," 387.

47. The fifth month was also the time for the first planting of the new rice crop, a sacred period filled with ceremonies to protect the crop and foster a good harvest. Reiko Mochinaga Brandon reports that the young girls selected to transplant the precious seedlings first gathered in a hut beneath a roof layered with iris (believed to drive away evil). During the village rice-planting ceremonies, boys engaged in competitions of various kinds. Brandon suggests that these symbolized competition in rice growing. Brandon, *Country Textiles of Japan*, 17.

48. Kaempfer, *Kaempfer's Japan*, 114.

49. Matthew Welch, "Shōki the Demon Queller," in *Japanese Ghosts and Demons: Art of the Supernatural*, ed. Stephen Addiss (New York: George Braziller in association with the Museum of Art, University of Kansas, 1985), 83.

50. See, for example, Brandon, *Country Textiles of Japan*, 17.

51. I am grateful to Insoo Cho, who first suggested this identification. Dr. Cho is the former chief curator of the Hoam Museum in Seoul, Korea, and is currently assistant professor (art history), University of Southern California, Los Angeles.

52. Emperor Gaozu followed the Sui dynasty system in which court officials of the sixth and seventh ranks wore a green outer robe with a silver belt. His successor Taizong (r. 626–649) elaborated the system, with dark green for the sixth rank and light green for the seventh. Although there are numerous references in the literature to officials who failed to be promoted bemoaning their green robes, the rank was respectable. See Mary M. Dusenbury, "The Color of Power: China," in Mary M. Dusenbury, "Radiance and Darkness: Color at the Heian Court" (Ph.D. diss., University of Kansas, 1999), 86.

53. This account follows that in the *Tianzhongji*, a sixteenth-century anthology of anecdotes about popular beliefs, that quoted from an earlier text (now lost). See Mary H. Fong, "A Probable Second 'Chung Ku'uei' by Emperor Shun-chih of the Ch'ing Dynasty," *Oriental Art* 23 (1977): 427–428.

54. There are extant copies of letters of thanks for imperial gifts of New Year's portraits of Zhong Kui painted by the Tang scholar Liu Yuxi (772–842). See ibid., 428 and n. 40.

55. The practice of placing images of protective deities on the doors of houses at the beginning of each new year can be documented in China from the late second century CE. The abundant evidence in Song dynasty literature of the sale of printed door-god images during the New Year's holiday indicates that, at least by this time, the use of protective door gods was common practice. Sung-nien Po and David Johnson, *Domesticated Deities and Auspicious Emblems: The Iconography of Everyday Life in Village China; Popular Prints and Papercuts from the Collection of Po Sung-nien* (Berkeley: Chinese Popular Cultures Project, University of California, 1992), 105.

56. Fong, "A Probable Second 'Chung Ku'uei,'" 428–439. See also Susan Bush and Hsio-yen Shih, comp. and ed., *Early Chinese Texts on Painting* (Cambridge, Mass.: Harvard University Press, 1985).

57. This figure style, as Fong points out, is derived from the tradition of Chan painting ("A Probable Second 'Chung Ku'uei,'" 423).

58. The scroll is scattered; this section belongs to the Masuda collection.

59. Welch, "Shōki the Demon Queller," 86–87.

60. Ibid., 83–84.

61. See "Two Sisters" by Baron von Stillfried, reproduced in Felice Beato, *Once Upon a Time: Vision of Old Japan*, trans. Linda Coverdale (New York: Friendly Press, 1986), 70. The two sisters sleep together under a *yogi* made from a *yūzen* kimono, heavily padded. A separate piece of *yūzen* fabric is employed to widen the *yogi*; dark indigo fabric (probably cotton) at collar and cuffs and light green fabric at the bottom of the collar band are also used to lengthen the garment. The book is a translation of *Mukashi, mukashi, 1863–1883*, a record of photographs taken by Felice Beato and Baron Raimund von Stillfried during this period.

62. Brandon, *Country Textiles of Japan*, 23–24.

63. Ibid., 33.

64. For a discusssion of these textiles, see Mary Dusenbury, "*Kasuri*: A Japanese Textile," *Textile Museum Journal* 17 (1978): 42–44.

65. See Keiko Kobayashi, "The Effect of Western Textile Technology on Japanese *Kasuri*: Development, Innovation, and Competition," *Textile Museum Journal* 40, 41 (2001–2002): 3–34.

66. For the history of *kasuri* weaving, see Mary Dusenbury, "*Kasuri*," in *Beyond the Tanabata Bridge*, ed. Rathbun, 57–74; "*Kasuri*: A Japanese Textile," 41–64; and Amanda Mayer Stinchecum, "A Common Thread: Japanese *Ikat* Textiles," *Asian Art* 3, no. 1 (Winter 1990): 37–61.

67. The use of *itajime* to pattern *kasuri* threads in the late Edo period is puzzling. Until recently, it seemed as if this somewhat unusual and complicated technique sprang, fully developed, into use in the nineteenth century, when it was first employed to pattern *kasuri* threads, and also to make imitation *shibori* cloth. Although there are several splendid polychrome textiles (called *kyōkechi*) in the eighth-century Shōsōin Repository at Tōdaiji in Nara that were quite likely patterned in a process similar to *itajime*, the technique seems to have virtually disappeared after the Heian period. Isolated references to *beni itajime* (safflower *itajime*) in Kyoto were about the only clues to its continued existence until a startling discovery in 1980 in Izumo. As the Itakura family was rebuilding the family house, they found a large number of *itajime* boards that had been used to pattern cloth in the storehouse, as well as indigo vats buried under its dirt floor. In the early Edo period, the Itakura family had been wealthy merchants who dealt in *sarashi momen* (bleached cotton that was used for dyeing). Eventually they also became indigo dyers, and family records indicate that they produced indigo-dyed *itajime*-patterned cloth beginning in 1817, at the latest. See "Ai Itajime" (Indigo Board Clamping) in the section under "Izumo" in *Senshoku to Seikatsu* (Summer 1981): 86–88.

In his brief report on "Ai Itajime," Yoshioka Tsuneo stated his belief that the demise of *kyōkechi* was directly related to the development of *katazome* dyeing in the Kamakura period. It is possible, however, that some of the textiles that scholars believe were patterned with stencils and some type of resist paste were actually dyed using *itajime*. Nevertheless, there is a long historical gap with no evidence to date of *itajime* dyeing of cloth. There is also no evidence to suggest how *itajime* came to be used to pattern *kasuri* wefts in the second quarter of the nineteenth century in Yamato and Ōmi.

68. Yoshida Mitsukuni et al., *Genshoku senshoku daijiten* (Great illustrated dictionary of textiles) (Kyoto: Tankōsha, 1977), 75. Since this was published in 1977, references have been found to the production of *itajime* in Ōmi in the 1830s.

69. Twenty-seven highly skilled women could tie the *kasuri* threads for ten *tan* (kimono lengths, approximately thirteen feet) of Ōmi *jōfu* (high-quality *asa* cloth from Ōmi) in a day. Using *itajime*, a single worker could produce as much. *Genshoku senshoku daijiten*, 75.

70. The kingdom of Ryūkyū first paid tribute to the Ming court in 1372. After the invasion by Satsuma in 1609, Ryūkyū sent tribute both to China and to Japan. Although Satsuma's control was severe, Ryūkyū officially remained a sovereign country until it was annexed by the Meiji government in 1879.

71. Louise Cort, "Bast Fibers," in *Beyond the Tanabata Bridge*, ed. Rathbun, 41.

72. Amanda Mayer Stinchecum notes that the absence of unequivocal references to *bashō* before the mid-sixteenth century, and the fact that the plants do not grow in the wild but are always clustered near human settlements (or the remains of human settlements), suggests that the plant was not indigenous to the islands, but was introduced sometime before these first references. See Stinchecum, "Textiles of Okinawa," in *Beyond the Tanabata Bridge*, ed. Rathbun, 78–79. A more traditional view holds that a fabric identified only as *sheng ji xiabu* in an inventory of the first tribute goods sent from Ryūkyū to the Ming court in 1392 probably refers to raw or glossed banana fiber cloth. See Kamakura Yoshitarō, "Textiles," in Kawakita Michiaki et al., *National Museum of Modern Art, Kyoto: Craft Treasures of Okinawa*, trans. and adapted from *Okinawa no kōgei* by Erika Kaneko (London: Serindia Publications, 1978), 261.

73. Stinchecum, "Textiles of Okinawa," 87; and Kamakura, "Textiles," 261.

74. Cort, "Bast Fibers," 39.

75. Ibid., 41. For a general description in English of the process of producing thread from the fiber banana, see Reiko Mochinaga Brandon and Barbara B. Stephan, *Textile Art of Okinawa* (Honolulu: Honolulu Academy of Arts, 1990), 4; and Amanda Mayer Stinchecum, "Unlined Robe" (Catalogue 154b), in Robert Moes, *Mingei: Japanese Folk Art* (Alexandria, Virginia: Art Services International, 1995), 239. For a detailed description with photographs, see *Kijōka no bashōfu* (*Kijōka banana fiber cloth*), *Ningen Kokuhō serizu* (Living National Treasures series), vol. 41 (Tokyo: Kodansha, 1977).

76. See Kamakura, "Textiles," 261.

77. Although commoners had been permitted to wear cotton in the winter at least as early as 1873, Sasamori Gisuke (1845–1915) observed, twenty years later, that the common people wore *bashōfu* garments exclusively. Sasamori was a former official from Aomori Prefecture in northern Japan, who traveled to Okinawa in 1893. Stinchecum, "Textiles of Okinawa," 86.

78. Tanaka Toshio and Tanaka Reiko. *Okinawa orimono no kenkyū: retsuji zuroku* (*Study of Okinawan weaving: pictorial record of cloth fragments*) (Kyoto: Shikōsha, 1976), 4.

79. Takimoto Kazuko, for example, in conversations with the author, 1974–1980.

80. The Shōsōin Repository at Tōdaiji in Nara contains at least two eighth-century textiles that use a two-color ply as part of a pattern of horizontal stripes. These fragments, which are woven comparatively coarsely, appear as isolated examples in the Shōsōin collection, and apparently had no influence on the subsequent repertory of Japanese weaving techniques. See Kaneo Matsumoto, *Jōdaigire: 7th and 8th Century Textiles in Japan from the Shōsōin and Hōryūji* (Kyoto: Shikosha, 1984), 130, fig. 108.

81. Tanaka Toshio first went to Okinawa in 1939 as part of a team of experts sponsored by the Nihon Mingei Kyōkai (Japan Folkcraft Movement). After three more research trips, the husband-and-wife team published a two-volume study. See Tanaka Toshio and Tanaka Reiko, *Okinawa orimono no kenkyū* (*Study of Okinawan weaving*) and *Okinawa orimono no kenkyū: retsuji zuroku*, 2 vols. (Kyoto: Shikosha, 1976). The statement is found on page 4 of the second volume.

82. Tanaka and Tanaka, *Okinawa orimono no kenkyū: retsuji zuroku*, cats. 37, 36, 35, 34, 29, and 3 (in the order discussed in the present text).

83. See, for example, the one-page synopsis on *bingata* dyeing in a biographical dictionary of Japan's Living National Treasures. "Bingata," in *Ningen Kokuhō jiten*, 118.

84. Sakihara Mitsugu, *A Brief History of Early Okinawa Based on The Omoro Sōshi* (Tokyo: Honpo Shoseki Press, 1987), 165. In time, the range of colors was expanded, and the ranks of officials were distinguished by the colors of their *bashōfu* court robes.

85. Kamakura, "Textiles," 268.

86. After King Sattu sent the first tribute from Ryūkyū to the Ming court in 1372, Emperor Hongwu (r. 1368–1398) sent "thirty-six" families (probably a formulaic number) from Fujian to Ryūkyū. These Chinese families settled on the islands in 1392, and they (and their descendants) served the court as navigators, shipwrights, interpreters, teachers, diplomats, and ministers. See Robert K. Sakai and Sakihara Mitsugu, "Okinawa," in *Encyclopedia of Japan* (New York and Tokyo: Kodansha International, 1983), 85.

87. See Kamakura Yoshitarō, "Okinawan History and Handicrafts," in the National Museum of Modern Art, Kyoto, *Craft Treasures of Okinawa*, 223–232, and "Textiles," 261–272.

88. Kamakura quotes from the *Mizaisei*, compiled in 1715, apparently a sort of census and record of tax liabilities ("Textiles," 270).

89. Kamakura, "Textiles," 268–269.

90. For a discussion of crop failures and famine, see Conrad Totman, *Early Modern Japan* (Berkeley, Los Angeles, and London: University of California Press, 1993), 236–245.

91. Michiyo Morioka, "Sashiko, Kogin, and Hishizashi," in *Beyond the Tanabata Bridge*, ed. Rathbun, 110.

92. Ibid.

93. Ibid.

94. Quoted in ibid.

95. For a handsome example of a seventeenth- or eighteenth-century *kasane hanpi* used in the Bugaku dance, see Kasuga Shrine, ed. *Bugaku Treasures from the Kasuga Shrine* (Tokyo: Otsuka Kogeisha, 1984), cat. 36-1.

96. This *dōfuku* is not to be confused with the highly decorated, straight short coats associated with warlords of the late Muromachi and Momoyama periods (a homophone written with different characters).

97. For an example of an Edo period aristocrat's *dōfuku*, see Kawakami Shigeki, *Kuge no ifuku (Court costume)*, *Nihon no bijutsu* 8, no. 339 (August 1994): 63, fig. 129.

98. Hino Saishiko, *Nihon fukushokushi (History of Japanese costume)* (Tokyo: Kōshunkaku, 1963), 117–118 and ill. 114.

99. *Genshoku senshoku daijiten*, 752.

100. Takemura Akihiko, *Fukusa: Japanese Gift Covers* (Tokyo: Iwasaki Bijutsu-sha, 1991), 101, 124, 213. See also Mary V. Hays and Ralph E. Hays, *Fukusa: The Shojiro Nomura Fukusa Collection* (Oakland, Ca.: Mills College Art Gallery, 1983).

101. Takemura, *Fukusa*, 135–136.

102. For a discussion of Nishijin, see "Nishijin," in *Genshoku senshoku daijiten*, 794; and "Jacado ki," in same, 505–506. See also Helen Benton Minnich in collaboration with Shojiro Nomura, *Japanese Costume and the Makers of Its Elegant Tradition* (Rutland, Vermont and Tokyo: Charles E. Tuttle, 1963), 176–180, 319–320; and Adachi, *The Living Treasures of Japan*, 24–27.

103. Yokoi Yūhō, "Kesa Kudoku," in Yokoi Yūhō with Daizen Victoria, *Zen Master Dōgen* (New York and Tokyo: Weatherhill, 1976), 93.

104. Ibid., 88.

105. Ibid., 89.

106. Ibid., 103–104.

107. Ibid., 105.

108. Yokoi with Victoria, *Zen Master Dōgen*, 101; and Kyūma Keichō, *Kesa no kenkyū (A study of kesa)* (Tokyo: Daihūrin Kakuhan, 1967), 20. In Japan today, all aspects of constructing, wearing, and handling a *kesa* continue to be surrounded with detailed regulations. Kyūma lays out the regulations concerning *kaśāya* in the following categories: shape (garment and interior field), color, size, stitching techniques, construction, number (and size) of basic garments, and use (see *Kesa no kenkyū*, 20–25).

109. See Roderick Whitfield and Anne Farrer, *Caves of the Thousand Buddhas: Chinese Art from the Silk Route* (New York: George Braziller, 1990), 114–115.

110. The former are now in the Hōryūji Hōmotsukan on the grounds of the Tokyo National Museum, and the latter in the Shōsōin Repository of Tōdaiji in Nara.

111. Gafu Izutsu, conversation with Marie Lyman, April 7, 1981, as quoted in Marie Lyman, "Distant Mountains: The Influence of *Funzō-e* on the Tradition of Buddhist Clerical Robes in Japan," *Textile Museum Journal* (1984): 26.

112. *See the Konkōmyō saishō ō gyō (Suvarnaprabhāsottama-rāja Sūtra*, or *Sūtra of the Sovereign Kings of the Golden Light Ray)*, in William Theodore de Bary, ed., *The Buddhist Tradition in India, China and Japan* (New York: Vintage Books, 1972), 269–270. Following the association of the corner patches with the Four Guardian Kings, the two tabs that appear at the upper center of most *kesa* have been interpreted variously as referring to the two guardian Deva kings, Brahmā and Indra; or, alternately, to Mañjuśrī (Monju in Japanese) and Samantabhadra (Fugen), two bodhisattvas who often flank the historical Buddha in triad configurations. The central panel of the *kesa* thus has sometimes been seen as a representation of the Buddha. For a discussion of the Four Guardian Kings, see Louis Frédéric, *Buddhism*, trans. Nissim Marshall, Flammarion Iconographic Guides (Paris and New York: Flammarion, 1995), 241–246.

113. Robert Treat Paine and Alexander Soper, *The Art and Architecture of Japan* (New York: Viking Penguin, 1987), 30. Some Buddhist sects, such as Tendai and Shingon, refer to the corner patches as *Shitennō*. Others (Sōtō Zen, for example) simply call them *kakuchō*, or "corner layers." See Lyman, "Distant Mountains," n. 8. Kyūma Keichō, in his *Kesa no kenkyū*, refers to corner patches simply as *kakuchō*.

114. Shitennōji is one of three major temples constructed in the late sixth and very early seventh centuries. Shōtoku Taishi also built Wakakusadera (forerunner of Hōryūji), with a figure of Bhaishajyaguru (Yakushi in Japanese), the Buddha of Healing, as the main icon. Soga Umako, uncle of Empress Suiko and an important power behind the throne, built Asukadera, dedicated to the historical Buddha Śākyamuni and completed in 596. See Penny Mason, *History of Japanese Art* (New York: Harry N. Abrams, 1993), 41.

115. See Frédéric, *Buddhism*, 241 ff.

116. See *Shōsōin-ten (Exhibition of Shōsōin Treasures)* (Nara: Nara National Museum, 1987), 32, cat. 15; and *Shōsōin-ten (Exhibition of Shōsōin Treasures)* (Nara: Nara National Museum, 1991), 12, cat. 1.

117. See Lyman, "Distant Mountains," 32, fig. 9.

118. Qingchou Zhengcheng (known in Japan as Seisetsu Shōchō, 1274–1339) came to Japan in 1327. The *kesa* is owned by Chōshōin in Kyoto. The *kesa* worn by Kūkoku Myōō (1328–1407) is owned by Jiseiin in Kyoto. Both are reproduced in Alan Kennedy, "*Kesa*: Its Sacred and Secular Aspects," *Textile Museum Journal* (1983): 72–73; and in *Nihon no bijutsu*, no. 90 (1974): pl. 132 and 57.

119. See Helmut Brinker and Hiroshi Kanazawa, *Zen: Masters of Meditation in Images and Writings*, tr. Andreas Leisinger, *Artibus Asiae* Supplementum 40 (Zurich: Artibus Asiae Publishers, 1996), 163–164.

120. The Edo-period manual is the *Zuzō shuchi*, published in block-printed form in 1806. See Alan Kennedy, *Japanese Costume: History and Tradition* (Paris: Adam Biro, 1990), 123. Kyūma illustrates the proper construction of corner patches in *Kesa no kenkyū*, 131.

121. See Minnich and Nomura, *Japanese Costume*, 197.

122. Sharon Shore, Conservation Report, 1998.

123. Frédéric, *Buddhism*, 241–242.

124. Although the sixteen-petal chrysanthemum was an imperial motif, it was sometimes employed by others, with or without imperial permission.

125. Oliver Impey, "Reflections Upon the Crafts of Meiji Period Japan with Reference to the Collection of the

Ashmolean Museum," *Oriental Art* 42, no. 3 (Autumn 1996): 11.

126. A mid-eighth-century banner preserved in the Shōsōin Repository at Tōdaiji in Nara, for example, depicts a standing peacock with grasses and a flowering tree. The image is rendered in a difficult double-faced embroidery technique, in which the image appears identically on the front and back of the banner. See Matsumoto, *Jōdaigire*, 120–121, pl. 100.

127. The other two species are the white-naped crane and the hooded crane. See Mary Griggs Burke, "The Delights of Nature in Japanese Art," *Orientations* 27, no. 2 (February 1996): 57.

128. The following discussion is based on the work of James Edward Ketalaar. See, in particular, his "Interpreting Persecution: Law of the Buddha, Law of the King," in his book, *Of Heretics and Martyrs in Meiji Japan: Buddhism and Its Persecution* (Princeton: Princeton University Press, 1990), 5–14.

129. Walter Muir Whitehill, *Museum of Fine Arts, Boston: A Centennial History* (Cambridge, Mass: The Belknap Press of Harvard University Press, 1970), 113.

Catalogue of the Collection

Several technical terms have been used in their broadest meanings:

Brocade refers to patterned polychrome textiles with patterning formed by one or more supplementary wefts (or warps).

Compound weave refers to textiles in which patterning is formed by the use of two or more sets of warps and/or wefts; the structure of one face does not necessarily affect that of the other.

Damask refers to patterned monochrome textiles in which the patterning is formed by the interplay of warp and weft in differing directional orientations. Thus it includes twill patterning on a twill, satin, or plain weave ground; satin patterning on a twill, satin, or plain weave ground; and plain weave patterning on a twill or satin ground.

Supplementary weft indicates a patterning weft that is not part of the basic structure of the fabric.

GENERAL NOTES

Dimensions are given in inches followed by centimeters; length (or height) is given first, followed by width. Textiles in the collection have been measured both in inches and in centimeters, and rounded slightly; therefore inch and centimeter measures may not be precisely equivalent mathematically.

Only length measurements are given for Chinese skirts, which have pleats and a wrap-around design, and are therefore inherently flexible in width as worn.

The terms "gold-wrapped thread" and "silver-wrapped thread" refer to metallic alloys with the appearance of gold or silver. The term "metallic foil" is used only when the metal has tarnished so much that it appears neither gold nor silver. None of these threads has been analyzed for metallic content.

The object titles given here are longer and more descriptive than those given in the main text.

An asterisk (*) indicates that there is an entry for this textile in the main text.

SOUTH ASIA
INDIA/PAKISTAN

Notes: "Mirror glass" indicates small pieces of glass or mica "mirrors" set onto a cloth with embroidery stitches. "Mirrorwork" (*shisha*) indicates the process of setting the mirror glass. Stitches include a variety of looped and flat types.

COSTUME

Woman's Headcloth with scattered flowers and borders of flowering plants
Pakistan (Sind)
19th or 20th century
Silk embroidery on cotton ground
Embroidery (stem) on mottled green plain weave ground
103 x 45 in.; 261 x 115.5 cm
Source Unknown, 0000.124

Woman's Headcloth with eight-petalled flowers in meandering rows and geometric borders
India (Karnataka)
19th or early 20th century
Silk embroidery on cotton ground
Embroidery (detached interlacing) on red plain weave ground
89 x 54 in.; 226 x 37.5 cm
Source Unknown, 0000.125

Embroidered Bag with floral motifs
India
19th or early 20th century
Silk
Embroidery on red satin ground
3 x 1.5 in.; 7.5 x 4.5 cm
Source Unknown, 0000.2366

Woman's Headcloth with vertical rows of red fan-shaped flowers on green base with borders of flowering plants
Pakistan (Sind)
19th or early 20th century
Silk embroidery on cotton ground
Embroidery (satin, chain stitch) on tan plain weave ground
79 x 16.5 in.; 200.5 x 42 cm
Source Unknown, 1927.5

**Woman's Shawl* (Abocchnai) with crowded rows of red fan-shaped flowers on green base with borders of flowering plants* (Plate 3, p. 25)
Pakistan (Sind)
Late 19th or early 20th century
Silk embroidery on fine cotton ground
Embroidery (stem, chain stitch) on off-white plain weave ground
75.5 x 51.5 in.; 191 x 131 cm
The William Bridges Thayer Memorial, 1928.848

Woman's Headcloth with lattice formed by tan unembroidered ground with interstices filled with pairs of green curved motifs on red embroidered ground
India/Pakistan (Punjab)
19th century
Silk embroidery on coarse cotton ground with mica mirrors
Embroidery (*phulkari*) on tan plain weave ground
91.5 x 53 in.; 232 x 139 cm
The William Bridges Thayer Memorial, 1928.849

Woman's Headcloth (Bochini) with central medallion, quadrants of widely spaced geometric motifs, and borders of flowering plants
India (Kutch) or Pakistan (Sind)
19th century
Silk embroidery on cotton ground with mica mirrors
Embroidery (couching, chain) on tan plain weave ground
82.5 x 63 in.; 210 x 160 cm
The William Bridges Thayer Memorial, 1928.850

Woman's Headcloth with red central medallion, radiating bands with medallions, and borders of flowering plants
Pakistan (Sind) or vicinity
19th century
Silk embroidery on cotton ground
Embroidery (chain, satin) on off-white plain weave ground
81 x 45.5 in.; 203.5 x 116 cm
The William Bridges Thayer Memorial, 1928.851

Woman's Headcloth with central medallion, green radiating bands with medallions, and borders of green plants
Pakistan (Sind)
19th or early 20th century
Silk and sequins
Embroidery (satin, chain) on red plain weave ground
76 x 47 in.; 191 x 120 cm
The William Bridges Thayer Memorial, 1928.852

*Woman's Headcloth (Odhani) with elaborate central medallion and regular rows of flowering plants on blue ground with outer red border set with mirrors
(Plate 1, p. 24)
India (Banni district, Kutch, Gujarat)
Late 19th or early 20th century
Silk and mica
Embroidery (chain stitch and mirrorwork) on blue satin ground
67 x 75 in.; 170 x 190.5 cm
The William Bridges Thayer Memorial, 1928.854

Woman's Headcloth with all-over casual design of simple pointed flowers (Fig. 2, detail)
India (Kutch, Gujarat)
19th or early 20th century
Silk embroidery on cotton ground
Embroidery (stem) on brown plain weave ground
113 x 51.5 in.; 288 x 131 cm
The William Bridges Thayer Memorial, 1928.855

Woman's Skirt (Ghaghara) with alternating vertical rows of dancing women and peacocks in trees
India (Gujarat)
19th or early 20th century
Silk and gold-wrapped thread
Gold brocade (discontinuous supplementary weft) and embroidery on red satin ground
35 x 36 in.; 89 x 91.5 cm
The William Bridges Thayer Memorial, 1928.865

Embroidered Bodice (Choli) with rows of six-petalled flowers
India (Kutch)
19th or early 20th century
Silk with cotton ties and insets
Embroidery on blue and orange satin grounds
11.5 x 29.5 in.; 29.5 x 75 cm
The William Bridges Thayer Memorial, 1928.870

Woman's Bodice (Choli) with paired birds and flowering plants
India/Pakistan
19th or early 20th century
Cotton and mirror glass
Embroidery on indigo plain weave ground
18.5 x 29 in.; 47 x 74.8 cm
The William Bridges Thayer Memorial, 1928.871

*Woman's Tunic (Aba) (Plate 6, detail, p. 34)
India (Banni district, Kutch, Gujarat)
19th or early 20th century
Silk and mirror glass
Embroidery (chain stitch and mirrorwork [shisha]) on mustard yellow satin ground
40.5 x 40.5 in.; 103 x 103 cm
The William Bridges Thayer Memorial, 1928.872
Note: This aba has a small Marshall Field and Co. tag attached to it with a handwritten inscription: "antique embroidered silk dress" and "over 100 years."

*Woman's Tunic (Aba) (Plate 4, p. 30)
India (Banni district, Kutch, Gujarat)
Late 19th or early 20th century
Silk and mirror glass
Embroidery (a variety of looped and flat stitches, mirrorwork [shisha], and detached interlacing) on red satin ground
43.5 x 41.3 in.; 110.5 x 105 cm
The William Bridges Thayer Memorial, 1928.873

*Woman's Tunic (Aba) (Plate 5, p. 32)
India (Gujarat)
19th or early 20th century
Silk and mirror glass
Embroidery (a variety of looped and flat stitches, and mirrorwork [shisha]) on deep blue satin ground
49.5 x 41.5 in.; 126 x 105.5 cm
The William Bridges Thayer Memorial, 1928.874

*Child's Hooded Cap with dancing women, peacocks, elephants, and flowering plants (Plate 7, p. 35)
India (Kutch or Saurastra, Gujarat)
19th or early 20th century
Silk
Embroidery (chain and other looped stitches) on red satin ground
17.3 x 9.3 in.; 44 x 24 cm
The William Bridges Thayer Memorial, 1928.875

*Woman's Headcloth (Orhni) with geometric design of paired central x-shaped crosses on squares, with quadrant and border variants of cross-on-square motif
(Plate 2, p. 25)
India (Bikaner, Rajasthan)
19th or early 20th century
Wool, cotton, and applied mirrors
Cotton embroidery on deep red wool plain weave ground
86 x 41 in.; 218.5 x 104 cm
The William Bridges Thayer Memorial, 1928.879

Shawl with rows of gold boteh at borders and four boteh at interior corners
India (Delhi region)
20th century
Wool and gold-wrapped thread
Embroidery (couching) on blue machine-woven twill ground
86 x 47 in.; 219 x 120 cm
Gift of Dr. & Mrs. Alfred E. Farah, 1978.20

HOUSEHOLD FURNISHINGS

Square Panel with densely packed rows of birds and flowers
India (possibly embroidered by Chinese community in India)
19th or early 20th century
Silk
Embroidery (satin) on red satin ground with green, yellow, and red outer borders
32 x 30 in.; 82 x 76 cm
Source Unknown, 0000.2325

Household Furnishing with freely executed interior floral borders and corner semi-circles enclosing a red central square and colored tabs on two sides
Northwest India or Pakistan (Sind)
19th or early 20th century
Silk embroidery on cotton ground
Embroidery (stem) on green plain weave ground around red center
23 x 22 in.; 58 x 56 cm
Source Unknown, 0000.2348

Bed Furnishing (Palempore) with tree-of-life design and crowded borders and interior corners depicting a variety of birds and flowers
India
19th century
Cotton
Block printing, resist and mordant dyeing on tan plain weave ground
35.5 x 53 in.; 90 x 135 cm
Source Unknown, 0000.2349

Bed Furnishing (Palempore) with tree-of-life design and crowded borders and interior corners depicting a variety of birds and flowers
India
19th century
Cotton
Block printing, resist and mordant dyeing on tan plain weave ground
35.5 x 53 in.; 90 x 135 cm
Source Unknown, 0000.2351

Household Furnishing (reconstructed from woman's headcloth) with central medallion and aligned rows of flowering plants with pieced colored satin borders
(Plate 8, p. 37)
India
19th century
Silk
Embroidery (chain) on yellow satin ground
57 x 78.5 in.; 145 x 199 cm
The William Bridges Thayer Memorial, 1928.853

Household Furnishing (reconstructed from woman's headcloth) with dancing women and peacocks
(Plate 9, p. 38)
India
19th century
Silk
Embroidery (chain stitch) on satin ground
40.5 x 76.5 in.; 103 x 194 cm
The William Bridges Thayer Memorial, 1928.856

Household Furnishing with birds, flowers, and prancing animals
India (Saurastra) or Pakistan (Sind)
19th or early 20th century
Silk embroidery on silk ground
Embroidery (detached interlacing) on deep blue satin ground with red tie-dye and other borders, and lining of stamped gold dots on blue gauze sari material
41 x 31 in.; 104.5 x 78.5 cm
The William Bridges Thayer Memorial, 1928.878

Embroidered Panel with geometric motifs
India (Kutch) or Pakistan (Sind) (Plate 10, p. 41)
19th or early 20th century
Cotton
Embroidery (detached interlacing) on indigo plain weave ground
41 x 21.5 in.; 104.5 x 54.5 cm
The William Bridges Thayer Memorial, 1928.881

Bed Furnishing with central field of scrolling flowers surrounded by deep borders with large boteh *patterns*
India (?) or Iran (?)
19th or early 20th century
Cotton
Block printing on diaper-pattern ground
82 x 77.5 in.; 208 x 196.5 cm
The William Bridges Thayer Memorial, 1928.1256

WOVEN TEXTILES

Woven Fragment (end panel of a sari?) with all-over flower and vine motifs
India (Varanasi?)
19th century
Silk and gold-wrapped thread
Compound weave
27.5 x 31 in.; 70 x 78.5 cm
The William Bridges Thayer Memorial, 1928.857

Brocade Cloth with rows of gold circular motifs and scattered flowers
India
19th or early 20th century
Silk and gold-wrapped thread
Brocade on pink plain weave ground
99 x 31 in.; 312 x 79 cm
The William Bridges Thayer Memorial, 1928.858

Patola (fragile with losses)
India (Gujarat)
19th century
Silk and metal-wrapped thread
Ikat
W. 50.8 in.; 129 cm
The William Bridges Thayer Memorial, 1928.860

Woven Fragment with Krishna as cowherd with cows and suckling calves in borders of scrolling vines
India
19th century
Silk and silver-wrapped thread
Silver brocade on yellow satin ground
12 x 66 in.; 30.5 x 167.8 cm
The William Bridges Thayer Memorial, 1928.864

Fragments of Sari with ivory-on-ivory floral patterns
India
19th or early 20th century
Silk
Discontinuous supplementary patterned twill on ivory gauze ground
a and b: 45 x 42 in.; 115.5 x 107 cm
c and d: 45 x 39.5 in.; 115.5 x 101 cm
Gift of Mrs. Gertrude Welch, 1932.48a,b,c,d

FLAT EMBROIDERED

Embroidered Panel with widely spaced, alternating vertical rows of flowering plants and diamonds, with interior border of dense geometric shapes and mirrors
India/Pakistan (Punjab)
19th or early 20th century
Silk embroidery on cotton ground with applied mirrors
Embroidery (stem, mirrorwork) on indigo plain weave ground
96 x 47 in.; 271.5 x 120 cm
The William Bridges Thayer Memorial, 0000.131

Embroidered Panel with large, central gold star with unidentified border motifs projecting into central field
India
20th century
Heavy gold-wrapped cotton floss on wool
Embroidery (couching) on navy plain weave ground
96 x 47 in.; 271.5 x 120 cm
Source Unknown, 0000.1106

Printed and Embroidered Fragments (border panels?) with boteh
India (?)
19th or early 20th century
Silk and metal-wrapped thread on cotton ground
Heavy silk floss and metal-wrapped thread embroidery (couching) on printed plain weave ground
a: 11.5 x 45 in.; 29.5 x 114.5 cm
b: 12 x 45 in.; 30.5 x 114.5 cm
Source Unknown, 0000.2345a,b

Embroidered Panel with widely spaced, alternating vertical rows of flowering plants and diamonds, with interior border of dense geometric shapes and mirrors
India/Pakistan (Punjab)
19th or early 20th century
Silk embroidery on cotton ground
Embroidery (stem) on brown plain weave ground
96 x 45.3 in.; 272 x 115.5 cm
Source Unknown, 0000.2346

White-on-White Embroidered Fabric with flowering plants and floral clusters (for European market)
(Plate 11, detail, p. 43)
India
19th or early 20th century
Cotton on raw silk
Embroidery (double-face satin stitch) on plain weave ground
324 x 33.5 in.; 823 x 85 cm
Source Unknown, 0000.2433

PRINTING/DYEING

Calico Fragment with staggered rows of black-outlined boteh *with emerging flowering vines*
India (?)
19th century
Cotton
Block printing on red plain weave ground
11.3 x 16.5 in.; 28.8 x 42 cm; plus 9.5 in., 24 cm folded under
Source Unknown, 0000.2382

Prayer Mat or Household Furnishing (possibly for tourist trade)
India
Early 20th century
Cotton
Block printing on plain weave ground
41.3 x 60.3 in.; 105 x 153 cm
The William Bridges Thayer Memorial, 1928.867

Prayer Mat or Household Furnishing (possibly for tourist trade)
India
Early 20th century
Cotton
Block printing on plain weave ground
58.5 x 42.5 in.; 149 x 108 cm
The William Bridges Thayer Memorial, 1928.868

Household Furnishing with central medallion in floral field with borders and calico lining
India
19th or early 20th century
Cotton
Block printing on plain weave ground
46 x 34.5 in.; 117 x 86 cm
The William Bridges Thayer Memorial, 1928.869

Bandanna
India
Early 20th century
Silk
Block printing on plain weave ground
36.3 x 32.5 in.; 92 x 83 cm
Gift of Mrs. E. M. Hopkins, 1930.15

SOUTH ASIA
KASHMIR AND INDIA/PAKISTAN (PUNJAB)

KASHMIR SHAWLS

Embroidered Kashmir Shawl (Plate 19, p. 71)
India/Pakistan (Punjab)
19th century
Cashmere/wool
Embroidery on twill ground
47 x 46 in.; 119.5 x 117 cm
The William Bridges Thayer Memorial, 1928.451

Kashmir Shawl
Kashmir
19th century
Wool with cashmere ground
Twill tapestry and embroidery
54.5 x 54.5 in.; 138.5 x 138.5 cm
The William Bridges Thayer Memorial, 1928.454

Embroidered Kashmir Shawl (Plate 21, p. 73)
India/Pakistan (Punjab)
19th century
Wool
Embroidery on twill ground
67 x 66 in.; 170.3 x 167.8 cm
The William Bridges Thayer Memorial, 1928.455

Embroidered Kashmir Shawl (Plate 20, p. 72)
India/Pakistan (Punjab)
Sikh period (1819–1846)
Cashmere/wool
Embroidery on twill ground
71.5 x 69 in.; 179.5 x 175.5 cm
The William Bridges Thayer Memorial, 1928.460

Kashmir Shawl—Chandar, Khatraaz Style
Iran
19th century
Cashmere/wool
Twill tapestry with fine wool or cashmere
embroidery
69.5 x 70 in.; 176.8 x 178.5 cm
The William Bridges Thayer Memorial, 1928.462

Kashmir Shawl
India/Pakistan (Punjab)
19th century
Cashmere/wool
Twill tapestry and embroidery
68 x 66 in.; 167.3 x 172.4 cm; fringe: 2 in.; 5 cm
The William Bridges Thayer Memorial, 1928.464

Kashmir Shawl (Plate 15, p. 62)
Kashmir
ca. 1840
Wool with cashmere end tabs
Twill tapestry and embroidery
56 x 119 in.; 142.5 x 302.5 cm; fringe: .8 in.; 2 cm
The William Bridges Thayer Memorial, 1928.748

Kashmir Shawl
Kashmir
ca. 1840
Cashmere/wool
Twill tapestry and embroidery
53 x 64 in.; 134.7 x 162.7 cm
The William Bridges Thayer Memorial, 1928.750

Kashmir Shawl (Plate 12, p. 56–57)
Kashmir
1820s
Cashmere
Twill tapestry
125 x 49 in.; 317.5 x 124.5 cm
The William Bridges Thayer Memorial, 1928.751

Kashmir Shawl (Plate 16, p. 64)
Kashmir
Third quarter of 19th century
Cashmere/wool
Twill tapestry and embroidery
124 x 54 in.; 320 x 137 cm
The William Bridges Thayer Memorial, 1928.752

Kashmir Shawl (Plate 17, p. 65)
Kashmir
Third quarter of 19th century
Cashmere/wool
Twill tapestry and embroidery
125 x 56 in.; 316.8 x 142.3 cm
The William Bridges Thayer Memorial, 1928.754

Kashmir Shawl (Plate 13, p. 58–59)
Kashmir
1815–1830; reconstructed late 19th or early 20th
century
Cashmere
Twill tapestry and embroidery
117 x 25 in.; 297.3 x 63.6 cm
The William Bridges Thayer Memorial, 1928.756

Kashmir Shawl
Kashmir
19th century
Cashmere/wool
Twill tapestry
34.8 x 23 in.; 88.3 x 58.5 cm
The William Bridges Thayer Memorial, 1928.757

Kashmir Shawl
Kashmir or India/Pakistan (Punjab)
after 1860
Wool
Twill tapestry and embroidery
70 x 70 in.; 177.5 x 177.5 cm
The William Bridges Thayer Memorial, 1928.790

Kashmir Shawl (Plate 14, p. 60)
Kashmir
Second quarter of 19th century
Cashmere/wool with some silk thread for piecing
Twill tapestry and embroidery
131.5 x 55 in.; 333.5 x 140 cm; fringe: 1.5 in.; 4 cm
The William Bridges Thayer Memorial, 1928.965

Kashmir Shawl (Plate 18, p. 68)
India/Pakistan (Kashmir or the Punjab)
ca. 1870
Cashmere/wool
Twill tapestry and embroidery
83 x 81 in.; 210 x 205 cm; fringe: .5 in.; 1.3 cm
The William Bridges Thayer Memorial, 1928.971

Kashmir Shawl
India/Pakistan (Kashmir or the Punjab)
(1860–1875)
Cashmere/wool
Twill tapestry and embroidery
72 x 72 in.; 183 x 183 cm
Gift of E. Helen Pendleton, 1977.5

IRAN

Textile Fragment (Plate 28, p. 90)
Iran
Qajar period, 18th or 19th century
Silk and metal-wrapped silk thread
Brocaded plain weave (discontinuous
supplementary weft patterning)
12 x 8.5 in.; 30.5 x 21.8 cm
Source Unknown, 0000.173

Textile Fragment (Plate 23, p. 86)
Iran
Qajar period, 19th century
Silk and metal strips
Cut and voided velvet (right selvage)
4.5 x 9 in.; 11.8 x 23 cm
Source Unknown, 0000.175

Textile Fragment
Iran
Second half of 19th century
Silk with metal-wrapped silk core on plain weave
cotton ground
Supplementary weft patterning
12.5 x 3.5 in.; 32 x 9 cm
Source Unknown, 0000.178

Brocade Fragment
Iran
Late 19th century
Silk on cotton ground
Brocaded plain weave (discontinuous supplementary weft with weft floats on back)
8 x 5.5 in.; 20.5 x 14 cm
Source Unknown, 0000.181

Textile Fragment with warp stripes of warp resist
(Plate 27, p. 89)
Iran
Safavid period, first half of 18th century
Silk and metal-wrapped silk thread
Brocaded satin (discontinuous supplementary weft
patterning) with warp-resist stripes
23 x 15.3 in.; 58 x 39 cm
The William Bridges Thayer Memorial, 0000.183

Textile Fragment, Timurid style (Plate 34, p. 97)
Iran or Central Asia
15th century
Silk
Compound weave (satin lampas: satin weave with
weft-faced twill; one selvage)
13 x 10 in.; 33 x 25.5 cm
Source Unknown, 0000.683

Textile Fragment (Plate 24, p. 87)
Iran
Safavid period, 17th century
Silk and metal-wrapped silk thread
Compound weave with metal ground (discontinuous and continuous supplementary weft patterning
with weft floats on back)
10.3 x 10 in.; 28 x 25.3 cm
Source Unknown, 0000.2084

Textile Fragment (Plate 26, p. 89)
Iran
Qajar period, 19th century
Silk and metal-wrapped silk thread
Compound weave with metal ground (continuous
complementary weft patterning)
10.3 x 7.3 in.; 26 x 19.5 cm
Source Unknown, 0000.2085

Textile Fragment (Plate 22, p. 86)
Iran
Qajar period, 19th century
Silk and metal strips
Cut and voided velvet (right selvage)
7 x 4.5 in.; 18 x 11.5 cm
Source Unknown, 0000.2089

Textile Fragment (Plate 29, p. 90)
Iran
Qajar period, 19th century
Cotton, ink, and pigments (also dye?)
Plain weave, printed and painted
13 x 9 in.; 33 x 23 cm
Source Unknown, 0000.2381

Ceremonial Horse Cover (Plate 25, p. 88)
Iran
Safavid period, 18th century
Silk and metal-wrapped silk thread
Compound weave with metal ground (complementary weft patterning)
54.5 x 34 in.; 138.5 x 86.5 cm
The William Bridges Thayer Memorial, 1928.877

Textile Fragment
Iran
Early 19th century
Silk and metal-wrapped silk thread
Brocaded satin (complementary weft patterning)
5.3 x 6.8 in.; 13.3 x 17.3 cm
The William Bridges Thayer Memorial, 1928.1040

Textile Fragment
Iran
Late 18th or early 19th century
Silk with traces of metal-wrapped silk thread
Compound weave (complementary weft patterning)
8.3 x 10 in.; 21 x 25.5 cm
The William Bridges Thayer Memorial, 1928.1041

Textile Fragment
Iran (?)
Late 19th or early 20th century
Silk and wool
Compound weave (lampas)
9.8 x 17.5 in.; 25 x 44.5 cm
The William Bridges Thayer Memorial, 1928.1042

Brocade Fragments (two)
Iran
19th century
Silk patterning on plain weave cotton ground
Brocaded plain weave (taffeta; supplementary
discontinuous weft)
a: 17.5 x 4 in.; 20 x 10.3 cm
b: 16.5 x 11 in.; 42 x 28 cm
The William Bridges Thayer Memorial,
1928.1043a,b

Qalemkar
Iran (Isfahan)
Mid-20th century
Heavy cotton
Polychrome block printing on plain weave ground
94 x 66 in.; 237 x 167.5 cm
Gift of Forrest E. Jones, 1974.120

CARPETS

Carpet (Plate 31, p. 93)
Iran (Senna)
Qajar period, 19th century
Wool on mercerized (?) cotton warp
Knotted pile on striped warp
66.5 x 53 in.; 169 x 134.5 cm
Source Unknown, 0000.2021

Carpet (Plate 32, p. 95)
Iran (Tabriz)
Qajar period, 19th century
Silk pile on cotton warp and weft
Knotted pile
70 x 51 in.; 177.8 x 129.5 cm
Source Unknown, 0000.2022

Carpet
Iran (Heriz) (Plate 33, detail, p. 96)
Qajar period, late 19th century
Wool pile on cotton warp and weft
Knotted pile, symmetrical knot
176 x 140 in.; 447 x 355.5 cm
Source Unknown, 0000.2423

Kilim (Plate 30, detail, p. 91)
Iran (Zarand, near Kermanshah)
Qajar period, 19th century
Wool weft, cotton warp
Tapestry weave (discontinuous weft, plain weave
structure)
168 x 68 in.; 426.8 x 172.8 cm
The William Bridges Thayer Memorial, 1928.820

INDONESIA

Sarong
Indonesia (Java)
20th century
Cotton
Batik on plain weave ground
81.5 x 40.3 in.; 207 x 102 cm
Source Unknown, 0000.2358

Sarong
Indonesia (Java)
19th–20th century
Cotton
Batik on plain weave ground
78.5 x 41.5 in.; 200 x 106 cm
Source Unknown, 0000.2360

Batik Square
Indonesia (Java)
20th century
Cotton
Batik on plain weave ground
37.5 x 40.3 in.; 95 x 102 cm
Source Unknown, 0000.2362

Batik Square
Indonesia (Java)
20th century
Cotton
Batik on plain weave ground
40.3 x 40.3 in.; 102 x 102 cm
Source Unknown, 0000.2369

Sarong
Indonesia (Java)
19th–20th century
Cotton
Batik on plain weave ground
96 x 41.3 in.; 244 x 105 cm
Gift of Professor and Mrs. Roger Barber, 1990.15

CHINA

COSTUME

*Square Shawl for European Market with rows of large
red flowers on pink ground*
China
Qing dynasty, late 19th century
Silk
Double-face embroidery on pink ground
51.5 x 47 in.; 131 x 120 cm;
knotted fringe: 16 in.; 41 cm
Source Unknown, 0000.133

Woman's Padded Jacket with flowering plants
China
20th century
Silk
Blue-grey damask
32.5 x 58.5 in.; 83 x 158 cm
Source Unknown, 0000.1029

Long pao with gold patterning on orange-red ground
(Plate 36, p. 120)
China
Qing dynasty, 19th century
Silk and gold-wrapped thread
Brocade (supplementary weft on plain weave
ground)
54 x 85 in.; 137.2 x 216 cm
Source Unknown, 0000.1030
Literature: *Catalogue of the Oriental Collection*,
Helen Foresman, Spencer Museum of Art, 66–70

*Woman's Blue Silk Embroidered Jacket with bats and
peonies*
China
Qing dynasty, 19th century
Silk and gold-wrapped thread
Embroidery (satin, seed, and couching) on satin
ground
42.5 x 62 in.; 108 x 158 cm
Source Unknown, 0000.1031

Woman's Pleated Wedding Skirt (Plate 49, p. 145)
China
Qing dynasty, 19th century
Silk, gold-wrapped thread, and applied ribbons with
cotton waistband
Embroidery (satin, couching) on red damask
ground with appliqué on white satin border panels
L. 36.8 in.; 93.5 cm
The William Bridges Thayer Memorial,
0000.1032a,b (Thayer #2960)

Woman's Embroidered Vest with Rank Badges
(Plate 43, p. 135)
China
Qing dynasty, 19th century
Silk, gold- and silver-wrapped thread, and metal
bangles
Embroidery (satin, seed, couching, chain stitch) on
blue satin ground with applied knotted net, tassels,
and bangles
35.3 x 25 in.; 89.5 x 63.5 cm
The William Bridges Thayer Memorial, 0000.1033
(Thayer #2960)

Woman's Velvet Jacket (Plate 58, p. 163)
China
Qing dynasty, 19th century
Silk
Cut velvet on satin ground
36.8 x 71 in.; 93 x 180 cm
The William Bridges Thayer Memorial, 0000.1034
(Thayer #2947, 1150)

Man's Embroidered Long pao (Plate 37, p. 122)
China
Qing dynasty, 19th century
Silk and gold-wrapped thread
Embroidery (satin, seed, couching) on blue plain
weave ground
54 x 88 in.; 137 x 223.5 cm
Source Unknown, 0000.1035
Literature: *Catalogue of the Oriental Collection*,
66–70
Conserved in 1998 by Sharon Shore, Caring for
Textiles

Man's Kesi Long pao
China
Qing dynasty, 19th century
Silk, gold- and silver-wrapped threads, and *sumi* ink
Kesi with blue ground
L. 55 in.; 140 cm
The William Bridges Thayer Memorial, 0000.1039
(Thayer #2953)

*Woman's Rust-Colored Velvet Jacket with bats,
swastika, and auspicious characters*
China
Qing dynasty, 19th century
Silk
Cut velvet (garment was woven to shape)
33 x 70 in.; 84 x 178 cm
The William Bridges Thayer Memorial, 0000.1040

*Black Velvet Vest with three clusters of fruit and flowers
and wide border of auspicious symbols* (Plate 59, p. 164)
China
Qing dynasty, late 19th or early 20th century
Silk
Cut velvet (garment was woven to shape)
30 x 32 in.; 76 x 81 cm
Source Unknown, 0000.1042

Woman's Yellow Damask Jacket
China
Qing dynasty, 19th century
Silk
Appliqué and applied ribbons on damask ground
35.5 x 74.5 in.; 90 x 189 cm
The William Bridges Thayer Memorial, 0000.1043
(Thayer #2960)

Woman's Kesi Robe with butterflies on red ground
(Plate 56, p. 155)
China
Qing dynasty, 19th century
Silk and gold-wrapped thread
Kesi tapestry, embroidery (couching, seed), and
painting
57 x 55 in.; 145 x 139.7 cm
The William Bridges Thayer Memorial, 0000.1044
(Thayer #2956)
Label: "Importer R. Bensanoth, Chicago"

*Chao fu (Plate 35, p. 112)
China
Qing dynasty, 19th century
Silk, gold-wrapped thread, and peacock feathers
Embroidery (satin, seed, couching) on blue-black
plain weave ground
55 x 85.5 in.; 140 x 217 cm
Source Unknown, 0000.1045
Literature: *Handbook of the Collection, Helen
Foresman Spencer Museum of Art*, 152 (ill.); *Catalogue
of the Oriental Collection*, 67–70

*Woman's Pleated Wedding Skirt (Plate 50, p. 146)
China
Qing dynasty, 19th century
Silk, gold-wrapped thread, and applied ribbons with
cotton waistband
Embroidery (satin, couching) and appliqué on
orange-red damask ground
L. 37 in.; 94 cm
Source Unknown, 0000.1047

Woman's Blue Summer Pants
China
Qing dynasty, 19th century
Silk, gold-wrapped thread, and applied ribbons with
cotton waistband
Embroidery (satin, couching) on ground of pat-
terned twill on plain weave, with horizontal gauze
weave every sixth row
38 x 47.5 in.; 96.5 x 121 cm
The William Bridges Thayer Memorial, 0000.1048
(Thayer #2960)

Woman's Pale Blue Summer Pants with black
appliqué
China
Late Qing dynasty, 19th–early 20th century
Silk with cotton waistband
Looped braids and black satin ribbon appliqued
on blue damask ground with gauze every eighth
weft row
38.5 x 27 in.; 98 x 68.5 cm
Source Unknown, 0000.1049

*Woman's Pleated Skirt (Plate 51, p. 148)
China
Qing dynasty, 19th century
Silk and applied ribbons with cotton waistband
Embroidery (satin, seed) on yellow damask ground
L. 40 in.; 101 cm
The William Bridges Thayer Memorial, 0000.1050
(Thayer #29597)

Theatrical Robe
China
Qing dynasty, 19th century
Silk and silver-wrapped thread
Embroidery (satin, running, couching) on yellow
satin ground
L. 61.5 in.; 156 cm
The William Bridges Thayer Memorial, 0000.1123
(Thayer #2952)

Theatrical Collar
China
Qing dynasty, 19th or 20th century
Silk, gold-wrapped thread, metal, feathers, mirror
glass, and glass
Embroidery (couching, satin, satin with superim-
posed net structure) on pink satin ground with
knotted net fringe
38 x 24 in.; 96.5 x 61 cm
The William Bridges Thayer Memorial, 0000.1124

Long pao
China
Qing dynasty, 19th century
Silk with gold- and silver-wrapped thread
Embroidery (couching, seed, satin) and appliqué on
blue plain weave ground
57.5 x 54.5 in.; 146.5 x 138.5 cm
Source Unknown, 0000.1801

Child's Jacket
China
Qing dynasty, 19th century
Silk
Embroidery (satin, seed) and applied ribbon on yel-
low damask ground
L. 20.5 in.; 52 cm
The William Bridges Thayer Memorial, 0000.2417
(Thayer #2959)

*Egret Rank Badges (pair) (Plate 41, p. 170)
China
Qing dynasty, 19th century
Silk, ink, gold- and silver-wrapped thread
Kesi and painting on deep blue ground
11.8 x 11.5 in.; 30 x 29.3 cm
11.5 x 12 in.; 29.3 x 30.5 cm
The William Bridges Thayer Memorial, 1928.47
and 1928.48

*Woman's Brown Velvet Jacket with paired dragons in
roundels (Plate 60, p. 165)
China
Qing dynasty, 19th century
Silk
Cut velvet
30.5 x 57.5 in.; 77.5 x 146.5 cm
The William Bridges Thayer Memorial, 1928.55

Woman's Pleated Skirt
China
Qing dynasty, 19th century
Silk and gold-wrapped thread
Embroidery (satin, couching) on yellow ground
L. 29.5 in.; 75 cm
Source Unknown, 1941.31 and 1941.32a

*Daoist Priest's Robe (Jiangyi) (Plate 44, p. 137)
China
Qing dynasty, 18th or 19th century
Silk and gold-wrapped thread
Kesi with pale peach ground
55.5 x 67.8 in.; 141 x 172 cm
Gift of Mrs. Elizabeth Ellis, 1946.28
Literature: *Catalogue of the Oriental Collection*, 70

*Woman's Pleated Skirt (Plate 52, p. 149)
China
Qing dynasty, 19th century
Silk, gold-wrapped thread, sequins, and applied
ribbons
Embroidery (couching, satin) and gold patterning
on red damask ground
L. 38.8 in.; 98.5 cm
Gift of Mrs. Jacob Grant Strickler, 1946.31a,b

Mourner's Jacket and Hood
China
20th century
Bast fiber with woven cotton ties
Very loose plain weave (with "spin-ply joins")
Jacket: 33 x 36 in.; 84 x 91.5 cm
Hood: 27 x 15.5 in.; 68.5 x 39.5 cm
Gift of Mrs. R. Boese, 1950.40a,b

Wedding Skirt
China
Qing dynasty, 19th century
Silk, gold-wrapped thread, and brass bells
Embroidery (couching, satin, seed), applied rib-
bons, and knotted net on red satin ground
L. 38.3 in.; 99 cm; with fringe: 45 in.; 114 cm
Gift of Mrs. Evelyn S. Classen, 1951.3a

Dancer's Cloud Collar with layered, shaped, and
embroidered lappets of white, yellow, blue, and red
China
Qing dynasty, 19th or 20th century
Silk, gold-wrapped thread, and stone disks
Embroidery (satin, stem) on satin grounds with
braided and knotted hanging ornaments, tassels,
and applied ribbons
19.5 x 41 in.; 49.5 x 104 cm
ribbons extend 35.5 in.; 90.2 cm
Gift of Mrs. Evelyn S. Classen, 1951.3b

*Golden Pheasant Rank Badges (pair)
(Plate 42, p. 170)
China
Qing dynasty, late 19th century
Silk, gold- and silver-wrapped thread
Embroidery (satin, couching) on blue-black satin
ground
12.5 x 12.5 in.; 32 x 32 cm
Gift of the Cooper Union through Oberlin College,
1954.347

*Woman's Skirt Panels (pair) (Plate 53, p. 150–151)
China
Qing dynasty, 19th century
Silk, gold-wrapped thread, and ribbons
Embroidery (satin, couching, seed) on yellow satin
weave ground
waistbands are missing
30 x 44 in.; 76 x 112 cm
Gift of the Cooper Union through Oberlin College,
1954.350a,b

Woman's Blue Embroidered Coat with three large, casual roundels of red and pink flowering branches with smaller scattered flowers in pairs
China
20th century
Silk and gold-wrapped thread
Embroidery (satin, seed) on blue crepe ground
L. 39 in.; 99 cm
Gift of Mr. James Campbell, 1966.24

Woman's Pleated Skirt
China
Qing dynasty, 19th century
Silk, gold- and silver-wrapped thread
Embroidery (couching) with applied ribbons on red damask and patterned gauze ground
36 x 35.5 in.; 91.5 x 90.3 cm;
35.5 x 90.3 in.; 34.5 x 87.5 cm
Gift of Mr. James Campbell, 1966.27a,b

*Woman's Long pao (Plate 38, p. 124)
China
Qing dynasty, 19th century
Silk, gold- and silver-wrapped thread
Kesi tapestry with embroidery (couching, satin stitch) on red ground
57.3 x 87 in.; 145.5 x 221 cm
Gift of Mrs. Ethyl C. Wellman, Topeka, 1968.13
Literature: Catalogue of the Oriental Collection, 66–70

Woman's Vest with phoenix and dragons
China
Qing dynasty, late 19th or 20th century
Silk and gold-wrapped thread
Embroidery (couching, satin stitch) on blue-black twill ground with gold lattice border; some aniline dyes, including lavender
L. 32.3 in.; 82 cm
Gift of Lettie G. Archer, 1969.55.1

Woman's Long pao with phoenix and dragons in abbreviated cosmos
China
Qing dynasty, 19th century
Silk and gold-wrapped thread
Embroidery (satin, couching) on dark blue satin ground
L. 40.8 in.; 103.5 cm
Gift of Lettie G. Archer, 1969.55.2

*Woman's Pleated Skirt (Plate 54, p. 152)
China
Qing dynasty, early 20th century
Silk and gold-wrapped thread with cotton waistband
Embroidery (satin, couching) on purple twill ground with gold lattice borders
L. 37.8 in.; 96 cm
Gift of Lettie G. Archer, 1969.55.3
Probably either a theatrical skirt or a rental wedding skirt

*Woman's Embroidered Coat with peonies in large and small clusters and central floral roundel
(Plate 55, p. 154)
China
Qing dynasty, 19th century
Silk, gold-wrapped thread, and ribbons
Embroidery (satin, couching, seed, appliqué) shades of blue on red satin ground with embroidered black satin borders
45.5 x 48 in.; 115.8 x 122 cm
Gift of Dr. and Mrs. Alfred E. Farah, 1978.19
Literature: The Register 5, no. 6: 79 (ill.)

*Woman's Cut Velvet Coat with all-over peonies, peaches, bats, and butterflies (Plate 61, p. 167)
China
Qing dynasty, 19th century
Silk, gold-wrapped thread, and applied ribbons
Cut velvet; copper-colored velvet patterning on blue satin ground with embroidered (satin, couching) satin borders and cuffs
47 x 55.5 in.; 119.5 x 141 cm
Gift of Dr. and Mrs. Robert P. Woods, 1982.121

*Woman's Bamboo-Patterned Robe (Plate 57, p. 157)
China
Quig dynasty, late 19th or early 20th century
Silk with gold-wrapped thread
Embroidery (couching) on blue satin ground with lavender borders and applied ribbons
51.8 x 54.5 in.; 131.5 x 139 cm
Gift of Dr. and Mrs. Robert P. Woods, 1982.122

*Child's Long pao (Plate 39, p. 127)
China
Qing dynasty, late 18th–early 19th century
Silk, gold- and silver-wrapped thread
Kesi, embroidery (couching), and painting on blue ground
36 x 47 in.; 91.5 x 120 cm
Given in Memory of James H. Walker, Jr. by his Family, 1993.351

*Phoenix Rank Badge (Plate 40, p. 129)
China
Ming dynasty, late 15th–early 16th century
Silk and gold-wrapped thread
Kesi
13.3 x 14.5 in.; 33.5 x 37 cm
Museum Purchase: R. Charles and Mary Margaret Clevenger Fund, 1999.199

Woman's Embroidered Robe with dragons and cranes in abbreviated cosmos
China
Qing dynasty, 19th century
Silk and gold-wrapped thread
Embroidery (satin, couching, seed) on red satin ground
42 x 68.5 in.; 107 x 174 cm
Gift of Mrs. James H. Walker, 2001.201

Woman's Embroidered Shoes (pair)
China
ca. 1916
Silk, cotton, paper, commercial trim, and unknown fabric-covered hard material for sole and heel
Embroidery (satin) on red damask; fabric and inner core are held together with quilting stitches
3.3 x 1.3 x 2.5 in.; 8.5 x 3.5 x 6 cm
Gift of Mr. Floyd C. Williams in memory of his wife Violet, 2001.203

ACCESSORIES

Long Embroidered Pocket with geometric designs in grid on one side and flowers on the other, interrupted by horizontal embroidered bands of dense blue and white flowers
China
Late Qing dynasty, 19th–early 20th century
Silk
Embroidery (counted satin stitch, satin) with applied ribbon on concealed ground
18.8 x 5.8 in.; 48 x 15 cm
Source Unknown, 0000.1070

Summer Hat (yellow circular hat with red cords radiating from central metal knob)
China
Late Qing dynasty, 19th–early 20th century
Wool, cotton, and metal knobs
Loosely woven twill with twisted cord fringe, ribbon, and two metal balls
Diam. 11.3 in.; 28.5 cm
Gift of Mrs. R. Boese, 0000.1175

Embroidered Fan Case with gold and blue scrolling vines
China
Late Qing dynasty, 19th–early 20th century
Silk, gold-wrapped thread, and glass beads
Embroidery (couching) with applied glass beads and plaited strap on off-white satin ground
18.3 x 2.5 in.; 46.5 x 6.5 cm
Source Unknown, 0000.1189

Detached Pocket with Tassels and design of butterflies and grasses
China
Late Qing dynasty, 19th–early 20th century
Silk
Embroidery (satin, seed) with ornamental knots, applied ribbon, braids, and tassels on white satin ground
17.5 x 3.3 in.; 44.5 x 8.5 cm
Source Unknown, 0000.1192

Manchu Woman's Hat
China
Late Qing dynasty, 19th–early 20th century
Silk, cotton, and metal
Folded and shaped blue-black satin with red cord wrapping above metal base, and ornamental openwork gold-colored bar at top
9 x 17.5 x 3.3 in.; 23 x 44.5 x 8.5 cm
Source Unknown, 0000.1193

Round Collar (black satin with central ribbon depicting row of red-crested cranes, with seven pendent lobes with flowers on red satin ground edged with black)
China
Late Qing dynasty, 19th–early 20th century
Silk and gold-wrapped thread
Embroidery (counted satin stitch, couching) with applied ribbon and cording on satin ground
12.5 x 12.8 in.; 32 x 32.5 cm
The William Bridges Thayer Memorial, 0000.1196

Tie or Pendent Ornament, widening double-sided length of blue-black silk with scrap of white silk at pointed end, embroidered with bird and partial roundel
China
Late Qing dynasty, 19th–early 20th century
Silk with gold-wrapped thread
Embroidery (satin, couching) on black satin ground
14 x 1.5 in.; 36 x 4 cm
Source Unknown, 0000.1197

Collar (?) with beaded floral design, possibly for European market
China
Late Qing dynasty, 19th–early 20th century
Silk, glass beads, and metal
Embroidery (beading) on pink satin ground surrounded by black satin with metal crab-shaped clasps and chain
20.8 x 3.5 in.; 53 x 9 cm
The William Bridges Thayer Memorial, 0000.1198

Juyi-Shaped Ornament with attached pompoms and butterfly
China
Late Qing dynasty, 19th–early 20th century
Silk, gold-wrapped thread, wire, and paper
Embroidery (couching, satin) with applied cord, pompoms, leaves, and butterfly on satin ground; butterfly is layered paper covered with fabric and gold leaf; pompoms appear as fruit on attached embroidered leaves on red damask ground
21 x 4.5 in.; 53.5 x 11.5 cm
Source Unknown, 0000.1199

Gourd-Shaped Leather Pouch with green braided drawstring
China
Late Qing dynasty, 19th–early 20th century
Leather, metal clasp, gold-wrapped thread, and cotton cord
Braiding and stitching on brown/black leather
6.3 x 4.3 in.; 16 x 11 cm;
w. of extended drawstrings: 12.5 in.; 32 cm
Gift of Mrs. R. Boese, 1950.27

Money Belt with endless knot and other geometric patterns
China
20th century
Cotton
Embroidery (stem, running needle-woven cord stitch, machine stitching) with braided loops on lavender plain weave ground with braided cord loops
11 x 4.8 in.; 28 x 12.5 cm; l. with cloth ties: 37.5 in.; 95.5 cm
Gift of Mrs. R. Boese, 1950.54

Black Velvet Hat with braided purple trim and central knob with pendent tassels
China
20th century
Silk
Applied cording, tassels, fringe, netting, and satin-covered balls on black velvet ground
6.5 x 16.5 in.; 8.8 x 22.5 cm, excluding pendent tassels
Gift of Dr. and Mrs. Robert P. Woods, 1982.123

FLAT EMBROIDERED

Cushion Cover
China
Qing dynasty, 19th century
Silk
Embroidery (counted thread) on concealed ground
26.5 x 26.5 in.; 67.5 x 67.5 cm
Source Unknown, 0000.1024

Embroidered Bed Cover with flowers and grasses
China
Late 19th or 20th century
Silk and gold-wrapped thread
Embroidery (satin, couching, appliqué) and applied ribbon on yellow damask ground
66 x 58.5 in.; 168 x 148.8 cm
Source Unknown, 0000.1051

Embroidered Panel (Household Furnishing) with peonies and auspicious symbols
China
Qing dynasty, 19th century
Silk and gold-wrapped thread
Embroidery (satin, seed, running, couching) and applied ribbon on yellow damask ground framed in embroidered black silk
18.5 x 10.5 in.; 46 x 26.8 cm
Source Unknown, 0000.1052

Embroidered Panel with narrative scene of boy on qilin
China
Qing dynasty, late 19th or early 20th century
Silk and gold-wrapped thread
Embroidery (satin, seed, chain, couching) and applied ribbon on blue satin ground
30.5 x 18.8 in.; 77 x 47.5 cm
The William Bridges Thayer Memorial, 0000.1053

Embroidered Panel with roundels of blue peonies on salmon ground
China
Qing dynasty, 19th or early 20th century
Silk
Embroidery (satin) on salmon damask with checkered end borders
36 x 15 in.; 91.5 x 38 cm
Source Unknown, 0000.1054

Embroidered Panel with roundels of red peonies on blue ground
China
Qing dynasty, 19th or early 20th century
Silk
Embroidery (satin) on blue damask with checkered end borders
34.5 x 13.5 in.; 88 x 34.5 cm
Source Unknown, 0000.1056

Embroidered Panel with roundels of red peonies and butterflies on yellow ground
China
Qing dynasty, 19th or early 20th century
Silk
Embroidery (satin) on yellow damask with checkered end borders
33 x 11 in.; 84 x 28.5 cm
Source Unknown, 0000.1057

Embroidered Panel with roundels of blue peonies on salmon ground
China
Qing dynasty, 19th or early 20th century
Silk
Embroidery (satin) on salmon damask with checkered end borders
36 x 14.5 in.; 91.5 x 37 cm
Source Unknown, 0000.1058

Embroidered Panel with roundels of red peonies, polychrome flowers, and butterflies on green ground
China
Qing dynasty, 19th or early 20th century
Silk
Embroidery (satin) on green damask with checkered end borders
33 x 13.5 in.; 85 x 34.5 cm
Source Unknown, 0000.1059

Embroidered Medallion with peonies and butterflies
China
Qing dynasty, 19th or early 20th century
Silk
Embroidery (satin) on black satin ground
Diam. 11 in.; 28 cm
Source Unknown, 0000.1060

Embroidered Medallion with deer, cranes, bats, flowers, and landscape elements
China
Qing dynasty, 19th or early 20th century
Silk
Embroidery (satin) on black satin ground
Diam. 11 in.; 28 cm
Source Unknown, 0000.1061

Paper Medallion with applied embroidered motifs of human figure with flora and fauna
China
Qing dynasty, 19th or early 20th century
Paper and silk
Silk embroidery (satin, couching) on satin; cut-out embroidered motifs are glued to a paper roundel
Diam. 7.3 in.; 18.5 cm
Source Unknown, 0000.1062

Unidentified (pair of costume appurtenances?)
China
Qing dynasty, 19th or early 20th century
Silk, gold-wrapped thread, and applied ribbons with narrow cotton band extending past edges of fabric at one end
Embroidery (seed, couching) on off-white damask ground
L. 31 in.; 79 cm; w. 27.5 in.; 70 cm (wide end), 5 in.; 13 cm (narrow end)
The William Bridges Thayer Memorial, 0000.1063 and 0000.1064

Embedded Medallion with flora and fauna
China
Qing dynasty, 19th or early 20th century
Silk
Embroidery (satin) on blue-black satin ground
Diam. 11 in.; 28 cm
Source Unknown, 0000.1065

Embroidered Panel with phoenixes and peonies
China
Qing dynasty, 19th or early 20th century
Silk
Embroidery (satin) and applied ribbon on
red/orange satin ground
27.3 x 23 in.; 69.3 x 58.5 cm
The William Bridges Thayer Memorial, 0000.1066

Embroidered Borders (pair) with flowers and butterflies
China
Qing dynasty, 19th or early 20th century
Silk and gold-wrapped thread
Embroidery (satin, couching) on blue satin ground;
each border is embroidered on a wider length of
blue satin, probably designed to be cut from the
fabric before use
41.5 x 13.5 in.; 106 x 34.5 cm (two panels stitched
together)
Source Unknown, 0000.1067

Embroidered Borders for a formal garment with gold-
on-black fret pattern
China
Qing dynasty, 19th century
Silk and gold-wrapped thread
Embroidery (couching) on satin weave ground
28 x 5.3 in.; 71.3 x 13.5 cm
28 x 4.8 in.; 71.3 x 12 cm
21 x 7.8 in.; 53.5 x 19.8 cm
Source Unknown, 0000.1071–1073 (see also
1954.351)

*Embroidered Sleeve Borders with peacocks and flower-
ing trees (pair) (Plate 46, p. 143 left)
China
Qing dynasty, 19th century
Silk
Embroidery (satin) on yellow satin ground
39.5 x 3.3 in.; 100.5 x 8.3 cm (each)
Source Unknown, 0000.1074 and 0000.1088

Embroidered Sleeve Borders with butterflies and
flowering branches (pair) (Plate 48, p. 143 center)
China
Qing dynasty, late 19th or early 20th century
Silk and gold-wrapped thread
Embroidery (satin, couching) on salmon satin
ground
35 x 4.3 in.; 89 x 11 cm (each)
Source Unknown, 0000.1075 and 0000.1076

*Embroidered Borders (pair) (Plate 48, p. 143 right)
China
Qing dynasty, late 19th century
Silk
Embroidery (satin) on off-white damask ground
43 x 3.5 in.; 110 x 9 cm
Source Unknown, 0000.1077 and 0000.1080

*Embroidered Sleeve Borders with peonies and butter-
flies (pair) (Plate 47, p. 143 center)
China
Qing dynasty, 19th century
Silk
Embroidery (satin) on off-white patterned ground
(supplementary weft floats on plain weave ground)
38 x 3.5 in.; 96.5 x 9 cm
Source Unknown, 0000.1078 and 0000.1081

Embroidered Sleeve Borders with peacocks, birds,
flowers, and landscape elements (pair)
China
Qing dynasty, 19th century
Silk
Embroidery (satin) on light yellow satin ground
35 x 2.8 in.; 89 x 70 cm (each)
Source Unknown, 0000.1079 and 0000.1084

Embroidered Sleeve Borders with boy on qilin in land-
scape setting (pair)
China
Qing dynasty, 19th century
Silk and gold-wrapped thread
Embroidery (satin, couching) on off-white satin
ground
29 x 3.5 in.; 73.5 x 9 cm (each)
The William Bridges Thayer Memorial, 0000.1082
and 0000.1083

Embroidered Sleeve Borders with cranes, trees, and
flowers (pair)
China
Qing dynasty, 19th century
Silk
Embroidery (satin) on off-white satin ground with
damask at unembroidered ends
34 x 3.5 in.; 86.3 x 9 cm (each)
Source Unknown, 0000.1085 and 0000.1090

Embroidered Sleeve Borders with figures in landscape
(pair)
China
20th century
Silk
Embroidery (satin) on grey damask ground (with
white wefts and blue warps; weft floats appear
white against a grey ground)
26 x 4 in.; 66 x 10 cm (each)
Source Unknown, 0000.1086 and 0000.1087

Embroidered Sleeve Border with peonies and bats
China
Qing dynasty, 19th century
Silk and gold-wrapped thread
Embroidery (seed with a little couching) on salmon
satin ground
36 x 3.5 in.; 91.5 x 9 cm (width of each to folded edge)
Source Unknown, 0000.1089

Embroidered Panel with roundel of cranes in landscape
China
Qing dynasty, 19th century
Silk
Embroidery (satin) on two salmon-colored satin
panels sewn together
31 x 33 in.; 79 x 84 cm
Source Unknown, 0000.1092

Pair of Embroidered Hangings depicting Eight Daoist
Immortals
China
Qing dynasty, 19th century
Silk and gold-wrapped thread
Embroidery (satin, couching) on brown velvet
ground
42 x 6.8 in.; 107 x 17.5 cm (each)
Source Unknown, 0000.1120 and 0000.1121

Narrative Embroidered Panel (central panel depicting
women in a garden flanked by two text panels, with
two outside panels depicting peacocks in a garden
setting)
China
Qing dynasty, 19th century
Silk, gold-wrapped thread, cotton lining, and cotton
top band
Embroidery (satin, couching) and applied ribbon on
off-white satin ground
77.5 x 19 in.; 196 x 48.5 cm
Source Unknown, 0000.2198

Shaped Tab Ornament with boy on dragon,
attendants, floral and geometric motifs
China
Qing dynasty, 19th century
Silk and gold-wrapped thread
Embroidery (counted satin stitch, couching) with
applied braid, knotted netting, and tassels on
concealed ground
15.5 x 9 in.; 39.5 x 23 cm
Source Unknown, 0000.2319

Embroidered Sleeve Borders with dragons, bats, and
flowers (pair)
China
Late Qing dynasty, 19th–early 20th century
Silk and gold-wrapped thread
Embroidery (satin, seed, couching) on grey-green
damask
35.5 x 3.5 in.; 90.2 x 9 cm (each)
Gift of Mrs. Bryant, 0000.2321a,b

Embroidered Hanging (lower panel with standing male
figure with male and female attendants; upper panel
with large flowers and birds)
China
Late Qing dynasty, 19th–early 20th century
Silk, cotton, gold-wrapped thread, paint, hair, and
beads
Embroidery (satin, seed, couching), padding, and
piecing set into black satin ground
39.5 x 39.3 in.; 100.5 x 100 cm
The William Bridges Thayer Memorial, 0000.2324
(Thayer tag)

Embroidered Panel with three canopies
China
Late Qing dynasty, 19th–early 20th century
Silk and gold-wrapped thread with cotton band
at top
Embroidery (satin and couching) on black satin
ground
13 x 44 in.; 33.3 x 111.8 cm
The William Bridges Thayer Memorial, 0000.2326
(Thayer tag)

Embroidered Panel with woman and child on qilin *with attendants traveling through landscape*
China
Late Qing dynasty, 19th–early 20th century
Silk and metal disks with cotton band at top
Embroidery (satin, stem) with appliqué and applied ribbon, braid, knotted netting, fringe, and tassels on salmon satin ground
85 x 29 in.; 216 x 73 cm
The William Bridges Thayer Memorial, 1928.859

Embroidered Panel with phoenix, peonies, and butterflies in landscape setting
China
Late Qing dynasty, 19th–early 20th century
Silk
Embroidery (satin) and applied ribbon on orange/red satin ground with black border
36 x 25.5 in.; 91.5 x 65 cm
The William Bridges Thayer Memorial, 1928.862

Embroidered Hanging with elephant with smoking cauldron
China
20th century
Silk and gold-wrapped thread
Embroidery (satin, couching) on red satin weave ground
60.8 x 21.5 in.; 104.5 x 55 cm
Gift of the Cooper Union through Oberlin College, 1954.344

Embroidered Panel with large frontal dragon
China
Late Qing dynasty, 19th–early 20th century
Silk and gold-wrapped thread
Embroidery (satin, couching) and applied ribbon border on orange/red satin ground
25 x 21 in.; 63.5 x 53.5 cm
Gift of the Cooper Union through Oberlin College, 1954.345

Cushion Cover with Daoist symbols
China
Late Qing dynasty, 19th–early 20th century
Silk and gold-wrapped thread
Embroidery (satin, couching) on brown damask ground
26 x 26 in.; 66 x 66 cm
Gift of the Cooper Union through Oberlin College, 1954.346

Embroidered Fragment with flowers and butterflies
China
Qing dynasty, 19th century
Silk and gold-wrapped thread
Embroidery (satin, seed, couching) on (recycled?) salmon damask
14 x 10 in.; 35.5 x 25.5 cm
Gift of the Cooper Union through Oberlin College, 1954.349

Embroidered Borders for a formal garment with gold-on-black fret pattern (Plate 45, p. 141)
China
Qing dynasty, 19th century
Silk and gold-wrapped thread
Embroidery (couching) on satin ground
105 x 31 in.; 267.8 x 78.8 cm (backing cloth); 5.5 in.; 14 cm (approx. width of panels, varied lengths)
Gift of the Cooper Union through Oberlin College, 1954.351 (see also 0000.1071–1073)

Embroidered Hanging depicting boy with flute on dragon and girl on phoenix in clouds, and landscape flanked by large flower vase; border with musicians and dancers in garden setting
China
Qing dynasty, 19th century
Silk and gold-wrapped thread
Embroidery (satin, couching, seed) with applied ribbon on red/orange satin ground
81 x 20.5 in.; 129.5 x 52 cm
Gift of Swannie Smith Zink, 1962.19

Embroidered Panel with rank bird, auspicious symbols, and abbreviated landscape
China
Late Qing dynasty, 19th–early 20th century
Silk and gold-wrapped thread
Embroidery (satin, couching, seed) on blue-black satin ground
58.8 x 30.3 in.; 150 x 77 cm
Gift of Dr. and Mrs. Justin L. Mooney, 1965.12

Embroidered Panel made from long pao *segments with dragons in abbreviated cosmos*
China
Late Qing dynasty, 19th–early 20th century
Silk and gold-wrapped thread
Embroidery (satin, couching) on red plain weave ground
55.5 x 35 in.; 141 x 89 cm
Gift of Dr. and Mrs. Justin L. Mooney, 1965.13

Embroidered Panel with peonies and bats (sleeve border reconstructed as Household Furnishing)
China
Qing dynasty, 19th century
Silk with cotton backing
Embroidery (satin) on off-white satin ground with wide green satin border edged with white satin
34.5 x 6 in.; 87.6 x 15.2 cm
Gift of Rose K. Auerbach, 1967.40

Embroidered Panel with fish and flowering branches
China
20th century
Silk and gold-wrapped thread
Embroidery (satin, couching) on cream satin ground with embroidered black border
25.5 x 12.5 in.; 65 x 32 cm
Gift of Rose K. Auerbach, 1967.43

Embroidered Sleeve Border with peony in central urn surrounded by flowers
China
Qing dynasty, 19th century
Silk and gold-wrapped thread
Embroidery (seed, couching) on blue crepe ground with damask patterning
24.3 x 3.5 in.; 62 x 9 cm (to folded edges)
Gift of Rose K. Auerbach, 1967.45

Embroidered Medallions (pair) with peacock pairs and peonies
China
Qing dynasty, 19th century
Paper, silk, gold-wrapped thread, and peacock feathers
Embroidery (seed, couching) on paper
a: Diam. 9.5 in.; 24 cm
b: Diam. 9.3 in.; 23.5 cm
Given in Memory of James H. Walker, Jr. by his Family, 1993.359a,b

FLAT WOVEN

Woven Hanging with four dragons in a row with abbreviated cosmos
China
Qing dynasty, 19th or early 20th century
Silk and gold-wrapped thread
Supplementary weft on very loose satin ground with applied ribbons and borders
33.5 x 68.3 in.; 85 x 173 cm
The William Bridges Thayer Memorial, 0000.1069 (Marshall Field tag)

Woven Panel with standing man and his attendant in a scholar's study
China
Qing dynasty, 19th or early 20th century
Silk, gold-wrapped thread, and ink or dye
Kesi with painted details and thin satin edging
41.5 x 17.3 in.; 106 x 44 cm
Source Unknown, 0000.1093

Woven Panel with two scenes from a story (?)
China
Qing dynasty, 19th century
Silk, gold-wrapped thread, and ink
Kesi with painted details
42 x 11 in.; 106.8 x 28 cm
Source Unknown, 0000.1094

Woven Panel with rows of dragon medallions framed in textile borders
China
Qing dynasty, 19th century
Silk and gold-wrapped thread
Supplementary weft on satin ground
34.8 x 88.5 in.; 22 x 56 cm
Source Unknown, 0000.1095

Woven Panel with all-over ivory flowers and clouds on ivory ground
China
Qing dynasty, 19th century
Silk
Damask
39.5 x 100.5 in.; 13.5 x 34.3 cm
Source Unknown, 0000.1096

Four Woven Panels (each with three interior panels)
depicting a total of twelve lohan
China
Qing dynasty, 19th century
Silk, ink, and pigments
Kesi
35 x 9.3 in.; 89 x 23.5 cm
Source Unknown, 0000.1097–1099 and
0000.1118

Woven Panel with opera scene
China
Qing dynasty, 19th century
Silk, cotton, gold-wrapped thread, glass beads,
human hair, and ink
Kesi with painted details
67 x 112.5 in.; 170 x 286 cm
The William Bridges Thayer Memorial, 0000.1112

Woven Panel with two large peonies
China
Qing dynasty, 19th century
Silk, gold- and silver-wrapped thread
Supplementary weft on satin ground
40 x 14.5 in.; 102 x 37 cm
Source Unknown, 0000.1113

Woven Panel with scene of traveling scholar meeting
boy with buffalo in landscape
China
Late 19th or 20th century
Silk, gold- and silver-wrapped thread
Supplementary weft on satin weave ground
20.5 x 20 in.; 52.8 x 50.8 cm
Source Unknown, 0000.1116

Gauze Band with flying birds in gold leaf
China
Qing dynasty, 19th century
Silk
Patterned gauze with applied gold leaf
166 x 3.5 in.; 421.8 x 9 cm
Source Unknown, 0000.1117

Woven Panel with butterflies and flowers on fretwork
China
Qing dynasty, 19th century
Silk
Cut velvet
13 x 39.5 in.; 33.3 x 100 cm
Source Unknown, 0000.1119

Woven Panel (Chairback?) with four crane medallions
in floral border
China
Qing dynasty, 19th century
Silk
Compound weave with velvet ground
61.3 x 19.3 in.; 155.5 x 49 cm
Source Unknown, 0000.1122

Panel with scrollwork enclosing flowers
China
Qing dynasty, 19th century
Silk
Velvet (cut and uncut pile) on twill ground
55 x 18.5 in.; 140.5 x 47 cm
Source Unknown, 0000.2194

Hanging with twelve pointed tabs suspended from black
velvet panel and layered in three vertical rows with
floral motifs
China
Qing dynasty, 19th century
Cotton
Printing on velvet ground
48.5 x 14.8 in.; 123.5 x 37.5 cm
Source Unknown, 0000.2199

Textile Fragment with design of all-over flowers, bats,
and butterflies
China
Qing dynasty, 19th or early 20th century
Silk and gold-wrapped thread
Compound weave
21 x 28.3 in.; 53.5 x 72.8 cm
The William Bridges Thayer Memorial, 1928.863

Panel (from a long pao?) with dragons in abbreviated
cosmos
China
Qing dynasty, 19th or early 20th century
Silk, metal-wrapped thread, and pigment
Kesi with painted details
46.3 x 25.3 in.; 117.5 x 64 cm
Gift of Dr. and Mrs. Justin L. Mooney, 1965.14

Brocade Panel with all-over design of flowers, bats, and
butterflies
China
Qing dynasty, 19th or early 20th century
Silk
Brocade
26.8 x 8.3 in.; 68 x 21 cm
Gift of Rose K. Auerbach, 1967.41

Woven Panels (pair), each with two mounted warriors
at a gallop with raised weapons in abstracted mountain
landscape
China
Qing dynasty, 19th or early 20th century
Silk, gold-wrapped thread, and pigment
Kesi with painted details
13.3 x 8.8 in.; 34.5 x 22.5 cm (each)
Gift of Rose K. Auerbach, 1967.46a,b

Brocade Panel with two rows of auspicious symbols and
ribbon border
China
Qing dynasty, late 19th century
Silk and gold-wrapped thread
Brocade
25 x 8.3 in.; 63.5 x 21 cm
Gift of Rose K. Auerbach, 1967.48

Woven Panel (Chairback?) with dragons in
abbreviated cosmos
China
Qing dynasty, 19th or early 20th century
Silk, gold-wrapped thread, and ink
Kesi with painted details
55.5 x 16.8 in.; 141 x 42.5 cm
Gift of Rose K. Auerbach, 1967.50

Pieced Hanging ending in three pendent tabs with
pointed ends and designs of dragons, landscape
elements, and auspicious symbols
China
Qing dynasty, 19th or early 20th century
Silk and gold-wrapped thread
Compound weave
64.5 x 9 in.; 111.5 x 23 cm
Gift of Rose K. Auerbach, 1967.51

Woven Chairbacks (pair) with quadrants featuring a
dragon medallion, a peony medallion, unpatterned blue
ground, and three shishi (lion-dogs) in landscape
China
Qing dynasty, 18th or early 19th century
Silk and gold-wrapped thread
Kesi
36.5 x 19.3 in.; 92.8 x 49.5 cm
Given in Memory of James H. Walker, Jr. by his
Family, 1993.330a,b

PRINTING/DYEING

Flag
China
20th century
Silk and pigment
Screen printed
36.3 x 24 in.; 92 x 61 cm
Source Unknown, 0000.2318

ARMOR

Military Officer's Armor with ground of block-like
interlocking gold "γ" shapes on blue ground with metal
studs
China
Late Qing dynasty, 19th–early 20th century
Silk, gold-wrapped thread, metal, paper, bast fiber,
and felt
Embroidery (couching, stuffing, wrapping,
padding, satin) on double-weave ground (gold-
wrapped thread and blue silk on thinner brown
silk warp) with applied ribbons, cords, and velvet
borders
See individual entries below for dimensions of each
piece
Source Unknown, 0000.2330a–h and 0000.1161,
0000.1177, 0000.1178, 0000.2323

Armor (Loin Panel with lion-dog head at top and
bottom and central shou [longevity] character)
China
Late Qing dynasty, 19th–early 20th century
Silk, gold-wrapped thread, and metal
Embroidery (couching, stuffing, wrapping,
padding, satin) on double-weave ground with blue
silk lining and paper inner lining
26 x 9 in.; 66.3 x 23 cm
Source Unknown, 0000.1161

Armor (Case or Pouch with spoked medallion)
China
Late Qing dynasty, 19th–early 20th century
Silk, gold-wrapped thread, leather, and metal
Embroidery (couching, stuffing, wrapping, padding, satin) on double-weave ground with leather trim and metal fittings
10.5 x 9.5 x 3 in.; 27 x 24.3 x 7.8 cm
Source Unknown, 0000.1177

Armor (Strap)
China
Late Qing dynasty, 19th–early 20th century
Silk, cast metal attachments, and unidentified core filler
Paired warp twining or plaiting
61 x 1.5 in; 155 x 4 cm
Source Unknown, 0000.1178

Armor (Legging with leather and metal central spoked medallion)
China
Late Qing dynasty, 19th–early 20th century
Silk, gold-wrapped thread, leather, and metal with paper inner lining
Applied leather, cord, metal ornaments, "jewels," and metal fittings on double-weave ground
22 x 12 in.; 56 x 30.5 cm
Source Unknown, 0000.2323

Armor (Jacket with central medallion of paired dragons and waves)
China
Late Qing dynasty, 19th–early 20th century
Silk, gold-wrapped thread, and metal studs with paper inner lining
Embroidery (satin, couching) with applied studs, cords, ribbon, and black velvet edging on double-weave ground
30.5 x 79 in.; 77.5 x 101 cm
Source Unknown, 0000.2330a

Armor (Leg Coverings; skirt-like pair of leg coverings with common waistband and central embroidered medallion of frontal dragon with flaming pearl on each)
China
Qing dynasty, 19th or early 20th century
Silk, gold-wrapped thread, and metal with cotton waistband and paper lining
Embroidery (couching, satin) with applied ribbon, cords, and black velvet edging on double-weave ground
40 x 51 in.; 101.5 x 129.5 cm
Source Unknown, 0000.2330b

Armor (Epaulets with central embroidered dragon and pearl roundel on each)
China
Qing dynasty, 19th or early 20th century
Silk, gold-wrapped thread, metal plates and studs
Embroidery (couching, satin) with applied metal studs and black velvet edging on double-weave ground
15.3 x 18 in.; 38.8 x 46 cm
Source Unknown, 0000.2330c,d

Armor (Chest Medallion)
China
Qing dynasty, 19th or early 20th century
Gold and silver-colored metals with dragon pattern surrounding central "jewel"; paper and felt lining
Diam. 5.8 in.; 14.5 cm
Source Unknown, 0000.2330e,f

Armor (Patch worn attached to front center of jacket with loops and toggles)
China
Qing dynasty, 19th or early 20th century
Silk, gold-wrapped thread, and metal studs
Applied studs, ribbon, and velvet edging on double-weave ground
6.3 x 7.5 in.; 16 x 19 cm
Source Unknown, 0000.2330g

Armor (Underarm Protector)
China
Late Qing dynasty, 19th–early 20th century
Silk, gold-wrapped thread, and metal studs
Applied studs, ribbon, and velvet edging on double-weave ground
10 x 11.5 in.; 25.5 x 29.5 cm
Source Unknown, 0000.2330h

THREE DIMENSIONAL FIGURES

Daoist Immortal Lu Dongbin
China
Qing dynasty, 19th century
Silk, cotton, paper, pigment, and gold foil
Various construction techniques; fabric is damask with painted details
17.5 x 8 in.; 44.5 x 20.5 cm
The William Bridges Thayer Memorial, 0000.1146

Daoist Immortal Cao Guojiu
China
Qing dynasty, 19th century
Silk, cotton, paper, pigment, and gold foil
Various construction techniques; fabric is damask with painted details
18.5 x 9 in.; 46 x 23 cm
The William Bridges Thayer Memorial, 0000.1147

Daoist Immortal Zhong Liquan
China
Qing dynasty, 19th century
Silk, wire, gold-wrapped thread, paper, pigment, and gold foil
Various construction techniques; fabric is satin with painted details
17 x 8 in.; 43.3 x 20.5 cm
The William Bridges Thayer Memorial, 0000.1148

Daoist Immortal Zhang Guolao
China
Qing dynasty, 19th century
Silk, wire, gold-wrapped thread, paper, pigment, and gold foil
Various construction techniques; fabric is damask with painted details
17 x 8.5 in.; 43.3 x 22.8 cm
The William Bridges Thayer Memorial, 0000.1149

Daoist Immortal Li Tieguai
China
Qing dynasty, 19th century
Silk, cotton, paper, pigment, and gold foil
Various construction techniques; fabric is damask with painted details
17 x 7 in.; 43.3 x 18 cm
The William Bridges Thayer Memorial, 0000.1150

Daoist Immortal Shou Lao
China
Qing dynasty, 19th century
Silk, cotton, paper, pigment, and gold foil
Various construction techniques; fabric is damask with painted details
17 x 11 in.; 43.3 x 28 cm
The William Bridges Thayer Memorial, 0000.1151

Daoist Immortal He Xiangu
China
Qing dynasty, 19th century
Silk, cotton, gold-wrapped thread, paper, pigment, and gold foil
Various construction techniques; fabric is damask with painted details
16.5 x 7 in.; 42 x 17.8 cm
The William Bridges Thayer Memorial, 0000.1152

Daoist Immortal Han Xiangzi
China
Qing dynasty, 19th century
Silk, cotton, gold-wrapped thread, paper, and pigment
Various construction techniques; fabric is satin with painted details
16.5 x 6.5 in.; 42 x 16.3 cm
The William Bridges Thayer Memorial, 0000.1153

Panel with female figure
China
Qing dynasty, 19th century
Cotton, silk, pigment, and paper
Plain weave cotton panel with brocade and paper figures
13.8 x 8.8 in.; 35 x 22.3 cm
The William Bridges Thayer Memorial, 0000.1154

Panel with female figure
China
Qing dynasty, 19th century
Cotton, silk, pigment, and paper
Plain weave cotton panel with brocade and paper figures
13.8 x 8.8 in.; 35 x 22.3 cm
The William Bridges Thayer Memorial, 0000.1155

Panel with female figure
China
Qing dynasty, 19th century
Cotton, silk, pigment, and paper
Plain weave cotton panel with brocade and paper figures
13.8 x 8.8 in.; 35 x 22.3 cm
The William Bridges Thayer Memorial, 0000.1156

Panel with female figure
China
Qing dynasty, 19th century
Cotton, silk, pigment, and paper
Plain weave cotton panel with brocade and paper figures
13.8 x 8.8 in.; 35 x 22.3 cm
The William Bridges Thayer Memorial, 0000.1157

JAPAN

COSTUME (EXCLUDING WEDDING)

Kimono-Shaped Gown with fringed sash, design of flowering cherries at hem, sleeves, and left shoulder, and mon (crest) (for Western market?)
Japan
20th century
Silk
Embroidery (satin with plied threads) on black crepe ground with red lining
53 x 47.5 in.; 135 x 121 cm
Source Unknown, 0000.1126

Fringed Sash (for Kimono-Shaped Gown above) with design of flowering cherries at ends
Japan
20th century
Silk
Embroidery (satin with plied threads) on black crepe
101 x 6 in.; 257 x 15 cm;
with fringe: 110 x 6 in.; 280 x 15 cm
Source Unknown, 0000.1127

Kimono with small checkerboard design for man or elderly woman
Japan
20th century
Silk
Narrow white horizontal and vertical lines on deep indigo plain weave ground
54.5 x 51.5 in.; 138 x 131 cm
Source Unknown, 0000.1133

Man's Black Hanten (Jacket) with half-lining of grey horizontal stripes on burgundy ground
Japan
20th century
Silk
Crepe with black braided cord tie with tassels
45.5 x 51.5 in.; 116 x 130 cm
Source Unknown, 0000.1135

Man's Obi
Japan
20th century
Silk
Shibori tie-dye on black crepe; shape of resisted dots is unusual (oval with more white at one end than the other)
134 x 19.5 in.; 340 x 47.5 cm
Source Unknown, 0000.1137

Obi with phoenix and floral roundels and zigzag squares with inner geometric patterns
Japan
Mid-20th century
Silk, gold- and silver-wrapped thread
Jacquard with embroidery (eyes of phoenix)
158 x 12.8 in.; 402 x 32.5 cm
Gift of Mrs. Carly Eddy Hinrichsen, 1964.100

Woman's Underkimono with large patterns of asa no ha (hemp flower) on top and diagonal rows of red, green, and blue squares below
Japan
20th century (with recycled ground fabric)
Silk
Printing (probably screen printing) on recycled plain weave silk with vestiges of *honbitta* (all-over) tie-dye
58 x 48 in.; 148 x 122 cm; sleeve length: 28.5 in.; 73 cm
Gift of Mr. James Campbell, 1966.26

Noh Robe Fragments with brocaded autumn flowers on dangawari ground (Fig. 14, p. 199)
Japan
Edo period, 18th or early 19th century
Silk and gold-wrapped thread
Brocade (with polychrome long weft floats) on ground of gold patterned twill against *dangawari* ground (warp changes colors in vertical blocks)
Front panel and *eri* (collar band): 110 x 6.5 in.; 280 x 16.5 cm
Fragments: each approx. 14 x 16 in.; 35.5 x 40.5 cm
Given in Memory of James H. Walker, Jr. by his Family, 1993.349A–K

Noh Robe with crowded all-over patterns of large flowers (very fragile)
Japan
Edo period, 18th or 19th century
Silk and gold foil on paper
Brocade on satin ground
65 x 56.5 in.; 172.5 x 143.8 cm
Given in Memory of James H. Walker, Jr. by his Family, 1993.352

Woman's Outer Kimono with pine, bamboo, and cranes, and padded hem
Japan
20th century, ca. 1953
Silk, gold- and silver-wrapped thread
Embroidery (couching, satin) on blue satin ground
68 x 48.5 in.; 175.8 x 123 cm;
sleeves: 13 x 24.5 in.; 33 x 62.3 cm
Gift of Mrs. John Manwaring in memory of Mr. and Mrs. Russell Gordon Smith, 1995.38

COSTUME FROM TŌHOKU

Nizuri Vest (Plate 80, p. 245)
Japan (Tsuruoka district, Yamagata Prefecture)
Early 20th century
Cotton
Sashiko stitching on plain weave ground
22.5 x 12.5 in.; 57 x 31.8 cm
Museum Purchase: The Barbara Benton Wescoe Fund, 1993.8

Kogin Overgarment (Plate 81, p. 246)
Japan (Tsugaru peninsula, Aomori Prefecture)
Late 19th century
Asa (bast fiber) and cotton
Kogin (cotton counted thread embroidery) on plain weave *asa* ground
37 x 21 in.; 94 x 53.3 cm
Museum Purchase: The Barbara Benton Wescoe Fund, 1993.9

COSTUME FROM OKINAWA

*Bashō (Banana Fiber) Garment with cotton stripes in the warp in brown, light blue, natural white, and mūdei (two-color ply) on natural tan ground
(Plate 78, p. 238)*
Japan (Okinawa)
20th century, before 1945
Bashō (banana fiber) and cotton
Plain weave
42.5 x 22.5 in.; 106.3 x 56.3 cm
Museum Purchase: The Barbara Benton Wescoe Fund, 1993.14

Bingata Fragment with small polychrome floral motifs (Plate 79, p. 241)
Japan (Okinawa)
Second half of 19th century
Ramie, dyes, and pigments
Bingata dyeing (small stencils, paste resist, free-hand painting, immersion dyeing); light indigo plain weave ground
25.3 x 14 in.; 63 x 35 cm
Museum Purchase: The Barbara Benton Wescoe Fund, 1993.15

WEDDING TEXTILES

*Wedding Obi Panels with phoenixes and pine trees
(Plate 85, p. 254)*
Japan
Meiji period (1868–1912)
Silk and silver-wrapped thread
Jacquard
27.5 x 89.5 in.; 70 x 227.3 cm (each)
Source Unknown, 0000.1107 and 0000.1110

Woman's White Wedding Kimono
Japan
Mid-20th century
Silk with metallic thread in crests
Damask
72.5 x 49.5 in.; 184 x 126 cm; sleeve length: 37 in.; 94 cm
Gift of Mrs. David W. Isaac, 1990.26

Wedding Obi with autumn grasses on gold and silver ground (Plate 86, p. 255)
Japan
Mid-20th century
Silk with paper-backed gold and silver foil and silver-wrapped thread
Jacquard with row of simple gauze every .9 cm
162 x 12.5 in.; 412 x 32 cm
Gift of Mrs. David W. Isaac, 1990.27

Fukusa (Ceremonial Gift-Wrapping Cloth) with painted design of mushrooms in one corner
Japan
Meiji period, ca. 1900
Silk, ink, and pigments
Painting with plied green cord stitched 3.8 cm from edge of white plain weave ground; green corner tassels
27.3 x 26.5 in.; 69.3 x 67.5 cm
Given in Memory of James H. Walker, Jr. by his Family, 1993.346

*Fukusa *with gold and polychrome design of partially-opened boxes for* kai awase *(shell-matching game) with their thick, red, braided cords and tassels and scattered shells* (Plate 82, p. 249)
Japan
Edo period, late 18th or 19th century
Silk and gold-wrapped thread
Embroidery (couching, satin, stem) with applied red braided cords on dark blue satin with red crepe edge and lining
35.3 x 27.3 in.; 89.5 x 69.2 cm
Given in Memory of James H. Walker, Jr. by his Family, 1993.353

*Fukusa *with kai awase boxes and red cords (one box with pine design; one with flowering plum)*
(Plate 83, p. 250)
Japan
Edo period, late 18th or 19th century
Silk and gold-wrapped thread
Embroidery (couching, satin, stem) with applied red braided cords on dark blue satin with red crepe edge and lining, and one extant corner tassel (of four)
33.3 x 27.3 in.; 84.5 x 69.2 cm
Given in Memory of James H. Walker, Jr. by his Family, 1993.354

*Fukusa *with pair of gold and red lobsters*
(Plate 84, p. 251)
Japan
Edo period, late 18th or 19th century
Silk and gold-wrapped thread
Embroidery (couching, chain) on dark blue satin ground with red crepe edge and lining and four corner tassels
29 x 28 in.; 73.8 x 71.3 cm
Given in Memory of James H. Walker, Jr. by his Family, 1993.355

KATAZOME AND TSUTSUGAKI

Katazome *Fragment with ochre, blue, and white gourds, boxes, and seal script*
Japan
20th century
Cotton
Katazome *on brown plain weave ground
10.8 x 8 in.; 27.5 x 20 cm
Source Unknown, 0000.1128

Kimono Fragment with blossoms and pine branches
Japan
Late 19th–20th century
Silk
Stencil and paste-resist dyeing on crepe ground
10 x 10.3 in.; 25.5 x 26 cm
Source Unknown, 0000.1136

*Katazome Futonji *(Quilt Cover) Panel with design of chrysanthemums and *karakusa *scrolling vines*
(Plate 67, p. 216)
Japan
19th or 20th century
Cotton
Katazome *(stencil and paste-resist dyeing) on indigo plain weave ground
61 x 12.5 in.; 155 x 31.7 cm
Museum Purchase, 1992.82

*Katazome Futonji *Panel with design of carp, waves, and floating chrysanthemums* (Plate 68, p. 217)
Japan
19th or 20th century
Cotton warp, *asa *and cotton wefts
Katazome *on indigo weft-faced plain weave ground
56 x 12.5 in.; 142 x 31.4 cm
Museum Purchase, 1992.83

*Katazome Yukata *Panel with design of flowering gourds* (Plate 69, p. 219)
Japan
19th or 20th century
Cotton
Katazome *in imitation of *shibori *on indigo plain weave ground
27.5 x 12 in.; 69.9 x 30.8 cm
Museum Purchase, 1992.84

Tsutsugaki Futonji *Panel with pine, crane, tortoise, and floral medallions*
Japan
20th century
Handspun cotton
Tsutsugaki *(free-hand paste-resist dyeing and painting) on indigo plain weave ground
48 x 62.3 in.; 158.1 x 122 cm
Museum Purchase, 1992.85

*Woman's *Katazome Jacket with small, light blue, overall motifs of scattered leaves and diagonal lines, with light and dark brown striped, bast fiber lining*
(Plate 70, p. 221)
Japan
Late 19th or 20th century
Hemp, cotton, and tree-bast fiber
Katazome *on indigo plain weave ground
37 x 23 in.; 92.5 x 58 cm
Museum Purchase: The Barbara Benton Wescoe Fund, 1993.10

*Hekizan *(artist's dates unknown)* (Plate 71, p. 223)
Boy's Day Banner
Japan
Edo period, late 18th–19th century
Handspun cotton with dyes and pigments
Tsutsugaki *and painting on indigo plain weave ground
165 x 72 in.; 419.1 x 182 cm
Museum Purchase: The Barbara Benton Wescoe Fund, 1993.12

*Yogi *(Padded Kimono-Shaped Bedcovering) with phoenix, paulownia, and bamboo* (Plate 72, p. 226)
Japan (western region)
Late 19th–early 20th century
Cotton, dyes, and pigments
Tsutsugaki *and painting on indigo plain weave ground
65 x 32 in.; 162.5 x 80 cm
Museum Purchase: The Barbara Benton Wescoe Fund, 1993.13

STENCILS

*Stencil for Yukata *with swallows in flight against net pattern* (Plate 62, p. 210)
Japan
Edo period, ca. 1826–1834
Mulberry paper laminated with persimmon tannin with silk mesh backing
Cutting techniques: *hikibori, dōgubori, tsukibori*
21.5 in. x 16.5 in.; 54.8 x 42 cm
Source Unknown, 0000.2959

*Stencil for Yukata *with water chestnut quatrefoils on narrow vertical stripes* (Plate 64, p. 212)
Japan
Late Meiji or early Taishō period, early 20th century
Mulberry paper laminated with persimmon tannin with silk mesh backing
Cutting techniques: *tsukibori, hikibori, kiribori, dōgubori*
21.5 x 16.5 in.; 54.8 x 42 cm
Source Unknown, 0000.2960

*Stencil for Yukata *with chrysanthemums and insect-eaten paulownia (?) leaves on striped ground*
(Plate 63, p. 211)
Japan
Meiji or early Taishō period, late 19th–early 20th century
Mulberry paper laminated with persimmon tannin with silk mesh backing
Cutting techniques: *tsukibori, hikibori, kiribori*
21 x 16.8 in.; 54.3 x 42.5 cm
Source Unknown, 0000.2961

*Stencil for Yukata *with bows and birds*
(Plate 65, p. 213)
Japan
Taishō period (1912–1926)
Mulberry paper laminated with persimmon tannin with silk mesh backing
Cutting techniques: *tsukibori, hikibori *with applied dots
21.8 x 16.8 in.; 55 x 42.8 cm
Source Unknown, 0000.2962

Stencil with all-over floral motifs
Japan
20th century
Mulberry paper laminated with persimmon tannin with mesh backing
20 x 17.3 in.; 51 x 44 cm
Gift of Dr. and Mrs. George A. Colom, 2000.158

Stencil with small huts in landscape and abstracted flowers, leaves, and clouds
Japan
20th century
Mulberry paper laminated with persimmon tannin with mesh backing
23.3 x 17.3 in.; 59 x 44 cm
Gift of Dr. and Mrs. George A. Colom, 2000.159

Stencil with repeated woven basket design
Japan
20th century
Mulberry paper laminated with persimmon tannin with mesh backing
21.3 x 17.5 in.; 54 x 44.5 cm
Gift of Dr. and Mrs. George A. Colom, 2000.160

*Stencil for *Yukata* or Kimono with *komon* pattern
Japan (Plate 66, p. 214)
Meiji or Taishō period, late 19th–early 20th century
Mulberry paper laminated with persimmon tannin
Cutting technique: *dōgubori*
7.8 x 16.5 in.; 19.5 x 42 cm
Gift of Elizabeth Sherbon, Professor of Dance
1961–75, 2000.182

KASURI

*Kasuri Futonji *Panel with white crosses and "log cabin" pattern in vertical stripe on indigo ground*
Japan (Plate 74, p. 231)
19th–20th century
Cotton
Warp and weft *kasuri*, plain and "log cabin" weaves on indigo ground
60.5 x 39 in.; 153.6 x 99 cm
Museum Purchase, 1992.78

*Kasuri Futonji *Panel with reserved stripes in the warp and weft on indigo ground* (Plate 75, p. 232)
Japan
19th–20th century
Cotton
Warp and weft *kasuri* on indigo plain weave ground
56.5 x 13 in.; 143.6 x 33 cm
Museum Purchase, 1992.79

*Kasuri Futonji *Panel with fans and interlocking squares* (Plate 76, p. 233)
Japan
19th–20th century
Cotton
Warp and weft *kasuri* (hand tying and *e-dai*) on indigo plain weave ground
61 x 12.8 in.; 155 x 32.4 cm
Museum Purchase, 1992.80

*Kasuri Futonji *Panel with flaming pearl motif in interstices of zigzag pattern of small squares* (Plate 77, p. 234)
Japan
19th–20th century
Cotton
Weft *kasuri* on indigo plain weave ground
61 x 12.8 in.; 155 x 32.4 cm
Museum Purchase, 1992.81

*Child's *Kasuri Furisode *with small motifs of butterflies, chrysanthemums, and waves among well and rice field designs* (Plate 73, p. 230)
Japan, probably Ōmi area of Shiga Prefecture
Early 20th century
Ramie
Warp and weft *kasuri* including *itajime* on indigo plain weave ground
37 x 12 in.; 92.5 x 30 cm
Museum Purchase: The Barbara Benton Wescoe Fund, 1993.11

BUDDHIST TEXTILES

Woven Panel with geometric and floral motifs
Japan
Edo period, 18th or 19th century
Silk
Supplementary weft on satin ground, loosely woven
50 x 13 in.; 127 x 33 cm
Source Unknown, 0000.681

Temple Furnishing with alternating patches of geometric and floral motifs with exterior floral border and interior corner patches of border material
Japan
Meiji period, late 19th century (with some older fabric)
Silk and gold foil on flat paper strips
Compound weaves and patchwork
61.5 x 11.3 in.; 154 x 30 cm
The William Bridges Thayer Memorial, 0000.1139
(Thayer tag)

Seven-Panel Kesa (Priest's Robe) with design of asa no ha (hemp flowers)
Japan
Edo period, 18th century?
Silk, gold- and silver-wrapped thread
Patterned twill and patchwork; fabric with design of hemp flowers was cut into patches and reassembled into the large central rectangle; outer border and patches at corners of inner rectangle have design of flowering vines (compound weave)
80 x 43.5 in.; 203.5 x 111 cm
Source Unknown, 0000.2190

Buddhist Textile Fragment with complex geometric design of roundels in interlocking octagons connected with fretwork at horizontal and vertical connecting points, and fillers of tortoise-shell motifs, flowers, clouds, etc.
Japan
19th or early 20th century
Silk
Compound weave and patchwork
16.8 x 14 in.; 43 x 35.5 cm
Gift of Rose K. Auerbach, 1967.42

Patchwork Temple Furnishing with polychrome design of fans on faded red ground
Japan
Edo or Meiji period, 19th century
Silk and gold foil on paper
Compound weave and patchwork
39 x 13.3 in.; 99 x 34 cm
Gift of Rose K. Auerbach, 1967.44

Ohi (Priest's Stole) with silver chrysanthemum roundels on red ground with border of green brocade and replaced interior corner patches (Plate 89, p. 267)
Japan
Muromachi or Momoyama period, 16th century (central panel); constructed in the Edo period, 18th century with late-19th-century replacement corner patches
Silk, gold and silver foil on flat paper strips
Brocaded twill (supplementary weft on twill ground), figured twill, and patchwork
48 x 12 in.; 122 x 30.5 cm
Gift of Rose K Auerbach, 1967.49

Temple Furnishing or Ohi with orange, blue, and white floral motifs and streamers on green ground
Japan
Edo or Meiji period, 19th century
Silk and metal foil on flat paper strips
Compound weave; fabric was cut and repieced
66 x 12.8 in.; 168 x 32.5 cm
Gift of Rose K. Auerbach, 1967.52

*Ohi *with stylized coral, flaming pearls, and waves* (Plate 88, p. 265)
Japan
Edo period, 18th–19th century
Silk and metallic foil on flat paper strips
Compound weave with vertically ribbed ground; fabric was cut and repieced; the Four Guardian Deities are depicted on the corner patches
61.3 x 12.3 in.; 155.8 x 31.8 cm
Given in Memory of James H. Walker, Jr. by his Family, 1993.347

Temple Furnishing with sprinkles of gold and silver clouds and floating lotus leaves on orange/red ground
Japan
Edo period, dated by inscription to 1810
Silk, silver and gold leaf, and *sumi* ink
Stencilled and painted designs on orange/red plain weave ground; patterned after ground cloth was cut and pieced into this shape of central square with border
27 x 20.5 in.; 68.5 x 67.3 cm
Given in Memory of James H. Walker, Jr. by his Family, 1993.356

*Seven-Panel Kesa *with abstract floral motif in nested jagged diamond ground* (Plate 87, p. 262)
Japan
Edo period, second half of 17th century
Silk and metallic foil on flat paper strips (in corner patches)
Cut and repieced green brocaded satin; corner patches were probably woven in China during the Ming dynasty (16th century)
45 x 89 in.; 114.5 x 226 cm
Museum Purchase: The Barbara Benton Wescoe Fund, 1995.13
Formerly in collection of Traphagen School

TEXTILES FOR EXPORT

Embroidered Panel with cranes and irises (Plate 91, p. 271)
Japan
Meiji period (1868–1912)
Silk and gold-wrapped thread
Embroidery (satin, couching, running, seed) on off-white damask ground
53 x 65 in.; 134.6 x 166.1 cm
Source Unknown, 0000.1111

Embroidered Panel with crane and irises (Plate 90, p. 270)
Japan
Meiji period (1868–1912)
Silk and gold-wrapped thread
Embroidery (satin, couching, running, seed) on off-white damask ground
56 x 39 in.; 143.6 x 97.5 cm
Source Unknown, 0000.2432

HOUSEHOLD FURNISHINGS

Borders and Backing for Hanging Scroll with gold-colored bamboo and ground
Japan
20th century
Silk
Jacquard
40 x 13 in.; 101.5 x 33 cm
Source Unknown, 0000.1125

Summer Space Divider or Mosquito Net with chrysanthemum roundels
Japan
20th century
Silk
Plain weave patterning on off-white gauze ground
82 x 124 in.; 208.5 x 315 cm
Source Unknown, 0000.1131

Noren (Door Hanging) with two blue horizontal stripes on off-white ground
Japan
19th–20th century
Silk
Crepe
13 x 28.5 in.; 33 x 72.5 cm
Source Unknown, 0000.1138

FLAT WOVEN FRAGMENTS

Kimono Panel with orange roundels and checkerboard segments
Japan
Edo period, 18th–19th century
Silk
Embroidery (satin, couching) on pale indigo satin ground
46 x 10 in.; 117 x 25.5 cm
Source Unknown, 0000.1055

Women's Kimono Panels with butterflies and gourd roundels in alternating rows
Japan
19th or early 20th century
Silk and remains of paper backing for gold or silver foil
Supplementary weft on plain weave ground
60 x 13.5 in.; 153 x 35 cm
51 x 13.5 in.; 137 x 35 cm
74.5 x 13.5 in.; 187 x 35 cm
Source Unknown, 0000.1100–1102

Woven Panels with rows of chrysanthemums and leaves on reddish brown ground
Japan
Edo or Meiji period, 19th century
Silk and gold foil on flat paper strips
Compound weave
49 x 27.5 in.; 124 x 70 cm
19.5 x 17 in.; 49.8 x 43.3 cm (largest dimensions)
The William Bridges Thayer Memorial, 0000.1105 (Thayer tag) and 0000.2827

Velvet Panel with bamboo leaves and stripes
Japan
Edo or Meiji period, 19th century?
Silk
Velvet, cut and uncut pile
39.5 x 12.5 in.; 100.5 x 31 cm
Source Unknown, 0000.1108

Woven Panel with chrysanthemum roundels on red ground
Japan
Edo or Meiji period, 19th century
Silk and gold foil on flat paper strips
Compound weave
35.5 x 13 in.; 90.3 x 33 cm
Source Unknown, 0000.1109

Velvet Panels with purple and gold stripes on ground of wheels, butterflies, and peonies in lattice
Japan
19th–20th century
Silk
Velvet, cut and uncut pile
74 x 20.5 in.; 162.5 x 52 cm
74 x 20.5 in.; 162.5 x 52 cm
Source Unknown, 0000.1132 and 0000.1143

Woven Panels with center seam and silver-grey all-over pattern of cranes and chrysanthemums in rows
Japan
Edo or Meiji period, 19th century
Silk and metal-wrapped thread
Patterned twill
54 x 50 in.; 137 x 127 cm
Source Unknown, 0000.1140 (Marshall Field tag)

Pieced Panel of Woman's Kimono Remnants with woven design of butterflies and branches
Japan
Edo or Meiji period, 19th century
Silk
Supplementary weft on plain weave ground
62 x 13 in.; 158 x 33 cm
Source Unknown, 0000.1141

Triangular Fragment with red and white chrysanthemum roundels on green and gold lattice (two pieces stitched together)
Japan
Edo or Meiji period, 19th century(?)
Silk and gold foil on flat paper strips
Compound weave with brown handspun cotton lining
39 x 39 in.; 99 x 99 cm;
selvage to selvage: 26.5 in.; 67.5 cm
The William Bridges Thayer Memorial, 0000.1142 (Thayer tag)

Woven Fragment with checkerboard of squares of alternating geometric and leaf patterns
Japan
19th–early 20th century
Silk
Velvet (cut and uncut pile) and compound weave structure
15.3 x 10.3 in.; 39 x 26 cm
The William Bridges Thayer Memorial, 1928.7066 (Thayer tag [removed])

Woven Panel with lion-dog, peonies, and tortoise-shell pattern on orange ground
Japan
Edo or Meiji period, 19th century
Silk and metallic foil on paper strips
Compound weave
25 x 8 in.; 63.5 x 20.5 cm
The William Bridges Thayer Memorial, 1928.7073

Woven Fragment with dragons and clouds
Japan
Edo or Meiji period, 19th century
Silk and gold foil on paper strips
Compound weave
11 x 36 in.; 28 x 91.5 cm
The William Bridges Thayer Memorial, 1928.7077 (Thayer tag)

Woven Panel with red chrysanthemums and flowers on red ground
Japan
20th century
Silk
Twill patterning on loose, plain weave crepe ground
40.5 x 17.5 in.; 103 x 45 cm
Gift of Mrs. F. B. Dains, 1945.27

Embroidered Panel (probably kosode fragment) with realistic squirrels on grapevine
Japan
Meiji period, late 19th century
Silk and gold-wrapped thread
Embroidery (satin, stem, couching) on blue satin ground
33 x 35 in.; 84 x 89 cm
Given in Memory of James H. Walker, Jr. by his Family, 1993.348

TEXTILE SAMPLE BOOKS

Textile Sample Books (Fig. 12a, p. 197)
Japan
Edo or Meiji period, 19th century
Silk, gold- and silver-wrapped thread, gold and silver foil on flat paper strips; textiles are mounted on paper
Compound woven silks with some embroidery
14.5 x 24 in.; 37 x 56 cm
Transfer from Cincinnati Museum of Art, 1995.32.1–4

Textile Sample Book, accordion style (Fig. 12b, p. 197)
Japan
Edo or Meiji period, 19th century
Silk, gold and silver foil, and cotton on paper
Compound woven silks on one side, *katazome* printed cottons on the other
16 x 12 in.; 41.8 x 30.5 cm
Transfer from Cincinnati Museum of Art, 1995.33

KOREA

Canopy commissioned for provincial tour by
Chinese official Kim with inscribed names of
donors
Korea
Chosŏn dynasty, 1886
Silk
Embroidery (satin) on white and blue satin
grounds (for the border)
Diam. 77.5 in.; 197 cm
Source Unknown, 0000.1026

Embroidered Panel with crane in roundel framed
by square floral border and surmounted by three
smaller cranes
Korea
20th century
Silk and gold-wrapped thread with cotton band
Embroidery (satin, couching) on red satin
ground
37.5 x 36.3 in.; 94 x 97 cm
The William Bridges Thayer Memorial,
0000.1068

Glossary

bast fiber: Any fiber obtained from the inner stem or bark of plants, including linen (flax), hemp, ramie, and wild bast fibers such as *fuji* (wisteria), *ohyō* (elm), *kuzu* (arrowroot), *shina* (linden), *irakusa* (nettle), and *kōzo* (mulberry). Except for flax, all of these traditionally were used in Japan.

binding system: System of interlacement of warp and weft threads that form the structure of the cloth. There are three basic binding systems: plain weave, twill, and satin.

brocade: Loosely defined term used to describe a weave structure in which a supplementary set of warps or wefts is used to create a polychrome pattern supplementary to the foundation weave. Brocade wefts may be discontinuous, limited to the areas of the pattern where they are required. They are often glossy silk or metallic.

compound weave: Loosely defined term used to describe weave structures in which patterning is achieved by the use of two or more sets of warps and/or wefts; the structure of one face does not necessarily affect that of the other.

damask: Generally a weave structure in which the pattern is formed by two distinct binding systems with different directional orientations. One binding system generally reads as pattern and the other as ground. Damask weaves are usually monochromatic; the pattern is visible because of the different ways that light reflects off the differing directional orientations of pattern and ground. The term most often refers to structures based on two satin systems, one with predominant warp and the other with predominant weft. In this volume the term is used more broadly to include structures based on twill patterning on a twill, satin or plain weave ground; satin patterning on a twill, satin or plain weave ground; and plain weave patterning on a twill or satin ground.

detached interlacing: Needle technique in which the artisan first sets up scaffolding warps on the surface of the ground fabric, and then darns wefts into the warps, creating separate layers of plain weave fabric that float over the surface of the ground fabric.

drawloom: Handloom designed to permit the automatic repetition of complex patterns. In addition to the regular set of harnesses, a drawloom is equipped with a figure or pattern harness with a set of long cords attached to different warp threads (or sets of threads). The loom usually has a high frame to accommodate the figure cords; a "drawboy" pulls the cords in coordination with the weaver, who is seated at a bench in front of the loom.

gauze: Weave structure in which warp threads twist around each other, held in place by the weft. In simple gauze, only adjacent warps intertwine; in figured or complex gauze, warps move from their original positions in a series of diagonal interlacements to form an openwork pattern in the cloth. Gauze interlacements create small openings in the finished cloth, resulting in a cool fabric often used for summer garments.

harness: Loom component. Generally a rectangular frame, the harnesses hold the heddles. One set of warp elements is threaded through the heddles in each harness. Plain weave requires two harnesses; twill, a minimum of three harnesses; and satin, a minimum of five harnesses. The harnesses are generally attached to treadles. The weaver controls the structure and pattern of the cloth by depressing one or more treadles which, in turn, raise or lower the appropriate harnesses.

heddles: Loom components made of string or metal, heddles have "eyes" or openings through which warps are threaded when the loom is set up. The manipulation of the heddles raises or lowers groups of warps to create a "shed," the opening through which the weft is passed to weave the cloth. Heddles are generally hung from a set of harnesses to facilitate manipulating them as a group.

jacquard loom: Mechanized loom invented by Joseph Marie Jacquard in the late eighteenth century that was designed to replace the drawloom. A set of punched cards moves forward automatically to raise the appropriate pattern threads as the weaver works the treadles. A jacquard loom is faster and more efficient than a draw loom, does not require a drawboy, and reduces the possibility of careless errors during the weaving process.

mordant: Chemical substance, often a metallic compound, that combines with the dye to form an insoluble compound, thus fixing the color in the thread or cloth.

plain weave: The most basic weave structure in which each warp and weft intersect at right angles in an over-under alternation. Plain weave is one of three basic binding systems.

reed: Loom component consisting of a long, narrow frame with finely-spaced dividers, designed to keep warp threads properly spaced; usually made of bamboo, wood, or metal. On some looms, the reed also serves as a beater, pressing a new weft into the web of the woven cloth.

"S" and "Z" spin and ply: The terms "s" and "z" refer to the direction of twist given to fiber as it is spun into thread, or to the direction of ply when two threads are twisted together. The reference is to the direction of the center stroke of the letter.

satin: Basic weave structure derived from a broken twill and based on a unit of five or more warps and wefts. The weft passes over four or more warp ends and under the next, in a sequence in which none of the floats or binding points is aligned on the diagonal. Usually woven in silk, the weave structure creates a fabric that is lustrous on the front face. Satin is one of three basic binding systems.

shed: At the loom, the space made by the separation of warps into two layers to permit the passage of the weft.

supplementary warp or weft: Patterning warp or weft that is not part of the basic structure of the fabric.

tapestry: Weaving technique in which discontinuous wefts of various colors each operate in a discrete pattern area, generally in a plain weave structure.

tie-dye (*shibori* in Japan; *bandhani* in India): A resist dyeing technique in which cloth is patterned after weaving by tying, binding, or stitching selected areas to reserve them from the dye.

treadles: Loom components consisting of long pedals attached to the harnesses of a loom. Operated by the weaver's feet, treadles raise or lower appropriate groups of warp threads.

twill: Basic weave structure with a diagonal orientation. The simplest twill structure is based on a unit of three warps and wefts, in which weft threads pass over two warp threads and then under one, never passing over the same combination of warps in succeeding rows. If the sequence proceeds regularly from row to row, a left- or right-oriented diagonal appears in the cloth; if the sequence is irregular (as in "broken twill"), the alignment is jagged and not diagonal. Twill is one of three basic binding systems.

warp: Parallel elements that run longitudinally in loom or fabric. Warp threads are set on the loom before weaving begins.

weft: Thread that is passed from side to side (selvage to selvage) through succeeding sheds to interweave with the warp.

SOUTH ASIA

aba: Also *abha*; *abho*; "A"-shaped tunic with tight-fitting sleeves worn by women of several different groups in northwest India and Pakistan.

abocchnai: (Tharri) Woman's headshawl. Also called *odhani* in Hindi.

asli tus: The highest-quality fleece used for weaving Kashmir shawls. *Asli tus* traditionally came from the Himalayan Ibex (*Capra ibex*), which lives in the wild above fourteen thousand feet, primarily in Ladakh and western Tibet.

bandhani: Tie-dye technique of patterning cloth by tying or binding selected areas to reserve them from the dye.

boteh: (Persian) Design element consisting of the cone or paisley motif found on nineteenth-century Kashmir shawls. The *boteh* is derived from floral and flowering plant motifs popular at the Safavid court in Iran and the Mughal court in India.

buta: (Arabic) Means "shrub" or "flowering bush." The term used in Kashmir to denote the flower-filled cone motifs found on Kashmir shawls.

calico: Cotton fabric with colorful patterns achieved through various surface design techniques, including block-printing, painting, and mordant and resist dyeing. See also chintz.

chintz: Mordant-printed or -painted cotton fabric with colorful patterns. In English the term has come to mean highly glazed, patterned cotton, usually with floral motifs; chintz is often used for household furnishings.

ikat: Fabric name derived from the Indonesian word *mengikat*, meaning "to tie or bind." Patterning technique in which the design on the cloth is created by partially dyeing the warp and/or weft yarns before weaving. Traditionally, thread or other material is wound tightly around the sections of yarns to be reserved. Also refers to cloth patterned by this technique. Called *kasuri* in Japan.

kani: Interlocking twill tapestry, the technique used to pattern Kashmir shawls. In *kani* weaving, discontinuous wefts of various colors each operate in a discrete pattern area; wefts interweave with the warp in a twill structure, and interlock with wefts in adjacent areas.

Kashmir shawl: Shawl from Kashmir or neighboring areas, made of cashmere or other fleece, and patterned with distinctive cone-shaped floral motifs (*buta*, *boteh*). Popular in Europe from the late eighteenth century through the 1870s, and copied on draw and jacquard looms at many European weaving centers, including Paisley in Scotland. Early Kashmir shawls were long and narrow, with simple, colorful borders of *buta* motifs and a large central area left unpatterned and undyed to emphasize the luster of the off-white cashmere fiber. As the shawls gained popularity in Europe, Kashmiri weavers mixed the more plentiful (and less expensive) sheep's wool with cashmere or used it alone. In the course of the nineteenth century, the shawls became wider and border motifs increasingly encroached on the main body of the garment, leaving only a medallion of unpatterned cloth in the center.

Mirrorwork: See *shisha*

naqqash: Artisan who drew the patterns for a Kashmir shawl; a highly respected professional.

odhani: Also *odhni*, *orhni*. Woman's long shawl worn over the head and shoulders in north and northwest India and Pakistan.

pallov: Border of a Kashmir shawl.

pashm: Fleece from the cashmere goat (*Capra hircus*). Most high-quality Kashmir shawls were woven from the fleece of this Central Asian species of mountain goat, which lives at an elevation of about ten thousand feet in the mountains of Ladakh, Tibet, and Chinese Turkestan. The goats were combed in the spring to harvest the lustrous soft undercoat.

pashmina: Cloth woven of *pashm* fiber.

rafugar: Highly skilled needleworkers who received the segments of a Kashmir shawl, woven on different looms, joined them together like a jigsaw puzzle, and embellished the design as necessary to hide the joins and make the parts work together as a whole.

shisha: Decorative technique in which small mirrors are stitched on cloth, usually as part of detailed embroidered decoration. Mirrors add sparkle to the cloth, and in many places are believed to divert harm (or the "evil eye").

talim: Shorthand notation for weavers of Kashmir shawls indicating the sequence of weft colors and number of warps across which they extend to produce a given pattern.

talim-guru: Artisan who produced the shorthand notation (*talim*) for weavers of a Kashmir shawl.

tarah-guru: Artisan who called the colors of a pattern for a Kashmir shawl. Starting at the bottom of the black-and-white drawing prepared by the *naqqash*, the *tarah-guru* called out each color and the number of warps across which it extended, working across each row from the bottom of the design to the top. The *tarah-guru* worked in tandem with the *talim-guru*, who transcribed his rapid chant into a shorthand notation (*talim*) for the weavers.

toji: Tiny bobbin resembling an eyeless needle that carried the colored weft threads used in weaving a Kashmir shawl. A complex Kashmir pattern required hundreds of *tojis*.

CHINA

chao fu: Audience robe. The most formal Qing-dynasty official robe, the *chao fu* is distinguished in shape by its straight bodice, tripartite narrow sleeves ending in flared "horse hoof" cuffs, distinctive shaping of the right overlap of the bodice, and attached, pleated skirt.

chaogua: Long embroidered vest designed to be worn as the outermost garment of a Manchu woman's formal costume. Longer than the Han woman's *xiabei*, the *chaogua* had straight hems with no hem embellishment and generally was worn over a *long pao*.

hanpi: See definition under Japan.

jiangyi: Daoist priest's robe; a large, rectangular outer garment, unstructured except for a slightly curved hemline. *Jiangyi* are usually made of silk and elaborately patterned.

kesi: Chinese silk tapestry. *Kesi* was used for garments and household furnishings.

long pao: Dragon robe; official garment less formal than the *chao fu*. A long, slightly "A"-shaped garment that was folded across the body from left to right, closing with a distinctive shaping of the edge of the overlap at the fastening; and with narrow, tripartite sleeves ending in flared "horse hoof" cuffs. Also called *qifu* or *jifu* (auspicious robe).

rong: Chinese silk velvet. Some early Chinese *rong* fabrics are not technically velvet by European definitions.

xiabei: Long embroidered vest designed to be worn as the outermost garment of a Han woman's formal costume. The *xiabei* fell to mid-calf and had deeply cut, triangular hems embellished with heavy fringe or with knotted netting, tassels, and metal bangles. It generally was worn over a long skirt and wide-sleeved robe that fell to mid-calf.

JAPAN

asa: Designates bast fibers in general. More specifically the term refers to hemp (*taima* or *hon asa*) and ramie (*karamushi* or *chōma*).

bashō: Fiber from the leaf of the fiber banana (*Musa sapientum* L., var. *liukiuensis* Matsumura). *Bashō* fiber is produced and woven in Okinawa to create *bashōfu*, or *bashō* cloth.

bashōfu: Cloth woven of *bashō* fiber.

e-dai: Also *osa-dai*, *ezu-dai*, *tane ito dai*, *sumi ito dai*; picture stand. Stand used to create complex *kasuri* patterns. The *e-dai* is a rectangular wooden frame with an open-topped reed fastened to the two longest sides. The distance between the reeds is equal to the projected width of the finished cloth, plus the necessary "take-up" (the extra width needed to account for the movement of the weft threads over and under the warp as they pass from selvage to selvage). To pattern wefts using an *e-dai*, a thick thread was wound back and forth between the openings of the reeds to simulate the passage of weft. When enough had been wound for one repeat of the design, the pattern was drawn or stenciled onto this guide thread, or *tane ito*, usually with sumi ink. The *tane ito* was then taken off the *e-dai* and stretched out on a large frame, such as a warping frame. Finally, the pattern weft threads were wound next to the *tane ito* and tied at the appropriate points, as indicated by the ink marks on the guide thread.

fukusa: Padded and lined silk cloths, often with tassels at the corners, used to cover formal gifts. Most are elaborately decorated with subjects that are symbolically appropriate for a particular significant event (such as a wedding), or with a single motif (such as a family crest) that could be used for any occasion throughout the year.

furisode: Swinging sleeves; form of *kosode* or kimono with long sleeves worn by young women and courtesans.

futon: Padded mats and coverlets used as bedding.

futonji: Cloth used to cover *futon*.

ginran: Textile with weft patterning in silver or a silver alloy, made by affixing "silver" leaf to paper or an animal substrate, cutting this into strips, and using the strips as a pattern weft.

hanpi: Hip- or knee-length sleeveless "coat" with a straight bodice and attached, often slightly flaring skirt. In the Nara period, *hanpi* sometimes had very short sleeves. There are more than thirty eighth-century hanpi in the Shōsōin Repository in Nara, which were either imported from Tang-dynasty China or modeled on Chinese prototypes.

itajime: Board-pressed; technique used to create complex *kasuri* patterns efficiently. Warp or weft threads were clamped between pairs of carved boards; when the boards were immersed in a dye bath, the sections of thread caught between the raised portions of the carved design resisted the dye. The patterns on *itajime kasuri* textiles generally have sharper, more distinct edges than those on hand-tied *kasuri*.

kasuri: Patterning technique in which the design on the cloth is created by partially resist-dyeing the warp and/or weft yarns before weaving. Also refers to cloth patterned by this technique. More generally known by the Malay-Indonesian term *ikat*.

katagami: Stencil paper. Made from the inner bark of the paper mulberry tree (*kōzo; Broussonetia kazinoki sieb*), *katagami* is constructed of two or more sheets of paper laid at right angles to each other and laminated with aged persimmon tannin (*kakishibu*).

katazome: Stencil dyeing. More accurately described as stencil and paste-resist dyeing, a technique of patterning cloth in which a design is brushed onto a cloth with rice paste through a stencil, reserving that section of the cloth from the dye. Most *katazome* textiles have repeating patterns.

kesa: The signature garment of a Buddhist priest; a large rectangle composed of an uneven number of columns of discrete pieces of fabric stitched together. Although the fabric pieces are often made of precious materials, the fact that they are patched together is designed to symbolize the Buddhist priest's vow of poverty. In Japan the *kesa* is worn over other clothing, usually draped over the left shoulder and under the right arm.

kinran: Textile with weft patterning in gold or a gold alloy, made by affixing "gold" leaf to paper or an animal substrate, cutting this into strips, and using the strips as a pattern weft.

kogin: Counted-thread embroidery. Also garments decorated with *kogin*, particularly those embroidered with white cotton thread on an indigo hemp or cotton ground from the Tōhoku district of northern Honshu, Japan's main island.

komon: Small pattern; small, all-over *katazome* patterns, and cloth patterned with *komon* designs.

kosode: Small sleeves; forerunner of the kimono, and similar to it in cut and construction. The name refers to the narrow wrist openings that distinguish the garment. A *kosode* may have long or short sleeves.

nizuri: Work vest worn mainly by women from the Tōhoku district of northern Honshu to protect their backs from heavy loads. *Nizuri* are often heavily stitched in the areas most subject to abrasion. Some are beautifully decorated with all-over geometric patterns of white cotton stitching on an indigo-dyed cotton or bast fiber ground.

nobori: Banner such as those placed outside houses on the annual Boys' Day Festival.

obi: Textile wrapped around the waist to fasten a kimono or other garment. The width and style of *obi* have varied from narrow cords to simple cotton belts worn with men's *yukata*, to the stiff, doubled, heavily brocaded *obi* worn with women's wedding kimono. Methods of tying also have followed the fashions of the times.

ohi: Buddhist priest's arm stole.

sashiko: Running embroidery stitch, particularly associated with white cotton patterns on an indigo cotton or bast fiber ground, as seen in garments of the Tōhoku district of northern Honshu.

shibori: Cloth that has been patterned after weaving by binding selected areas to reserve them from the dye. Tiny sections of the cloth may be pinched and wrapped with thread; large areas may be tied off and capped; the cloth may be folded (or wrapped) and bound; or it may be stitched with the stitching line pulled taut.

tane ito: Guide thread used in the *e-dai kasuri* process.

tsutsugaki: Drawing with a tube; hand-drawn paste-resist dyeing. The artisan outlines a pattern on the cloth with a rice paste resist squeezed through a tube (*tsutsu*); applies pigments, dyes, and mordants to the cloth with brushes; and then spreads resist paste over the design to protect it from subsequent immersion dyeing. *Tsutsugaki* textiles are characterized by bold, pictorial designs, usually on an indigo-dyed cotton ground.

yogi: Padded, oversized kimono used as a bed coverlet. *Yogi* have an extra panel in the back, making them large enough to cover two people.

yukata: Bath wear; cotton kimono used as an informal summer garment by men, women, and children.

yūzen: Type of resist dyeing on silk, developed in the late seventeenth century, which made it possible to create *kosode* or kimono with freely executed painterly designs in an array of sumptuous colors. Applied through a small tube of stencil paper, often fitted with a metal tip, a rice resist paste is used to outline the design. Dyes and pigments are applied to the cloth with brushes—some wide and flat, for coloring large areas and creating graduated washes of color (*hikizashi*); others small enough to paint in small details of the design (*irozashi*).

Selected Bibliography

SPENCER MUSEUM PUBLICATIONS

Catalogue of the Oriental Collection. Lawrence, Kansas: Spencer Museum of Art, 1980.

Handbook of the Collection, Helen Foresman Spencer Museum of Art. Lawrence, Kansas: Spencer Museum of Art, 1978.

The Register 5, no. 6 (1978).

SOUTH ASIA

Ain-i Akbari (The Institutes of Akbar). Compiled by Abul Fazl 'Allami (1551–1602). Translated from the original Persian by H. Blochmann. Edited by D. C. Phillott. Calcutta: Royal Asiatic Society of Bengal, 1927 i.e. 1939. Blochmann's translation was first published by the Asiatic Society of Bengal in three volumes, 1873–1894.

Ames, Frank. *The Kashmir Shawl and Its Indo-French Influence*. Woodbridge, Suffolk (England): Antique Collectors' Club, 1988 (1986).

Archer, Mildred, and Toby Falk. *India Revealed: The Art and Adventures of James and William Fraser 1801–35*. London: Cassell, 1989.

Baden-Powell, Baden Henry. *The Indian Village Community*. Delhi: Cosmo Publications, 1972.

Barnard, Nicholas. *Arts and Crafts of India*. London: Conran Octopus, 1993.

Bates, Charles Ellison. *A Gazetteer of Kashmir and the Adjacent Districts . . . .* New Delhi: Light and Life Publishers, 1980. Reprint of the 1873 edition published in Calcutta.

Bernier, François. *Travels in the Mogul Empire, 1656–1668*. London: Archibald Constable, 1891.

Birdwood, George Christopher Molesworth. *The Industrial Arts of India*. London: Chapman and Hall, ca. 1880.

Bunting, Ethel-Jane W. *Sindhi Tombs and Textiles: The Persistence of Pattern*. Albuquerque: The Maxwell Museum of Anthropology and the University of New Mexico Press, 1980.

Chandra, Moti. "Indian Costume and Textiles from the Eighth to the Twelfth Century." *Journal of Indian Textile History*, no. 5 (1960).

———. *Studies in Early Indian Painting*. London: Asia Publishing House, 1970.

———. *Trade and Trade Routes in Ancient India*. New Delhi: Abhinav Publications, 1977.

Crill, Rosemary. *Indian Embroidery*. London: Victoria and Albert Publications, 1999.

Das Gupta, Jyoti Bhusan. *Jammu and Kashmir*. The Hague: Martinus Nijhoff, 1968.

Deloch, Jean, ed. *Voyage en Inde du Comte de Modave 1773–1776*. Paris: École française d'extrême-orient, 1971.

Desai, Chelna. *Ikat Textiles of India*. Tokyo: Graphic-sha, 1988.

Dhamija, Jasleen, ed. *Crafts of Gujarat*. New York: Mapin International, 1985.

Dhamija, Jasleen, and Jyotindra Jain, eds. *Handwoven Fabrics of India*. Ahmedabad, India: Mapin Publishing, 1989.

Drew, Frederic. *The Jummoo and Kashmir Territories: A Geographical Account.* Graz, Austria: Akademische Druck-u. Verlagsanstalt, 1976. Originally published in 1875.

Duprés, Adrien. *Voyages en Perse faits dans les années 1807, 1808, 1809.* 2 vols. Paris, 1819.

Edwards, S. M. *Babur: Diarist and Despot.* London: A. M. Philpot, no date (between 1921 and 1936).

Elson, Vickie G. *Dowries from Kutch.* Los Angeles: Museum of Cultural History, University of California, 1979.

Fisher, Nora, ed. *Mud, Mirror and Thread: Folk Traditions of Rural India.* Ahmedabad, India and Santa Fe: Mapin Publishing Pvt. in association with Museum of New Mexico Press, 1993.

Forster, George. *A Journey from Bengal to England, through the Northern Part of India, Kashmire, Afghanistan, and Persia, and into Russia by the Caspian-Sea.* Punjab, Pakistan: [Patiala] Languages Dept., 1970. Originally published in London in 1798.

Fraser, James Baillie. *Journal of a Tour through Part of the Snowy Range of the Himalayan Mountains . . . .* Delhi and New Delhi: Neeraj Publishing House, distributed by D. K. Publishers' Distributors, 1982. Originally published in London in 1825.

———. *Narrative of a Journey into Khorasan, in the Years 1821 and 1822.* London: Longman, Hurst, Rees, Orme, Brown, and Green, 1825. Republished with a new introduction by Edward Ingram (New York: Oxford University Press), 1984.

Frater, Judy. "Elements of Style: The Artisan Reflected in Embroideries of Western India." In Nora Fisher, ed. *Mud, Mirror and Thread: Folk Traditions of Rural India.* Ahmedabad: Mapin Publishing in association with the Museum of New Mexico Press, 1993.

———. *Threads of Identity: Embroidery and Adornment of the Nomadic Rabaris.* Ahmedabad: Mapin International, 2003. First published ca. 1995.

Gilfoy, Peggy Stoltz. *Fabrics in Celebration from the Collection.* Indianapolis: Indianapolis Museum of Art, 1983.

Gillow, John, and Nicholas Barnard. *Traditional Indian Textiles.* London: Thames and Hudson, 1991.

Gittinger, Mattiebelle. *Master Dyers to the World.* Washington, DC: The Textile Museum, 1982.

Guy, John. *Woven Cargoes: Indian Textiles in the East.* New York: Thames and Hudson, 1998.

Guy, John, and Deborah Swallow, eds. *Arts of India: 1550–1900.* London: Victoria and Albert Museum, 1990.

Habib, Irfan, ed. *Akbar and His India.* Delhi: Oxford University Press, 1997.

Hacker, Katherine F., and Krista Jensen Turnbull. *Courtyard, Bazaar, Temple: Traditions of Textile Expression in India.* Seattle: University of Washington Press, 1982.

Harle, J. C. *The Art and Architecture of the Indian Subcontinent.* The Pelican History of Art. London: Penguin Books, 1990 (revised 1987).

Hiroshima Prefectural Art Museum, ed. *Textile Arts of Asia.* Hiroshima: Hiroshima Prefectural Art Museum, 1996.

Hügel, Baron Charles. *Travels in Kashmir and the Panjab.* London: John Petheram, 1845.

Ions, Veronica. *Indian Mythology.* London: Paul Hamlyn, 1975 (1967).

Irwin, John. "Indian Textiles in Historical Perspective." In Monroe Wheeler, ed. *Textiles and Ornaments of India.*

———. *The Kashmir Shawl.* London: Her Majesty's Stationery Office, 1973.

Irwin, John, and Margaret Hall. *Historic Textiles of India at the Calico Museum.* Vol. 1, *Indian Painted and Printed Fabrics.* Ahmedabad, India: S. R. Bastikar on behalf of Calico Museum of Textiles, 1971.

———. *Historic Textiles of India at the Calico Museum.* Vol. 2, *Indian Embroideries.* Ahmedabad, India: S. R. Bastikar on behalf of Calico Museum of Textiles, 1973.

Iwatate, Hiroko. *Desert Village, Life and Crafts: Gujarat, Rajasthan.* Tokyo: Yobisha, 1985.

Jacquemont, Victor. *Voyages dans l'Inde pendant les années 1828 á 1832.* 4 vols. Paris: Firmin Didot frères, 1841.

Jahangir, Emperor of Hindustan (1569–1627). *The Tuzuk-i-Jahangiri; or, Memoirs of Jahangir.* Translated by Alexander Rogers. Edited by Henry Beveridge. Delhi: Munshiram Manoharlal, 1968.

Journal of Indian Art 2, no. 18. October 1888.

Kahlenberg, M. H. "A Study of the Development and Use of the Mughal Patkā (sash) with Reference to the Los Angeles County Museum of Art Collection." In *Aspects of Indian Art: Papers Presented in a Symposium at the Los Angeles County Museum of Art, October, 1970.* Edited by Pratapaditya Pal. Leiden: E. J. Brill, 1972.

Krishna, Vijay. "Flowers in Indian Textile Design." *Journal of Indian Textile History*, no. 7 (1967).

Lee, Sherman E. *A History of Far Eastern Art.* Edited by Naomi Noble Richard. Englewood Cliffs and New York: Prentice Hall and Harry N. Abrams, 1994.

Leitner, G. W. *An Account of Shawl Weaving . . . from Linguistic Fragments Discovered in 1870, 1872 and 1879.* Lahore, Pakistan, 1882.

Lévi-Strauss, Monique. *The Cashmere Shawl.* New York: Harry N. Abrams, 1986.

Malleson, Colonel George Bruce. *Akbar and the Rise of the Mughal Empire.* Oxford: Clarendon Press, 1894.

Maxwell, Robyn. *Textiles of Southeast Asia: Tradition, Trade and Transformation.* Melbourne, Oxford, Auckland, New York: Australian National Gallery and Oxford University Press, 1990.

Mehta, Rustam J. *The Handicrafts and Industrial Arts of India.* Bombay: D. B. Taraporevala Sons, 1960.

———. *Masterpieces of Indian Textiles.* Bombay: D. B. Taraporevala Sons, 1970.

Moorcroft, William, and George Trebeck. *Travels in the Himalayan Provinces of Hindustan and the Panjab from 1819 to 1825.* 2 vols. Edited by H. H. Wilson. London: J. Murray, 1841.

Mukharji, T. N. *Art-Manufactures of India.* Calcutta: Superintendent of Government Printing, India, 1888.

Nabholz-Kartaschoff, Marie-Louise. *Golden Sprays and Scarlet Flowers: Traditional Indian Textiles from the Museum of Ethnography, Basel, Switzerland.* Kyoto: Shikosha, 1986.

Nath, Aman, and Francis Wacziarg, eds. *Arts and Crafts of Rajasthan.* London: Thames and Hudson, 1987.

Olsen, Eleanor. "The Textiles and Costumes of India: A Historical Review." *The Museum* 17. Summer/Fall 1965. (The Newark Museum).

Paine, Sheila. *Chikan Embroidery: The Floral Whitework of India.* Aylesbury, Bucks (England): Shire Publications, 1989.

Pal, Pratapaditya, ed. *Art and Architecture of Ancient Kashmir.* Bombay: Marg Publications, 1989.

———. *Aspects of Indian Art: Papers Presented in a Symposium at the Los Angeles County Museum of Art, October, 1970.* Leiden: E. J. Brill, 1972.

Peebles, Merrily. *Court and Village: India's Textile Traditions.* Santa Barbara, California: Santa Barbara Museum of Art, 1981.

Polo, Marco. *The Travels.* Translated by Ronald Lathan. New York: Penguin Books, 1958.

Potocki, Jan. *Voyages.* Introduction and Notes by Daniel Beauvois. Paris: Fayard, ca. 1980–. Originally published by Henrich Julius von Klaproth as *Voyage dans les steppes d'Astrakhan et de Caucase par le Comte Jean Potocki* (Paris, 1829).

Ross, Nancy Wilson. *Three Ways of Asian Wisdom.* New York: Simon and Schuster, 1972 (1966).

Rowland, Benjamin. *The Art and Architecture of India: Buddhist, Hindu, Jain.* The Pelican History of Art. New York: Penguin Books, 1984. First published in 1953; most recent revision by J. C. Harle in 1977.

Shah, Hajji Mukhtar. *A Treatise on the Art of Shawl Weaving*. Lahore, Pakistan: Koh-i-Nor Press, 1887.

Stockley, Beth, et al. *Woven Air: The Muslin and Kantha Tradition of Bangladesh*. London: Whitechapel, 1988.

Sufi, G. M. (Al-Hajj). *Kashmir, A History of Kashmir*. 2 vols. New Delhi: Light and Life Publishers, 1974. Originally published by the University of the Punjab (Lahore, Pakistan), 1949.

Swarup, Shanti. *The Arts and Crafts of India and Pakistan*. Bombay: D. B. Taraporevala Sons & Co., 1957.

Tavernier, Jean Baptiste. *Les six voyages de Jean Baptiste Tavernier . . . .* Paris: G. Clouzier, 1676–1677.

Temple, Sir Richard. *Journals Kept in Hyderabad, Kashmir, Sikkim, and Nepal*. Edited by Richard Carnac Temple. 2 vols. London: W. H. Allen, 1887.

Victoria and Albert Museum. *The Indian Heritage: Court Life and Arts under Mughal Rule*. London: Victoria and Albert Museum, 1982.

———. "Some Dated Textiles in the Victoria and Albert Museum." *Journal of Indian Textile History*, no. 5 (1960).

Vigne, G. T. *Travels in Kashmir*. 2 vols. London: H. Colburn, 1844.

Watson, J. Forbes. *The Textile Manufacturers and the Costumes of the People of India*. Varanasi, India: Indological Book House, 1982. Originally published in London (Printed for the India Office, by G. E. Eyre and W. Spottiswoode), 1866.

Watt, Sir George. *Indian Art at Delhi, 1903. Being the Official Catalogue of the Delhi Exhibition, 1902–1903*. Calcutta: The Superintendent of Government Printing, India, 1903.

Welch, Stuart Cary. *Gods, Kings, and Tigers: The Art of Kotah*. Munich and New York: Prestel, 1997.

———. *India: Art and Culture, 1300–1900*. New York: The Metropolitan Museum of Art and Holt, Rinehart and Winston, 1985.

Wheeler, Monroe, ed. *Textiles and Ornaments of India*. New York: The Museum of Modern Art, 1956.

Zimmer, Heinrich. *The Art of Indian Asia: Its Mythology and Transformations*. Completed and edited by Joseph Campbell. 2 vols. Bollingen Series, vol. 39. New York: Published for Bollingen Foundation by Pantheon Books, 1955.

IRAN

Amanat, Abbas, ed. *Cities and Trade: Consul Abbott on the Economy and Society of Iran, 1847–1866*. London: Ithaca Press, 1983.

Beattie, May H. "On the Making of Carpets." In D. King and D. Sylvester, *The Eastern Carpet in the Western World*. London: Arts Council of Great Britain, 1983, 106–109.

Bier, Carol. "The Legacy of Timur: A Small Rug at the Textile Museum." *International Carpet & Textile Review*, no. 9 (1996): 98–100.

———. *The Persian Velvets at Rosenborg*. Copenhagen: Rosenborg, 1995.

———, ed. *Woven from the Soul, Spun from the Heart: Textile Arts of Safavid and Qajar Iran (16th– 19th Centuries)*. Washington, DC: The Textile Museum, 1987.

Chenciner, Robert. "Persian Exports to Russia from the 16th to the 19th Century." *Iran* 30 (1992): 123–130.

Floor, Willem. *The Dutch and the Persian Silk Trade, in Safavid Persia*. Edited by Charles Melville. London and New York: I. B. Taurus, 1996.

Helfgott, Leonard M. *Ties That Bind: A Social History of the Iranian Carpet*. Washington, DC and London: Smithsonian Institution Press, 1994.

Herzig, Edmund M. "The Volume of Iranian Raw Silk Exports in the Safavid Period." *Iranian Studies* 25, nos. 1, 2 (1992): 61–79.

Lentz, Thomas W., and Glenn D. Lowry. *Timur and the Princely Vision: Persian Art and Culture in the Fifteenth Century*. Los Angeles and Washington, DC: Los Angeles County Museum of Art, the Arthur M. Sackler Gallery, and Smithsonian Institution Press, 1989.

McWilliams, Mary. "Catalogue Number 36 (Satin Lampas)." In *Woven from the Soul, Spun from the Heart: Textile Arts of Safavid and Qajar Iran (16th–19th Centuries)*. Edited by Carol Bier. Washington, DC: The Textile Museum, 1987, 206.

Neumann, Reingard. *Persische Seide: die Gewebekunst der Safawiden un Ihrer Nachfolger*. Leipzig: Seemann, 1988.

Sonday, Milton. "Pattern and Weaves: Safavid Lampas and Velvet." In *Woven from the Soul, Spun from the Heart: Textile Arts of Safavid and Qajar Iran (16th–19th Centuries)*. Edited by Carol Bier. Washington, DC: The Textile Museum, 1987, 57–83.

Tattersall, C. E. C. *Notes on Carpet-Knotting and Weaving*. London: Victoria and Albert Museum, 1969.

Tietzel, Brigitte. *Und Blumen Sing ich ungestort, von ihrem Shawl herunter: persische Seiden des 16.–18. Jahrhunderts aus dem Besitz des Deutschen Textilmuseums Krefeld*. Krefeld: Stadt Krefeld, 1988.

See also the entries "Abrisham" (Silk), "Carpets," and "Clothing," in Encyclopaedia Iranica, v. 1, pp. 229–47, Routledge & Kegan Paul, London, 1983; v. 4, pp, 834–96, Routledge & Kegan Paul, London, 1990; and v. 5, pp. 1–9, Mazda Publishers, Costa Mesa, CA, 1992.

CHINA

Bartholomew, Terese Tse. *The Hundred Flowers: Botanical Motifs in Chinese Art*. San Francisco: Asian Art Museum of San Francisco, 1985.

———. *Myths and Rebuses in Chinese Art*. San Francisco: Asian Art Museum of San Francisco, 1988.

Bernard, S. J. *Aux Portes de la Chine; les missionnaires du seizième siècle*. Tientsin: Hautes études, 1933.

Bray, Francesca. *Technology and Gender: Fabrics of Power in Late Imperial China*. Berkeley, Los Angeles, and London: University of California Press, 1997.

Brown, Claudia, with contributions by Robert D. Mowry, Martha Winslow Grimm, Janet Baker, and An-yi Pan. *Weaving China's Past: The Amy S. Clague Collection of Chinese Textiles*. Phoenix, Arizona: Phoenix Art Museum, 2000.

Burnham, Dorothy. *Cut My Cote*. Toronto: Royal Ontario Museum, 1973.

Burnham, Harold. *Chinese Velvets*. Toronto: University of Toronto Press, 1959.

Cammann, Schuyler. *China's Dragon Robes*. New York: The Ronald Press, 1952.

———. "The Development of the Mandarin Square." *Harvard Journal of Asiatic Studies* 8 (1944–1945): 71–130.

Cao Xueqin. *The Story of the Stone*. Translated by David Hawkes and John Minford. 5 vols. Bloomington, Indiana: Indiana University Press, 1973–1987.

Catalogue of the Shanghai Customs' Collection at the Austro-Hungarian Universal Exhibition. Shanghai: Imperial Maritime Customs Press, 1873.

Chang, T'ien-tsê. *Sino-Portuguese Trade from 1514– 1644; a synthesis of Portuguese and Chinese sources*. Leiden, E. J. Brill, 1933. Republished in 1969.

Cheng Weiji. *History of Textile Technology of Ancient China*. New York: Science Press, 1992.

Chung, Young Y. *The Art of Oriental Embroidery: History, Aesthetics, and Techniques*. New York: Charles Scribner's Sons, 1983.

Clothed to Rule the Universe: Ming and Qing Dynasty Textiles at the Art Institute of Chicago. Chicago: The Art Institute, 2000.

Cotton and Silk Making in Manchu China. Introduction by Mario Bussagli. Excerpts from Father J. B. Du Halde, S.J. New York: Rizzoli, 1980.

Crossley, Pamela Kyle. *The Manchus*. Cambridge, Mass. and Oxford: Blackwell Publishers, 1997.

Davis, Sir John Francis. *China: A General Description of That Empire and Its Inhabitants*. London: John Murray, 1857.

De Verboden Stad: Hofcultuur van de Chinese keizers (1644–1911) (The Forbidden City: Court Culture of the Chinese Emperors [1644–1911]). Rotterdam: Museum Boymans-van Beuningen, 1990.

Eberhard, Wolfram. *A Dictionary of Chinese Symbols*. Translated from the German by G. L. Campbell. London and New York: Routledge and Kegan Paul, 1986. First published in German as *Lexikon Chinesischer Symbole* (Cologne: Eugen Diederichs Verlag, 1983).

Elliott, Mark C. *The Manchu Way*. Stanford: Stanford University Press, 2001.

Fairbank, John K., Edwin O. Reischauer, and Albert M. Craig. *East Asia: The Modern Transformation*. Boston: Houghton Mifflin, 1965.

Ferguson, Donald. "Letters from Portuguese Captives in Canton" (written in 1534 and 1536). *The Indian Antiquary* 30, 31 (1901–2).

Fogel, Joshua. *The Literature of Travel in the Japanese Rediscovery of China: 1862–1945*. Stanford: Stanford University Press, 1996.

Gao Hanyu. *Chinese Textile Designs*. Translated by Rosemary Scott and Susan Whitfield. London: Viking, 1992. First published in Chinese as *Zhongguo lidai zhi ran xiu tulu* (Hong Kong: The Commercial Press, 1986).

Garrett, Valery M. *Mandarin Squares*. Oxford: Oxford University Press, 1990.

Gray, John Henry. *Walks in the City of Canton*. Hong Kong: De Souza and Co., 1875.

Grousset, René. *The Empire of the Steppes: A History of Central Asia*. Translated by Naomi Walford from the French edition of 1952. New Brunswick, New Jersey: Rutgers University Press, 1970. Originally published in French in 1939.

Hakluyt Society. *The Voyage of Jan Hughyen van Lonschoten to the East Indies*. Hakluyt Society, series 1, nos. 70, 71. London: Hakluyt Society, 1885.

Hays, Mary V. "Chinese Women's Skirts of The Qing Dynasty." *The Bulletin of the Needle and Bobbin Club* 72, nos. 1, 2 (1989): 4–41.

Ho, Ping-ti. *Studies on the Population of China: 1368–1953*. Cambridge, Mass.: Harvard University Press, 1959.

Hsia Nai. *Jade and Silk in Han China*. Edited and translated by Chu-tsing Li. The Franklin D. Murphy Lectures, vol. 3. Lawrence, Kansas: The Helen Foresman Spencer Museum of Art, 1983.

Jackson, Beverly and David Hugus. *Ladder to the Clouds: Intrigue and Tradition in Chinese Rank*. Berkeley: Ten Speed Press, 1999.

Jacobsen, Robert D. *Imperial Silks: Ch'ing Dynasty Textiles in the Minneapolis Institute of Arts*. Minneapolis: The Minneapolis Institute of Arts, 2000.

de Jesus, C. A. Montalto. *Historic Macao*. Hong Kong: Kelly and Walsh, Ltd., 1902.

Kuhn, Dieter. "Textile Technology: Spinning and Reeling." In *Science and Civilisation in China*. Edited by Joseph Needham. Vol. 5, part 9. Cambridge: Cambridge University Press, 1988.

Lee, Sherman E. *A History of Far Eastern Art*. Edited by Naomi Noble Richard. Englewood Cliffs and New York: Prentice Hall and Harry N. Abrams, 1994.

Legge, James, trans. *Li Chi Book of Rites (Liji)*. Edited by Ch'u Chai and Winberg Chai. 2 vols. New Hyde Park, New York: University Books, 1967.

———. *The Shoo King or The Book of Historical Documents (Shujing)*. Taipei: Southern Materials Center, 1985. Originally published in London by Oxford University Press in 1865.

Little, Stephen, with Shawn Eichman. *Taoism and the Arts of China*. Chicago: The Art Institute of Chicago in association with University of California Press, 2000.

Matsumoto, Kaneo. *Jōdaigire: 7th and 8th Century Textiles in Japan from the Shōsōin and Hōryūji*. Kyoto: Shikosha, 1984.

Medhurst, W. H. *The Foreigner in Far Cathay*. London: Edward Stanford, 1872. Reprinted in 1977 by Chinese Materials Center, San Francisco.

Medley, Margaret. *The "Illustrated Regulations for Ceremonial Paraphernalia of the Ch'ing* [Qing] *Dynasty."* London: Han-Shan Tan, 1982. Reprinted from *Transactions of the Oriental Ceramic Society* 31 (1958–1959): 95–104.

Pang, Mae Anna. *Dragon Emperor: Treasures from the Forbidden City*. Melbourne: National Gallery of Victoria, 1988.

Reischauer, Edwin O., and John K. Fairbank. *East Asia: The Great Tradition*. Boston: Houghton Mifflin, 1960.

Satowl, Ernest M., ed. *The Voyage of John Sais to Japan, 1613*. London: Hakluyt Society, series 2, no. 5, 1900.

Shen Fu. *Six Records of a Floating Life*. Translated by Leonard Pratt and Chiang Su-hui. London: Penguin Books, 1983.

Shōsōin-ten. English title: *Exhibition of Shōsōin Treasures*. Nara: Nara National Museum, 1974, 1978, 1989, 1991, 1992.

Stack, Lotus. *The Pile Thread*. Minneapolis: Minneapolis Museum of Art, 1991.

Stodulski, L. P., D. Nauman, and M. Kennedy. "Technical Appendix: Analysis of Precious Metal Threads." In Peggy Gilfoy, *Fabrics in Celebration from the Collection*. Indianapolis: Indianapolis Museum of Art, 1983.

Store, Joyce. *The Thames and Hudson Manual of Dyes and Fabrics*. London: Thames and Hudson, 1978.

Sun, E-tu Zen. "Sericulture and Silk Textile Production in Ch'ing China." In W. E. Willmott, ed. *Economic Organization in Chinese Society*. Stanford: Stanford University Press, 1972.

Thorp, Robert L. *Son of Heaven: Imperial Arts of China*. Seattle: Son of Heaven Press, 1988.

Vollmer, John. *Clothed to Rule the Universe: Ming to Qing Dynasty Textiles at the Art Institute of Chicago*. Chicago: The Art Institute of Chicago, 2000.

———. *Decoding Dragons*. Eugene, Oregon: Museum of Art, University of Oregon, 1983.

———. *Five Colours of the Universe*. Edmonton: The Edmonton Art Gallery, 1980.

———. *In the Presence of the Dragon Throne*. Toronto: Royal Ontario Museum, 1977.

———. "Manchu Style and Ethnic Identity." In *Secret Splendors of the Chinese Court*. Edited by Imelda Gatton Degraw. Denver: Denver Art Museum, 1981.

Wang Binghua, Ji Xianlin, Ahmat Rashid, Hes Duxiu, Li Wenying, Lu Enguo, Yu Wanli, Xu Wenkan, and Han Kangxin. *The Ancient Corpses of Xinjiang: The Peoples of Ancient Xinjiang and Their Culture*. Chinese title: *Xinjiang gu shi: gu dai Xinjiang ju min ji qi wen hua*. In Chinese and English. Translated by Victor H. Mair. Ürümqi, Xinjiang: Xinjiang ren min chu ban she, 2002.

Watt, James C. Y., and Joyce Denney. "Tapestry-Woven Panel." In "Recent Acquisitions: A Selection: 1994–1995." *Bulletin of the Metropolitan Museum of Art*, Fall 1995.

Wenwu, 1964, no. 11; 1972, no. 5:25–36; 1973, no. 5; 1978, no. 4; 1982, no. 2:28–32.

Wilkinson-Weber, Clare M. *Embroidering Lives: Women's Work and Skill in the Lucknow Embroidery Industry*. SUNY Series in the Anthropology of Work. Edited by June C. Nash. Albany: State University of New York Press, 1999.

Williams, C. A. S. *Outlines of Chinese Symbols and Art Motifs*. Rutland, Vermont and Tokyo: Charles E. Tuttle, 1974. Based on the third revised edition printed in Shanghai in 1941.

Williams, S. Wells. *A Chinese commercial guide, consisting of a collection of details and regulations respecting foreign trade with China, sailing directions, tables, etc.* Canton: Printed at the Office of the Chinese Repository, 1856.

Willmott, W. E., ed. *Economic Organization in Chinese Society*. Stanford: Stanford University Press, 1972.

Wilson, Verity. *Chinese Dress*. London: Victoria and Albert Museum, 1986.

———. "Cosmic Raiment: Daoist Traditions of Liturgical Clothing." In *Orientations*, May 1995.

———. "Studio and Soirée: The Use and Misuse of Chinese Textiles in a European Setting." In *Textiles in Trade*. Proceedings of the Textile Society of America. Los Angeles: Textile Society of America, 1990, 217–222.

Zhao Feng. *Treasures in Silk: An Illustrated History of Chinese Textiles*. Hong Kong: ISAT/Costume Squad, 1999.

Zhao Feng, ed. *Recent Excavations of Textiles in China*. Hong Kong: ISAT/Costume Squad Ltd., 2002.

Zhao Qiguang. "Dragon: The Symbol of China." *Oriental Art*, Summer 1991: 72–80.

Zhou Xun and Gao Chunming. *5000 Years of Chinese Costumes*. San Francisco: China Books and Periodicals, 1987.

JAPAN

Adachi, Barbara. *The Living Treasures of Japan*. Tokyo, New York, and San Francisco: Kodansha International, 1973.

Beato, Felice. *Once Upon a Time: Vision of Old Japan*. Translated by Linda Coverdale. New York: Friendly Press, 1986.

Blakemore, Frances. *Japanese Design Through Textile Patterns*. New York and Tokyo: John Weatherhill, 1978.

Brandon, Reiko Mochinaga. *Country Textiles of Japan: The Art of Tsutsugaki*. New York and Tokyo: Weatherhill, 1986.

Brandon, Reiko Mochinaga, and Barbara B. Stephan. *Textile Art of Okinawa*. Honolulu: Honolulu Academy of Arts, 1990.

Brinker, Helmut, and Hiroshi Kanazawa. *Zen: Masters of Meditation in Images and Writings*. Translated by Andreas Leisinger. *Artibus Asiae* Supplementum 40. Zurich: Artibus Asiae Publishers, 1996.

Burke, Mary Griggs. "The Delights of Nature in Japanese Art." *Orientations* 27, no. 2 (February 1996): 54–61.

Bush, Susan, and Hsio-yen Shih, comp. and ed. *Early Chinese Texts on Painting*. Cambridge, Mass: Harvard University Press, 1985.

Cort, Louise Allison. "Bast Fibers." In *Beyond the Tanabata Bridge: Traditional Japanese Textiles*. Edited by William Jay Rathbun. New York: Thames and Hudson in association with the Seattle Art Museum, 1993.

———. "The Changing Fortunes of Three Archaic Japanese Textiles." In *Cloth and Human Experience*. Edited by Annette B. Weiner and Jane Schneider. Washington, DC and London: Smithsonian Institution Press, 1989.

De Bary. William Theodore, ed. *The Buddhist Tradition in India, China and Japan*. With the collaboration of Yoshito Hakeda and Philip Yampolsky and with contributions by A. L. Basham, Leon Hurvitz, and Ryusaku Tsunoda. New York: Vintage Books, 1972. Originally published by the Modern Library in 1969.

Dower, John W. *The Elements of Japanese Design; A Handbook of Family Crests, Heraldry and Symbolism*. New York and Tokyo: Walker/Weatherhill, 1971.

Dusenbury, Mary. "The Art of Color." In *Beyond the Tanabata Bridge: Traditional Japanese Textiles*. Edited by William Jay Rathbun. New York: Thames and Hudson in association with the Seattle Art Museum, 1993.

———. "Kasuri." In *Beyond the Tanabata Bridge: Traditional Japanese Textiles*. Edited by William Jay Rathbun. New York: Thames and Hudson in association with the Seattle Art Museum, 1993.

———. "The Color of Power: China." In Mary M. Dusenbury. "Radiance and Darkness: Color at the Heian Court." Ph.D. diss., University of Kansas, 1999.

———. "*Kasuri*: A Japanese Textile." *Textile Museum Journal* 17 (1978).

———. "Tree-Bast Fiber Textiles of Japan." *Spin-Off* 10 (Fall 1986): 35–39.

———. "A Wisteria Grain Bag." In *Textiles in Daily Life: Proceedings of the Third Biennial Symposium of the Textile Society of America*. Earleville, Maryland: The Textile Society of America, 1992.

Dusenbury, Mary, Hiroi Nobuko, and Nagano Gorō. *Textiles of Old Japan: Tree-Bast Fiber Textiles and Old Kasuri*. San Francisco: San Francisco Craft and Folk Art Museum, 1985.

Eberhard, Wolfram. *A Dictionary of Chinese Symbols*. Translated from the German by G. L. Campbell. London and New York: Routledge and Kegan Paul, 1986. First published in German as *Lexicon chinesischer Symbole* (Cologne: Eugen Diederichs Verlag, 1983).

Endō Motoo. *Nihonshokuninshi (A history of Japanese artisans)*. Tokyo: Yūzankaku, 1967.

Fong, Mary H. "A Probable Second 'Chung Ku'uei' by Emperor Shun-chih of the Ch'ing Dynasty." *Oriental Art* 23 (1977).

Fontein, Jan, ed. *Living National Treasures of Japan: An Exhibition Organized by the Committee of the Exhibition of Living National Treasures of Japan*. Exhibition shown at Museum of Fine Arts, Boston; The Art Institute of Chicago; and Japanese American Cultural and Community Center, Los Angeles. Publication information unrecorded (1982?).

Frédéric, Louis. *Buddhism*. Translated by Nissim Marshall. Flammarion Iconographic Guides. Paris and New York: Flammarion, 1995.

Fukui Sadako. *Nihon no kasuri bunkashi (A cultural history of kasuri in Japan)*. Kyoto: Kyoto Shōin, 1973.

Gluckman, Dale Carolyn, and Sharon Sadako Takeda. *When Art Became Fashion: Kosode in Edo-Period Japan*. Los Angeles: Los Angeles County Museum of Art, 1992.

Hauser, William. "The Kinai Cotton Trade." *The Journal of Asiatic Studies*, Vol. 33, No. 4. August 1974.

Hays, Mary V., and Ralph E. Hays. *Fukusa: The Shojiro Nomura Fukusa Collection*. Oakland, California: Mills College Art Gallery, 1983.

Hino Saishiko (?). *Nihonfukushokushi (A history of Japanese costume)*. Tokyo: Kōshunkaku, 1963.

ICU Hachiro Yuasa Memorial Museum, Reiko Hara, Kazuko Saito, and Hiroko Nagai, eds. *Some no katagami: monyō no tenkai (Japanese paper stencil designs)*. Tokyo: Hachiro Yuasa Memorial Museum, International Christian University, 1985.

ICU Hachiro Yuasa Memorial Museum, J. E. Kidder, Jr., Akiko Fukuno, Reiko Hara, and Kazuko Saito, eds. *Aizome (Japanese indigo textiles)*. Tokyo: Hachiro Yuasa Memorial Museum, International Christian University, 1987.

Impey, Oliver. "Reflections Upon the Crafts of Meiji Period Japan with Reference to the Collection of the Ashmolean Museum." *Oriental Art* 42, no. 3 (Autumn 1996).

Jackson, Anna. *Japanese Country Textiles*. London: Victoria and Albert Museum, 1997.

Japan Photographers Association. *A Century of Japanese Photography*. New York: Pantheon Books, 1980.

Kaempfer, Engelbert. *Kaempfer's Japan: Tokugawa Culture Observed*. Edited, translated, and annotated by Beatrice M. Bodart-Bailey. Honolulu: University of Hawai'i Press, 1999.

Kahlenberg, Mary Hunt, ed. *The Extraordinary in the Ordinary: Textiles and Objects from the Collections of Lloyd Cotsen and the Neutrogena Corporation*. New York: Harry N. Abrams in association with the Museum of International Folk Art, Museum of New Mexico, 1998.

Kaiyama Kyusaburo. *The Book of Japanese Design: Banshoku shin hinagata bijutsu oyo*. Translation and commentary by Sylvia Price Mueller. New York: Crown Publishers, 1969.

Kamakura Yoshitarō. "Okinawan History and Handicrafts" and "Textiles." In Kawakita Michiaki, et al. *National Museum of Modern Art, Kyoto: Craft Treasures of Okinawa*. Translated and adapted from *Okinawa no kōgei* by Erika Kaneko. London: Serindia Publications, 1978. Catalogue of an exhibition held at the National Museum of Modern Art, Kyoto in 1974.

Kasuga Shrine, ed. *Bugaku Treasures from the Kasuga Shrine*. Nara: Kasuga Shrine, 1984. Printed in Tokyo by Otsuka Kogeisha.

Kata-gami: Japanese Stencils in the Collection of the Cooper-Hewitt Museum. Washington, DC: Smithsonian Institution, 1979.

Katonah Museum of Art. *Object as Insight: Japanese Buddhist Art and Ritual*. Katonah, New York: Katonah Museum of Art, 1995.

Kawakami Shigeki. *Kuge no ifuku (Court costume)*. *Nihon no bijutsu* (Arts of Japan) 8, no. 339 (August 1994).

Kawakami, Shigeki, ed., with contributions by Hiroyuki Kano, Shigeki Kawakami, and Meiko Nagashima. *Kyoto Style: Trends in 16th–19th Century Kimono*. Translated by Mami Hild. Kyoto: Kyoto National Museum, 1999.

Kawakita Michiaki et al., *National Museum of Modern Art, Kyoto: Craft Treasures of Okinawa*. Translated and adapted from *Okinawa no kōgei* by Erika Kaneko. London: Serindia Publications, 1978.

Kennedy, Alan. *Japanese Costume: History and Tradition*. Paris: Adam Biro, 1990.

———. "*Kesa*: Its Sacred and Secular Aspects." *Textile Museum Journal*, 1983.

Ketelaar, James Edward. *Of Heretics and Martyrs in Meiji Japan: Buddhism and Its Persecution*. Princeton: Princeton University Press, 1990.

Kijōka no bashōfu (Kijōka banana fiber cloth). Ningen Kokuhō serizu (Living National Treasures series), vol. 41. Tokyo: Kodansha, 1977.

Kitamura Tetsugen. *Nihon fukushokushi (A History of Japanese costume)*. Tokyo: Iseikatsu Kenkyūkai, 1973.

Kobayashi Keiko. "The Effect of Western Textile Technology on Japanese *Kasuri*: Development, Innovation, and Competition." *Textile Museum Journal* 40, 41 (2001–2002): 3–34.

Kuo, Susanna. *Katagami: Japanese Textile Stencils in the Collection of the Seattle Art Museum*. Seattle: Seattle Art Museum, 1985.

Kyoto National Museum. *Some no katagami* (Stencil paper for dyeing). Kyoto: Kyoto National Museum, 1968.

Kyūma Keichō. *Kesa no kenkyū (A study of kesa)*. Tokyo: Daihōrin Kakuhan, 1967.

Leupp, Gary P. *Servants, Shophands, and Laborers in the Cities of Tokugawa Japan*. Princeton: Princeton University Press, 1992.

Lyman, Marie. "Distant Mountains: The Influence of *Funzō-e* on the Tradition of Buddhist Clerical Robes in Japan." *Textile Museum Journal* (1984): 25–42.

Manthorpe, Victoria, ed. *Travels in the Land of the Gods (1898–1907): The Japan Diaries of Richard Gordon Smith*. New York: Prentice Hall Press, 1986.

Mason, Penny. *History of Japanese Art*. New York: Harry N. Abrams, 1993.

Matsumoto, Kaneo. *Jōdaigire: 7th and 8th Century Textiles in Japan from the Shōsōin and Hōryūji*. Kyoto: Shikosha, 1984.

Mellott, Richard. "Katazome, Tsutsugaki, and Yūzenzome." In *Beyond the Tanabata Bridge: Traditional Japanese Textiles*. Edited by William Jay Rathbun. New York: Thames and Hudson in association with the Seattle Art Museum, 1993.

Minnich, Helen Benton, in collaboration with Shojiro Nomura. *Japanese Costume and the Makers of Its Elegant Tradition*. Rutland, Vermont and Tokyo: Charles E. Tuttle, 1963.

Mizoguchi, Saburō. *Design Motifs*. Translated and adapted by Louise Allison Cort. Arts of Japan, vol. 1. New York and Tokyo: Weatherhill/Shibundo, 1968.

Moes, Robert. *Mingei: Japanese Folk Art from the Brooklyn Museum Collection*. New York: Universe, 1985.

———. *Mingei: Japanese Folk Art from the Montgomery Collection*. Alexandria, Virginia: Art Services International, 1995.

Morioka Michiyo. "Ainu Textiles" and "Sashiko, Kogin, and Hishizashi." In *Beyond the Tanabata Bridge: Traditional Japanese Textiles*. Edited by William Jay Rathbun. New York: Thames and Hudson in association with the Seattle Art Museum, 1993.

Morioka Michiyo, and William Jay Rathbun. "Tsutsugaki and Katazome." In *Beyond the Tanabata Bridge: Traditional Japanese Textiles*. Edited by William Jay Rathbun. New York: Thames and Hudson in association with the Seattle Art Museum, 1993.

Mowry, Robert, and Nancy Berliner. "Prajnaparamita Sutra from the Qisha Tripitaka." In *Latter Days of the Law: Images of Chinese Buddhism 850–1850*. Edited by Marsha Weidner. Lawrence, Kansas: Spencer Museum of Art in association with University of Hawaii Press, 1994.

The Mustard Seed Garden Manual of Painting: Chieh Tzŭ Yuan Hua Chuan, 1679–1701. Translated and edited by Mai-mai Sze. Princeton: Bollingen Series, Princeton University Press, 1956. Facsimile edition of the 1887–1888 Shanghai edition.

Nagano Gorō and Nobuko Hiroi. *Orimono no genfūkei*. English title: *Base to Tip: Bast-Fiber Weaving in Japan and Its Neighboring Countries*. Kyoto: Shikosha, 1999. In Japanese with a substantive summary English translation by Monica Bethe including charts, index, glossary, and captions.

Nagasaki, Iwao. "The Tradition of Folk Textiles in Japan." In *Beyond the Tanabata Bridge: Traditional Japanese Textiles*. Edited by William Jay Rathbun. New York: Thames and Hudson in association with the Seattle Art Museum, 1993.

Nakano Eisha, with Barbara B. Stephan. *Japanese Stencil Dyeing: Paste-Resist Techniques*. New York and Tokyo: John Weatherhill, 1982.

Nihon Mingeikan. *Okinawa no bi (The beauty of Okinawa)*. Tokyo: Nihon Mingeikan, 1981.

Ningen Kokuhō jiten (Dictionary of Living National Treasures). Edited by Minami Kunio, Yanagibashi Makoto, and Ōtaki Mikio. Tokyo: Unsōdō, 1998.

Oda Hideo. "Kasuri gijutsu no kenkyū (A study of kasuri techniques)." In *Senshoku to seikatsu*, Summer 1974.

Ogasawara Sae. *Kasuri*, vol. 309, *Nihon no bijutsu* (Kasuri, vol. 309 of Arts of Japan). February 1992.

Okakura Kakuzō. *The Book of Tea*. Rutland, Vermont: Charles E. Tuttle, 1956.

Okamura Kichiemon. "*Nihon no kasuri*." In *Nihon no kasuri*, vol. II, *Senshoku no bi* (Kasuri in Japan, vol. II of The Beauty of Textiles), Kyoto: Shikōsha, 1981.

Okanobori Sadaharu. *Monyō no jiten (Dictionary of pattern)*. Tokyo: Tokyodō Shuppan, 1968.

Paine, Robert Treat, and Alexander Soper. *The Art and Architecture of Japan.* New York: Viking Penguin, 1987.

Po, Sung-nien, and David Johnson. *Domesticated Deities and Auspicious Emblems: The Iconography of Everyday Life in Village China; Popular Prints and Papercuts from the Collection of Po Sung-nien.* Berkeley: Chinese Popular Cultures Project, University of California, 1992.

Rathbun, William Jay. "Kasuri, Shiborizome, and Koshi Patterns" and "Okinawan Weaving and Dyeing." In *Beyond the Tanabata Bridge: Traditional Japanese Textiles.* Edited by William Jay Rathbun. New York: Thames and Hudson in association with the Seattle Art Museum, 1993.

Sakai, Robert K., and Mitsugu Sakihara. "Okinawa." In *Encyclopedia of Japan.* New York and Tokyo: Kodansha International, 1983.

Sakihara, Mitsugu. *A Brief History of Early Okinawa Based on The Omoro Sōshi.* Tokyo: Honpo Shoseki Press, 1987.

Shaver, Cynthia. "Sashiko: A Stitchery of Japan." In *Beyond the Tanabata Bridge: Traditional Japanese Textiles.* Edited by William Jay Rathbun. New York: Thames and Hudson in association with the Seattle Art Museum, 1993.

Shaver, Cynthia, Noriko Miyamoto, and Sachio Yoshioka. *Hanten and Happi: Traditional Japanese Work Coats.* Sumi Collection. Kyoto: Shikosha, 1998.

Shimizu, Yoshiaki, ed. *The Shaping of Daimyo Culture: 1185–1868.* New York: George Braziller in association with National Gallery of Art, Washington, 1988.

Shively, Donald H. "Sumptuary Regulation and Status in Early Tokugawa Japan." *Harvard Journal of Asiatic Studies* 25 (1964–1965): 123–164.

Shōsōin-ten. English title: *Exhibition of Shōsōin Treasures.* Nara: Nara National Museum, 1974, 1978, 1989, 1991, 1992.

Smith, Thomas C. *The Agrarian Origins of Modern Japan.* Stanford: Stanford University Press, 1959.

Stinchecum, Amanda Mayer. "A Common Thread: Japanese Ikat Textiles." *Asian Art* 3, no. 1 (Winter 1990).

———. *Kosode: 16th–19th Century Textiles from the Nomura Collection.* New York: Japan Society and Kodansha International, 1984.

———. "Textiles of Okinawa." In *Beyond the Tanabata Bridge: Traditional Japanese Textiles.* Edited by William Jay Rathbun. New York: Thames and Hudson in association with the Seattle Art Museum, 1993.

Sugihara Nobuhiko. "Nihon no katazome ni tsuite." In *Nihon no katazome.* Edited by the National Museum of Modern Art. Tokyo: The National Museum of Modern Art, 1980.

———. "Some no katagami." In Kyoto National Museum. *Some no katagami.* Kyoto: Kyoto National Museum, 1968.

Takahashi Yōji, ed. "Nihon no nuno: genshi nuno tanbō" *(Japanese cloth: an inquiry into primitive cloth).* Taiyō (The Sun). *Nihon no kokoro* (Spirit of Japan), no. 67 (Autumn 1989).

Takemura, Akihiko. *Fukusa: Japanese Gift Covers.* Tokyo: Iwasaki Bijutsusha, 1991.

Tanaka Toshio and Tanaka Reiko. *Okinawa orimono no kenkyū (Study of Okinawa weaving)* and *Okinawa orimono no kenkyū: retsuji zuroku (Study of Okinawan weaving: pictorial record of cloth fragments).* 2 vols. Kyoto: Shikosha, 1976.

Till, Barry, and Paula Swart. *Kesa: The Elegance of Japanese Monks' Robes.* Victoria, Canada: Art Gallery of Greater Victoria, 1996.

Tokugawa Yoshinobu. *The Tokugawa Collection of No Robes and Masks.* Transl. and adapted by Louise Allison Cort and Monica Bethe. New York: Japan Society 1977.

Tonomura Kichinosuke. *Kurashiki Mingeikan zoroku.* English title: Catalogue of Kurashiki Museum of Folk Craft. Vol. 1. Kurashiki: Kurashiki Mingeikan, 1973. In Japanese with an English introduction and some captions in English.

Totman, Conrad. *Early Modern Japan.* Berkeley, Los Angeles, and London: University of California Press, 1993.

The Victoria and Albert Museum. *Japanese Stencils.* Exeter: Webb and Bower with the Trustees of the Victoria and Albert Museum, London, and Carroll, Dempsey and Thirkell, 1988.

Weidner, Marsha, ed. *Latter Days of the Law: Images of Chinese Buddhism 850–1850.* Lawrence, Kansas: Spencer Museum of Art in association with University of Hawaii Press, 1994.

Welch, Matthew. "Shōki the Demon Queller." In *Japanese Ghosts and Demons: Art of the Supernatural.* Edited by Stephen Addiss. New York: George Braziller in association with the Spencer Museum of Art, University of Kansas, 1985.

Whitehill, Walter Muir. *Museum of Fine Arts, Boston: A Centennial History.* Cambridge, Mass.: The Belknap Press of Harvard University Press, 1970.

Whitfield, Roderick, and Anne Farrer. *Caves of the Thousand Buddhas: Chinese Art from the Silk Route.* New York: George Braziller, 1990.

Williams, C. A. S. *Outlines of Chinese Symbols and Art Motifs.* Rutland, Vermont and Tokyo: Charles E. Tuttle, 1974. Based on the third revised edition printed in Shanghai in 1941.

Winkel, Margarita. *Souvenirs from Japan: Japanese Photography at the Turn of the Century.* London: Bamboo Publishing, 1991.

Yamanaka Norio. *The Book of Kimono.* Tokyo, New York, and London: Kodansha International, 1982.

Yamanobe Tomoyuki. *Some (Dyeing). Nihon no bijutsu* 7, no. 11 (1966).

Yanagi Sōetsu. *The Unknown Craftsman: A Japanese Insight into Beauty.* Adapted by Bernard Leach. Foreword by Shōji Hamada. Tokyo: Kodansha, 1972.

Yokoi Yūhō, with Daizen Victoria. *Zen Master Dōgen.* New York and Tokyo: Weatherhill, 1976.

Yoshida Mitsukuni, et al. *Genshoku senshoku daijiten (Great illustrated dictionary of textiles).* Kyoto: Tankōsha, 1977.

Yoshioka Sachio, ed. *Katagami, katazome: Yoshioka korekushon.* English title: Katagami, Katazome: *Paper Stencils for Dyeing: The Yoshioka Collection.* In Japanese and English. Kyoto: Shikosha, 1989.

Zwalf, W., ed. *Buddhism: Art and Faith.* New York: Macmillan, 1985.

Index

Page numbers in *italics* refer to illustrations